A DISCIPLINE DIVIDED

A DISCIPLINE DIVIDED

SCHOOLS AND SECTS IN POLITICAL SCIENCE

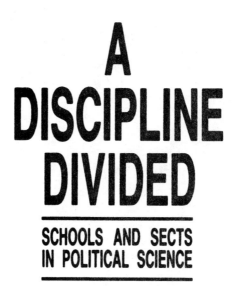

GABRIEL A. ALMOND

SAGE Publications
International Educational and Professional Publisher
Newbury Park London New Delhi

For information address:

SAGE Publications, Inc.
2455 Teller Road
Newbury Park, California 91320
E-mail: order@sagepub.com

SAGE Publications Ltd.
6 Bonhill Street
London EC2A 4PU
United Kingdom

SAGE Publications India Pvt. Ltd.
M-32 Market
Greater Kailash I
New Delhi 110 048 India

Printed in the United States of America

Library of Congress Cataloging-in-Publication Data

Almond, Gabriel Abraham, 1911-
A discipline divided : schools and sects in political science / by Gabriel A. Almond.
p. cm.
Bibliography: p.
Includes index.
ISBN 0-8039-3301-0. — ISBN 0-8039-3302-9 (pbk.)
1. Political science. I. Title.
JA71.A475 1989
320—dc20 89-34774
CIP

96 97 98 99 00 01 12 11 10 9 8 7 6

Contents

Preface

This book brings under one set of covers articles and papers that I have written in recent years. The justification for doing this is that they have a certain coherence and timeliness. They are concerned with two broad and important professional themes: the nature of political science as science, and the problem of generations and professional memory.

There is a long-standing polemic in political science between those who view the discipline as a hard science—formal, mathematical, statistical, experimental—dedicated to the cumulation of tested "covering laws," and those who are less sanguine and more eclectic, who view all scholarly methods, the scientific ones as well as the softer historical, philosophical, and legal ones, as appropriate and useful. This second school—to which I adhere—takes the position that relationships in the social sciences are less predictable than in the hard sciences, since the data of the social sciences—human actions and events—are governed by memory, learning, aspiration, and goal seeking. These qualities of human culture and behavior tend to limit us to the discovery of soft and "erodible" regularities, and the most appropriate metamethodological assumption is the "falsificationist" one. That is, we have the obligation of constantly monitoring our conclusions, and if they survive repeated tests, we may view them as unfalsified, until the next test.

The second theme—the topic of Part II, that of generations and professional memory—is concerned with the problem of transmission of the methods and findings of the political science discipline across generations. The chapters that appear in Part II suggest the conclusion that the discontinuity between the scholarly generations post-1965 and those that preceded them is an especially large one. The normal propensity of each generation to caricature and simplify the work of its parents and teachers, in order to establish independent intellectual ground on which to stand, has in the post-1965 generation assumed greater than usual proportions. There is a very real question as to whether this generation has so broken with its past that it may be condemned to repeat its mistakes, to say nothing of being unable to benefit from its positive accomplishments.

Let me offer a word or two of introduction to the several papers included in this volume. In Part I, "Separate Tables: Schools and Sects in Political Science" is essentially a lament about the atrophy of civil discourse in political science, the fragmentation of the field into ideological and methodological camps. It identifies the camps and suggests the problems of reestablishing consensus.

The second chapter, "Clouds, Clocks, and the Study of Politics," written in collaboration with Stephen Genco over a decade ago, was an effort to correct the then spreading view that political science and the social sciences were indistinguishable from the "hard" sciences. Starting from Karl Popper's argument regarding the heterogeneity of reality and the special characteristics of human culture and behavior, the chapter defends an alternative view of the nature of political science as science, and supports a strategy of disciplinary support and development open to both the older institutional, philosophical, and historical approaches and the newer "scientific" ones; to the "applied" side of the discipline as well as the "pure."

Chapter 3, "Model Fitting in Communism Studies," written in collaboration with Laura Roselle, responds to a methodological argument advanced by Giovanni Sartori in the early 1970s, that it was a mistake to transfer models from American studies to European, communist, and Third World studies, that this "conceptual traveling" had the effect of distorting and "misforming" the political reality it was supposed to illuminate. Such a criticism would be apt only if the models and metaphors were taken as reflecting reality rather than being employed in a trial-and-error fashion. The chapter reviews the history of model fitting in communism studies, showing how this drawing on the models of other branches of the political science discipline gradually took on this trial-and-error approach. A review of this history demonstrates the heuristic and constructive value of this model-fitting procedure, showing that the use of the totalitarian, structural-functional, cultural, developmental, pluralist, corporatist, bureaucratic decision-making, patron-client models, and so on, got at different aspects of communist political reality, that they represented an analytic repertory useful in capturing the unique properties of communist systems, the differences among them, and their dynamic and developmental patterns.

"Rational Choice Theory and the Social Sciences" (Chapter 4) was written on the occasion of the thirtieth anniversary of the publication of Anthony Downs's *Economic Theory of Democracy*, one of the earliest products of the rational choice movement in political science. The chapter seeks to place the rational choice movement of the last decades in historical context, relating it to earlier political metaphors, spelling out its powers and its weaknesses. Its power derives from the simplicity and clarity of its assumptions, lending itself to formal and mathematical formulation. Its weakness lies in its failure to come to grips with the variety and complexity of human goal seeking. The chapter reports early indications that these problems are being recognized.

Chapters 5 and 6 deal with the concept of political culture. Chapter 5 briefly reviews the intellectual history of the political culture concept, evaluates the current polemics about its explanatory power, and discusses the ways in which political culture affects and is affected by political structure and process, and the ways in which historical experience may shape it. Chapter 6 "proves" the case for the importance of political culture as an explanatory variable, by examining the persistence of prerevolutionary, precommunist beliefs and values in those countries that have carried out the most systematic and sustained programs designed to eliminate capitalist, liberal, ethnic, and national beliefs and values, and to replace them with "communist" or "socialist" culture.

In Part II, Chapters 7 and 8 demonstrate that just at the time when political theorists and political leaders in the communist countries are rediscovering or discovering for the first time the importance of pluralism, some of our own scholars appear to have lost connections to its meaning and history. Chapter 7 is a review of Suzanne Berger's *Organizing Interests in Western Europe: Pluralism, Corporatism, and the Transformation of Politics*. This book, drawing substantially on European scholars, fails to treat in any way the large American literature dealing with interest groups in the United States and abroad that appeared in the decades from the 1920s to the 1960s, and it also fails to link with the theoretical literature on pluralism of the late nineteenth and early twentieth centuries. The neostatist movement discussed in Chapter 8, "The Return to the State," through its failure to search the literature, repeats the exaggerations of the sovereignty-pluralism debate of the turn of the century.

Chapters 9 and 10 are efforts to correct the exaggerations of the "dependency" literature in its treatment of the political development research of the 1950s and 1960s. Chapter 9, "The Development of Political Development," challenges the dependency charge of ethnocentrism, that the development literature forecast the triumph of capitalist democracy in the Third World. Examination of the development literature shows it to have been quite circumspect in appraising Third World prospects. The dependency movement in turn is shown to be vulnerable to the criticism of failing to accord explanatory power to domestic forces in Third World countries. Chapter 10, "The International-National Connection," challenges the argument advanced in some of the contemporary development literature, that the comparative politics discipline has sought to explain the development of states purely in terms of domestic factors or forces. While the dominant tradition has this domestic bias, the chapter demonstrates the existence of a solid, if minor, tradition that stresses the importance of the international security, economic, and cultural environments in the shaping of the politics and public policy of nation-states. This tradition would include the pre-World War I work of John R. Seeley and Otto Hintze, the early post-World War II work of Gershenkron, Hirschman, Peacock, and Wiseman, up to the recent studies of Lijphart, Tilly, Gurewitch, Skocpol and Katzenstein.

The appendices deal with the University of Chicago so-called behavioral school of political science, in which I was fortunate enough to be trained. They may serve to evoke, and perhaps demythologize, the "culture" of the Chicago school. My biographical memorial of Harold D. Lasswell may illuminate the unusual creativity of one of the leading members of this intellectual community. Where he fit in the Chicago school, and what the members of this school were like in their younger days, is suggested by selections from my oral history now on file in the archives of the American Political Science Association. It may provide some sense of reality about this community of scholars who worked together at the University of Chicago in the two decades from 1920 until 1940.

GABRIEL A. ALMOND

PART I

Political Science as Science

1

Separate Tables: Schools and Sects in Political Science

> Miss Cooper: Loneliness is a terrible thing don't you agree?
> Anne: Yes, I do agree. A terrible thing . . .
> Miss Meacham: She's not an "alone" type.
> Miss Cooper: Is any type an "alone" type, Miss Meacham . . ?
> (From Terence Rattigan's *Separate Tables*, 1955, 78, 92)

In *Separate Tables*, the hit of the 1955 New York theatrical season, the Irish playwright, Terence Rattigan, used the metaphor of solitary diners in a second-rate residential hotel in Cornwall to convey the loneliness of the human condition. It may be a bit farfetched to use this metaphor to describe the condition of political science in the 1980s. But in some sense the various schools and sects of political science now sit at separate tables, each with its own conception of proper political science, but each protecting some secret island of vulnerability.

It was not always so. If we recall the state of the profession a quarter of a century ago, let us say in the early 1960s, David Easton's (1953) and David Truman's (1955) scoldings of the profession for its backwardness among the social science disciplines had been taken to heart by a substantial and productive cadre of young political scientists. In 1961 Robert Dahl wrote his *Epitaph for a Monument to a Successful Protest*, reflecting the sure confidence of a successful movement, whose leaders were rapidly becoming the most visible figures in the profession. Neither Dahl nor Heinz Eulau, whose *Behavioral Persuasion* appeared in 1963, made exaggerated or exclusive claims for the new political science. They expressed the view that the scientific approach to the study of political phenomena had proven itself, and that

---

it could take its place alongside political philosophy, public law, and institutional history and description, as an important approach to the study of politics. As the part of the discipline "on the move," so to speak, it created some worry among the older subdisciplines. An appropriate metaphor for the state of political science at that time perhaps would be the "young Turk-old Turk" model, with the young Turks already beginning to gray at the temples. But we were all Turks.

Now there is this uneasy separateness. The public choice people seek an anchorage in reality, a "new institutionalism," to house their powerful deductive apparatus; the political econometricians want to relate to historical and institutional processes; the humanists cringe at the avoidance of political values by "scientism," and suffer from feelings of inadequacy in a world dominated by statistics and technology; and the radical and "critical" political theorists, like the ancient prophets, lay about them with anathemas against the behaviorists and positivists, and the very notion of a political science professionalism that would separate knowledge from action. But their anti-professionalism must leave them in doubt as to whether they are scholars or politicians.

The uneasiness in the political science profession is not of the body but of the soul. In the last several decades the profession has more than doubled in numbers. American-type political science has spread to Europe, Latin America, Japan, and more interestingly to China and the USSR. Political science has taken on the organizational and methodological attributes of science – research institutes, large-scale budgets, the use of statistical and mathematical methods, and the like. Political science has prospered materially, but it is not a happy profession.

We are separated along two dimensions: an ideological one, and a methodological one (see Figure 1.1). On the methodological dimension there are the extremes of soft and hard. At the soft extreme are Clifford Geertz (1972) types of "thickly descriptive," clinical studies. As an example of this kind of scholarship, Albert Hirschman (1970) celebrated the John Womack (1969) biography of the Mexican guerrilla hero, Emiliano Zapata, with its almost complete lack of conceptualization, hypothesizing, efforts to prove propositions, and the like. Despite this lack of self-conscious social science, Hirschman argues, the Zapata study was full of theoretical implications of the greatest importance. Leo Strauss (1959) and his followers in political philosophy with their exegetical approach to the evocation of the ideas of political philosophers come pretty close to this soft extreme as well, but while Womack's kind of work leaves everything but narrative and description to implication, Straussian exegesis involves the discipline of the

		Ideological Dimension	
		Left	Right
Methodological Dimension	Hard	HL	HR
	Soft	SL	SR

Figure 1.1.

explication of the great texts, ascertaining their "true" meaning through the analysis of their language.

Somewhat away from the soft extreme, but still on the soft side of the continuum, would be political philosophical studies more open to empirical evidence and logical analysis. Recent work such as that of Michael Walzer on justice (1983) and obligation (1970), Carole Pateman on participation (1970) and obligation (1979) would be illustrative. Here there is more than a simple, rich evocation of an event or personality, or precise exegesis of the ideas of political philosophers. A logical argument is advanced, often tested through the examination of evidence, and developed more or less rigorously.

At the other extreme of the methodological continuum are the quantitative, econometric, and mathematical modeling studies; and the most extreme would be the combination of mathematical modeling, statistical analysis, experiment, and computer simulation in the public choice literature. Theories of voting, coalition making, decision-making in committees, and in bureaucracies, involving the testing of hypotheses generated by formal, mathematical models would exemplify this hard extreme.

On the ideological continuum on the left we have four groups in the Marxist tradition—the Marxists properly speaking, the "critical political theorists," the *dependencistas*, and the world system theorists, all of whom deny the possibility of separating knowledge from action, and who subordinate political science to the struggle for socialism. At the conservative end of the continuum are the neoconservatives, who favor among other things a free market economy and limits on the power of the state, as well as an aggressive anti-communist foreign policy.

If we combine these two dimensions we end up with four schools of political science, four separate tables—the soft-left, the hard-left, the soft-right, and the hard-right tables. Reality, of course, is not quite this neat. The ideological and methodological shadings are more complex, more subtle. To elaborate our metaphor a bit but still within the refectoral realm, since the overwhelming majority of political scientists are somewhere in the center—

"liberal" and moderate in ideology, and eclectic and open to conviction in methodology—we might speak of the great cafeteria of the center, from which most of us select our intellectual food, and where we are seated at large tables with mixed and changing table companions.

The outlying tables in this disciplinary refectory are strongly lit and visible, while the large center lies in shade. It is unfortunate that the mood and reputation of the political science discipline is so heavily influenced by these extreme views. This is in part because the extremes make themselves highly audible and visible—the soft left providing a pervasive flagellant background noise, and the hard right providing virtuoso mathematical and statistical displays appearing in the pages of our learned journals.

The Soft Left

Suppose we begin with the soft left. All of the subgroups of the soft left share in the meta-methodological assumption that the empirical world cannot be understood in terms of separate spheres and dimensions, but has to be understood as a time-space totality. "Critical theory," as developed by Horkheimer, Adorno, Marcuse, and others of the "Frankfurt School," rejects the alleged detachment and disaggregating strategy of mainstream social science. The various parts of the social process must be seen "as aspects of a total situation caught up in the process of historical change" (Lukacs, quoted in David Held, 1980, 164). The student as well as that which he studies is involved in struggle. Hence objectivity is inappropriate. "Positivists fail to comprehend that the process of knowing cannot be severed from the historical struggle between humans and the world. Theory and theoretical labor are intertwined in social life processes. The theorist cannot remain detached, passively contemplating, reflecting and describing 'society' or 'nature'" (Held, 165). To understand and explain one must have a commitment to an outcome. There is no political *science* in the positivist sense, that is, a political science separable from ideological commitment. To seek to separate it is a commitment to support the existing, historically obsolescent order.

The more orthodox Marxists such as Perry Anderson (1976), Goran Therborn (1977), Philip Slater (1977), and others, while sharing the meta-methodology of the "Critical school," go further and argue that unless one accepts historical materialism in the fullest reductionist sense of explaining the political realm in class struggle terms, one ends up failing to appreciate the relationship between theory and "praxis."

As we consider the composition of the soft left our fourfold metaphor of separate tables begins to break down. The Marxist theorists of several persuasions – the "critical theorists," the "dependency" writers, and "world system" theorists – make quarrelsome table companions. What they all share is a common belief in the unity of theory and praxis, in the impossibility of separating science and politics. As a logical consequence, positivist political science, which believes in the necessity of separating scientific activity from political activity, loses contact with the overriding unity of the historical process and is mindlessly linked to the status quo. Positivist political science fails to take into account the historical dialectic which makes the shift from capitalism to socialism inevitable.

Fernando Cardoso, the leading theorist of the dependency school, contrasts the methodology of dependency theory with the North American social science tradition in the following language:

> We attempt to reestablish the intellectual tradition based on a comprehensive social science. We seek a global and dynamic understanding of social structures instead of looking only at specific dimensions of the social process. We oppose the academic tradition which conceived of domination and social-cultural relations as "dimensions" analytically independent of one another and together independent of the economy, as if each one of these dimensions corresponded to separate features of reality. . . . We use a dialectical approach to study society, its structures and processes of change. . . . In the end what has to be discussed as an alternative is not the consolidation of the state and the fulfillment of "autonomous capitalism," but how to supersede them. The important question, then, is how to construct paths toward socialism. (Cardoso and Faletto, 1979, ix and xxiv)

Political science can be science, then, only if it is fully committed to the attainment of socialism.

One of the leading American expositors of the "dependency" approach, Richard Fagen, draws the implications of Cardoso's views for the academic community concerned with development issues. Real progress in development scholarship has to be associated with a restructuring of asymmetric international power relations and "a much more difficult and historically significant assault on capitalist forms of development themselves. . . . Only when this crucial understanding infuses the nascent academic critique of the global capitalist system will we be able to say that the paradigm shift in mainstream U.S. social science is gathering steam and moving scholarship closer to what really matters" (1978, 80).

Two recent interpretations of the history of American political science show that this "soft-left" critique of mainstream work in the discipline has taken on some momentum. David Ricci in *The Tragedy of Political Science* (1984) traces the emergence of a liberal scientific school of political science in post-World War II America, a movement dedicated, according to Ricci, to proving the superior virtue of liberal pluralistic values and assumptions by the most precise methods. The validity of this complacent "empirical political theory" constructed by such political scientists as David Truman, Robert Dahl, C. E. Lindblom, the University of Michigan group of voting specialists, and others, was undermined in the disorders of the late 1960s and early 1970s, and in the associated discrediting of American politics and public policy. Ricci draws the implication of this behavioral-postbehavioral episode, as demonstrating that political science as empirical science without the systematic inclusion of moral and ethical values and alternatives, and a commitment to political action, is doomed to disillusion. Political science has to choose sides; failing to do so results in its withdrawal into specialized preciosity, and futility.

Ricci's soft leftism is of the humanist moderate left variety. That of Raymond Seidelman (1985) is a more sharply radical treatment of the history of American political science. In a book entitled *Disenchanted Realists: Political Science and the American Crisis, 1884–1984,* Seidelman develops the thesis in detail that there have been three trends in American political theory—an institutionalist trend, a democratic populist trend, and a relatively short-lived "liberal political science" trend, initiated in the 1920s and 1930s by the University of Chicago school, and flowering in the United States in the post-World War II years roughly until the 1970s. The institutionalist trend is the Hamiltonian-Madisonian tradition embodied in the constitutional system, so constructed that it would frustrate the will of majorities. Separation of powers theory is based on a distrust of popular propensities. Contrasted with this tradition of American political theory is the democratic populist trend manifested in early agrarian egalitarianism, abolitionism, populism, and the like. This second Thomas Paine tradition is anti-statist, anti-government and was discredited by the rise of industrial-urban society and the necessity for strong central government.

The third tradition was based on a belief in the possibility of a science of politics which would help produce a powerful national state, manned by trained experts pursuing constructive and coherent public policies, and supported by virtuous popular majorities. This third tradition dream of a great constructive political science has been dispelled on both the political and the science sides. Political reality has turned into a disarticulated set of elite-dominated "issue networks" and "iron triangles," incapable of pursuing consistent and effective public policies; and the science has turned into a set of disembodied specialties lacking in linkage to politics and public policy. Seidelman concludes:

> Historically, political science professionalism has only obscured fundamental conflicts and choices in American public life, for it has treated citizens as objects of study or clients of a benign political paternalism. . . . Until political scientists realize that their democratic politics cannot be realized through a barren professionalism, intellectual life will remain cleaved from the genuine if heretofore subterranean dreams of American citizens. Political science history has confirmed this separation, even as it has tried to bridge it. Modern political science must bridge it, if delusions are to be transformed into new democratic realities. (241)

The burden of the soft left, thus, is an attack on political science professionalism. It is a call to the academy to join the political fray, to orient its teaching and research around left ideological commitments—in particular, moderate or revolutionary socialism.

The Hard Right

The hard right, on the other hand, is ultra-professional at the methodological level, deploying a formidable array of scientific methodologies—deductive, statistical, and experimental. There is a tendency to view softer historical, descriptive, and unsophisticated quantitative analysis as pre-professional, as inferior breeds of political science, although in recent years there has been a notable rediscovery of political institutions, and an effort to relate formal deductive work to the empirical tradition pioneered by Gosnell, Herring, and V. O. Key.

William Mitchell (1988), in a recent review of the public choice movement in political science, distinguishes between the two principal centers, which he calls the Virginia and Rochester schools. The Virginia school, influential mainly among economists, was founded by James Buchanan and Gordon Tullock. The founder of the Rochester school, more influential among political scientists, was William Riker. Both schools tend to be skeptical of politics and bureaucracy and are fiscally conservative. But the Virginia school views the market unambiguously as the benchmark of efficient allocation. The Virginians according to Mitchell display a "firm conviction that the private economy is far more robust, efficient, and perhaps equitable than other economies, and much more successful than political processes in efficiently allocating resources. . . . Much of what has been produced by the [Virginian] Center for Study of Public Choice, can best be described as contributions to a theory of the failure of political processes . . . inequity, inefficiency, and coercion are the most general results of democratic policy formation" (106–107). Buchanan proposed an automatic deficit reduction plan years before the adoption of the Gramm-Rudman-Hollings proposal; and he was the author of an early version of the proposed constitutional budget-balancing amendment. Buchanan, in two books–*Democracy in Deficit: The Political Legacy of Lord Keynes* (Buchanan and Wagner, 1977), and *The Economics of Politics* (1978)–presents a view of democratic politics in which voters act in terms of their short-run interests, that is to say, oppose taxes and favor material benefits for themselves; politicians naturally play into these propensities by favoring spending and opposing taxing; and bureaucrats seek to extend their power and resources without regard to the public interest.

These theorists differ in the extent to which they believe that the short-run utility-maximizer model captures human reality. Some scholars employ the model only as a way of generating hypotheses. Thus Robert Axelrod, using deductive modeling, experimentation, and computer simulation, has made important contributions to our understanding of how cooperative norms emerge, and in particular how norms of international cooperation might develop from an original short-run utility-maximizing perspective (1984). Douglass North (1981), Samuel Popkin (1979), Robert Bates (1988), and others combine rational choice modeling with sociological analysis in their studies of Third World development and historical process.

That this view is on the defensive is reflected in recent comments of scholars with unquestionable scientific credentials. Thus Herbert Simon challenges the rational choice assumption of this literature:

> It makes a difference to research, a very large difference, to our research strategy whether we are studying the nearly omniscient *homo economicus* of rational choice theory or the boundedly rational *homo psychologicus* of cognitive psychology. It makes a difference for research, but it also makes a difference for the proper design of political institutions. James Madison was well aware of that, and in the pages of the *Federalist Papers,* he opted for this view of the human condition; "As there is a degree of depravity in mankind which requires a certain degree of circumspection and distrust, so there are other qualities in human nature which justify a certain portion of esteem and confidence:"–a balanced and realistic view we may concede, of bounded human rationality and its accompanying frailties of motive and reason. (303)

James March and Johan Olsen attack the formalism of the public choice literature: "The new institutionalism is an empirically based prejudice, an assertion that what we observe in the world is inconsistent with the ways in which contemporary theories ask us to talk. . . . The bureaucratic agency, the legislative committee, and the appellate court are arenas for contending social forces, but they are also collections of standard operating procedures and structures that define and defend interest" (1984, 738). They similarly question the rational self-interest assumption of the public choice literature, arguing,

> Although self-interest undoubtedly permeates politics, action is often based more on discovering the normatively appropriate behavior than on calculating the return expected from alternative choices. As a result, political behavior, like other behavior, can be described in terms of duties, obligations, roles, and rules. (744)

The Soft Right

In the soft-right cell there are miscellaneous conservatives of an old and a "neo" variety, who tend to be traditional in their methodologies and on the right side of the ideological spectrum. But the followers of Leo Strauss in political theory are a distinctive breed indeed. Their methodological conservatism is unambiguous. The enlightenment and the scientific revolution are the archenemy. High on their list of targets is the value-free and ethically neutral political science of Max Weber. As Leo Strauss put it, "Moral obtuseness is the necessary condition for scientific analysis. The more serious we are as social scientists the more completely we develop within ourselves a state of indifference to any goal, or to aimlessness and drifting, a state of what may be called nihilism" (1959, 19). But political *science* is not only amoral, it is not really productive of knowledge. Again Leo Strauss, "Generally speaking, one may wonder whether the new political science has brought to light anything of political importance which intelligent political practitioners with a deep knowledge of history, nay intelligent and educated journalists, to say nothing of the old political scientists, did not know at least as well beforehand" (in Storing, 1962, 312).

The Straussians reject all "historicist" and "sociology of knowledge" interpretations of political theory. The true meaning of philosophical texts is contained in what has been written. The political philosopher must have the skill and insight necessary to explicate this original meaning. The ultimate truth can be located in the writings of the original classic philosophers, and particularly in the writings of Plato – in his Socratic rationalism shorn of all contingency. Truths transcend time, place, and context. Post-Machiavellian political philosophy has led to moral relativism and the decay of civic virtue; "behavioral" political science is the debased product of this moral decline.

In the recent celebrations of the 200th anniversary of the Constitution, the Straussians, as one might expect, were in the vanguard of the "original intent" school of constitutional interpretation. Gordon Wood, in a recent review of the Straussian literature on the Constitution (1988), points out that for such Straussians as Gary McDowell and Walter Berns the whole truth about the Constitution is contained in the constitutional text, and perhaps the record of the debates, and the Federalist Papers. Wood points out that the Straussian commitment to "natural right" leads them to distrust of all historically derived rights, "particularly those recently discovered by the Supreme Court" (1988, 39). For some Straussians the natural right to property postulated by the Founders may be grounds for rolling back the modern welfare state. The moral model regime for many Straussians is the Platonic aristocracy, or as second-best, Aristotelian "mixed government." Their program of action is a call for an intellectual elite which will bring us back to first principles.

The Hard Left

There is finally a hard-left school, which employs scientific methodology in testing propositions derived from socialist and dependency theories. However, the moment one makes explicit and testable the assumptions and beliefs of left ideologies, one has gone part of the way toward rejecting the anti-professionalism of the left. And this is reflected in the nervousness of leading socialist and dependency theorists over quantification and the testing of hypotheses. Thus Christopher Chase-Dunn, one of the leading world system quantifiers, pleads with his colleagues, "My concern is that we not become bogged down in a sterile debate between 'historicists' and 'social scientists,' or between quantitative and qualitative researchers. The 'ethnic' boundaries may provide us with much material for spirited dialogue, but a real understanding of the world system will require that we transcend methodological sectarianism" (1982, 181). The leading dependency theorists such as Cardoso and Fagen raise serious questions regarding the validity of "scientific type, quantitative" studies of dependency propositions. For reasons not clearly specified such research is "premature," or misses the point. Thus they probably would not accept as valid the findings of the Sylvan, Snidal, Russett, Jackson, and Duvall (1983) group, which tested a formal model of "dependencia" on a worldwide set of dependent countries in the 1970–75 period, and came up with mixed and inconclusive results. Nevertheless, the dependency and world system quantifiers and econometricians, including political scientists and sociologists such as Chase-Dunn (1982), Richard Rubinson (see Rubinson and Chase-Dunn, 1979), Albert Bergesen (1980), Volker Bornschier and J. P. Hoby (1981), and others, are carrying on quantitative studies oriented toward the demonstration of the validity of world system and dependency propositions.

Getting Our Professional History Straight

Most political scientists would find themselves uncomfortable seated at these outlying tables. Having become a major academic profession only in the last two or three generations, we are not about to cast off our badges of professional integrity by turning our research and teaching into political advocacy. This is reflected in the partial defection from anti-professionalism by the hard left, who insist that assertions about society and politics can be tested by formulating them explicitly and precisely, and using statistical methods where appropriate.

Similarly, most of us are troubled at the preemption by the public choice and statistical political scientists of the badge of professionalism, and their demotion of the rest of us to a prescientific status. And this concern is shared by some of the most reputable and sophisticated of our more rigorous political scientists, who are currently engaged in relating to and rehabilitating the older political science methodologies, such as philosophical, legal, and historical analysis, and institutional description.

And there are few political scientists indeed who would share the view that all political science since the sixteenth century is a deviation from the true path, and that the sole route to professionalism is through the exegesis of the classical texts of political theory.

It is noteworthy that each of these schools or sects presents us with a particular version of the history of the political science discipline. Whoever controls the interpretation of the past in our professional history writing has gone a long way toward controlling the future. The soft left has almost preempted the writing of professional political science history in recent years. I believe they may have succeeded in convincing some of us that we have deviated from the true path. Both Ricci and Seidelman would have us believe that modern political science with its stress on methodology and objectivity could only develop in the United States, where for a brief interval it appeared that liberal democracy and an objective professionalism were possible. As this American optimism abates, and as party and class antagonism sharpens inevitably, they argue, a politically neutral political science becomes untenable. According to this view political science must again become an active part of a political and, for some, a revolutionary movement.

The view of professional history presented by the hard right is a very foreshortened one. According to this view, prior to the introduction of mathematical, statistical, and experimental methodologies there was no political science and theory in the proper sense.

But the large methodologically eclectic majority of political scientists, and those who are committed to the control of ideological bias in the conduct of professional work—what I call the "cafeteria of the center"—ought not to concede the writing of disciplinary history to any one of these schools. The history of political science does not lead to any one of these separate tables, but rather to the methodologically mixed and objectivity-aspiring scholarship of the center.

It is not correct to argue that political science deviated from classical political philosophy in the sixteenth and seventeenth centuries, and that it has been on the wrong path ever since. Nor is it correct to attribute to American political science the effort to separate political theory from political action. The Straussians cannot legitimately claim exclusive origin in classical Greek philosophy. The scientific impulse in political studies had its beginnings among the classical Greek philosophers. Robert Dahl, for my money, is a more legitimate follower of Aristotle than is Leo Strauss.

There is a political sociological tradition going all the way back to Plato and Aristotle, continuing through Polybius, Cicero, Machiavelli, Hobbes, Locke, Montesquieu, Hume, Rousseau, Tocqueville, Comte, Marx, Pareto, Durkheim, Weber and continuing up to Dahl, Lipset, Rokkan, Sartori, Moore, and Lijphart, which sought, and seeks, to relate socioeconomic conditions to political constitutions and institutional arrangements, and to relate these structural characteristics to policy propensities in war and peace.

Our founding fathers belonged to this tradition. Alexander Hamilton observed in *Federalist 9*, "The science of politics . . . like most other sciences, has received great improvement. The efficacy of various principles is now well understood, which were either not known at all, or imperfectly known to the ancients" (1937). And in *Federalist 31* Hamilton deals with the perennial question of just how scientific moral and political studies could be. He concludes,

> Though it cannot be pretended that the principles of moral and political knowledge have, in general, the same degree of certainty with those of the mathematics, yet they have much better claims in this respect than . . . we should be disposed to allow them. (189)

It is worth noting that the hard science-soft science polarity, which we have been led to assume is a recent phenomenon attributable to the heresy of the American behavioral movement, has in fact been endemic to the discipline since its origins.

In the nineteenth and early twentieth centuries, Auguste Comte, Marx and Engels and their followers, Max Weber, Emile Durkheim, Vilfredo Pareto, and others treated politics in larger social science perspectives, with lawlike regularities and necessary relationships. At the turn of the twentieth century John Robert Seeley and Otto Hintze, Moissaye Ostrogorski, and Roberto Michels all produced what they considered to be "scientific laws" of politics – Seeley and Hintze on the relationship between external pressure and internal freedom in the development of the nation states of Western Europe; Ostrogorski, on the incompatibility of the mass-bureaucratic political party and democracy which he derived from a comparative study of the rise of the British and American party systems; and Michels, on the "iron law of oligarchy," the propensity in large bureaucratic organizations for power to gravitate to the top leadership, which he derived from his "critical" case study of the Social Democratic party of Germany. More recently, Duverger's "law" of the relationship between the electoral and party systems also came from Europe.

Among the early pioneers of modern professional political science it was common practice to speak of this branch of scholarship as a "science" from the very beginning. Thus Sir Frederick Pollock and John Robert Seeley, the first lecturing from Oxford and the Royal Institution, the second from Cambridge, entitled their books *The History of the Science of Politics* (1890) and *An Introduction to Political Science* (1896), respectively. What these early writers meant by "science" varied from case to case. Pollock distinguishes between the natural and moral sciences:

> The comparative inexactness of the moral sciences is not the fault of the men who have devoted their abilities to them, but depends, as Aristotle already saw, on the nature of their subject matter. (5)

For John Robert Seeley political science was to be a body of propositions drawn from historical knowledge. He expected a takeoff in the development of political science because of the development of historiography in the nineteenth century. If the moderns were to do so much better than Locke, Hobbes, and Montesquieu, it was because their historical data base was much richer.

For Seeley, who introduced political science into the Cambridge Tripos, it meant learning to "reason, generalize, define, and distinguish . . . as well as collecting, authenticating, and investigating facts." These two processes constituted political science. "If we neglect the first process, we shall accumulate facts to little purpose, because we shall have no test by which to distinguish facts which are important from those which are unimportant; and of course, if we neglect the second process, our reasonings will be baseless, and we shall but weave scholastic cobwebs" (1896, 27–28).

There were two schools of thought in the nineteenth and early twentieth century social sciences regarding the degree or kind of science that was possible. The work of Auguste Comte, Karl Marx, and Vilfredo Pareto makes no distinction between the social and the "natural" sciences. Both groups of sciences sought uniformities, regularities, laws. On the other hand, the notion of a social science which would consist of "a closed system of concepts, in which reality is synthesized in some sort of permanently and universally valid classification, and from which it can again be deduced" was viewed as entirely meaningless by Max Weber:

> The stream of immeasurable events flows unendingly towards eternity. The cultural problems which move men form themselves ever anew and in different colors, and the boundaries of that area in the infinite stream of concrete events which acquires meaning and significance for us, i.e. which becomes an "historical individual" are constantly subject to change. The intellectual contexts from which it is viewed and scientifically analyzed shift. (1949, 80)

The "lawfulness" of human interaction is of a different order for Max Weber. The subject matter of the social sciences – human action – involves value orientation, memory and learning, which can only yield "soft" regularities, "objective possibilities," and probabilities. Cultural change may attenuate or even dissolve these relationships. Similarly, Durkheim viewed cultural phenomena as too complex and open to human creativity to lend themselves to the same degree of causal certainty as the natural sciences.

During the first decades of professional political science in the United States – from 1900 to the 1930s – two scholars, Merriam and Catlin, the first as American as apple pie, the second a temporarily transplanted Englishman—took the lead in advocating the introduction of scientific methods and standards in the study of politics. Merriam's contribution was primarily programmatic, and promotional. He advocated, recruited personnel, and funded a particular research program at the University of Chicago. He also was a founder of the Social Science Research Council. Catlin wrote on methodological questions, differentiating between history and political science, and locating political science among the social sciences.

In his 1921 manifesto, "The Present State of the Study of Politics," Merriam advocated the introduction of psychological insights into the study of political institutions and processes, and of the introduction of statistical methods in an effort to enhance the rigor of political analysis. Nowhere in this early call to professional growth and improvement is there anything approximating a discussion of scientific methodology. He proposed to *do* political science rather than talk about it. And indeed, in the decades following at the University of Chicago, a research program unfolded exemplifying Merriam's stress on empirical research, quantification, and social-psychological interpretation. The scholars produced by this program constituted a substantial part of the nucleus of the post-World War "behavioral movement."

George Catlin may have been the first to speak of a "behaviorist treatment of politics" (1927, xi), and in his argument about a science of politics seems to dispose of all of those objections which would differentiate social and human subject matters from those of natural science. But he is hardly sanguine about the prospects of science.

> Politics must for the present confine itself to the humble task of collecting, where possible measuring, and sorting the historical material, past and contemporary; and following up probable clues to the discovery of permanent forms and general principles of action. . . . It is reasonable to expect that political science will prove to be more than this, that it will give us some insight into the possibility of controlling the social situation, and will show us, if not what it is wise to do, at least what, human nature being what it is, it is unwise to do, because such action will cut across the grain of the social structure and athwart the lines of activity of the deeper forces which have built up this structure. (1927, 142–43).

Thus Bernard Crick's (1959) argument that it was the behavioral movement in American political science, and particularly the Chicago school that was responsible for leading political science down the garden path of scientism cannot bear careful examination of the sources. In both Europe and America meta-methodological opinion has been divided on this question. It would be hard to find more hard-science-oriented scholars than Comte, Marx, Pareto, and Freud. Durkheim and Weber, while fully committed to the pursuit of science, clearly recognized that the social scientist dealt with a subject matter less tractable to covering-law hard-science forms of explanation. This polemic diffused to the United States in the course of the twentieth century.

Crick's attribution of this scientific orientation to Chicago populists does not hold up when we examine the evidence. One has to read the Tocqueville correspondence (1962) to appreciate how close that brilliant interpreter of American democracy, a century before the Chicago school saw the light of day, came to doing an opinion survey in his travels around the country. As he talked to a steamboat captain on the Mississippi, to farmers in the interior, to bourgeois dinner companions on the eastern seaboard, and to officeholders in Washington, D.C., sampling the American population was clearly on his mind. Karl Marx drew up a six-page questionnaire for the study of the living conditions, working conditions, attitudes, and beliefs of the French working class in the early 1880s. A large number of copies were distributed to socialists and working-class organizations. The data gathered were to be used in the forthcoming general election (1880). In Max Weber's working papers for his study of the peasantry in East Prussia there is evidence that he planned and partially executed a survey of Polish and German peasant attitudes. And in his study of comparative religion he used a formal two-by-two table—worldliness-unworldliness, asceticism-mysticism—as a way of generating hypotheses about the relationship between religious ethics and economic attitudes.

Most of the important discoveries in the development of statistics were made by Europeans. La Place and Condorcet were Frenchmen; the Bernoulli family were Swiss; Bayes, Galton, Pearson, and Fisher were Englishmen; Pareto was an Italian; Markov a Russian. The first "public choice" theorist was the Scotsman, Duncan Black (1958). The view that the quantitative approach to social science analysis was peculiarly American doesn't stand up to the historical record. What was peculiarly American was the improvement in, and the application of, quantitative methods as in survey research, content analysis, aggregate statistical analysis, mathematical modeling, and the like, and the pursuit in empirical depth of psychological and sociological hypotheses largely generated in the European social science literature.

At the darkest moment in European history—in the 1930s—there was a strong infusion of European social science into the United States through refugees such as Paul Lazarsfeld, Kurt Lewin, Marie Jahoda, Wolfgang Kohler, Hans Speier, Erich Fromm, Franz Neumann, Otto Kircheimer, Leo Lowenthal, Franz Alexander, Hannah Arendt, Hans Morgenthau, Leo Strauss, and many others. It should be quite clear from this litany of names that this emigration carried the various social science polemics within it, and that the counterposition of a European and an American approach to social science around the issue of humanist vs. scientific scholarship will simply not bear the light of day. There is clear continuity from the European background to the growth of the social sciences and political science in the United States.

This broad tradition of political science, beginning with the Greeks and continuing up to the creative scholars of our own generation, is the historically correct version of our disciplinary history. The critical and Marxist schools throw in the professional sponge. Confronting this simplistic temptation we need to have a deep-rooted and unshakable firmness in our commitment to the search for objectivity. The call for "relevance" associated with "postbehavioralism" implies a greater concern for policy implications in our scholarly work, but it cannot imply a commitment to a particular course of political action. A political scientist is not necessarily a socialist, and surely not a socialist of a particular kind.

The version of disciplinary history presented to us in Straussian political philosophy cannot be taken seriously. The hard-nosed public choice version of our history mistakes technique for substance. Mainstream political science is open to all methods that illuminate the world of politics and public policy. It will not turn its back on the illumination we get from our older methodologies just because it now can employ the powerful tools of statistics and mathematics.

We have good grounds for professional pride in the development of political science in the last decades. And as Americans we have made important contributions to an age-old, worldwide effort to bring the power of knowledge to bear on the tragic dilemmas of the world of politics.

References

Anderson, Perry. 1976. *Considerations on Western Marxism*. London: New Left Books.

Axelrod, Robert. 1984. *The Evolution of Cooperation*. New York: Basic Books.

Bates, Robert. 1988. *Macro-Political Economy in the Field of Development*. Duke University Program in International Political Economy, Working Paper No. 40 (June).

Bergesen, Albert. 1980. "The Class Structure of the World System." In *Contending Approaches to World System Analysis*, ed. William R. Thompson. Beverly Hills, CA: Sage Publications.

Black, Duncan. 1958. *The Theory of Committees and Elections*. Cambridge: Cambridge University Press.

Bornschier, Volker, and J. P. Hoby. 1981. "Economic Policy and Multi-National Corporations in Development: The Measurable Impacts in Cross National Perspective." *Social Problems*, 28: 363-377

Bornschier, Volker, C. Chase-Dunn, and R. Rubinson. 1978. "Cross-national Evidence of Effects of Foreign Aid and Investment on Development." *American Journal of Sociology*, 84(3): 207-222.

Buchanan, James. 1978. *The Economics of Politics*. Lancing, West Sussex: Institute of Economic Affairs.

Buchanan, James, and Richard Wagner. 1977. *Democracy in Deficit: The Political Legacy of Lord Keynes*. New York: Academic Press.

Cardoso, Fernando, and Enzo Faletto. 1979. *Dependency and Development in Latin America*. Berkeley: University of California Press.

Catlin, George E.G. 1927. *The Science and Method of Politics*. Hamden, CT: Anchor Books.

Chase-Dunn, Christopher. 1982. "Commentary." In *World System Analysis: Theory and Methodology*, ed. Terence Hopkins and Immanuel Wallerstein. Beverly Hills, CA: Sage Publications.

Crick, Bernard. 1959. *The American Science of Politics*. Berkeley: University of California Press.

Dahl, Robert A. 1961. "The Behavioral Approach in Political Science: Epitaph for a Monument to a Successful Protest." *American Political Science Review*, 55(Dec.): 763-772.

Easton, David. 1953. *The Political System*. New York: A. A. Knopf.

Eulau, Heinz. 1963. *The Behavioral Persuasion in Politics*. New York: Random House.

Fagen, Richard. 1978. "A Funny Thing Happened on the Way to the Market: Thoughts on Extending Dependency Ideas." *International Organization*, 32(1): 287-300.

Geertz, Clifford. 1972. *The Interpretation of Cultures*. New York: Basic Books.

Hamilton, Alexander. 1937. *The Federalist*. Washington, DC: National Home Library Foundation.

Held, David. 1980. *Introduction to Critical Theory: Horkheimer to Habermas*. Berkeley: University of California Press.

Hirschman, Albert. 1970. "The Search for Paradigms as a Hindrance to Understanding." *World Politics*, 22(3, March): 329-343.

March; James, and Johan Olsen. 1984. "The New Institutionalism: Organizational Factors in Political Life." *American Political Science Review*, 78(3 Sept.): 734-750.

Marx, Karl. 1880. "Enquiete Ouvriere." *La Revue Socialiste* (20 April).

Merriam, Charles E. 1921. "The Present State of the Study of Politics." *American Political Science Review*, 15(May): 173-185.

Mitchell, William. 1988. "Virginia, Rochester, and Bloomington: Twenty-five Years of Public Choice and Political Science." *Public Choice*, 56: 101-119.

North, Douglass. 1981. *Structure and Change in Economic History*. New York: W. W. Norton.

Pateman, Carole. 1970. *Participation and Democratic Theory*. Cambridge: Cambridge University Press.

Pateman, Carole. 1979. *The Problem of Political Obligation*. Chichester: Wiley.

Pollock, Frederick. 1890. *The History of the Science of Politics*. London: Macmillan.

Popkin, Samuel. 1979. *The Rational Peasant*. Berkeley: University of California Press.

Rattigan, Terence. 1955. *Separate Tables*. New York: Random House.

Ricci, David. 1984. *The Tragedy of Political Science*. New Haven, CT: Yale University Press.

Riker, William. 1982. *Liberalism Against Populism*. San Francisco: Freeman.

Rubinson, Richard, and C. Chase-Dunn. 1979. "Cycles, Trends, and New Departures in World System Development." In *National Development and World Systems*, ed. J. W. Meyer and M. T. Hannan. Chicago: University of Chicago Press.

Seeley, John Robert. 1896. *An Introduction to Political Science*. London: Macmillan.

Seidelman, Raymond. 1985. *Disenchanted Realists: Political Science and the American Crisis, 1884–1984*. Albany: State University of New York Press.

Simon, Herbert. 1985. "Human Nature in Politics: The Dialogue of Psychology with Political Science." *American Political Science Review*, 79(2 June): 293–304.

Slater, Philip. 1977. *Origin and Significance of the Frankfurt School: A Marxist Perspective*. London: Routledge & Kegan Paul.

Strauss, Leo. 1959. *What Is Political Philosophy*? Glencoe, IL: Free Press.

Strauss, Leo. 1972. "Political Philosophy and the Crisis of Our Time." In *The Post Behavioral Era*, ed. George Graham and George Carey. New York: Holt, Rinehart & Winston, pp. 217–242.

Sylvan, David, Duncan Snidal, Bruce M. Russett, Steven Jackson, and Raymond Duvall. 1983. "The Peripheral Economies: Penetration and Economic Distortion, 1970–1975." In *Contending Approaches to World System Analysis*, ed. William Thompson. Beverly Hills, CA: Sage Publications.

Therborn, Goran. 1977. *The Frankfurt School in Western Marxism: A Critical Reader*. London: New Left Books.

Tocqueville, Alexis de 1962. *Journey to America*. New Haven, CT: Yale University Press.

Truman, David. 1955. "The Impact of the Revolution in Behavioral Science on Political Science." *Brookings Lectures*. Washington, DC: Brookings Institution, pp. 202–231.

Walzer, Michael. 1970. *Obligations*. Cambridge, MA: Harvard University Press.

Walzer, Michael. 1983. *Spheres of Justice*. New York: Basic Books.

Weber, Max. 1949. *The Methodology of the Social Sciences* (translated by E. A. Shils and H. A. Finch). Glencoe, IL: Free Press.

Womack, John. 1969. *Zapata and the Mexican Revolution*. New York: A. A. Knopf.

Wood, Gordon S. 1988. "The Fundamentalists and the Constitution." *New York Review of Books* (18 Feb.).

2

Clouds, Clocks, and the Study of Politics

with Stephen Genco

In its eagerness to become scientific, political science has in recent decades tended to lose contact with its ontological base. It has tended to treat political events and phenomena as natural events lending themselves to the same explanatory logic as is found in physics and the other hard sciences. This tendency may be understood in part as a phase in the scientific revolution, as a diffusion, in two steps, of ontological and methodological assumptions from the strikingly successful hard sciences: first to psychology and economics, and then from these bellwether human sciences to sociology, anthropology, political science, and even history. In adopting the agenda of hard science, the social sciences, and political science in particular, were encouraged by the neopositivist school of the philosophy of science which legitimated this assumption of ontological and meta-methodological homogeneity. More recently, some philosophers of science and some psychologists and economists have had second thoughts about the applicability to human subject matters of strategy used in hard science. It may be useful to bring these arguments to the attention of political scientists.

Popper's Metaphors

Karl Popper, who along with R. B. Braithwaite, Carl Hempel, and Ernest Nagel has argued the thesis of meta-methodological homogeneity, more recently has stressed the heterogeneity of reality, and its unamenability to a single model of scientific explanation. He uses the metaphor of clouds and

---

From Gabriel A. Almond, "Clouds, Clocks, and the Study of Politics," *World Politics*, Vol. 29, No. 4.

clocks to represent the commonsense notions of determinacy and indeterminacy in physical systems. He asks us to imagine a continuum stretching from the most irregular, disorderly, and unpredictable "clouds" on the left to the most regular, orderly, and predictable "clocks" on the right. As the best example of a deterministic system near the clock-extreme, Popper cites the solar system. Toward this end of the continuum we would find such phenomena as pendulums, precision clocks, and motor cars. As an example of a system near the other, indeterminate, end of the continuum, he cites a cluster of gnats or small flies in which each insect moves randomly except that it turns back toward the center when it strays too far from the swarm. Near this extreme we would find gas clouds, the weather, schools of fish, human societies, and, perhaps a bit closer toward the center, individual human beings and animals.

The Newtonian revolution in physics popularized the notion—which was to persist for approximately 250 years—that this commonsense arrangement was in error. The success of Newton's theory in explaining and predicting a multitude of celestial and earthbound events by his laws of motion led most thinkers—although not Newton himself—to embrace the position that the universe and all its parts were by nature clocklike and in principle completely predictable. Phenomena that had the appearance of indeterminacy were viewed as being merely poorly understood; in time, they also were expected to be found regular and predictable. Thus the reigning model of science after Newton affirmed that all nature was governed by deterministic laws or, to put it in Popper's metaphor, "*all clouds are clocks*—even the most cloudy of clouds."[1]

In the 1920s, the development of quantum theory challenged this clocklike model of nature and supported the view that indeterminacy and chance were fundamental to all natural processes. With this discovery, Popper's metaphor was inverted; now the dominant view held that "to some degree *all clocks are clouds*; or in other words, that *only clouds exist*, though clouds of very different degrees of cloudiness."[2] Many scientists and philosophers greeted this change of model with relief, since it seemed to free them from the nightmare of determinism that denied the efficacy of human choices and goals.

But Popper goes on to argue his central point, that "*indeterminism is not enough*" to account for the apparent autonomy of human ideas in the physical world. "If determinism is true, then the whole world is a perfectly running flawless clock, including all clouds, all organisms, all animals, all men. If, on the other hand, Pierce's or Heisenberg's or some other form of indeterminism is true, then sheer *chance* plays a major role in our physical world. But is chance really more satisfactory than determinism?"[3]

Popper answers in the negative. Although physicists and philosophers have tried to build models of human choice based upon the unpredictability of quantum jumps,[4] he rejects these as being too circumscribed. He acknowledges that "the quantum-jump model may be a model for . . . snap decisions. . . . But are snap decisions really so very interesting? Are they characteristic of human behavior—of *rational* human behavior?" He concludes: "I do not think so. . . . What we need for understanding rational human behavior—and indeed animal behavior—is something *intermediate* in character, between perfect chance and perfect determinism—something intermediate between perfect clouds and perfect clocks. . . . For obviously what we want is to understand how such non-physical things as *purposes, deliberations, plans, decisions, theories, intentions*, and *values*, can play a part in bringing about physical changes in the physical world."[5]

Popper's method of arriving at a solution to this problem seems, like the problem itself, to be relevant to politics and political science. His conjecture is that the problem is essentially one of *control*; i.e., the control of behavior and other aspects of the physical world by human ideas or mental abstractions. Thus he states that "the solution must explain freedom; and it must also explain how freedom is not just chance but, rather, the result of a subtle interplay between *something almost random or haphazard*, and *something like a restrictive or selective control*—such as an aim or standard—though certainly not a cast-iron control." Accordingly, he restricts the scope of acceptable solutions to those that "conform to *the idea of combining freedom and control*, and also to *the idea of 'plastic control,'* as I shall call it in contradistinction to a 'cast-iron' control."[6]

Popper reaches an evolutionary solution to this problem—one that stresses trial-and-error elimination, or variation and selective retention.[7] Only such a theory can accommodate plastic control, and thus human freedom. Once this is seen, the problem of the relationship between ideas and behavior becomes solvable: "For the control of ourselves and of our actions by our theories and purposes is *plastic* control. We are not *forced* to submit ourselves to the control of our theories, for we can discuss them critically, and we can reject them freely if we think that they fall short of our regulative standards. Not only do our theories control us, but we can control our theories (and even our standards): there is a kind of *feedback* here."[8]

Popper concludes: "We have seen that it is unsatisfactory to look upon the world as a closed physical system—whether a strictly deterministic system or a system in which whatever is not strictly determined is simply due to chance; on such a view of the world human creativeness and human freedom can only be illusions. . . . I have therefore offered a different view of the world—one in which the physical world is an open system. This is compatible with the view of the evolution of life as a process of trial-and-error elimination; and it allows us to understand rationally, though far from fully, the emergence of biological novelty and the growth of human freedom."[9]

Thus Popper tells us that the models of explanation appropriate to the physical sciences will not enable us to come to grips with human and cultural phenomena, and that while we can increase our understanding of them, we cannot explain them fully because of their creative and emergent properties.

The Ontological Properties of Politics

Popper's essay presents us with three ways of conceptualizing social reality—as a clock, as a cloud, and as a system of plastic controls. Political reality, which it is the task of political science to explain, is clearly best captured by the third conceptualization. It consists of ideas—human decisions, goals, purposes—in constant and intense interaction with other ideas, human behavior, and the physical world. At the center of this complex system are *choices and decisions*—decisions to command, obey, vote, make demands. The political universe has organization; elites make decisions to command or not to command, what to command, how to implement commands. Citizens and subjects make decisions to comply, how to comply, or not to comply; to make demands, how to make demands, or not to make demands. That is the heart of politics, the subject matter our discipline is committed to exploring and understanding.

The relations among these events are not simply reactive, as are the encounters of physical objects; they are not readily amenable to cause-and-effect "clocklike" models or metaphors. Basically, this is because the behavioral repertoires of elites and citizens are not fixed repertoires. The actors in politics have memories; they learn from experience. They have goals, aspirations, calculative strategies. Memory, learning, goal seeking, and problem solving intervene between "cause" and "effect," between independent and dependent variable.

Political decisions are not made and implemented in a vacuum; they are subject to a complex array of *constraints* and *opportunities*. These constraints—the necessities of politics—range from the relatively hard variety represented by environmental or ecological limits to the quite soft variety illustrated by passing fashions and fads. Constraints define the "operational milieu" of political actors[10] and exhibit varying degrees of manipulability.

Some, like geography or the level of technology, are difficult to alter even in the long run; in the short run, they are practically nonmanipulable. Others, like cultural values and public opinion, are relatively easy to manipulate in some circumstances, more intractable in others. But manipulation is very rarely impossible in principle. Even relatively hard environmental constraints—such as the relation between material resource needs and population—can sometimes be altered as a consequence of man's creative, adaptive capacities. The agricultural revolution some 10,000 years ago multiplied by many times the number of people capable of being sustained in a given space, and the industrial revolution of the last two centuries multiplied it by many times again.

These ontological properties of political affairs are plain for all to see; they are not matters on which reasonable persons can differ. Social scientists who—for whatever philosophical or methodological reasons—deny them and view human behavior as simply reactive and consequently susceptible to the same explanatory logic as "clocklike" natural phenomena are trying to fashion a science based on empirically falsified presuppositions. That becomes clear when their explanatory schemes are thought of in terms of their own behavior as scientists. Insofar as they acknowledge the importance of scientific memory, scientific creativity, calculative strategies, goal seeking, and problem solving in their own work, they must in some degree acknowledge these qualities in the human and social material they investigate and seek to explain.

The implication of these complexities of human and social reality is that the explanatory strategy of the hard sciences has only a limited application to the social sciences. Models, procedures, and methodologies created to explore a world in which clocklike and cloudlike characteristics predominate will capture only a part of the much richer world of social and political interaction. Thus a simple search for regularities and lawful relationships among variables—a strategy that has led to tremendous successes in the physical sciences—will not explain social outcomes, but only some of the conditions affecting those outcomes.

Because the properties of political reality differ from those of physical reality, the properties of political *regularities* also differ from those of physical regularities. The regularities we discover are soft. They are soft because they are the outcomes of processes that exhibit plastic rather than cast-iron control. They are embedded in history and involve recurrent "passings-through" of large numbers of human memories, learning processes, human goal-seeking impulses, and choices among alternatives. The regularities we discover appear to have a short half-life. They decay quickly because of the memory, creative searching, and learning that underlie them. Indeed, social science itself may contribute to this decay, since learning increasingly includes not only learning from experience, but from scientific research itself.

The softness and historical boundedness of political theories can be illustrated by a few examples. Political scientists are justifiably proud of their theory of voting behavior. It is the closest thing to a scientific theory that we have. It has generated a set of what appear to be "covering laws"—demographic and attitudinal correlates of the voting decision, inductively arrived at. The deductive Downsian model of the consequences for party systems of different distributions of voter attitudes looks like an even more basic law of politics. But even a casual review of the findings of voting research in the last thirty years shows how unstable these regularities are, and how far short of hard science our efforts to stabilize them must inevitably fall. Modern research on voting behavior made its greatest progress in studies of American elections in the 1950s and early 1960s, a period of rapid economic growth and low-intensity politics. Students of American voting behavior in that period maintained they could explain and predict American voting behavior on the basis of "party identification" and "candidate image"; issues seemed to play only a secondary role.[11] The result of this effort to produce a hard causal explanation was a psychological theory of voting behavior based on party identification and candidate image. But this theory was soon to be challenged by studies done in the early 1970s which include data from the 1930s and late 1960s. These earlier and later periods show American voters as making their choices on the basis of candidates' issue positions to a far greater extent than was true of the 1950s and early 1960s. Recent writers speak of the "decomposition" of the party system, of the individuation of voting behavior, and of the "ideologization" of American politics.[12] And one of the leading collaborators of the Michigan group which produced the original party-identification theory now acknowledges that the demographic and attitudinal correlates of voting behavior are only loosely related, and that the only kind of theory we can aspire to is "some orderly specification of the conditions under which they vary."[13]

Political socialization theory is still engaged in a futile effort to impute relatively fixed values and weights to agents of socialization—family, school, workplace, media of communication, adult experiences, and the like.[14] Like voting research, socialization research in its thrust toward parsimonious scientific explanation has overlooked the larger historical context and the inherent instability of variables. Jennings and Niemi,[15] in one of the most sophisticated studies of political socialization ever undertaken, report that the impact of parents and teachers on the political attitudes of high school seniors was surprisingly weak. They failed to register the fact that the high school seniors they were sampling were the class of 1965, the first cohort of the post-World War II baby boom. It was a generation which to a considerable extent socialized itself, and it turned socialization theory upside down in the late 1960s by providing the cultural innovators of the youth rebellion. Like voting behavior theory, socialization theory is now slowly acknowledging the inherent instability of variables. The impact of the agents of socialization varies with changes in demographic and social structure, technology, and political events and issues. All that we can aspire to is a collection of propositions specifying the conditions under which these impacts tend to vary.

Perhaps the most vulnerable of these thrusts into hard science were the efforts of students of American politics in the early 1960s to discover the relationships between politics and public policy. The problem had been set by earlier work which argued that characteristics of the political system—party competition, voter participation, apportionment, and the like—had important consequences for public policy as measured by the level of public expenditures, and particularly by welfare expenditures. A series of statistical studies comparing the political, economic, and public policy characteristics of the American states in the 1950s and early 1960s proceeded to demonstrate that these political variables had little independent impact on the policy variables. When controlled for level of economic development, the effect of these political differences was washed away. This finding led to the remarkable conclusion that economic and other environmental variables explain public policy much better than political variables.[16]

There are two aspects of this research in public policy that are noteworthy for our purposes. The first is the extraordinary constriction of the time and space perspectives in this effort to test a global proposition concerning the relationships among economics, politics, and public policy. The fact that these were the American states in the 1950s—a period of political stability—rather than in the 1930s, did not register as limiting the kinds of inferences that could be drawn. Political scientists studying these problems brought no historical perspective to bear on their research—no memories of war, revolution, and depression, and of their well-known relationships to politics and public policy. Second, there was no recognition of the fact that environmental variables cannot directly produce public policy, that political choice must in the nature of the case intervene between them, and that historically this intervention has been very large indeed.

Social mobilization theory has sought to explain and predict trends toward politicization, democratization, and de-ideologization from trends toward urbanization, industrialization, communication, and education—only to discover that when these relationships are examined historically, human intractability and inventiveness, as well as sheer chance, complicate these patterns enormously.[17] The prophet of the end of ideology[18] has become the prophet of the postindustrial society[19] and, currently, the prophet of social disjunctions and cultural exhaustion.[20] Social scientists are finding that they do a better job of explaining when they follow the course of history, using sophisticated methodologies to isolate necessary sequences and constraints, but always aware of the role of chance and human inventiveness in producing the outcomes they are seeking to explain.

In their fascination with powerful regularities and uniformities that have the properties of causal necessity or high probability, social scientists have overlooked the fact that much of social and political change has to be explained neither by strong regularities nor by weak regularities, but by accidental conjunctions—by events that had a low probability of occurring. The concatenation of particular leaders with particular historical contexts is a matter of chance—of fortune—rather than necessity. Scholars can explain why Russia was ripe for revolution in 1917; and they can explain some aspects of Lenin's personality and operational code; but they cannot explain *why* the two conjoined to produce the Bolshevik Revolution, only *that* they conjoined by chance. The problem is similar to that of the biologist seeking to explain the emergence of a new species. He can describe an ecological niche in terms of constraints and opportunities; but for the niche to be occupied, the chance occurrence of an appropriate mutation or set of mutations is required.

Although in some respects the problem is similar to that of the biologist, it differs in fundamental ways. The interplay between the constraints of the ecological niche and the randomness of the process of mutation, to be sure, is a matter of trial and error. The search process is a random one, and largely genetic. In human affairs, the search process in addition has important conscious, planful aspects. It involves not only the chance concatenation of a revolutionary political niche with a Lenin, but with a scheming, contriving, willing, improvising Lenin, constantly probing, testing, and learning about the constraints and opportunities within the niche he is striving to occupy. Once he does occupy it, he transforms the niche and the population occupying it in ways that will constrain (but again not *determine*) future adaptive efforts. If we are to understand political reality, we have to come to grips not only with its determinate aspects but, most particularly, with its creative, adaptive, problem-solving aspects. For it is this last characteristic which is the essentially human property, and which is the unique mechanism and explanatory challenge of the social sciences.

The Clock Model of Political Science

The now dominant, "behavioral" tradition in political science tends to rest on three epistemological and methodological assumptions which it has taken from the hard sciences: (1) that the purpose of science is the discovery of regularities in, and ultimately laws of, social and political processes; (2) that scientific explanation means the deductive subsumption of individual events under "covering laws"; and (3) that the only scientifically relevant relationships among events in the world are those that correspond to a physicalistic conception of causal connection. These assumptions are highly interrelated, and each carries important substantive implications for the study of politics.

(1) The emphasis on generalizations in political science must first be understood in historical context. When David Easton argued in 1953 that "knowledge becomes critical and reliable when it increases in generality and internally consistent organization, when, in short, it is cast in the form of systematic generalized statements applicable to large numbers of particular cases,"[21] he was speaking against a tradition of ideographic, descriptive, noncumulative, and institutional case studies that had dominated much of the discipline (with a few notable exceptions) for several decades. A similar concern animated the behavioral polemics of Truman and others in the early 1950s.[22] The long-term result of this praiseworthy attempt to shift emphasis from description to explanation, however, has been the enshrining of the notion of generalization as the *sine qua non* of the scientific aspirations of the profession. This is perhaps most readily apparent in the recently burgeoning "scope and methods" literature. For example, Scarrow, in his *Comparative Political Analysis*, announces that "generalizations are the hallmark of all scientific endeavor,"[23] while Conway and Feigert, in *Political Analysis: An Introduction*, declare that "the function of science is generally perceived as being the establishment of general laws or theories which explain the behavior with which the particular discipline is concerned."[24] Even a sophisticated study, such as Przeworski's and Teune's *Logic of Comparative Social Inquiry*, states somewhat dogmatically: "The pivotal assumption of this analysis is that social science research, including comparative inquiry, should and can lead to general statements about social

phenomena. This assumption implies that human and social behavior can be explained in terms of general laws established by observation. Introduced here as an expression of preference, this assumption will not be logically justified."[25]

The substantive impact of this emphasis on generalizations is to focus the attention of research on regularities, uniformities, and stable patterns of association in political processes at the expense of unique or low-probability events or political outcomes. As Frohock expresses it in *The Nature of Political Inquiry*, "Science is concerned with establishing causal relations and general laws. To do this the social scientist must concentrate on systematic patterns of human conduct. Only as an event is a recurring instance of a general class can it be treated scientifically."[26]

We are not arguing here for the view that regularities do not occur in political processes or that valid generalizations cannot be made. As we noted above, political regularities—albeit soft—clearly exist and are crucial to political inquiry. Rather, our criticism is aimed at positions that see regularities and generalizations as the *only* proper objects of scientific political inquiry. This seems to us an unnecessary delimitation of the scope of the discipline's subject matter. If political reality is best viewed as a conjunction of choice and constraint, and as a source of both regularity and innovation, then political science should not be limited to a consideration of only part of this reality. A pure focus on generalizations as "the hallmark of all scientific endeavor" would seem to condemn it to just such a limitation.

(2) The concern with generalizations and regularities—and the concomitant willingness to limit the scope of political science to only those aspects of political reality that are generalizable—is closely associated with a particular conception of *explanation* in political inquiry. This position is also reflected in the "scope and methods" literature. Alan Isaak, in his *Scope and Method of Political Science*, declares that political scientists must accept the "scientific fact of life" that "every sound explanation and prediction contains at least one generalization; without generalizations there could be no explanations or predictions."[27] Similarly, Conway and Feigert argue, "Explanations in science require . . . laws or theories which are well established. . . . Explanation occurs when the facts to be explained can be deduced as a logical consequence of the laws or theory and . . . other known facts."[28]

The model of explanation alluded to here is the so-called covering law or deductive-nomological (D-N) model developed in the philosophy of science by R. B. Braithwaite,[29] Carl Hempel,[30] and others. The basic idea underlying this model is that something is explained when it has been shown to be a member of a more general class of things. "To explain something is to exhibit it as a special case of what is known in general."[31] This is achieved, according to the model, when the particular case is deduced from a more general law (or set of laws) that "covers" it and all other relevantly similar cases. That is why generalizations play such a fundamental role in deductive explanations.

The explanatory power of the D-N model derives from the fact that deduction from covering laws *logically necessitates* that which is deduced. The deduction "explains" by telling us that, on the basis of what we already know (the generalization), the case in question was to be expected: it *had* to occur the way it did.[32] This notion of "it was to be expected" stands at the center of the deductive conception of explanation, and accounts for the close association between explanation and prediction in the model.[33] For adherents of the D-N model, an explanation that would not be equally capable of supporting a prediction would not qualify as a true explanation.[34] It is not surprising, therefore, that closed deterministic systems—"clock models" in Popper's terminology—are most amenable to D-N explanation. As Hempel puts it: "The best examples of explanations conforming to the D-N model are based on physical theories of deterministic character. . . . [T]he laws specified by such a theory for the changes of state are deterministic in the sense that, given the state of that system at any one time, they determine its state at any other, earlier or later, time."[35]

It is clear that the D-N model loses its usefulness to the degree that there are *exceptions* to the law or laws warranting the explanation in question. If we cannot legitimately maintain that "all *A*'s are *B*'s" and must settle for a law asserting only that "some *A*'s are *B*'s," then the deductive link is dissolved and our explanation of the occurrence of *B* continues to be problematic. This state of affairs, however, is just what is implied by the notion of plastic control. Plasticity means that we can expect, in principle, that there will be exceptions to any generalizations we might form about the phenomena that are of interest to us. Thus the more our subject matter exhibits plastic control, the less it will be amenable to simple D-N explanations.

(3) The notion of causality is closely associated with the idea of covering-law explanation by both political scientists and philosophers of science. R. B. Braithwaite, for example, describes causality strictly in terms of covering laws: "The statement that some particular event is the effect of a set of circumstances involves the assertion of a general law; to ask for the cause of an event is always to ask for a general law which applies to the particular event."[36]

This formulation is echoed by political scientists. Thus Robert Dahl argues, "If we wish to explain an event, *E*, in a strictly causal manner, we consider *E* as an effect and bring it under some generalization of the form: 'Every event *C* is accompanied later by an event *E*.' . . . The *C* is called the cause, *E* the effect."[37] Similarly, Isaak maintains, "If saying that '*A* causes *B*' is tantamount to '*B* always follows *A*,' then they are both reducible to 'If *A*, then *B*.' In other words, we can express what is traditionally known as a causal relationship without using the term cause."[38]

All of these characterizations rest on the notion of causality as an *explanatory* concept. But how is this explanatory status acquired? As can be seen from even a cursory exposure to the literature on causation and conditions,[39] the concepts "cause" and "effect" are broad and ambiguous. One element of their meaning seems to stand out in any account, however: the principle of "same cause, same effect."[40] As Hempel puts it, "As is suggested by the principle 'same cause, same effect,' the assertion that [a given set of] circumstances jointly caused a given event implies that whenever and wherever circumstances of the kind in question occur, an event of the kind to be explained takes place."[41] Or, in Abraham Kaplan's slightly more cautious formulation: "Causal connection is usually analyzed in terms of some relation of implication: the grammar of the 'if-then' conjunction is at least a starting point. If the cause occurs, then its effects occur."[42] It is this element of "same cause, same effect" that confers explanatory power on causal relations in the world. Without it, "causality" becomes simply another problematic and essentially unexplained relationship between two or more things, events, or processes.

This philosophical characterization of the relationship between cause and effect is closely related to Popper's notion of cast-iron control. The cause *produces* the effect, and the existence of the cause is the *explanation* of the effect. A world of pure cause and effect, as narrowly defined by this identification of causality with covering-law explanation, would be a world without exceptions, a world that could not be other than what it is. Such a world, we feel, is completely alien to the world of politics, in which the potential for surprise and innovation is inherent in many, if not most, situations.

In spite of the inflexibility and aridity of the explanatory concept of causality, however, many political scientists have attempted to couch their analyses of political phenomena in terms of the notions of cause and effect. The result is often an odd mixture of formalized definitions and unrelated empirical substance. As an example of such a mixture, we might take a brief look at one branch of political analysis that has made considerable use of causal formulations—the literature on the concept of power. Here the relationship of cause and effect is explicitly invoked as a metaphor for a necessary, dependent connection between events. For example, Herbert Simon has stated that "for the assertion '*C* has power over *R*,' we can substitute the assertion, '*C*'s behavior causes *R*'s behavior.' If we can define the causal relation, we can define influence, power or authority, and *vice versa*."[43] Similarly, Andrew McFarland asserts that "definitions of power or influence based on such concepts as force, incentives or utilities, and minimum winning coalitions are . . . reducible to causal terms."[44] More recently, Jack Nagel has defined power as follows: "A power relation, actual or potential, is an actual or potential causal relation between the preferences of an actor regarding an outcome and the outcome itself."[45] And Robert Dahl, in the latest edition of his *Modern Political Analysis*, seems to maintain (although with some caveats) his long-standing view that causation is fundamental to understanding power and influence relations: "When we single out influence from all other aspects of human interaction in order to give it special attention, what interests us and what we focus attention on is that one or more of the persons in this interaction get what they want, or at least get closer to what they want, by causing other people to act in some particular way. We want to call attention to a *causal relationship* between what *A* wants and what *B* does."[46]

How is the word "cause" being used in these definitions? Clearly it is not being used as an explanatory concept, in the sense described by philosophers of science. For an explanation to be truly causal in that sense, as we have seen, the relationship in question would have to be (1) cast-iron, (2) generalizable, and (3) amenable to covering-law explanation. None of these properties would seem to apply to power relationships. There is no "necessity" inherent in the outcome of an attempt to assert power over another person, as there is in a causal connection between two physical objects. The target of the power attempt may, for any number of reasons, act differently than the power wielder would have him act. This is because a power relationship does not involve cast-iron control; instead, it is an interaction of two choosing and mutually constraining individuals, each with his own resources, goals, purposes, interests, and strategies. The intentions and resources of the first certainly constrain the choices and actions of the second, but they do not determine those choices and actions in any sort of cast-iron sense.

This "looseness of fit" between the behavior and intentions of actors involved in an attempt to exercise power means that their relationship is not readily generalizable; neither is it particularly amenable to strict covering-law explanation. As Hart and Honor have put it: "The statement that one person did something because . . . another threatened him, carries no implication or covert assertion that if the circumstances were repeated, the same action would follow; nor does such a statement require for its defense, as ordinary causal statements do, a generalization."[47] These considerations lead us to conclude that the power relationship is not causal, at least not in the explanatory sense of the term.[48]

This conclusion would seem, in one sense, to be shared by Dahl and many of the other political scientists who use causal language in their definition of power. If we examine their empirical analyses of power relations in real-world political situations rather than their definitions, we find careful and precise examinations of the complex interactions that contribute to outcomes, without reliance on simplistic notions of "same cause, same effect." In such substantive analyses—as opposed to definition making—plasticity is recognized and indeterminateness is often handled with sophistication and insight.

What we seem to observe in this particular area of political research, then, is a rhetorical or metaphorical—rather than explanatory—usage of causal language in formalizations and definitions. This accounts for the lack of a subsequent commitment to actual causal analysis in substantive research. The somewhat incongruous gap can perhaps best be explained as an attempt on the part of political scientists to create a "halo effect" around their theoretical formulations. Our longing for full scientific status has led us to create a kind of "cargo cult," fashioning cardboard imitations of the tools and products of the hard sciences in the hope that our incantations would make them real.

These three elements of the implicit logic that informs much of political science research today appear to imply a substantive model of the political world which closely resembles the deterministic "clock model" outlined by Popper. That is not to say that any political scientists actually *see* the political world this way; no doubt we would all agree that it often *appears* to be quite porous, irregular, and unpredictable. Rather, it is to say that the arsenal of meta-methodological principles and procedures we have borrowed from the physical sciences—or, more correctly, from a certain philosophical perspective on the physical sciences—has come to us with an array of substantive assumptions that all proclaim the principle "all clouds are clocks." If we search only for generalizations and regularities in political processes, if we couch our explanations only in terms of the covering-law model, and if we view political relationships as ultimately causal in nature, we are committing ourselves—whether we recognize it or not—to a disciplinary research program designed to strip away the cloudlike and purposive aspects of political reality in order to expose its "true" clocklike structure. If politics is *not* clocklike in its fundamental structure, then the whole program is inappropriate. We believe this to be the case: the current quandary in political science can to a large extent be explained by the fact that, by themselves, "clock-model" assumptions are inappropriate for dealing with the substance of political phenomena.

The Adoption of the Clock Model and Its Effects on Political Research and Pedagogy

The movement toward hard science in the study of politics is a phase in the scientific revolution of the last several decades. The great breakthroughs in physics and biology, and the extraordinary increases in research funding as science became a national asset, created a mood of sanguine expectations. It is not surprising that political scientists sought to share in this exciting and remunerative adventure.

Political science was invited to imitate the hard sciences by some of the more influential philosophers of science on the grounds that political reality lent itself to the same powerful methods that had proven so effective in physics and biology. That is one of the basic tenets of the logical positivist tradition in the philosophy of science,[49] and has been a starting point for many books and articles designed to show the social sciences and history how to achieve a "truly" scientific status.[50] In addition, there was immediate evidence of the success of the hard-science strategy within the social sciences themselves. Psychology and economics had been the first disciplines in the social sciences to move in this direction, demonstrating the possibilities of experimental methods, sophisticated quantitative methods, computer simulation, and mathematical modeling. The combination of philosophical legitimation and the demonstrated progress of psychology and economics was impossible to resist.

As a consequence of these legitimations and demonstration effects, the incentive structure of political science began to encourage an orientation modeled on the physical sciences. The pressures for conformity can be measured in terms of prestige, journal publications, fellowships, and grants. Major sources of research funding and graduate fellowships, such as the National Science Foundation, have been dominated by the hard sciences; the social science divisions have been junior partners in these agencies, and the political science section has been the most junior of all. Projects that have the appearance of hard science have had the inside track for gaining substantial research support.

Perhaps the most important consequence of this imitation of hard science has been an emphasis on method as the primary criterion for judging the quality of research in political science. Today, the leading research traditions tend to be defined by their methodologies rather than their substantive foci. One result of this principle of organization—although certainly not a necessary consequence of it—has been that the value of this work seems to be measured primarily by its technical virtuosity, and only secondarily by the importance of the problems treated or illuminated.

In the last two decades there has been a tremendous drive toward quantification in political science. Riker celebrated this trend in a recent communication to the *American Political Science Review* when he commented that some two-thirds of the articles in recent issues of that journal were based on quantitative analysis employing sophisticated statistics.[51] Quantification has undoubtedly contributed to major advances in political science and other social sciences. But it has also led to a significant number of pseudoscientific exercises that exhibit the form but not the substance of research in the physical sciences. Such studies become more prevalent when the use of quantification is treated as an end in itself rather than as a means toward understanding concrete political problems. Irrelevant quantification has recently been the subject of searching critiques in international relations,[52] comparative politics,[53] policy studies,[54] and elsewhere.

Quantitative analysis in political science has moved increasingly toward more sophisticated statistical methods. But the structure of the data in social science research often comes into conflict with the assumptions underlying confirmatory statistical theory. The problems involved in applying complex statistical methods to nonrandom, nonlinear, or nonadditive data should not be minimized.[55] Much of the inferential power of these methods is lost when the structure of the data does not conform to the rigid requirements of the theory. These difficulties have proven formidable enough to lead some statisticians, such as John Tukey, at Princeton, to devise alternative data-analytic techniques that, although not nearly as powerful as the most advanced statistical methods, are more compatible with the idiosyncratic characteristics of social and political data.[56] Here we seem to have fallen into a trap comparable to that of the early phases of Third World development, when "high technologies" were introduced into poor agricultural countries without regard for their disruptive consequences. We are discovering that an intermediate level of statistical technology, which takes into account the special characteristics of social data, is more appropriate to the social sciences than are the very sophisticated methods.

Running parallel to this emphasis on statistics in political science is an interest in mathematics and the construction of simple, logically rigorous models. This approach has been advocated in comparative politics by Holt and Richardson, who argue that "political scientists must turn to mathematics" if the discipline is to progress scientifically. They are careful to distinguish this path from the statistical one: "In making an appeal for more mathematics, we are not talking about statistics. . . . [S]tatistics provides a science with a basis for rigorous *induction*. Our critique suggests that the crying need in comparative politics is for more rigorous deduction and this is where mathematics, not statistics, is relevant."[57] This statement is echoed by A. James Gregor, Oran Young,[58] and many others.

The difficulty with mathematical models is that they usually measure up poorly to the complexities of the phenomena being modeled. For example, Oran Young, who strongly advocates the use of modeling methods in international relations, has candidly observed that "the inherent hazard of this procedure is that its products may display little relevance to the real world of international relations for the indefinite future."[59] Holt and Richardson, on the other hand, argue that a mathematically oriented political science must necessarily take a radically circumscribed view of political reality, cutting itself free from problem solving: "A science that is heavily committed to dealing with socially and morally relevant problems finds little use for this kind of paradigm or for the commitment to mathematics that it requires. For political science to advance, it must shed this professional commitment to solving social and moral problems."[60]

One aspect of the mathematical approach to politics deserves special mention: the use of rational-choice models to explain political behavior. These models are particularly interesting because they take the most intractable elements of political processes – the individual and collective choices of political actors – and try to treat them deterministically. Some analysts have argued that if political science is ever to be a true science, the notion of rationality must be its central concept. For example, Riker and Ordeshook draw an explicit analogy between rationality on the one hand and the notion of mechanism on the other:

> It is clear that the assumption of rationality and the assumption of mechanism play comparable roles in the explanation of the social and physical world. The mechanical assumptions assert that there is something about things that assures us they will (usually) move regularly, and the rationality assumption asserts that there is something about people that makes them behave (usually) in a regular way. In each case, the function is to generalize about the regularity.[61]

The kind of regularities Riker and Ordeshook are concerned with here are of a special type–"postulated" as opposed to "observed" regularities. Granting that choices in empirical situations usually fail to exhibit the degree of regularity necessary for warranting deductive explanations and theories, Riker and Ordeshook choose to build a theory of politics on the foundations of how people *would* act *if* they were rational utility maximizers. This, of course, leads to a theory that fails to model political reality well. But the substantive loss is considered acceptable in light of the methodological gain: "The method of postulated regularity is positively more efficient, because it permits the easy generation of hypotheses and offers a single and parsimonious explanation of behavior."[62]

The popularity of rational-choice models in political science would be puzzling to anyone who was not familiar with the current hierarchy of methodological and substantive priorities in the field. But with this hierarchy in mind, some particularly perplexing exercises become understandable. For example, in the recently published *Handbook of Political Science*, J. Donald Moon contributes a piece on "The Logic of Political Inquiry."[63] This article begins very promisingly by articulating the D-N model of explanation as well as an important alternative to it, the interpretive model, which explains behavior in terms of motives, intentions, rules and norms, etc. Noting serious defects in both models, Moon turns to the task of synthesizing the two in order to create a more comprehensive framework for political explanation. But the "synthesis" turns out not to be a synthesis at all; instead it consists of a *substitution* of a rational actor "model of man" for the interpretive model of explanation. This eliminates the "looseness" and lack of regularity of empirical choice that is captured by the interpretive model and substitutes for it "presuppositions [that] specify the decisional premises of the actors which, together with descriptions of their situations, provide the rationale for the actions which bring about the overall pattern of social behavior . . . that . . . theorists desire to explain."[64]

Like the regularities of interest to Riker and Ordeshook, these "presuppositions" are postulated (specified) *a priori*. They replace the contingent aspects of empirical choice and action with causal and lawlike assumptions. Thus choices are reduced to an algorithm specifying a necessary outcome from a necessary utility calculation. The net result of this substantive reduction is a definition of choice in terms of cause-and-effect relationships; which is to say, a definition of choice that denies the existence of choice! Certainly this conclusion would appear strange if we were not familiar with the current priority of method over substance in political science. As it is, we can see that Moon is struggling with the task of fitting his recalcitrant subject matter to the strict exigencies of a methodological notion of necessity that bears little resemblance to the realities of political choice.

The stress on reductionist explanation, quantification, and formalization has also led to an overloading of graduate curricula. If a political scientist must be a statistician, psychologist, and sociologist, then some of the traditional curriculum has to be set aside in order to make room for these newer disciplines and techniques. Anyone who has taught in a major graduate department of political science in the last twenty years will recall this inexorable process of narrowing and technicizing of the curriculum; the foreign-language requirements have been reduced, the field examination requirements have dropped from five to four to three, perhaps even to two. By the mid-1960s, it had become possible for someone to become a Ph.D. in political science with little if any knowledge of political theory, political history, foreign political systems, international relations, and even much about American politics and government. As Hayward Alker has recently remarked: "Training graduate students intensively in multivariate quantitative methods such as factor analysis makes less time available for developing a sophisticated awareness of what has classically been thought and said about political life. . . . Thus modern training is particularly inappropriate for understanding modern politics in which many questions about systems restructuring are continually raised."[65]

Accompanying this narrowing and technicization of the graduate curriculum has been a demoralization of the older intellectual traditions in the social sciences and in political science. Political theory and philosophy, public law and public administration, and descriptive institutional analysis have all become defensive, peripheral, and secondary subject matters. As a result, a large part of the political science tradition is no longer being transmitted effectively to younger generations.

What we suggest here is that "science" is not a set of methods extracted from mathematical physics, as the neopositivist philosophers might have us believe; it is ultimately a commitment to explore and attempt to understand a given segment of empirical reality. The means employed in pursuing this goal should be secondary: in "good" science, methods are fit to the subject matter rather than subject matter being truncated or distorted in order to fit it to a preordained notion of "scientific method." This is the lesson that social scientists should have learned from the physical sciences. Instead, they have ignored it and, in the process, have undermined what Abraham Kaplan has called the "autonomy of inquiry."[66] If social science is to redeem itself, "social scientists need to construct their own notions of 'good science,' their own methodological approach appropriate to their particular subject matter. . . . This view implies giving up the notion that there is some close analogy in the social sciences to basic research in the physical sciences."[67]

Second Thoughts in Psychology and Economics

Much of the knowledge our discipline has acquired of "scientific method" has been filtered through the two "pace-setting" disciplines in social science – psychology and economics. If we look closely at the present state of these disciplines, which have pioneered in the use of statistical methods, mathematical models, and experimentation, we find evidence of some doubt and disillusionment.

Psychology, much like political science, has over the last couple of decades entertained a nearly constant "great debate" concerning the conceptual and methodological principles underlying the discipline. How should man, as the subject matter of psychology, be conceptualized? What kind of knowledge should psychology hope to acquire, and how can this knowledge best be pursued? Lately, some participants in this debate have become more and more critical of the established orthodoxy and have begun to question previously sacrosanct assumptions. These critics are not the inevitable dissenting minority in any discipline, but include some of the recognized leaders in the profession – leaders who, in fact, have been instrumental in creating the very conceptions they now question.

The problem of the "image of man" in psychology has been taken up many times. A particularly trenchant and lucid discussion was offered by Isidor Chein in his 1962 presidential address to the Society for the Psychological Study of Social Issues. Chein argued that "among psychologists . . . the prevailing image of Man is that of an impotent reactor, with its responses completely determined by two distinct and separate, albeit interacting, sets of factors: (1) the forces impinging on it and (2) its constitution (including in the latter term . . . momentary psychological states)."[68] He held that this image is obviously false, that psychologists can cling to it only "by violating our cardinal obligation as scientists – to maintain faith in our subject matter, to support scrupulously that which we observe, and to observe fully without willful bias."[69]

What this image denies, and what observation clearly attests to, is that man is "an *active, responsible agent*, not simply a *helpless, powerless* reagent." Chein continues: "I am saying that we should not permit ourselves to be seduced, as so many of us have been, by those pretentious high order conceptualizations of Psychology that would deny Man the quality that is inalienably his, the quality of freedom—and, in the denial, make Man, as a psychological agent, inaccessible."[70]

This argument bears a strong resemblance to Popper's. The determinist assumption of "cast-iron control" over choice and action is rejected for a conception that allows for the autonomy of human action in creating, as well as in responding to, the world. Interestingly enough, Chein claims to be a determinist—in the sense of viewing every event as having necessary and sufficient conditions—but argues that motives and purposes share in the determination of human actions, thus bringing them under direct human control. Like Popper, therefore, Chein is concerned with the question of how "mental events" such as purposes, deliberations, and plans, can play a part in bringing about change in the physical world.

In his presidential address before the American Psychological Association in 1975, Donald Campbell called on psychologists to show a bit of epistemic humility, and to recognize that "all scientific knowledge is indirect, presumptive, obliquely and incompletely corroborated at best." He went on to argue that reductionism in psychology must be seen as a first step in a long-term research strategy, not as an end in itself:

> Considering the complexities of our field and our models from the history of the successful sciences, a strategy of deliberate initial oversimplification has to be recommended to psychology. But this guarantees that in the early stages of development the theoretical orthodoxy will be misleadingly reductionistic, will portray humans as more simple machines than they actually are. If psychologists at such a stage were to lose the perspective that this view was a product of their long-term strategy, were instead to exaggerate the degree of perfection of their current theories, and were to propagate these immature theories as final truth, the net result could be destructive of popular values. . . . Here again, a science requiring the strategy of deliberate initial oversimplification may recruit scholars overeager to adopt a demeaning, mechanistic, reductionistic view of human nature.[71]

Today, at least some psychologists have managed to move beyond the mechanistic image of man, and are pursuing research based upon a more realistic and useful conception. Among the newer approaches in social psychology, for example, is "attribution theory," which examines the assumptions and working hypotheses that constitute the "naive psychology" of ordinary people as they interpret their own behaviors and the actions of others. Lee Ross, one of the leaders in this field, has summed up the significance of this approach:

> The current ascendancy of attribution theory in social psychology culminates a long struggle to upgrade that discipline's conception of man. No longer the stimulus-response (S-R) automaton of radical behaviorism, promoted beyond the rank of information processor and cognitive consistency seeker, psychological man has at last been awarded a status equal to that of the scientist who investigates him. For man, in the perspective of attribution theory, is an intuitive psychologist who seeks to explain behavior and to draw inferences about actors and their environments.[72]

What of psychology's second problem, the kind of knowledge it can expect to attain about man? That issue has recently been given careful consideration by the educational psychologist Lee Cronbach. Reflecting on his experience in experimental social psychology over the last two decades, Cronbach asks the question, "Should social science aspire to reduce behavior to laws?" He observes that "social scientists generally, and psychologists in particular, have modelled their work on physical science, aspiring to amass empirical generalizations, to restructure them into more general laws, and to weld scattered laws into coherent theory. That lofty aspiration is far from realization."[73]

The essential difficulty with this methodology, Cronbach argues, is that social science laws, unlike physical laws, seem to be highly mutable. As he puts it, "Generalizations decay." Further, "At one time a conclusion describes the existing situation well, at a later time it accounts for rather little variance, and ultimately it is valid only as history. The half-life of an empirical proposition may be great or small. The more open a system, the shorter the half-life of relations within it are likely to be." He compares the task of building theories in this way with a mechanical assembly problem: "It is as if we needed a gross of dry cells to power an engine and could make one a month. The energy would leak out of the first cells before we had half the battery completed. So it is with the potency of our generalizations."[74]

At the end of this article, which recounts two decades of aspiration toward a nomological psychology, Cronbach writes:

> Social scientists are rightly proud of the discipline we draw from the natural science side of our ancestry. Scientific discipline is what we uniquely add to the time-honored ways of studying man. Too narrow an identification with science, however, has fixed our eyes upon an inappropriate goal. The goal of our work, I have argued here, is not to amass generalizations atop which a theoretical tower can some day be erected. . . . The special task of the social scientist in each generation is to pin down the contemporary facts. Beyond that, he

shares with the humanistic scholar and the artist in the effort to gain insight into contemporary relationships, and to realign the culture's view of man with present realities.[75]

Economics, like psychology and social psychology, has also been having its troubles in recent years. The critical themes have been surprisingly consistent; the field is seen as isolated and inbred, with its formal models bearing very little resemblance to the empirical world with which economists are supposed to be concerned. These criticisms have for quite some time been the stock-in-trade of such established gadflies of the profession as Gunnar Myrdal and John Kenneth Galbraith. Myrdal, for example, has argued that economists have failed to produce relevant knowledge because of an inappropriate commitment to the methods of the simpler natural sciences:

> In recent decades . . . there has been a strenuous, even strained, effort among my economic colleagues to emulate what they conceive of as the methods of the natural sciences by constructing utterly simplified models, often given mathematical dressing. . . .
>
> It should be clear, however, that this adoption of a form, which the natural scientists, in more simple, pointed questions, can use for analysis and presentation, does not really make the social sciences more scientific, if that form is not adequate to social reality and therefore, not adequate for the analysis of it.[76]

Similarly, Galbraith used the occasion of his 1972 presidential address to the American Economic Association to chide the profession for its failure to come to grips with practical economic problems: "Neo-classical or neo-Keynesian economics, though providing unlimited opportunities for demanding refinement, has a decisive flaw. It offers no useful handle for grasping the economic problems that now beset the modern society. . . . No arrangement for the perpetuation of thought is secure if that thought does not make contact with the problems that it is presumed to solve."[77]

These doubts and concerns have lately become a bit more widespread. Marc Roberts, a younger economist, asserts that "a significant proportion of recent theoretical work in economics has been of little scientific value. Many papers explore questions posed not by the world itself, but by someone else's model."[78] These views seem to be shared by some of the most respected leaders of the economic establishment. Oskar Morgenstern, in an important paper published in 1972, argues that economics is in a crisis because it lacks the concepts, methods, and philosophy it needs to deal adequately with social and political reality. Following a discussion of current equilibrium theory, Morgenstern observes:

> The contrast with reality is striking; the time has come for economic theory to turn around to "face the music."
>
> There is, of course, always the possibility and the temptation of proving all sorts of theorems which have no empirical relevance whatsoever. . . . Yet the ultimate criterion is whether what the theorem asserts is what is found in reality. One cannot help but be reminded of Hans Christian Andersen's story of the Emperor's clothes.[79]

Wassily Leontief, who won the Nobel Memorial Prize for the invention of input-output analysis, has struck an even more pessimistic note. In his presidential address to the AEA, given two years before Galbraith's, Leontief argued that "the uneasiness [in economics] is caused not by the irrelevance of the practical problems to which present-day economists address their efforts, but rather by the palpable *inadequacy* of the scientific means with which they try to solve them. . . . Uncritical enthusiasm for mathematical formulation tends often to conceal the ephemeral substantive content of the argument behind the formidable front of algebraic signs." He concluded that "in no other field of empirical inquiry has so massive and sophisticated a statistical machinery been used with such indifferent results."[80]

The problems in economics, as in psychology, would seem to be primarily substantive. Morgenstern, sounding much like Popper, points to the failure of economics to deal seriously with the nonphysical aspects of economic processes:

> The overwhelming emphasis on the physical aspects of the economic process . . . seems one-sided when we realize that it is plans, decisions, preferences, states of information, expectations, etc., etc., that determine the movement and significance of the physical components of the whole economic phenomenon. We are far from having more than broad notions of how to describe and measure their share in a concrete situation. Do we even have a good methodology we could apply?[81]

It used to be, and apparently still is in much of economic theory if not practice, that these decisions and expectations could be discounted because they tended to cancel one another out in the classical market situation. Today, however, many economists attribute a large part of the discipline's empirical dilemma to a failure to appreciate how extensively political decisions now override the mechanisms of the market. Galbraith observes that "in place of the market system, we must now assume that for approximately half of all economic output there is a power or planning system."[82] The effect of this injection of planning into the economic process has been to upset the predictive capabilities of economic theory. Robert Heilbroner, in commenting on the inability of economics to predict the course of a national economy, remarks that "it may be that this is less possible than it was, because the economy itself now is so much more a creature of decision making, and so much less the outcome of sheer interplay of impersonal forces, that prediction becomes inherently more difficult."[83]

This major problem in economics would seem to have important implications for political science. For what the economists are saying is that to the extent their subject matter is becoming more *political*, it is becoming less susceptible to scientific and formalistic methodologies. The impact of decisions, of the possibility of shifting the economy in new directions, undermines the regularity of the impersonal forces that previously allowed for successful predictive and modeling exercises. This conclusion does not augur well for those who envision an eventually formalized political science. Indeed, the tendency seems to be in the opposite direction; economics may be becoming more like political science!

A second and related problem economists have had to deal with deserves mention: the problems of decaying generalizations. Like psychology, economics has been unsuccessful in its attempt to build lasting empirical models of its subject matter. As Leontief puts it:

> In contrast to most physical sciences, we study a system that is not only exceedingly complex but also in a state of constant flux. I have in mind not the obvious change in the variables . . . that our equations are supposed to explain, but the basic structural relationships described by the form and the parameters of these equations. In order to know what the shapes of these structural relationships actually are at any given time, we have to keep them under continuous surveillance.[84]

These second thoughts in economics and psychology illustrate the degree to which the two bellwether disciplines are now reassessing their earlier explanatory strategies and meta-methodological commitments. Clearly, their attempts to deal with the complexities of social reality in terms of a model of scientific method borrowed from the physical sciences have run into more difficulties than they had expected. The ambivalence of this effort to bring the human enterprise under the categories and logic of the hard sciences has been captured by the economist and social philosopher Albert Hirschman, who points out in a recent book—in a section titled "A Passion for the Possible"—that "most social scientists conceive it as their exclusive task to discover and stress regularities, stable relationships, and uniform sequences" rather than recognizing "the multiplicity and creative disorder of the human adventure." He maintains that the social scientists would be surprised and even "distraught if their search for general laws were crowned with total success," and concludes, "Quite possibly . . . all the successive theories and models in the social sciences, and the immense efforts that go into them, are motivated by the noble, if unconscious, desire to demonstrate the irreducibility of the social world to general laws! In no other way would it have been possible to affirm so conclusively the social world as the realm of freedom and creativity."[85]

The philosophy of science itself is experiencing a process of reevaluation and reorientation similar to that taking place in psychology and economics. The article by Popper that we have used as a metaphorical guide for our own thinking is but one example of a more general trend in the field exemplified by this work[86] and that of Polanyi,[87] Hanson,[88] Kuhn,[89] Quine,[90] Lakatos,[91] Toulmin,[92] and many others. Today, the preeminent position held by logical positivism in the philosophy of science seems to be weakening. Philosophers of science no longer see their role as one of legislating the "rules" of science; they are more likely to pursue descriptive and explanatory modes of research. Science is viewed as an activity or a process, not simply as a logical product. Accordingly, an appreciation is beginning to develop for the degree to which science—humankind's loftiest intellectual achievement—is grounded and dependent upon basic common sense and informal as well as formalized substantive knowledge.[93] Philosophers are learning more about how science grows and how it prospers. The newer literature in the philosophy of science is rich in insights and implications for the enterprise of social science.

Implications

If the whole of social reality has distinctive properties rendering it unamenable to simple deductive-nomological forms of explanation, this is especially the case for the study of politics, which, of all the social sciences, focuses most directly on collective goal-seeking and adaptive processes. A political science solely concerned with the search for regularities that constrain choice would miss the distinctive aspect of political reality, which is the effort to escape from constraints, to discover value-optimizing solutions to problems in the context of constraints.

The anthropologist John W. Bennett recommends an approach to anthropological theory and research that is oriented around the concept of adaptation:

> Instead of abstractions from behavior, like culture or the reductive formulas of psychology or genetics, [adaptation] focuses on human actors who try to realize objectives, satisfy needs, and find peace while coping with present conditions. In their coping, humans create the social future in the sense of generating new problems or perpetuating old ones and may even modify the biological construction of the population in the process. . . . By analyzing the factors that guide the choice of strategies, we gain knowledge of the possibility and direction of change and the relation of human behavior to the milieus.[94]

We would argue that what Bennett has to say about anthropology applies with even greater force to political science: "The important phenomena for an adaptational anthropology are dynamic human purposes, needs and wants." The emphasis ought to shift "toward strategic coping, that is, the attempt to realize individual and social objectives through the mobilization of social and material resources. This category of human behavior has become dominant in the contemporary world with its interdependence and growing constraints on free action."[95]

Duncan MacRae argues a similar thesis regarding the development of the social sciences in the last several decades:

> They [the social sciences] have evolved from an earlier form of social analysis, less specialized and recondite, by imitating the natural sciences . . . many social scientists have become convinced that the most effective path to useful application lies through objective research and theory construction, free from the complications of ideological and philosophical dispute. They have thus developed distinct technical terminologies and methods of research, specialized journals and programs of graduate instruction. Through these devices they have separated the discourse of specialists from that of the general public, and the communications of the individual specialists from one another. The course of the social sciences during the past several decades has thus been guided by the model of natural science—however distinct they may seem from it to natural scientists themselves.[96]

MacRae's solution to this problem of the withdrawal of the social sciences from social problem solving is to introduce into the university a "discipline of policy analysis" which will combine social theories and analysis with disciplined ethical discourse. He believes that the present situation of cognitive and valuative fragmentation in the disciplines of social science can be overcome only by an institutional solution—the introduction of research and teaching departments of policy analysis and applied social science.[97]

We have somewhat less faith in organizational solutions, and are convinced that the discipline of political science—which has tended to abandon the task MacRae now wishes to assign to a special discipline—is still capable of reasserting a central role in the study and evaluation of public policy. The powerful attraction of the example of the natural sciences has begun to fade as our efforts have fallen short of our aspirations. Despite the prominence of the trend among our methodologists, in our leading journals, and in some of our leading centers of graduate instruction, the overwhelming majority of the profession in the United States and abroad actively resists the model, experiences a sense of obsolescence because of its prominence, or is indifferent to it. Most of the published work in political science settles for goals less ambitious than nomothetic explanation. This work includes descriptive or historical accounts or case studies making limited use of theoretical frameworks and generalizations, and contributes to the aims of understanding, interpreting, and exploring political reality and policy alternatives which MacRae identifies as crucial to policy analysis.

One might make the case that the search for greater rigor in our understanding of politics might have made more progress if its claims and expectations had been less extreme, less exaggerated, less difficult to square with a recalcitrant reality. A more cautious approach to scientific progress, recognizing the peculiarities of human and social reality, might have resulted in a more general acceptance of appropriate quantification, of the heuristic value of formal-mathematical formulation, experimental methods, and the like.

It is of interest that a quarter of a century ago, in the aftermath of World War II, when the movement toward science in the social disciplines was just beginning, this relationship between the search for regularities and man's efforts to discover value-optimizing solutions to his predicaments was more clearly understood. One has only to compare an early "scope and methods" book with the more recent ones cited above. Some twenty-five years ago, many of the pioneers of the behavioral movement in the social sciences contributed to a volume titled *The Policy Sciences: Recent Developments in Scope and Method*. In the leading chapter, Harold Lasswell stated his priorities: "If our policy needs are to be served, what topics of research are most worthy of pursuit? . . . What are the most promising methods of gathering facts and interpreting their significance for policy? How can facts and interpretations be made effective in the decision-making process itself?" The same essay celebrated the introduction of scientific methods into the social sciences—statistics, mathematical modeling, and related approaches. But this scientific hardening of method was set in the context of problem solving, value clarification, and the enhancement of the human condition. Lasswell looked upon method as making possible acts of "creative imagination" which might move mankind in constructive directions away from the tyrannies and catastrophes of the 1930s and 1940s.[98]

The connection between the search for regularities and political creativity—clearly seen by that generation freshly returned from Washington and the military theaters of World War II—was gradually lost in the decades that followed. The "methods" message of Lasswell's sermon was heard and acted upon with the mixed results we have reviewed, but the "policy science" message largely fell on deaf ears for reasons we have suggested above.

What is under attack here is the pecking order, and the particular set of priorities and resource allocations, which has come to dominate the profession in the last decades. These priorities and allocative policies, and this pecking order, are legitimated not by success in the explanation of political reality, but by the example and the demonstration effect of the hard sciences. A pecking order in which mathematization and sophisticated statistical analysis are viewed as the only sources of "real" or "powerful" theory, while theories produced from the interplay of imagination and induction are treated as "heuristic" or "weak" theory, cannot be justified by the explanatory performance of the former. Theories are inherently weak in the human sciences—both those that look "strong" because they look like the theories of physics, economics, or psychology, and those that look "weak" because they derive hypotheses from the examination of individual cases or historical experience.

Another aspect of the pecking order which is under criticism here is the distinction between pure and applied political science. Even in the hard sciences, the comparative intellectual payoffs of so-called pure and applied research are not at all clear-cut. Important discoveries often emerge out of applied research. In the social sciences, including political science, this difference loses its meaning since the special characteristic of social reality is man's adaptive behavior. The part of the discipline that calls itself pure political science, searching for powerful and enduring regularities, has missed the essential point of its subject matter. At best it illuminates the context of political decisions; but it leaves unexplored the adaptive searching process, the policy options, and their consequences. Surely the study of public policy—viewed as efforts to adapt to, cope with, modify, and overcome constraints—is as basic and pure an undertaking as is the search for constraining regularities. Indeed, we might argue that the essence of political science—insofar as it is to be defined by the essence of the politics it studies—is the analysis of choice in the context of constraints. That would place the search for regularities, the search for solutions to problems, and the evaluation of these solutions on the same level. They would all be parts of a common effort to confront man's political fate with rigor, with the necessary objectivity, and with an inescapable sense of identification with the subject matter which the political scientist studies.

Our policies of research support and professional training need to be freed from imitating the hard sciences. Policy studies, institutional studies, and philosophically sophisticated evaluative studies are claimants on research support with as much legitimacy as is currently accorded mathematical, statistical, and psychological and sociological reductionist studies. Knowledge of political substance in its institutional, historical, and philosophical aspects has to be reestablished on an equal footing with sophisticated methodologies and reductionist knowledge in our programs of graduate training. A whole library of meta-methodological handbooks and primers imposing the model of hard science on political reality has to be reevaluated in a new light. These volumes do not represent the "true path" to scientific progress; rather, they are a historical deviation, a flirtation with mistaken metaphors that temporarily captured the imagination of social scientists. Their historical importance is thus great, but their relevance to practical research problems in the social sciences is limited. To progress scientifically, the social disciplines require their own philosophy of science based on explanatory strategies, possibilities, and obligations appropriate to human and social reality.

Notes

1. Karl R. Popper, "Of Clouds and Clocks: An Approach to the Problem of Rationality and the Freedom of Man," in Popper, *Objective Knowledge: An Evolutionary Approach* (Oxford: Clarendon Press 1972), 210; emphasis in original.
2. *Ibid.*, 213; emphasis in original.
3. *Ibid.*, 226; emphasis in original.
4. Arthur H. Compton, *The Freedom of Man* (New Haven: Yale University Press 1935).
5. Popper (fn. 1), 228, 229; emphasis in original.
6. *Ibid.*, 231–32; emphasis in original.

7. See Donald T. Campbell, "Variation and Selective Retention in Socio-cultural Evolution," *General Systems Yearbook*, XIV (1969).
8. Popper (fn. 1), 240–41; emphasis in original.
9. *Ibid.*, 254–55.
10. Harold Sprout and Margaret Sprout, *The Ecological Perspective on Human Affairs* (Princeton: Princeton University Press 1965).
11. Angus Campbell and others, *The Voter Decides* (Evanston, IL: Row, Peterson 1954); Campbell and others, *The American Voter* (New York: Wiley 1960).
12. Norman Nie, Sidney Verba, and John R. Petrocik, *The Changing American Voter* (Cambridge: Harvard University Press 1976), 345ff; Walter Dean Burnham, *Critical Elections and the Mainsprings of American Politics* (New York: Norton 1970).
13. Philip E. Converse, "Public Opinion and Voting Behavior," in Fred I. Greenstein and Nelson W. Polsby, eds., *Handbook of Political Science*, IV (Reading, MA: Addison-Wesley 1975), 126.
14. For a recent review of the literature, see David O. Sears, "Political Socialization," in Greenstein and Polsby (fn. 13), 93ff.
15. M. Kent Jennings and Richard G. Niemi, *The Political Character of Adolescence* (Princeton: Princeton University Press 1974).
16. See Thomas R. Dye, *Understanding Public Policy* (Englewood Cliffs, NJ: Prentice-Hall 1972), 243–48, for a review of this literature and a fuller formulation of these findings and inferences.
17. For a review of this literature, see Gabriel A. Almond, Scott C. Flanagan, Robert J. Mundt, eds., *Crisis, Choice and Change* (Boston: Little, Brown 1973), 8ff.
18. Daniel Bell, *The End of Ideology* (New York: Free Press 1960).
19. Daniel Bell, *The Coming of Post-Industrial Society* (New York: Free Press 1973).
20. Daniel Bell, *The Cultural Contradictions of Capitalism* (New York: Basic Books 1976).
21. Easton, *The Political System* (New York: Knopf 1953), 55.
22. David B. Truman, "The Impact on Political Science of the Revolution in the Behavioral Sciences," reprinted in Heinz Eulau, ed., *Behavioralism in Political Science* (New York: Atherton 1969).
23. Howard A. Scarrow, *Comparative Political Analysis: An Introduction* (New York: Harper & Row 1969), 33.
24. Margaret Conway and Frank B. Feigert, *Political Analysis: An Introduction* (Boston: Allyn & Bacon 1972), 17.
25. Adam Przeworski and Henry Teune, *The Logic of Comparative Social Inquiry* (New York: Wiley 1970), 4.
26. Fred M. Frohock, *The Nature of Political Inquiry* (Homewood, IL: Dorsey 1967), 141.
27. Isaak, *The Scope and Method of Political Science* (Homewood, IL: Dorsey 1969), 80.
28. Conway and Feigert (fn. 24), 27.
29. Braithwaite, *Scientific Explanation* (Cambridge: Cambridge University Press 1953).
30. Hempel, *Aspects of Scientific Explanation* (New York: Free Press 1965); see also Ernest Nagel, *The Structure of Science* (New York: Harcourt, Brace and World 1961).
31. Abraham Kaplan, *The Conduct of Inquiry* (San Francisco: Chandler 1964), 339.
32. *Ibid.*
33. Paul Diesing, *Patterns of Discovery in the Social Sciences* (Chicago: Aldine Atherton 1971), 164.
34. See Hempel (fn. 30), 367, where this position is maintained while its obverse—that a valid

prediction must also qualify as an explanation – is put aside. This modification of the so-called symmetry thesis of explanation and prediction has not always been appreciated by political scientists. See, e.g., Oran Young, "The Perils of Odysseus: On Constructing Theories in International Relations," in Raymond Tanter and Richard Ullman, eds., *Theory and Policy in International Relations* (Princeton: Princeton University Press 1972), 183.

35. Hempel (fn. 30), 351; see also Nagel (fn. 30), 323.
36. Braithwaite (fn. 29), 2; see also Hempel (fn. 30), 348–49.
37. Dahl, "Cause and Effect in the Study of Politics," in Daniel Lerner, ed., *Cause and Effect* (New York: Free Press 1965), 87.
38. Isaak (fn. 27), 95.
39. See, e.g., Ernest Sosa, *Causation and Conditionals* (Oxford: Oxford University Press 1975); Myles Brand, ed., *The Nature of Causation* (Urbana: University of Illinois Press 1976).
40. There are many disputes concerning the philosophical status of causality that go well beyond this consensual element of its meaning – for example, the problem of whether the causal connection represents a constant conjunction, logical necessity, or "natural" necessity; and the problem of the temporal ordering and contiguity of causes and effects. For a discussion of these in terms relevant to political science research, see Georg Henrik von Wright, *Explanation and Understanding* (Ithaca, NY: Cornell University Press 1971).
41. Hempel (fn. 30), 348–49.
42. Kaplan, "Noncausal Explanation," in Lerner (fn. 37), 146.
43. Simon, *Models of Man* (New York: Wiley 1957), 5.
44. McFarland, *Power and Leadership in Pluralist Systems* (Stanford: Stanford University Press 1969), 29.
45. Nagel, *The Descriptive Analysis of Power* (New Haven: Yale University Press 1975), 29.
46. Dahl, *Modern Political Analysis* (3rd ed.; Englewood Cliffs, NJ: Prentice-Hall 1976), 30; emphasis in original.
47. H. L. A. Hart and A. M. Honor, *Causation in the Law* (Oxford: Clarendon Press 1959), 52.
48. For further arguments along similar lines, see Terence Ball, "Power, Causation and Explanations," *Polity*, VIII (Winter 1975), 189–214.
49. See von Wright (fn. 40), chap. 1.
50. See, e.g., Nagel (fn. 30); Hempel (fn. 30), chap. 9; May Brodbeck, "Explanation, Prediction, and 'Imperfect' Knowledge," in Herbert Feigl and Grover Maxwell, eds., *Minnesota Studies in the Philosophy of Science: Vol. 3* (Minneapolis: University of Minnesota Press 1962); Richard S. Rudner, *Philosophy of Social Science* (Englewood Cliffs, NJ: Prentice-Hall 1966); Rudner, "Comment: On the Evolving Standard View in Philosophy of Science," *American Political Science Review*, Vol. 66 (September 1972).
51. William H. Riker, quoted in "Editorial Comment," *American Political Science Review*, Vol. 68 (June 1974), 733–34.
52. Edward R. Tufte, "Improving Data Analysis in Political Science," *World Politics*, XXI (July 1969).
53. Andrew Mack, "Numbers Are Not Enough," *Comparative Politics*, VII (July 1975).
54. Ralph E. Strauch, "A Critical Look at Quantitative Methodology," *Policy Science*, II (Winter 1976).
55. See, e.g., Hayward R. Alker, "The Long Road to International Relations Theory: Problems of Statistical Nonadditivity," *World Politics*, XVII (July 1966); Hubert M. Blalock, "Cor-

related Independent Variables: The Problem of Multicollinearity," in Edward R. Tufte, ed., *The Quantitative Analysis of Social Problems* (Reading, MA: Addison-Wesley 1970).

56. Tukey, *Exploratory Data Analysis* (Reading, MA: Addison-Wesley 1977); David C. Hoaglin, *A First Course in Data Analysis* (Reading, MA: Addison-Wesley, forthcoming).
57. Robert T. Holt and John M. Richardson, Jr., "Competing Paradigms in Comparative Politics," in Holt and John E. Turner, eds., *The Methodology of Comparative Research* (New York: Free Press 1970), 70.
58. Gregor, "Political Science and the Uses of Functional Analysis," *American Political Science Review*, Vol. 62 (June 1968), 425–39; Young (fn. 34).
59. *Ibid.*, 196.
60. Holt and Richardson (fn. 57), 70–71.
61. William H. Riker and Peter C. Ordeshook, *An Introduction to Positive Political Theory* (Englewood Cliffs, NJ: Prentice-Hall 1973), 11. A sympathetic yet sober evaluation of the utility of rational choice models for explaining and predicting coalition behavior is offered by Abram De Swann, *Coalition Theories and Cabinet Formations* (San Francisco: Jossey-Bass 1973).
62. Riker and Ordeshook (fn. 61), 11–12. By "explanation," we can only assume that Riker and Ordeshook mean "definition," since the postulation of rationality *defines* a (hypothetical) type of behavior, but does not *explain* it in any way.
63. Moon, "The Logic of Political Inquiry: A Synthesis of Opposed Perspectives," in Greenstein and Polsby (fn. 13), 1.
64. *Ibid.*, 194.
65. Alker, "Polimetrics: Its Descriptive Foundations," in Greenstein and Polsby (fn. 13), VII, 157.
66. Kaplan (fn. 31), 3.
67. Marc J. Roberts, "On the Nature and Condition of Social Science," *Daedalus*, Vol. 103 (Summer 1974), 61, 62.
68. Chein, "The Image of Man," *Journal of Social Issues*, XVIII (October 1962), 3.
69. *Ibid.* Similar arguments are made in Rom Harre and P. F. Secord, *The Explanation of Social Behavior* (Totowa, NJ: Rowman & Littlefield 1972).
70. Chein (fn. 68), 2; emphasis in original; 18.
71. Campbell, "On the Conflict Between Biological and Social Evolution and Between Psychology and Moral Tradition," *American Psychologist*, XXX (December 1975), 1120, 1121.
72. Ross, "The Intuitive Psychologist and His Shortcomings: Distortions in the Attribution Process," in L. Berkowitz, ed., *Advances in Experimental Social Psychology*, X (New York: Academic Press 1977), 174.
73. Cronbach, "Beyond the Two Disciplines of Scientific Psychology," *American Psychologist*, XXX (February 1975), 116, 125.
74. *Ibid.*, 122–23.
75. *Ibid.*, 126.
76. Gunnar Myrdal, *Against the Stream: Critical Essays on Economics* (New York: Vintage 1972), 143.
77. John K. Galbraith, "Power and the Useful Economist," *American Economic Review*, Vol. 63 (March 1973), 2.
78. Roberts (fn. 67), 60.
79. Morgenstern, "Thirteen Critical Points in Contemporary Economic Theory," *Journal of Economic Literature*, X (December 1972), 1164–65.

80. Leontief, "Theoretical Assumptions and Nonobserved Facts," *American Economic Review*, Vol. 61 (March 1971), 1, 2, 3; emphasis in original.
81. Morgenstern (fn. 79), 1187–88.
82. Galbraith (fn. 77), 4.
83. Quoted in Wade Greene, "Economists in Recession," *New York Times Magazine* (May 12, 1974), 64.
84. Leontief (fn. 80), 3.
85. Albert O. Hirschman, *A Bias for Hope* (New Haven: Yale University Press 1971), 27.
86. Popper (fn. 1); *Conjectures and Refutations* (New York: Basic Books 1963); *The Logic of Scientific Discovery* (New York: Basic Books 1959).
87. Michael Polanyi, *Personal Knowledge* (Chicago: University of Chicago Press 1958).
88. Norwood R. Hanson, *Patterns of Discovery* (Cambridge: Cambridge University Press 1958); *Observation and Explanation: A Guide to Philosophy of Science* (New York: Harper & Row 1971).
89. Thomas S. Kuhn, *The Structure of Scientific Revolutions* (Chicago: University of Chicago Press 1962).
90. W.V.O. Quine, *Ontological Relativity* (New York: Columbia University Press 1969).
91. Imre Lakatos, "Falsification and the Methodology of Scientific Research Programmes," in Lakatos and Alan Musgrave, eds., *Criticism and the Growth of Knowledge* (Cambridge: Cambridge University Press 1970).
92. Stephen Toulmin, *Human Understanding*, I (Princeton: Princeton University Press 1972); *Foresight and Understanding* (New York: Harper & Row 1961).
93. See Campbell (fn. 71).
94. Bennett, "Anticipation, Adaptation, and the Concept of Culture in Anthropology," *Science*, Vol. 192 (May 28, 1976), 847.
95. *Ibid.*, 850, 851.
96. MacRae, *The Social Function of Social Science* (New Haven: Yale University Press 1976), 3.
97. *Ibid.*, 277ff.
98. Daniel Lerner and Harold D. Lasswell, eds., *The Policy Sciences: Recent Developments in Scope and Method* (Stanford: Stanford University Press 1951), 3, 12.

3

Model Fitting in Communism Studies

with Laura Roselle

The interaction between political theory and area studies in the last several decades has taken the form of model fitting—crude, clumsy, and, sometimes sanguine at the outset, increasingly deft and experimental as time went on and experience accumulated. Soviet and East European (and now Chinese) political studies, of all area studies, have been more open to this model-fitting process. This may very well be due to the scarcity of data about communist societies, and the effort to enhance insight through experimenting with different theoretical perspectives.

The argument that we make in this chapter is that this model-fitting experience is not to be set aside as ethnocentrism and cultural imperialism on the one hand, or methodologically gauche "conceptual traveling . . . conceptual misformation . . . conceptual stretching . . . or conceptual straining" on the other.[1] Both Binder and Sartori miss the point. Binder surely does not accurately describe the works of his colleagues when he speaks of "modernization theory" as "an academic, and pseudo-scientific transfer of the dominant, and ideologically significant, paradigm employed in research on the American political systems" to foreign and particularly non-Western areas.[2] And Giovanni Sartori, in his praiseworthy pursuit of careful, precise, logically arranged conceptualization, suppresses the messy, everyday interaction between theory and data that lies at the heart of creative scholarship.[3]

An early example of self-conscious model fitting in political science was

---

Karl Deutsch's *The Nerves of Government*, which employed the analogy of a cybernetic system as a way of illuminating political processes and concepts.[4] The analogy of communications flows, feedback loops, and "steering" produced suggestive insights and hypotheses. Deutsch reviews the experiences with modeling in the history of political theory, citing the model of mechanism – of balance, tension, and equilibrium – in the theories of Machiavelli, Hobbes, Locke, Montesquieu, and the Founding Fathers; the model of organism in classical and Catholic political theory, in Rousseau, and Burke; the grand philosophy of history models – the cyclical model of growth and decay of Plato and Aristotle, of Spengler and Toynbee; and the enlightenment model of progress. He also briefly reviews contemporary social science modeling – formal mathematical systems of equations, game theory, Weberian ideal-typical analysis, and the like.

Deutsch deals primarily with large-scale "macro-models" of total societies, political systems, economies, the shape of history, though it is quite clear that he has in mind the experimental model-fitting process that we shall be describing. Models, he points out, have to be tested for relevance; they must be matched against reality. The "model-matching" process is the way to get at the shape of reality. Surely the history of science demonstrates the value of this trial-and-error, back-and-forth process, between physical and conceptual imagination, drawing analogies from one subject matter to another, and experimental tests of these physical or conceptual models against reality. The development of high-energy physics, modern cosmology, and molecular biology, with their "charm theories," their "string," "black hole," "meat ball," and "sponge" theories, their "double helix" theories, is illustrative.

The history of communism studies, more than any other of the area studies (except American studies, which are area studies too), reflects the growth of this methodological sophistication. The history of communism studies may be written in terms of these experiments with macro-modeling efforts to capture the whole phenomenon so to speak, and with micro-modeling of aspects of communist politics. The notion of modeling has more than one meaning. In quantitative studies the term *model* is reserved for relations that are expressible in mathematical equations. But the term is also used generically to refer to explanatory mental constructs. The mind has no choice in relating to, adapting to, or attempting to master reality, but to select, summarize, and compare the unfamiliar with the familiar. In what follows we discuss totalitarianism, developmental theories of communist systems, the various treatments of communist politics in terms of pluralism, interest group theory, bureaucratic politics, and patron-client relations, as applications of explanatory models coming from other parts of the political science discipline, as efforts to explain the puzzling, the unfamiliar, by the known, by the familiar. This use of the model concept is relatively clear-cut. An interest group explanation of Soviet or Chinese politics seeks to explain the political process and its outputs by the action and interaction of groups defined in some way. Do actions of groups and coalitions of groups add up to a particular decision process and policy outcome? Group process concepts have been used with some effect in studies of American and European politics. Do they explain political processes and policy decisions in communist systems?

But the interaction of communism studies with other parts of the political and social science disciplines is not simply via explanatory models. Communism studies have also been influenced by theoretical frameworks drawn from sociological, anthropological, and political theories such as structural-functionalism, decision process theory, modernization theory. We discuss these imports into communism studies as heuristic theories, as conceptual frameworks of variables that enable us to formulate questions and hypotheses. Thus structural-functionalism and decision process frameworks, by requiring communism specialists to assume the existence of political processes, led to the experimentation with specific schemes such as bureaucratic politics, interest group, and patron-client theory.

The Totalitarian Model

The first model used in the study of communism was "dictatorship." Indeed, the Soviet regime referred to itself as a "dictatorship of the proletariat" (or of its "vanguard," the Communist party), a stage in the development of communism, before the state gave way to simple administration in the post-class struggle phase, first of socialism, and then of communism. For political scientists in the 1920s and 1930s it was classed with Italian Fascism and National Socialism. The comparative government of the interwar period had two classes of political systems—democracies and dictatorships. Dictatorship was defined in essentially negative terms; it eliminated effective popular participation and representation, the rule of law, division and separation of powers.

The first inkling that something new was afoot was in some speeches of Mussolini in the mid-1920s, when he referred to Fascist Italy as *uno stato totalitario*, meaning by that, national unity, the elimination of opposition, and the end of special interest domination. As Fascist power became more penetrative and Nazi Germany came on the scene, the term became generic, at first including only Germany and Italy. In the later 1930s "there was at least some disposition" to include the Soviet Union, "a disposition which was muffled during the war period, but which revived with the onset of the cold war."[5] In the mood of World War II Japanese military authoritarianism was assimilated to the model.

Perhaps the first self-conscious recognition that totalitarianism was a new form of government was a lecture by the historian Carlton J.H. Hayes titled "The Novelty of Totalitarianism in the History of Western Civilization" delivered at a meeting of the American Philosophical Society in November 1939.[6] Hayes lists four novel characteristics of this governmental system: (1) its monopoly of all powers within society; (2) its mobilization of popular support; (3) its effective use of techniques of education and propaganda; and (4) its emphasis on national power and the use of force.

The two works, however, which established totalitarianism as a unique type of political system appeared in the aftermath of the Second World War: Hannah Arendt's *The Origins of Totalitarianism*, and Friedrich and Brzezinski's *Totalitarian Dictatorship and Autocracy.*[7] Both studies described totalitarianism as a uniquely twentieth-century occurrence and both singled out the combination of terror, coercion, propaganda, and manipulation as the distinctive instrument of totalitarian rule. Arendt sought the origins of the system in anti-Semitism, nationalism, and imperialism, while Friedrich and Brzezinski focused on the distinctive institution and practices of totalitarian rule. Perhaps Arendt's most important insight into the politics of totalitarianism was her thesis that rather than being a stable monocratic distribution of power, it was inherently arbitrary in the interest of maximizing power at the center. Generalizing from the Hitler and Stalin cases, she pointed out that the extraordinary concentration of power in their hands was associated with maintenance of several competing organizations—a mass party, a secret police, and military services—and the refusal to make stable delegations of power and function to any one of them.[8] Friedrich and Brzezinski presented a general model of totalitarian dictatorship based on six criteria: (1) an official, monopolistic ideology; (2) a single mass party; (3) terroristic police control; (4) a monopoly of the communication of ideas; (5) a monopoly of weapons; (6) a centrally directed economy. These six characteristics formed the "syndrome" of the pattern of interrelated traits common to totalitarian dictatorships.

During the decade of the 1950s the totalitarian model dominated Soviet studies. The leading texts tended to interpret Soviet institutions and political processes primarily, if not solely, in terms of this extreme concentration of power.[9] The focus was on the central role of the Communist party, the personal role of Stalin, and the reliance on political terror.

The totalitarian model ran into rough water in the 1960s. The changes in the Soviet Union that followed the death of Stalin, and the emergence and development of other communist systems, raised questions as to the model's applicability, first to the Soviet Union and, second, to other communist systems. The lessening of the use of terror under Khrushchev called into question, for example, the totalitarian model's emphasis on terror. The Sino-Soviet split, which came into the open during the early 1960s, led some scholars to doubt the applicability of the totalitarian model in the study of Communist China. The disorders in Eastern Europe in the 1950s created a similar problem.

There were noteworthy efforts during the 1960s to modify and amend the model. An early example is an article by Allen Kassof titled "The Administered Society: Totalitarianism Without Terror," written in 1964. Kassof observed that the "administered society is thus a variant of modern totalitarianism, with the important difference that it operates by and large without resort to those elements of gross irrationality . . . that we have come to associate with totalitarian systems in recent decades."[10] Carl Friedrich, in his revised edition of *Totalitarian Dictatorship*, deemphasized terror as well. Similarly, Arendt in a later edition of her book downplays terror as a necessary and permanent feature of this kind of regime.[11] These efforts at repair retained most of the early features of the model, but treated the terroristic and mobilizational aspects as modifiable in degree.

But the scholarly community was not ready to accept the concept with those minor repairs. There were too many problems with it: too many definitions; too much cold war coloration; failure to explain change over time; and failure to distinguish totalitarianism from other types of autocracy.[12] Linz tried to remedy this situation by distinguishing totalitarian regimes, which he confined to Hitler's Germany and Stalin's Russia, from "premobilizational" totalitarian regimes, and "post-totalitarian" regimes under which category he would include the contemporary Soviet Union.

Studies of communism in Eastern Europe and Communist China generally eschewed the use of the term *totalitarianism*. It is striking that Brzezinski simply does not use the term in his *The Soviet Bloc*;[13] and Townsend in the leading text on Communist China points out that the six criteria of Friedrich and Brzezinski did not fit well.[14] Control rested less on political terror than it did on persuasion and organization.

This intellectual history of communism studies reflects the earlier, more naive use of models; first, the effort to capture the essence of political reality in a simple model (and not in the self-conscious, Weberian "ideal type" sense), and then the disillusionment at the failure of the model accompanied by the rejection of all modeling in favor of the "barefooted empiricism" of area studies. Some of the papers in the Lucian Pye volume *Political Science and Area Studies* reflect this disappointment and disillusionment with theory.[15] But this disillusionment with theorizing was rejected, for example, by George Breslauer, who asserts the need for modeling even after the failure of the totalitarian model.[16] "Western frustration with the shortcomings of the totalitarian model has led to a backlash against the use of labels per se, but this is a shortsighted response. Labels can be useful, and one measure of their utility is the dimensions of the system to which they draw attention."[17] The importance of theory in the learning process is also stressed by Abbott Gleason, who pointed out,

> It is one thing to criticize the totalitarian model. It would be quite another if the rejectors had not already thoroughly absorbed its insights. . . . The insights of one generation, especially the crucial ones that define its vision of the world, are often sitting ducks for those who speak for the next generation. From a scholarly point of view, the rejection of the idea of totalitarianism may be crucial to whatever the successor generation of scholars achieves in the way of understanding the Soviet Union and other Communist states.[18]

There had, however, been a more conceptually imaginative multimodel minor trend in Soviet studies beginning in the 1950s. Barrington Moore in his perceptive study, *Terror and Progress, USSR*, employed three models in combination as a way of explaining and forecasting Soviet development.[19] Many aspects of Soviet political and economic life lent themselves to a patron-client, traditionalistic interpretation—factionalism, "cliquism," "familistic" behavior, and the like. Other aspects lent themselves to an industrializing rational-technical pattern of explanation. And finally, there were aspects that lent themselves to an ideological, totalitarian model of explanation. Moore argued that all three dynamisms were present in Soviet politics; their relative dominance varied by issue and sphere, and over time in response to external and internal pressures.

Daniel Bell published an article enumerating some ten different approaches to the study of Soviet politics including social, culture and personality theories, Marxist and non-Marxist industrialization theories, totalitarianism, geopolitical approaches, and the like.[20] He explores the ways these various approaches illuminate different aspects of Soviet politics, and advocates an eclectic approach in Soviet studies.

Alex Inkeles, more parsimoniously, suggests three models rather similar to those of Barrington Moore: (1) totalitarianism, (2) industrialization, and (3) developmental.[21] He points out that some aspects of Soviet development can be explained by the totalitarian model, some by the generic industrialization model, and some by the requirements of an effective national administrative structure and economic growth. He observes that other models, such as the national characterological, also have useful insights to offer.

But the move into experimental model fitting in communism studies actually began in the discontent in the subdiscipline as it moved into the post-Stalin era, when much of what was happening in the politics of communist countries could not be explained by the totalitarian model, when decentralizing, legalistic, and pluralist bargaining features began to manifest themselves. Abbott Gleason, for example, claims that "with passage of time the Soviet Union seems more and more understandable in terms of rather traditional categories."[22] Hence, it is not accidental that the first major alternative model to be tried out was that of pluralism or "interest group" theory. Similarly, it is not surprising that experimentation began with case studies of policy processes in efforts to test various models for fit. But before concluding the discussion of totalitarianism it should be noted that after having been set aside for some two decades, there has been a small step back toward acknowledgment of the usefulness of the totalitarian model. It is still widely viewed as quite appropriate in analyzing the historic Stalinist and Nazi systems, and as a tendency in contemporary communist countries.[23] The limited utility that the totalitarianism concept still retains is reflected in discussions in Frederic Fleron's *Communist Studies and the Social Sciences*, as well as in such leading texts as Barghoorn on Soviet politics, Jerry Hough and Merle Fainsod on Soviet politics, and James Townsend on Chinese politics.[24] Leonard Schapiro offers a history of the use of the totalitarian concept and makes an important argument in favor of its continued limited utility.[25] Joseph LaPalombara offers a trenchant review of this polemic and points out that the pluralist writers qualify their revisionism by acknowledgment of the unitary and coercive features of these regimes. He takes a skeptical view of pluralist reinterpretations, and adopts the modified view of totalitarianism of Juan Linz.[26]

Heuristic Theory and Frameworks

What follows in this chapter is a brief account of the interplay of political theory and communism studies since the 1960s. Not all of it can be strictly accommodated under the modeling metaphor. There have been conceptual imports into communism studies which are "mapping" or heuristic devices facilitating description and comparison, and thus ultimately contributing to explanation, but not in themselves explanatory competitors. System theory, structural functionalism, decision theory, and political culture theory are examples of these heuristic imports from political, sociological, psychological, and anthropological theory. They are conceptual frameworks suitable for the description and comparison of any political system, or explanatory variables as in the case of the political culture concept. Such frameworks and concepts enable us to do the job of explanation of politics and policy systematically and rigorously. They are of a different order from the patron-client model, interest group model, the bureaucratic politics model, and the like, which have been put forward as tentative explanations of communist political process. Thus a patron-client factional model of communist politics would explain it in terms of the rivalry and competition of patron-client factions concerned with power and patronage, with policy a secondary concern. An interest group model would seek to explain communist politics in terms of group conflict and bargaining over power and policy. A bureaucratic politics model of communism would explain power and policy in terms of propensities and standard operating procedures of bureaucratic organizations. A rational choice, game-theoretic model would seek to explain communist politics in terms of competing actors with different resources calculating short-term material interests and pursuing strategies and forming coalitions on the basis of those interests. Another heuristic export from social science theory has been political culture theory, which stresses the importance of subjective or psychological variables in the explanation of politics. Political culture theory has had an unusually successful "run" in communism studies, helping to explain the survival, even the vitality, of precommunist and noncommunist attitudes and values, despite powerful efforts to eliminate them.

Structural Functionalism and Decision Theories

The first major postwar text on Soviet politics, Fainsod's *How Russia Is Ruled*, dominated the field for more than a decade.[27] It was an authoritative, essentially historical-institutional-descriptive study oriented around the totalitarian model, though not minimizing important lines of cleavage and dissent. Barrington Moore's early study, *Soviet Politics*, is an impressive account of the interplay of ideology and historical circumstance in the shaping of the Soviet economic, social, and political system.[28] His *Terror and Progress*, to which we have already referred, is a logical extension of his argument in this earlier work that historical reality—internal and external—has produced a social system differing in fundamental ways from what was predicted in Soviet ideology. However, the categories he employs in this earlier work are essentially historical and institutional.

Three other texts that first appeared in the 1950s and early 1960s—those of Adam Ulam, John Hazard, and John Armstrong—also were essentially historical institutional studies.[29] While sociological and anthropological theory had some impact on the work of Barrington Moore in the 1950s, it was not until the appearance of David Easton's *The Political System*, Lasswell's *The Decision Process*, and Almond's "Comparative Political Systems" that system and functional concepts began to penetrate comparative politics and studies of communist systems.[30] Frederick Barghoorn's *Politics in the USSR* was the first major experiment in the application of functional categories in the analysis of Soviet politics, and James Townsend's *Politics in China* applies a similar functional scheme to Communist China's politics.[31]

Other text treatments of Soviet and Chinese politics have adapted in varying degrees to system-functional and decision process analysis. Thus Jerry Hough's adaptation of the Fainsod text involves employing a policy process perspective in the second half of the book, dealing with such themes as citizen participation and political inputs, agenda setting and support building, factional conflict and pluralist tendencies, policy initiation, policy debates, and the like. Hough justifies this shift in the volume's emphasis by arguing that "research and writing about Western governments has centered on the policy-process and the factors associated with responsiveness in political systems, and meaningful comparative political science requires that a conscious attempt be made to ask the same questions about the Soviet Union."[32] Mary McAuley's Penguin book, *Politics and the Soviet Union*, deals with the contemporary Soviet political system in terms of the new policy process approach, using a policy case study technique.[33] The influence of Dahl, Allison, Skilling, Almond, and Powell is evident in her work. The current edition of David Lane's *Politics and Society in the USSR* has two substantial chapters (7 and 8) presenting a system-functional approach to Soviet politics and the group basis of Soviet politics. In his preface he describes his approach in the following terms: "I have sought to bring together the fruits of research, conducted both in the West and in the USSR, to give a synoptic view of Soviet society studied from the viewpoint of the social sciences. While the political process is examined as a political 'system,' other more traditional ways of study, such as the description of political 'institutions' have not been excluded."[34] In his more recent textbook focused more particularly on politics, the approach used in analyzing the political process is also in part a system-functional one.[35] A more recent text on communist systems by Stephen White and others follows a system-structural, policy process format, and deals at length with the significance of political cultural factors in explaining differences in political patterns.[36] White and his colleagues suggest a trial-and-error model-fitting approach similar to the one developed in this chapter, but they deal only briefly with the totalitarian, modernization, and bureaucratic models.

The diffusion of system-functional concepts into continental European Soviet studies is reflected in the work of Georg Brunner, who relies heavily on the American literature for his concepts and categories. After reviewing other functional categorizations, he presents a threefold functional scheme: (1) basic decision, (2) implementation, and (3) control. On the structural side the party dominates the decision and control functions, while the state and social organizations perform the implementation function. A later chapter on interest groups does not quite fit into this scheme.[37]

Two important conceptual steps have been taken in these structural-functional and decision process studies. The first is the separation of the policy process from structure and institutions. To understand a single country's political process, to say nothing of comparing it with others, requires asking functional or process questions. How is policy made and implemented? What institutions and agencies are involved in what ways in the articulation, communication, and aggregation of demands, and the making and implementation of decisions? A purely historical, structural approach tends to impute particular functions to particular structures, whereas in actual fact the typical pattern is one of multifunctionality of structure. A structural approach to communist systems would leave us with the dilemma of how to characterize the significant changes in communist political processes which have occurred while institutions have substantially remained the same. The second conceptual step is to require students of communist systems to assume a political and policy process. Daniel Tarschys has shown how the adoption of systemic and functional notions in the 1960s directed the attention of communist scholarship to the input side of the political process, rendering the older model of a purely administered "output" society obsolete.[38] T. H. Rigby, in a study of the changing composition of party leadership and membership in the Soviet Union in the half century from 1917 to 1967, shows how these changes were related to policy initiation, aggregation, communication, socialization, and recruitment.[39]

The conceptual models that have been employed by students of communist politics have come from the Almond-Powell threefold scheme of system, process, and policy functions, or from administrative decision theory, which breaks the policy process down into phases that typically include agenda setting, issue analysis, decision making, implementation, evaluation, and termination.[40] Decision-theoretic approaches may be normative or prescriptive – that is, they may examine a decision process from the point of view of its rationality, the extent to which ends are clearly formulated, and means chosen to attain those ends – or explanatory, that is, they may examine the extent to which the decision process is rigorously described, and its phases explained and related to outcomes. Case studies of Soviet foreign policy-making may exemplify the prescriptive approach to foreign policy decision making. Examples of this approach would be the various studies of the Berlin crises of the 1948–62 period, the Middle East crises of the 1950s and 1960s, the Cuban missile crisis, and the Czech crisis. This work and the larger decision-theoretic literature is reviewed in Horelick et al.[41] The explanatory decision-theoretic approach is exemplified by William Potter, who breaks the decision process down into five phases: (1) initiation, (2) controversy, (3) formal decision, (4) implementation, and (5) termination.[42] Potter then evaluates the literature on Soviet foreign policy-making from the point of view of its effective coverage of these five phases. Aspaturian, in a recent analysis of Soviet foreign policy decision making, uses a similar scheme, but does not include termination.[43]

Political Culture

While interest in attitudes and values as an explanation for political behavior is an ancient theme in political theory, in recent decades research and theoretical speculation about political culture have been associated with four historical puzzles. The first of these was the fall of the Weimar Republic and the rise of National Socialism in Germany; the second, the decline of civic culture in Britain and the United States, and the rise of consensual democratic political culture in Germany in the 1960s and 1970s; the third development was the frustration of efforts to export democratic attitudes and practices to Third World countries. The fourth puzzle was the remarkable persistence in communist countries of ethnolinguistic-national particularisms, religious commitments, and political opposition and dissent, despite the enormous effort mounted in these countries to eliminate these propensities and replace them with a new Marxist-Leninist political culture.

The collapse of democracy in Germany in the 1930s shook confidence in the relationships among industrialization, education, and democratization. What could explain this brutalization of politics and opinion in a country that had excelled in its trained and talented labor force, in scientific discovery, technological invention, and in artistic creativity? The decline of consensual politics in Britain and the United States during the 1960s and the 1970s and its rise in Germany during the same decades raised questions about the stability and persistence of political attitudes, given sharp fluctuations in governmental effectiveness and performance. The rapid collapse of democratic institutions in Third World countries demonstrated the "stickiness" of traditional attitudes and values. Finally, the intermittent popping up of dissenting nationalistic, religious, ethnolinguistic, and political movements in communist countries, despite the sustained, massive, and penetrative efforts on the part of the communist elites to develop a homogeneous "communist man" political culture, stimulated political culture research and speculation among scholars specializing on these areas.

In fact the political culture bibliography in the last decade has more entries from communism studies than from other areas. The first full-length treatment of communist political culture, subculture, and political socialization was in Barghoorn's study of Soviet politics. Within a few years Richard Fagen published a study of the effort of the communist movement to create a new "Cuban man," urging that the concept of political culture be broadened to include behavior as well as attitudes.[44] This polemic over the definition of the political culture concept has been continued by Robert Tucker, Stephen White, and others.[45] In a thoughtful analysis of this issue, Archie Brown, drawing on anthropological debates about the definition of culture, shows that the more inclusive "kitchen sink" definition of culture has been increasingly set aside by anthropologists in recent decades in favor of a subjective definition (one limited to cognitive, affective, and evaluative factors) rather than including behavior and even artifacts. This shift among anthropologists "represents a recognition that making an analytical distinction between the cognitive world of the actors and the realm of events and transactions in which they engage points up the problematic nature of the relationship between the subjective and cognitive realm, on the one hand, and the behavior on the other, in a way conducive to reflection and research on the nature of the interactions."[46]

The bibliography dealing with communism and political culture theory in general terms includes Fagen, Tucker, Brown, Jack Gray, McAuley, Stephen White, and Almond, among others.[47] The main theoretical issues have to do with definition and methodology. What should be included under the political culture rubric; and, given the difficulties of access for the collection of data, how is it possible to determine the extent of persistence of precommunist or the creation of noncommunist propensities? Stephen White suggests an ingenious method of determining the significance of historical-cultural factors in the political life of communist countries.[48] He draws on John Stuart Mill's approach to comparative analysis, combining the methods of agreement and difference in contrasting the historical and contemporary experience of communist countries.

Barghoorn is the acknowledged pioneer in the treatment of political culture in the Soviet Union. All three editions of his *Politics in the USSR* deal with historical patterns, subcultural tendencies, elite political culture, and socialization and communication processes.[49] A book-length treatment of Soviet political culture by Stephen White emphasizes mass political culture, presenting substantial empirical data produced by Soviet social scientists on popular attitudes and beliefs.[50] He makes the argument that the acceptance of absolutism on the part of the Soviet masses is largely explained by Russia's pattern of absolutism. This point is disputed by Barghoorn, who insists that the extreme coercion and terror of the Stalin years as well as the monopoly of communication and organization are important contributing factors.

Another polemic in the Soviet political culture field deals with the nature of popular participation in Soviet politics. Barghoorn and Friedgut emphasize the mobilized and subject-participatory character of mass participation.[51] Di Franceisco and Gitelman, on the basis of a substantial number of interviews with Soviet emigres, assert that mass participation, while focused on the implementation side of the policy process, includes both a ritual conformity component and a quantitatively significant component of "particularized contacting" *à la* Verba and Nie.[52] In other words, there is greater activism in Soviet politics than is suggested in the notion of subject participation, but it takes the form of approaching party and governmental authorities on private and personal needs.

The political cultures of the Eastern European countries demonstrate the extraordinary staying power of nationalist and liberal tendencies, and traditional ethnic and religious propensities in the face of the most penetrative efforts to eliminate them or assimilate them into the Communist system. Czechoslovakia, Poland, Hungary, and Romania each in their own way have managed to force a compromise on the Soviet-backed Communist efforts to create homogeneous "socialist" cultures.[53] The Yugoslavian experience suggests how these sociopolitical systems might modify themselves if Soviet pressure were withdrawn.[54]

In this connection it is of interest that the concept of political culture has been widely adopted in the Soviet Union itself and with a definition not too far removed from that used in the West. While Soviet scholars assume that socialist political culture is the normative version of political culture toward which human history tends, they acknowledge the persistence of older historical tendencies, and the socialization processes that preserve them, in the Soviet Union, in the Eastern European countries, in the Third World and the West. Soviet scholars have used survey research particularly in the study of the political culture of youth in Russia.[55] Empirical studies of attitudes and opinion on political, ideological, and social issues have been carried out in a number of Eastern European countries as well.

The Developmental Model

Quite early in communism studies different versions of modernization and development theory were applied in efforts to explain and predict the course of political change. Thus the industrial development model was one of the three models used by Barrington Moore and Alex Inkeles in speculating about the dynamics of Soviet politics.[56] Huntington and Brzezinski, in their comparative study of the United States and the USSR, explained converging political tendencies in terms of the common impact of industrialization and modernization, while at the same time arguing that differing historical and ideological patterns would prevent a complete convergence.[57]

Social mobilization theory in its earlier version predicted that political mobilization would follow upon social mobilization (industrialization, urbanization, education, mass communication). Karl Deutsch, S. M. Lipset, James Coleman, Inkeles and Smith, and many others contributed to a literature that anticipated tendencies toward democratization in communist countries as they succeeded in industrializing.[58] The conceptual apparatus of modernization theory was applied to Eastern European communist countries by Jan Triska and his associates.[59] Paul Johnson, in particular, presented a set of hypotheses about the relationship among economic, social, and political modernization variables in Eastern European countries, and suggested a research design that might be used to test the validity of these hypotheses.[60]

Huntington explained the development of the "Leninist party" in terms of the political-economic dynamics of modernization. The Leninist party provided an organizational framework capable of containing a society, mobilized by industrialization, urbanization, spreading literacy, and the mass media.[61] Richard Lowenthal argued more than fifteen years ago that we ought to expect a profound alteration in the functions and operations of the

CPSU as it shifted from its earlier penetrative, mobilizing, and transformative role, to that of reaching and interacting with a basically transformed socioeconomic base. "Yet though the totalitarian institutional framework has been preserved, the basic relation between the political system and the development of society has been reversed. Formerly the political system was in command, subjecting an underdeveloped society to forced development and to a series of revolutions from above. Now the political system has to respond to the pressures generated by an increasingly advanced society."[62] Lowenthal anticipated a political transformation that would include the legitimation of policy conflict within a framework of bureaucratic rationality, but that would be marked by tension between pluralist impulses and efforts to contain them and avoid instability and the threat of systemic change. Kenneth Jowitt advanced the theory that there were only two routes to the modern world—the liberal route, historically unique and no longer available, and the Marxist-Leninist route of forced modernization. He saw no future for reformist incrementalism.[63] But in later writing as he reflected on the experience of such communist countries as Yugoslavia, Poland, and Romania, he introduces the category of neotraditionalism to explain the stagnation and corruption of communist regimes.[64]

Broadly speaking, the development model, the historical persistence-cultural model, and the ideological model have been the principal competitors in efforts to explain future political change in communist societies. The development model predicts that given industrial-technical development, historical-cultural differences and ideological differences would gradually lose their explanatory power to the point of insignificance. The historical-cultural persistence model argues that no matter how powerful and homogeneous these technocratic-industrial developments are, historical-cultural propensities would produce significant differences in development patterns. An ideological model argues that political ideological goals could both significantly modify historic-cultural propensities and contain the unintended consequences of technical-industrial change. It is a tribute to the originality of Barrington Moore's original formulation that this threefold approach still survives as the most inclusive explanation of the dynamics of communist systems and change.

Andrew Janos, in his recent *Politics and Paradigms*, goes beyond Barrington Moore, arguing that he and, indeed, the entire classical Marxian-Weberian-Parsonian modernization tradition can no longer explain developmental processes in the modern world, that a global division of labor and system of communications has been reached in which international political-economic forces have important explanatory power. Janos foresees a new paradigm which will recognize the looseness of the relationship between internal mobilization variables and cultural-political change.[65] Innovations and ideas

> float freely from society to society and from continent to continent . . . and as ideas move from core to periphery, they will encounter different configurations of interest, giving rise to different institutional responses and patterns of behavior. The ideas of modern secularism and popular sovereignty are cases in point. Whereas in the West they gave rise to parliamentary democracy, elsewhere the corresponding institutional expression is most frequently bureaucratic authoritarianism.[66]

Janos overlooks the fact that the international environment was of enormous importance in the shaping of the European states and their institutions, and that this has been recognized and elaborated in the work of Hintze, Tilly, and many others.[67] Similarly, the importance of international demonstration effect and of diffusion in Western development has been elaborated in Heclo and debated in Flora and Heidenheimer and others.[68] It is not clear how Janos's new paradigm differs from the positions taken by other development theorists, in particular those listed in his table who postulate different development outcomes attributable to differences in internal characteristics, historical timing, and international context.[69]

In an earlier, more focused treatment of the prospects for Soviet development, George Breslauer lists some five "images" of the Soviet future to be found in the literature of Soviet dissent and Western Soviet scholarship.[70] These are, working from left to right, socialist democracy, elitist liberalism, welfare state authoritarianism, Russite fundamentalism, and various forms of instability and fragmentation. On Dahl's polyarchy scale, socialist democracy would involve transformation in the direction of both participation and contestation; while elitist liberalism would represent movement in the direction of pluralism limited primarily to technocrats and intellectuals.[71] On the right, Russite fundamentalism would represent the coming to dominance of chauvinistic, anti-Semitic, anti-intellectual propensities present among some sections of the military, the police, and even some sections of the party. Breslauer finds a number of different varieties of instability predicted in the literature. These include ethnic fragmentation occurring in a context of economic stagnation, military conflict, and Russite favoritism; and recurrent political crises resulting from economic and political immobilism. Breslauer's left and center alternatives are similar to the predictions of the development school, which anticipated political mobilization and pluralist tendencies resulting from modernization; Russite fundamentalism is one version of the traditionalist or neotraditionalist alternative described in Moore, Jowitt, and others.

In the center of Breslauer's continuum is "welfare state authoritarianism," which approximates contemporary Soviet reality. Breslauer describes a "leftist" and "rightist" version of welfare state authoritarianism. The leftist version would involve a budgetary shift toward a consumer economy, expanded opportunity for ethnic minorities, opening up of the political process to some participation, and a narrower definition of political deviance; this moderate leftward movement would be associated with detente and increased foreign trade and cultural exchange. The rightist version would involve moves in contrary directions on all these dimensions. Breslauer expects the foreseeable future to oscillate between these two welfare authoritarian tendencies.

Pluralist Models

Discontent with the totalitarian model as a description of the communist political process led to a willingness to experiment with a family of pluralist models – interest group theory, corporatism, and issue network and policy community theories.

The concept of pluralism entered political science as an attack on the theory of sovereignty. The theory of sovereignty in turn emerged in the state-building processes of the fifteenth to nineteenth centuries, affirming and justifying the central state authority of the absolutist regimes. In its extreme form, as in Hobbes, the sovereign was viewed as the fashioner of law and as unlimited by any other source of law, human or divine. And in the middle and late nineteenth century in connection with the late development of the nation-state in Germany and Italy, and the general rise of trade unions, democratic, and socialist parties, a theoretical polemic developed affirming the ultimate sovereignty of the central state on the one hand, and the autonomy and legitimacy of such other institutions as churches, communities, regions, professions, and the family on the other. Otto Gierke, John Figgis, Leon Duguit, Harold Laski, Ernest Barker, and others argued that rather than viewing society as an association of individuals dominated by the central state, it ought to be viewed as an organization of co-equal and cooperating groups – churches, professional associations, trade unions, local communities, as well as the state.[72] These constituent groups had their own legitimacy, which ought not to be set aside by the central state. Such theorists as Bentley and Mary Parker Follett went even further, reducing government and the state to interest group phenomena, and viewing public policy as the product of the free play of group pressures.[73]

The relationship between this "pluralism" of political theory and the pluralist models that were employed in, and rose out of, the empirical interest group research of the decades since the First World War is more complex than is suggested in the work of Berger, Manley, and Krasner.[74] These empirical interest group approaches, as in Merriam and Schattschneider, did not attribute equality to the various interests, nor did they decry the "autonomy" of the state.[75] Samuel Huntington describes the history of American political science in terms of the succession of three paradigms – the progressive, the pluralist-conflictual, and the pluralist-consensual.[76] The progressive historians, such as Beard, Parrington, and Turner, interpreted American politics as a conflict between a narrow economic elite and a populist mass.[77] The early empirical pluralist tradition represented in the works of such political scientists as Merriam and Schattschneider took a critical view of the group interest basis of American politics, arguing that while groups influenced the government, business interests were far more powerfully organized and effective than other groups.

The pluralist-consensual model was developed in the work of Herring, Truman, and others, in the New Deal and post-Second World War period.[78] Here the pluralist model took into account the rise of organized labor and the development of the welfare state. Pluralism was viewed as a relatively open system in which workers as well as farmers and businessmen, blacks as well as whites, had access to the political process.

What the Herrings and Trumans did was to modify the earlier conflictual pressure group model of Merriam and Schattschneider. They saw interest groups as functional to democracy. In the contemporary debate about pluralism in American democracy, the earlier muckraking model has been forgotten. Thus we would have to correct John Manley's Pluralism I and II.[79] He really is contrasting Pluralism II with Pluralism III; and Pluralism II has much in common with Pluralism I. The Pluralism I of Merriam and Schattschneider is by no means the equilibrium, balanced model of Bentley and Latham. It is a model in which democracy is biased by a concentration of political resources in the business class; quite similar to the picture drawn in Lindblom's *Politics and Markets*, and Dahl's *Dilemmas of Democratic Pluralism*.[80]

The empirical models of pluralism in American political studies have been caricatured in still another respect. The political scientists of the decades of the 1930s to the 1960s produced a very large literature of the Congress, the presidency, and public administration. Thus the same writers associated with the pluralist position have also produced studies illustrative of the autonomy and importance of governmental institutions. Thus Pendleton Herring wrote *Presidential Leadership* and *Public Administration and the Public Interest*.[81] V. O. Key, Jr., wrote *The Administration of Federal Grants in Aid to the States*, and David Truman wrote *Administrative Decentralization*.[82] We may argue that prior to going abroad, interest group models were the focus of the principal polemic in American political studies.

In its voyages abroad, *pace* Sartori, interest group theory had a similarly constructive polemical and theoretical effect. In the 1950s and the 1960s interest group studies moved to the European and then to the Latin American areas. Henry Ehrmann and Almond chronicle the European trip, and Stepan and Schmitter the Latin American.[83] These last two voyages produced the corporatist models which we discuss below.

The Interest Group Model in Communist Studies

But interest group theory had one of its most interesting stopovers in communism studies. H. Gordon Skilling was one of the first students of communist countries to suggest that interest groups also function there as well.[84] In a later symposium a number of Soviet specialists applied interest group theory to various aspects of Soviet politics.[85] Some argued that not only do groups exist in communist systems, but that they initiate policy ideas in competition with other groups, and that Soviet leaders take the demands of groups into account in making policy. This was a sharp break from the totalitarian model, and its significance was emphasized in a new version of Fainsod's early book by Jerry Hough, who argued that "the basic insights of the interest group and factional conflict approaches about the presence of conflict in the Soviet policy process should be seen as a valuable supplement to other models and should not be considered controversial."[86] A flurry of attacks on Skilling's work and on Hough's more extreme version of the interest group approach to communism studies followed, suggesting that the approach was indeed controversial. Thus William Odom wrote "A Dissenting View," Andrew Janos took a "Second Look," and David Powell had problems "In Pursuit of Interest Groups in the Soviet Union."[87] LaPalombara in his "Monoliths or Plural Systems: Through Conceptual Lenses Darkly" implied that communism specialists were suffering from blurred vision.[88]

Some of these critics were assuming that Skilling had advanced the interest group approach as *the* explanatory model of Soviet politics. But as Skilling explains in his most recent discussion of the issue, "interest groups were not asserted to be the most significant feature of the Soviet polity, still less was policy considered an automatic product of group pressures."[89] Using the interest group model illuminated important aspects of Soviet politics. Skilling also argued that interest groups are compatible with an authoritarian system, although they are subject to restrictions imposed by the state. Some scholars doubted the appropriateness of the group concept in treating communist political phenomena. Griffiths, for example, spoke of "tendencies" rather than groups.[90]

One of the most constructive developments coming out of this polemic regarding the "totalism-pluralism" of communist systems was the resort to policy case studies as a way of testing the validity of the interest group approach. Thus Joel Schwartz and William Keech examined group influences in the educational policy processes in the Soviet Union; Philip Stewart has investigated the politics of industrial education; Peter Solomon has written about the politics of Soviet criminal policy, and Thane Gustafson has examined Soviet land and water policy.[91]

The interest group approach has also entered into the China field. Early examples would be the work of Oksenberg, Liu, and Esmein on the Cultural Revolution.[92] Goldman and Pye have also used group theory implicitly in their work on Chinese political processes.[93] Most group studies, however, were limited to the analysis of the Chinese political elite. David Goodman sought to remedy this situation in an edited symposium on groups and politics in the PRC.[94] Goodman notes the reliance in China studies on the use of the totalitarian model, although the term itself was rarely employed. He argues that experimentation with a group perspective may be "a necessary stage of development because it is thought probable that it will provide some obvious (and sharp) contrasts with the dominant totalitarian model(s)."[95] By initially focusing on elite behavior and not testing alternative pluralist models, China studies failed to generate the kinds of empirical data that had enriched Soviet and communism studies. The death of Mao and the example of Soviet studies set the stage for the incorporation and testing of interest group models in China studies. By focusing on groups one is able to focus on political process and the relationship between political and social systems. Contributors to this Goodman symposium presented case studies on the military, economists, teachers, peasants, workers, intellectuals, and the political elites.

An important contribution to the interest group literature, treating the various communist countries of Eastern Europe, is the study of the "blue-collar" workers edited by Jan Triska and Charles Gati.[96] The workers had previously been neglected in the literature. The book focuses on working-class attitudes and political behavior. There are a number of case studies of specific problems in East European countries. One theme is that in the absence of working-class organizations articulating their interests, informal and anomic activities predominate. Alex Pravda's contribution to the volume reports on labor disorders and strikes, through which workers attempt to articulate their interests.

Another group-focused contribution to the study of Eastern Europe is the symposium edited by Zvi Gitelman and Walter Connor, which examines public opinion and interest groups in the USSR, Poland, Czechoslovakia, and Hungary.[97] Gitelman argues that the "modernization of East European society has resulted in the partial emergence of publics–collectivities that confront issues, discuss them, and divide over them."[98] Knowledge of these groups, their attitudes, and propensities is essential to the understanding of the political processes of these countries.

In a lucid and comprehensive review of the debate about pluralism as it relates to Soviet studies, Archie Brown concludes that the work on interest group theory has greatly expanded our knowledge of the politics of communist countries. But the picture does not justify calling it pluralism. The groups are not open or autonomous.

Archie Brown acknowledges that Czechoslovakia in 1968, and Poland in 1980–81, were de facto pluralist-socialist states in the sense in which Dahl defines pluralism.[99] On the other hand, efforts to rescue pluralism by qualifying it as "institutional-pluralism" or "bureaucratic-pluralism" fail to distinguish communist patterns from noncommunist ones. Departmental particularism and bureaucratic crypto-politics are well-nigh universal phenomena.

Corporatism

One offshoot of the totalitarian-pluralist polemic was a search for a model that would combine features of both, and would take into account the empirical complexity of communist regimes. "Corporatism," a theme out of Latin American and European studies, has appeared promising to some students of communist countries. Corporatism, as a political theory, emerged in the nineteenth and early twentieth centuries in two versions: a "guild socialist" kind of corporatism elaborated in the work of the British political theorist G.D.H. Cole, and a corporatist version developed in Catholic political theory.[100] The pluralist version of corporatism led to various proposals for functional representation, such as adding a special legislative chamber to represent economic and professional "interests" to existing parliamentary chambers, or formally introducing interest representation into existing legislative chambers. There have been some experiments with functional representation in one or two European countries. The Catholic version, expressed first in the Papal Encyclical *Rerum Novarum*, issued in 1892, was the Church's answer to Marxist class struggle doctrine on the one hand and liberal capitalist individualism on the other. The social reality of mankind could not be expressed simply in class terms, nor in isolated individual terms, but rather in the complex of groupings in which men and women are associated–families, communities, regions, professions and occupations, and the like. The state must accommodate the legitimacy and autonomy of these groupings, and they must have a share in public decision making. The appropriation of corporatist ideas and institutional arrangements by Fascist Italy, Nazi Germany, as well as authoritarian Austria, Spain, and Portugal, discredited corporatism in the first postwar decades.

Contemporary corporatist theory rests on the discovery that in many European countries and in Latin America, interest group activity differs from the open, relatively unregulated competition familiar in American politics. Stein Rokkan and Robert Kvavik had made this point carlier with regard to the Scandinavian countries.[101] In these countries, in the Low Countries, in Austria, to a lesser extent in Germany, the interest group–government bargaining process is a more orderly, more regulated matter. It typically involves a limited number of economic-occupational organizations "recognized by the state" and "enjoying a representation monopoly within their respective categories."[102] It involves regularized bargaining over wage, price, and investment policy between these interest groups and relevant parts of the government bureaucracy. Cameron has demonstrated that this pattern of industrial and economic policy-making is associated with greater stability, slow but continuous economic growth, less inflation, and more substantial welfare benefits than is the case with the more competitive interest group countries such as the United States.[103] Katzenstein attributes this pattern of interest group relations to the vulnerability of small nations to international political, military, and economic threat and pressure, primarily since the great depression of the 1930s.[104] Schmitter distinguishes between societal and state corporatism, and it is the statist version of corporatism that has had some appeal to communism specialists.

Bunce and Echols viewed state corporatism rather than pluralism as a more apt description of the Soviet system under Brezhnev.[105] The evidence that they adduced is largely based on Brezhnev's efforts to balance and accommodate the interests of the party professionals, the industrial managers, the government bureaucracy, the scientists, and the agricultural sector, in the aftermath of the Khrushchev era. In a later discussion Valerie Bunce argues that corporatism in the Soviet political process fluctuates in relation to pressure on the Soviet economy. Thus in the early Brezhnev era there "was a mode of interest intermediation that sought to minimize conflict and maximize productivity by incorporating dominant economic and political interests directly into the policy process, while cultivating the support of the mass public through an expanding welfare state."[106] In the latter years of the Brezhnev regime pressure on Soviet resources from Eastern Europe, from increasing involvement in costly foreign ventures, and the accelerating arms race skewed the political process toward the military and heavy industry, foreclosing the bargaining power of light industries and labor. Bunce concludes that "corporatism does not live easily with large international commitments, both because of their costs and because of the contradictions in domestic class alliances that such commitments generate."[107] She disagrees with Archie Brown's argument that in the Soviet system these "interests" lack the legitimacy and autonomy that a corporatist regime would require—even in its statist version. According to Bunce periods of international relaxation and lowered military costs may move the Soviet polity in a corporatist direction with relatively open bargaining processes.

Hough objects to the application of the corporatist model to the Soviet case on the grounds that it ignores the fact that the state itself is segmented, and "that this segmentation has to be understood in terms of different societal interests."[108] Skilling complains that too little research has been done in terms of corporatism to test its utility.[109]

Archie Brown, along with Schmitter, Linz, and Stepan, has argued that the corporatist model may be applicable to Yugoslavia and perhaps other Eastern European communist countries.[110] With regard to the broad applicability of corporatism to the analysis of communist politics, Brown concludes tentatively that "a transition from a Communist Party state, organized to maintain the party's control within and vis-a-vis every other organization, to a corporatist one is not, in principle, impossible, and one could argue that in Yugoslavia, and perhaps in Hungary, we have begun to see a new type of corporatism emerging."[111]

Issue Networks and Policy Communities

Another model coming from American studies is "issue network" or "policy community" theory. This approach has its origins in the recognition that political processes vary according to issue or policy areas. The concept was first seriously advanced in Dahl's *Who Governs?*, in which he demonstrated that the structure of political power in New Haven varied according to the substance of the issues in conflict.[112] Theodore Lowi argued more explicitly that there were four relatively distinctive political process patterns according to whether the issues were extractive, regulative, distributive, or redistributive.[113] Freeman and others advanced the argument that there were many subgovernments or "iron triangles"–persistent relationships among administrative bureaus, congressional committees and their staffs, and interest group officials and technicians–that controlled access to the political process as it affected tax policy, welfare policy, health, transportation, conservation, defense, and other spheres of public policy.[114] Heclo viewed the "iron triangle" phenomenon as an unusual rather than a typical phenomenon, and preferred the looser formulation "issue networks" as more descriptive of the tripartite interaction among legislative, administrative, and interest group personnel.[115] His point was that the movement of policy specialists into and out of issue areas was too fluid to be captured by the "iron triangle" metaphor.[116] John Kingdon uses the term "policy community" to describe this loosely "corporatist" phenomenon; but it is not clear that this term differs very substantially in meaning from the issue network concept.[117]

An early application of issue network theory to Soviet studies was Zimmerman's "Issue Area and Foreign-Policy Process."[118] Perhaps the most extensive application of the issue network model is to be found in Nina Halpern's study of the role of economists in the making of Chinese economic policy.[119] She also provides an excellent review of the literature dealing with interest group, bureaucratic, and patron-client models. John Lewis makes an interesting connection between issue network and clientelist theory which we discuss below.[120]

Students of Soviet politics employ related concepts. Thus John Lowenhardt writes about "policy coalitions" in his study of Soviet decision making.[121] Hough associates his notion of institutional pluralism with issue "whirlpools" and complexes.[122] Political conflicts "tend to be compartmentalized with the debate in each policy area or whirlpool being largely limited to those whose careers are related to the issue, and others who have developed a special interest in it."[123] Skilling, on the other hand, views network theory as a variation on the interest group theme. It may, however, turn out to be a more appropriate model of communism studies since it does not carry the connotation of formal organization and autonomy.

Bureaucratic Politics

In the questioning about the "fit" of the totalitarian model in the 1960s another option that received attention was that of bureaucratic politics. Bureaucracy has been a central theme in the history of Marxism-Leninism. In Marx the state and bureaucracy were associated with class domination. Eliminate class, eliminate the state and bureaucracy. This was the Leninist utopia as well. Once class exploitation was eliminated, any washerwoman would be able to carry out the simple administrative tasks required in the communist society. In the early years of the Soviet Union, Lenin, and Trotsky in particular, viewed the emergence of Soviet bureaucracy as a threat to, or actual betrayal of, the revolution.

Early scholarship on Soviet politics also developed the bureaucratic theme. Barrington Moore's threefold scheme of tendencies in Soviet politics included bureaucratic politics as one of the three. This was the rational-technocratic impulse, the instrumental rationality of Max Weber, which Moore imputed to the emerging bureaucracy in the Soviet industrializing process. In the post-Stalin era, when some of the features of totalitarianism had subsided, the view was expressed that the technocratic bureaucracy now dominated the whole of Soviet society. Thus Alfred Meyer described the whole of the USSR as "a large bureaucracy comparable in its structure and functioning to giant corporations, armies, government agencies, and similar institutions."[124] The whole system, he claims, is a vast bureaucracy united by common goals which the central hierarchy guides and controls. Meyer's view of the role of bureaucracy in Soviet politics is similar in many ways to the view presented by those who describe the Soviet Union as an "administered" society, or as an "organized" or "command" society. Kassof sees, for example, one powerful ruling group as having a monopoly on the knowledge necessary to plan and coordinate the system. In Rigby's command society there is one group (the party and its leader) that has control, while the rest of the system is obedient and fulfills the ruling group's plans.[125] Armstrong also depicted hierarchical administration as being characteristic of the bureaucracy, but he insisted that the structure was not rigid and uniform.[126] In his comparison of bureaucracy in the Soviet Union and Western Europe he takes into account informal and personal relationships and utilitarian motivations common to both, as well as significant differences such as the relative lack of efficient communication in Soviet bureaucracy.

In *The Soviet Union and Social Science Theory*, Jerry Hough offers a critical review of the literature on bureaucratic politics.[127] He asks how bureaucrats and bureaucracy are to be defined as applying to the Soviet Union. Does the definition include the whole managerial stratum—political, governmental, military, industrial, scientific? The career patterns of all these managerial groups are similar, and Hough concludes that they are all parts of a bureaucracy. He then asks whether a bureaucratic model that stresses hierarchy and uniformity really captures the essence of the Soviet policy-making process. His conclusion is in agreement with Barghoorn's formulation that "we should not make the mistake of assuming that uniform socialization, centralized recruiting of executives, and the hierarchical structure of the political bureaucracy ensure unity of perspective or purpose among Soviet decision-makers. On the contrary, much evidence indicates that discord, conflict, and political infighting may play a larger, though concealed, role in one-party systems, than in democracies."[128]

Hough concludes that only case studies of Soviet institutions, and public policy areas, can begin to reveal the complexity of the Soviet decision-making process. He cites studies of industrial management by Granick, Berliner, and Azrael as examples of the kind of research likely to bring our understanding of Soviet politics to a higher level of resolution.[129]

The bureaucratic model has been frequently used in studies of Soviet foreign policy. Horelick, Johnson, and Steinbruner discuss the applicability of the bureaucratic politics model to Soviet decision making in their Rand study.[130] William Potter demonstrates the value of using an organizational decision-making approach in the study of Soviet foreign policy-making.[131] Distinguishing among the initiating, deliberating, legitimating, implementing, and terminating phases of foreign policy decision making enables one to locate the political actors in the relevant organizations, and spell out their roles in the decision process.[132] Jiri Valenta experimented with the bureaucratic politics paradigm in a case study of Soviet decision making in the Czech crisis of 1968.[133] Gail Lapidus recommends the use of a bureaucratic pluralist model in the analysis of Soviet policy toward China.[134]

The bureaucratic politics model has had an interesting encounter in Chinese political studies. Thus Lucian Pye points out that because of Chinese political cultural and structural factors, the bureaucratic politics model does not work well:

> Instead of having bureaucratic politics that involve the clashes of functionally specific interests, the Chinese political system remains a "bureaucratic polity," that is, a small hierarchically organized elite of officials whose attitudes, values, and personal relationships shape all decisions. In a bureaucratic polity, the decisionmakers do not have to respond to pressures from the society at large, and no interests outside of the state (or single party) hierarchy are allowed.[135]

There is an emphasis on personal relationships. Oksenberg and Lieberthal have both examined linkages in Chinese politics.[136] Oksenberg examined the communications process in particular, finding horizontal communications he did not expect to find which suggested the importance of informal, lateral interaction in Chinese politics. These questions among China specialists as to the aptness of the bureaucratic politics model lead to the "patron-client" model to which we now turn.

Patron-Client Relations

Each of these models in its exclusive form claims to be able to explain the output of political processes. A totalitarian model explains outputs as initiated by the central leader, and as implemented through the political process without significant modification. A pluralist model explains outputs as related to the strength of competing groups and their coalitions, and their access to the political process. A bureaucratic politics model explains outputs in terms of the standard operating procedures and policy propensities of bureaucratic agencies. It is the rare exception these days that any one of these models is advanced in exclusive terms.

The patron-client model came into prominence in the 1970s. What led to the experimentation with clientelism in communism studies was the evident importance of factionalism, power struggles, patronage, and corruption in these countries, and the failure of the totalitarian or pluralist models to account for these phenomena. Studies of this kind had emerged in the Soviet field independently of theory, as exemplified in the "kremlinology" studies. The most elegant example of this tradition was Robert Conquest's extraordinary analysis of "Soviet dynasties."[137] By the 1970s patron-clientelism as an analytical model had emerged all across the area disciplines, and there was a theoretical literature as well.

The patron-client model had its origin in anthropological and sociological theory, and it has been described and analyzed in a substantial ethnographic and historical literature covering the First, Second, and Third worlds, the present, the recent, and more remote pasts. James Scott's masterful bibliographical essay on clientelism includes more than a thousand items.[138] The principal theoretical analyses of political clientelism are to be found in the writings of Carl Lande and in his work reprinted in Schmidt et al., and in those of James C. Scott, Rene Lemarchand and Keith Legg, Eisenstadt and Lemarchand, and others.[139] The general theoretical point made in these writings is that the ultimate unit of political interaction in all societies is the *dyad*, the interaction of two persons, normally a dominance-dependence or patron-client relationship. Factions are made up of constellations of dyads with differing structures and different relationships, operating within such formal organizations as parties, interest groups, parliaments, and bureaucracies. Power and patronage are the currency of clientelist systems; policy is a secondary matter.

While factional power groups and cliques have been well known in Soviet studies since early on, it was not until the publication of a paper by Andrew Nathan, presenting a factional model for Chinese politics, that the explicit link-up with patron-client theory was made.[140] Two of the seminal influences on Nathan's work were Lande's study of clientelism in the Philippines and James Scott's paper on patron-client politics in Southeast Asia.[141] Nathan's analysis of politics in China was also substantially influenced by Nathan Leites's "operational code" analysis of factional politics in Fourth Republic France.[142] Nathan presents an operational code of Chinese factionalism which includes some fifteen propositions. These stress the essentially defensive and limited nature of factional struggle, the consensual basis of decision making, and the secondary nature of policy and ideology. While he found that analyzing the Cultural Revolution in these terms was illuminating, it was essential to recognize that

> factional struggle occurs within the context of a broad consensus of goals and methods. It would therefore be a mistake to identify the factionalism model with a crude power struggle theory, if the latter assumes that leaders are cynical in their ideological statements. But it would be equally foolish to believe that in China alone men's perspectives on ideological and policy issues are not influenced by their individual political vantage points. The occasional impres-

> sion that this is so may be the result of our knowing so much more about the issues than about the vantage points.[143]

In a thoughtful and theoretically informed monograph on clientelism in Chinese policy-making, John Lewis argues that "informal networks are pervasive in the Chinese policy process."[144] Citing the literature of anthropological network theory, which posits networks as universal units of social structure, Lewis first makes the point that "networks underlie all strategies for coalition building in political as well as other social situations."[145] He then distinguishes between dense and loose networks:

> In a relatively closed or "dense" network, the component members interact frequently, and network "gatekeepers" tightly control information from and to individuals outside the network including officials. Although dense networks may blunt or distort any leadership's implementation and monitoring of policies, the more extreme (or successful) forms of loose networks can also deflect centralized policy control since they can become alternative leadership systems of vast scope and influence. Dense networks of small scope can act as impenetrable fortresses, or to change the metaphor, as rival tribes, whereas large, loose networks can function as actual governing regimes. Both types of network coexist in China.[146]

There is substantial evidence that there are dense networks in China of the kind described by Lewis, and that they are viewed by the Deng regime as subversive of reformist and developmental plans. Locally based networks are able to establish "regional economic blockades." Privilege-seeking clientelism is pervasive throughout China, extending into the higher reaches of authority, and it frequently goes beyond privilege seeking and influence peddling into criminal behavior. Lewis hints at the importance of regime-supportive clientelism—using influence networks to enhance productivity and otherwise implement regime goals. Thus the struggle in Chinese communist politics would seem to be between power- and privilege-oriented clientelism and issue network clientelism, between power and privilege on the one hand and policy orientation on the other. Lewis argues:

> The task for Chinese studies beyond generating important questions, can start only with the aberrant behavior of networks. Eventually, however, we must deal directly with the roles that social networks play throughout the policy process. Often troublesome and destructive to policy implementation in the past, these networks may be the key to policy innovation and problem solving

in the future. To make this possible, China's national leaders have made the transformation of political networks a priority task.[147]

Lucian Pye, in his recent *Asian Power and Politics*, describes the varieties of patron-clientelism to be found in the politics of Asian countries, their dependence on different political cultures, and their consequences for power and politics in East, Southeast, and South Asia. He points out:

> In the East Asian societies which were once infused with Confucian values, political associations are themselves seen as being properly modelled after the family and the clan, and hence participants are expected to act as though they were banded together in a blood relationship. . . . The patterns in South and Southeast Asia, while not so explicitly modelled on the family, are also strongly group-oriented, but according more to the ties of patron-client relationships. In South Asia, and especially in India, this has meant that the politics of patronage generally prevails over the politics of policy implementation. In Southeast Asia the politics of entourages and cliques, of personal networks, and associations, are critical for the building of coherent national power structures. Thus even such hierarchical institutions as national bureaucracies and military establishments tend to be facades for pyramids of informal, but enduring, patron-client groupings.[148]

The importance of patron-client relations for Indian politics is suggested by Pye as explaining the absence of demoralization when grandiose plans go awry. "In this society of nurturing superiors and their dependent inferiors it is possible for people to find satisfying rewards in spite of failed grand designs."[149] The uniquely accommodative mode of adaptation to change that characterized Japanese historical development is explained by Lucian Pye as attributable to a propensity to build power "upward from the motivations of subordinate and local networks of relationships. . . . The same patterns of mutual dependency between superiors and subordinates were at work when the Japanese made their distinctive adaptations of Confucianism, and finally of American democracy. With each adaptation leaders and followers have deferred collectively to what they have taken to be a better, larger system, even while preserving the essence of their basic approach to power."[150]

A symposium published in *Studies in Comparative Communism* presents a patron-client analysis of Soviet politics by John Willerton with comments on Eastern Europe by Zygmunt Bauman, on China by John Burns, on Japan by Nobutake Ike, on advanced industrial societies by Keith Legg, and general comments by T. H. Rigby.[151] As evidence of the importance of patron-client networks in the Soviet Union, Willerton examines the clustering of members of the Central Committee around members of the Politburo.[152] Evidence of clustering into clientelistic networks is inferred from associated upward and downward shifts of Central Committee members as their patrons in the Politburo rise and fall.

Bauman confirms the importance of these lateral patronage linkages in Eastern European politics, but he is less confident of Willerton's measuring of these linkages simply by coinciding regional origins, and related upward and downward movements of upper and lower party figures.[153] John Burns reports the polemic in Chinese political studies that followed on Andrew Nathan's clientelistic interpretation of the Cultural Revolution. He argues that any clientelistic approach has to be reconciled with organizational, cultural, and ideological factors in explaining political behavior and public policy.[154] Nobutake Ike, in his discussion of clientelism in Japan, makes the general point that no political system can function without an element of trust, friendship, and personal loyalty, and that whenever and wherever there is distrust and insecurity, protective relationships form.[155] From this point of view the universality of clientelism may be safely assumed. The interesting question is how it combines with other criteria such as ideology and formal organization in the making of public policy. Finally, Rigby draws this useful symposium to a conclusion by pointing out that "patronage is a widespread, perhaps almost universal dimension of social systems, although it is perhaps only in feudal and quasi-feudal societies that it assumes a central organizing importance."[156] At the same time, he points out that

> it would be foolish to assume that the causes and character of clientelism in Western industrial bureaucracies and bureaucracies of Soviet type systems are identical. The point rather is that the systematic comparison may help elucidate just how far and in what respect the latter are *sui generis*. Further, to the extent that common features are established, the Western industrial bureaucracy literature may throw some light on the Soviet case, which is not open to direct field study.[157]

A symposium edited by Rigby and Harasymiw on leadership recruitment and clientelism in the Soviet Union and Yugoslavia brings together a great deal of information on the communist *nomenklatura* system of controlling and regulating staffing and promotion at the upper levels of the communist employment hierarchy.[158] It also deals with the ways in which clientelism works within this framework. Gyula Josza imaginatively likens patron-clientelism in the USSR to a *Seilschaft*, a roped party of mountain climbers.

He points out that in the Soviet Union and other communist countries patron-client studies have largely been confined to the upper levels of the hierarchy. The farther down one goes, the more inadequate biographical details become. He summarizes the data yielded in various studies of various central and local networks, and concludes that these networks are tolerated by top leaders since they may "contribute substantially to the functional capacity of the system in so far as they loosen the rigidity of rules and thereby ease the mutual blocking of each other's efforts by the different bureaucracies . . . and finally, they are able to patch up conflicts between local and central interests."[159]

This last collection of papers dealing primarily with the Soviet Union, John Lewis's treatment of this theme in the context of China studies, and Lucian Pye's concern with the ways in which difference in culture affect patterns of clientelism reflect the growing sophistication of communism studies.[160] Students of these phenomena now systematically place them in the context of theories of political recruitment and policy-making.

Other Models

There are, of course, other models that have been generated in the social sciences, and that have been tested only in limited ways in communism studies. Thus communications theory in at least two senses has been applied in Soviet and communism studies. In the first sense there is an overlap with bureaucratic or organization theory. Oksenberg and others (see above) have been concerned with the nature of information flows in the Chinese bureaucracy. The predominance of informal communication suggested to Oksenberg that factional and patron-client interactions might be dominating issue-oriented policy-making and implementation. Erik Hoffmann suggests that a combination of communications theory, organization theory, and role theory applied in communism studies would be productive of insights into the effectiveness of the Soviet polity and economy.[161] Thus the responsiveness and effectiveness of Soviet decision making would be dependent on flows of information from and to the international and domestic environments. The cybernetic model would lead one to observe the "feedback" and "steering" mechanisms of Soviet institutions. A predominance of vertical communication and restrictions on lateral communication in economic decisions might seriously affect efficiency and productivity by limiting feedback. A communications model would lead one to look for blocks and biases in Soviet information and communications processes, and to ask questions as to the effect of such blocks and biases on industrial policy, security policy, and the like.

Ellen Mickiewicz, viewing Soviet communications patterns developmentally, concludes that the older "two-step flow" theory, which was adapted to Soviet politics by Alex Inkeles, is no longer applicable to Soviet communication, just as it is no longer accorded validity in American studies.[162] A combination of mass education and the spread of electronic media, particularly television, has reduced the importance of opinion leaders and agitators. Hence the image of the Soviet polity as thoroughly penetrated and manipulated by the oral agitation of party local and cell leaders may no longer be applicable. The party cannot so thoroughly preempt the air waves; and the information transmitted by these means cannot be carefully interpreted by party members as was previously the case. Lacking the organizational means of directly penetrating policy processes, the Soviet mass public surely is not as important as in Western democracies; nevertheless there may be significant changes in Soviet policy processes attributable to the media revolution.

Very little use has been made of the public choice or rational choice model of political analysis in communism studies. This approach to political research, which applies models taken from economic theory to electoral, political, and legislative processes, and which has had substantial success in generating hypotheses about American political processes and institutions, has not as yet been given much of a test in foreign contexts. Economists specializing in the Soviet and other communist economies have done a certain amount of modeling of economic decisions in centrally managed economies. But a real test of this approach in illuminating communist political processes is still to be made. From this point of view William Welsh's game-theoretic analysis of the Hungarian Revolt of 1956 was an isolated research initiative, and his recommendations as to how the formal theory of games would have to be adapted to be useful in empirical research seem to have fallen on deaf ears.[163]

Conclusions

The literature we have reviewed describes a rich and complex interaction between communism studies and empirical political theory. Figure 3.1 suggests the sources and directions of this process of diffusion. From the social science disciplines—political science, sociology, social psychology, and anthropology—came the developmental and modernization models,

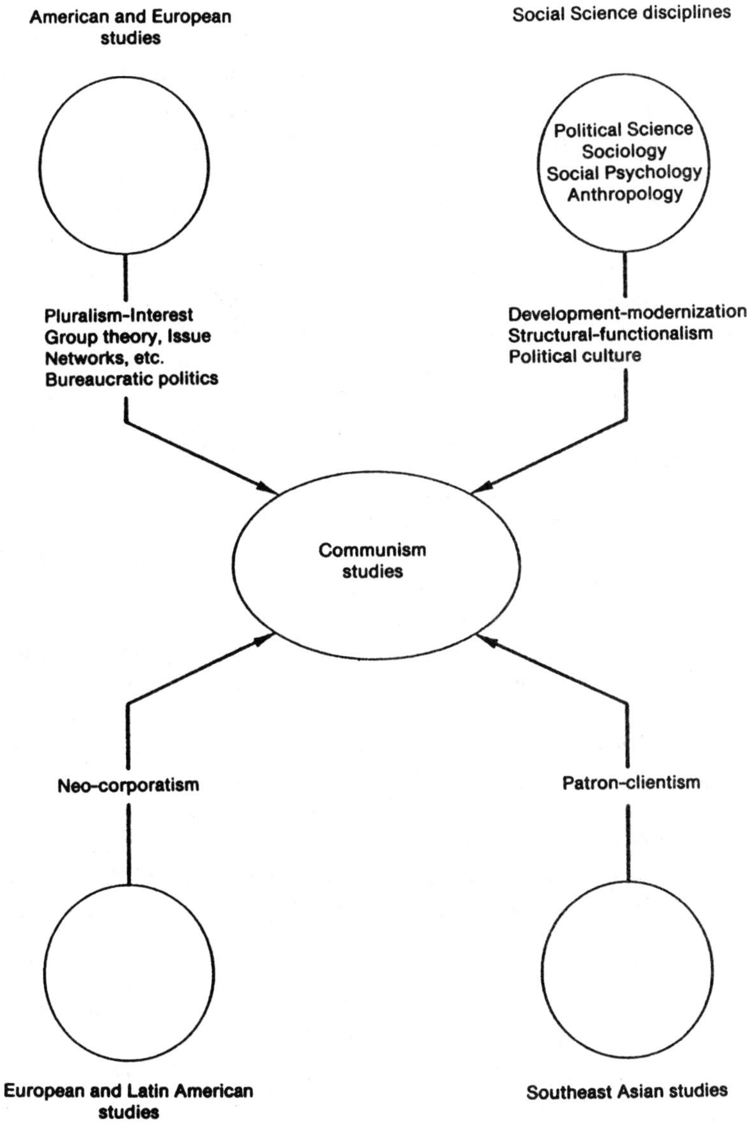

Figure 3.1. Diagramming Interaction Among Communism Studies, the Social Science Disciplines and Other Area Studies.

structural-functionalism, and political culture. From American and European political studies came the pluralist family of models—interest group theory, issue network and policy community theory—and the bureaucratic politics model. We might with equal justice attribute the bureaucratic model to Weberian sociological and political theory, but it came to communism studies via American models of organizational process and decision making. From European and Latin American studies came the neocorporatist model; and from Southeast Asian studies came the patron-client model. The only internally generated model in communism studies was the totalitarian one, and, as our discussion suggests, it still retains a limited utility.

How other area studies rank in openness to theoretical experimentation is a matter for separate and careful inquiry. A preliminary impression suggests that communism studies rank highest in this theoretical ecumenism, while Latin American studies would rank at the low end of the scale, though recent surveys suggest that this isolation may be abating.[164]

This conceptual experimentation in Western studies of communist systems has stirred up some curiosity among Soviet and Eastern European scholars. There is a kind of dialogue going on between Western scholarship and its counterparts. There have been more than echoes among Soviet political theorists of the concept of political culture. Political culture research has been defined by leading Soviet political scientists as one of the major subfields of political science, and a number of books have been published dealing with theoretical and empirical aspects of this theme.[165] Soviet political theorists are currently facing the problem of defining the state and the political system, and locating the state within the larger political system. They are seeking to escape from class reductionism, by attributing autonomy to the state, the capitalist state as well as the Soviet state. There is a partly covert, but occasionally overt, polemic around the issue of monism-pluralism. In a review of the writings of Soviet theorists on the state and the political system, Archie Brown argues:

> What makes the work of these writers both significant and controversial in the Soviet context is their attempt . . . to put on the scholarly agenda the real political process and real political relations within the Soviet Union and elsewhere, and to break away from the legalistic approach which has been far more dominant in Soviet writing on the state and on political institutions than the so-called legal-institutional approach ever was in Western political science prior to the "behavioral revolution."[166]

Soviet theorists have added their voices to the pluralistic polemic, in

Rousseauan and populist terms. Thus Archie Brown quotes Shakhnazarov, on the concept of pluralism:

> In recent times one has met with the assertion that socialist democracy is also pluralist in nature. It seems hardly necessary to use an alien concept to characterise the features of the political system of socialism which for a long time have been quite adequately defined in Marxist-Leninist scholarship by such concepts as the needs and interests of classes and social groups, the unity and diversity of these interests, the coincidence or contradiction between them, their defence and expression, coordination, etc. So far as a general definition is concerned, to that vague and ambiguous term, "pluralism," which may be interpreted in all sorts of ways, one ought to prefer the clear concept, "sovereignty of the people" (*narodovlastie*).[167]

On the broader issue of the creative impact on communism studies of this almost three-decade-long model-fitting experience, we are led to ask what alternative theories and methods might have been employed in efforts to explain communist political reality? There were, of course, the classic methodological antinomies, the nomothetic and the idiographic approaches to explanation – the search, on the one hand, for lawful regularities among variables, for necessary and sufficient causation; and on the other, there is the deep, Geertzian, "thickly descriptive," clinical search for the inward reality of individual cases.[168] Przeworski and Teune in their treatise on the comparative method go furthest in recommending the assimilation of area studies into general theory. In their own language, "the role of comparative research in the process of theory building and theory testing consists of replacing proper names of social systems (in this instance, countries) by the relevant variables."[169] From this point of view the Soviet Union, China, Poland, Czechoslovakia, etc. are of interest to us simply insofar as they can serve as experimental "trials" of the relationships among variables, on the one hand, or insofar as they can be explained by laws derived from comparative research, on the other.

If we suppose that a Przeworskian strategy had been adopted, the area study approach would have had to make do with that diminishing part of a nation's behavior not yet explained by general laws. Studies of communist countries would be reducible to events explainable and predictable by these generalizations. Aberrant events might lead to modifications in these generalizations, or to the addition of corollary theories. Albert Hirschman excoriates this extreme behavioral determinism in his "The Search for Paradigms as a Hindrance to Understanding."[170] In this paper Hirschman compares two then recently published books—John Womack's *Zapata and the Mexican Revolution*, and James Payne's *Patterns of Conflict in Colombia*.[171] The Payne study, based on interviews and questionnaires, forecasts with great certainty a depressing and conflictual future for Colombian politics and economics attributable to the venality and lack of program orientation of its politicians. Hirschman is critical of the extreme behavioral determinism of the Payne interpretation, and its failure to recognize the "open-endedness" of history. He does not reject the usefulness of "models, paradigms, and ideal types." Without such abstractions, he acknowledges, "we cannot even start to think."[172] It is the exaggerated belief in the complete explanatory and predictive power of these models that Hirschman is inveighing against.

Hirschman contrasts Womack's biography of Zapata with the approach in the Payne study. He says, "What is remarkable about the book is the continuity of the narrative and the almost complete, one might say Flaubertian, absence from its pages of the author who could have explained, commented, moralized, or drawn conclusions. Yet whoever reads through the book will have gained immeasurably in his understanding not only of the Mexican Revolution, but of peasant revolutions everywhere, and Womack's very reticence and self-effacement stimulate the reader's curiosity and imagination."[173] Hirschman's celebration of the Womack book, of course, makes the very best case for the clinical, in-depth, empathic approach to political studies. But in his zeal to give a well-earned spanking to Payne, Hirschman leaves not unmentioned but somewhat unelaborated the role played by models and theories in the growth of social knowledge. Womack may not have made his models explicit, but surely a Harvard Ph.D. in history in the 1960s could not have escaped some exposure to sociological and anthropological theory. As Hirschman pointed out, there is much theory implicit in it. And everyone seeking to exploit research such as that of Womack's would have had to explicate appropriate generalizations from his study, and compare and combine them with insights acquired from other studies. Had the Womack idiographic strategy been the only strategy pursued in communism studies we would have ended up with a great many in-depth, clinical studies, not adding up to conclusions—it would be neither a cumulative nor a progressive strategy.

Eckstein explores the methodological ground, left as *terra incognita* by Hirschman, between the idiographic and nomothetic extremes.[174] In an elegant essay on case studies, Eckstein describes five points on this continuum, or five types of case studies. The first—the idiographic-configurative—has already been exemplified in the Womack study; there are biographies of communist leaders, as well as historical studies, that would also exemplify this genre. The intellectual history of communism studies that we have been recounting exemplifies three of Eckstein's types of case studies: the "disciplined configurative," the "heuristic," and the "plausibility probe." Disciplined configurative studies are the least ambitious of these theory-oriented types of case studies. They apply theories to individual cases. Thus "frustration-aggression" theory may be applied to the frequency of disorder in a particular country, and may illuminate events in that country, and may even lead to questioning the theory if the expected interaction does not occur. If this type of case study theory is employed to illuminate the case, the feedback to the validation of the theory itself is fortuitous. Eckstein cites the application of structural-functionalism and political culture theory to individual country studies as examples of the disciplined configurative variety of case study. "Heuristic" case studies, on the other hand, are deliberate theory-testing undertakings. They may, and often do, involve a multiple case study strategy. The experience in communism studies with the family of pluralist theories exemplifies this type of case study strategy. Thus interest "group" theory has been rejected by some scholars, and "issue network" or political tendency theory proposed instead, on the basis of policy case studies. Valerie Bunce's testing of the corporatist model in the early and late Brezhnev era is another example of this strategy.

Eckstein's fourth type of case study–"the plausibility probe"– is related to the third type, and may actually be a preliminary step intended to estimate the promise of a theory before a substantial investment is made. The "crucial case study" is the most theoretically ambitious type of case study, involving the selection of a case least likely to support the theory. Roberto Michels's "Iron Law of Oligarchy" exemplifies this strategy.[175] If the tendency toward oligarchic domination in all organizations is a "scientific law," then it ought to hold even in situations where deliberate efforts are made to democratize political control. His study of the German Social Democratic party in the late nineteenth century–where ideology and institutional structure were supportive of democratic process–he viewed as a "crucial" test of the hypothesis. There do not seem to be any examples of crucial case studies in the communist field.

There have also been other substantive strategies pursued in communism studies. These would include the variety of monistic theories–those stemming from Marxism, or from Marxism-Leninism and propounded by communist political theorists; the culture-personality interpretations which were popular in the late 1940s and 1950s; the totalitarian model whose history we have reviewed above; and the modernization-convergence theories which held sway in the Khrushchev era. Our review of the literature makes it clear that all these theories fall substantially short of accounting for Soviet politics and political trends, and that the multimodel theoretical approach and the systematic theory-informed case study approach give us a more secure understanding of political patterns and potentialities.

But, if we are left with the eclectic, model-fitting approach as the preferred one, we still have to deal with the question of whether these various models fit together in a logic of explanation and, if so, what is the larger logic in which they fit. Ronald Amann in a recent article suggests such a multimodel logical concept of Soviet politics. He divides these interpretations of Soviet politics into Group A and Group B theories: "Group A theories place a heavy stress on the maximization of the power and privilege of the elite and of the nation over which they preside."[176] The variants of the Group A theories include (1) totalitarianism (a messianic, all-dominant elite); (2) state capitalism (an acquisitive elite exploiting public assets); and (3) neotraditionalism (systematic venal abuse of office). The variants of the Group B theories include (1) developmentalism, or institutional change impelled by technological imperatives and leading to democratization; (2) economic decentralization, in which a differentiated economy and society lead to bargaining propensities; and (3) state corporatism, in which major social groups are incorporated into a planned framework of bargaining and decision making. Broadly speaking, the Group A models present a pessimistic view of Soviet potentialities; they add up to the "evil empire" model of Ronald Reagan. There is little prospect for improvement in the climate of international politics. Group B theories, on the other hand, present the Soviet Union as moving to a more open and responsive system, and amenable to negotiation and compromise. Amann comes to the conclusion that none of the variants of the A or the B version of Soviet politics captures its essential characteristics. In their place Amann offers the notion of "hesitant modernizers" as describing the Soviet elite caught between system maintenance and reform. The modernization to which Amann refers includes movement away from extreme central planning in the direction of market incentives, enterprise autonomy, the encouragement of creativity and novelty, and in the political sphere a movement away "from traditional stress on discipline and obedience to greater reliance on material incentives and 'output participation.'"[177]

What Amann's analysis misses is the point that while neither conservative Group A theories nor liberal Group B theories fully capture the dynamics of Soviet politics, a strategy that employs them all in a battery, so to speak, can bring us closer to an understanding of how the system works, and how it might respond to different kinds of environmental changes. Both Group A theories and Group B theories, as well as some that Amann has overlooked, make some contribution to the illumination of communist politics. As we have seen in our brief intellectual history of communism studies, no one of the models could capture the whole of the political reality; but each one generated different questions about it, and brought into relief different aspects of Soviet politics.

Thus the family of pluralist models, in their interest group, issue network, policy community, corporatist, and political tendency versions, came to grips with the shortfall in the totalitarian conception. It enabled scholars to deal in a relatively orderly way with conflict and process in the making of Soviet policy. If political conflict Soviet style could not be accommodated to the interest group model, was the "issue network" concept, the policy community model, the "tendency" notion a better match? Functional and decision-theoretic concepts drew attention to the phasing of communist policy-making, the importance of initiation, the structure of policy-making and implementation, and the importance of termination.

The bureaucratic politics model drew attention to the enormous importance of formal organization in the politics of communist countries, but by itself it exaggerated the orderliness and hierarchy of these systems. Here the pluralist family of models and the patron-client model provided the needed correctives, drawing attention to the multiplicity of informal relationships–partly of a task-oriented variety, partly of a self-interested variety–which made it possible for these vast systems of interrelated formal organizations to function in response to leadership goals, on the one hand, or subverted them to personal demands for safety or advantage, on the other. Working with this battery of models, students of communist politics are in a position to observe how changes in the domestic and international environments of communist political systems are connected with changes in their political processes. They may bring out the point that under one set of environmental conditions pluralist or corporatist propensities may manifest themselves; while under another set, centralizing, bureaucratic tendencies may result; and under still a third set of conditions patron-client propensities may become dominant. This kind of model fitting points the way to dynamic and development theories of communist politics.

We should not exaggerate the accomplishments in communism studies that have resulted from this conceptual experimentation. On the eve of these developments–in 1963–Zbigniew Brzezinski and Samuel Huntington published their book, *Political Power: USA/USSR*.[178] It is to the great credit of these then young scholars that practically the entire armamentarium of theoretical innovations described above were applied in this trail-breaking study.

Thus (1) they present a functional or process scheme; (2) in different language they deal with political cultural differences; (3) they employ an interest group model, (4) a bureaucratic politics model, and (5) a patron-client model. And they present five case studies of public policy as a way of discovering the similarities and differences in the policy-making processes of the United States and the Soviet Union. Yet if one compares their treatments of these themes with comparable treatments in more recent work, it is evident that we have reached a higher level of conceptual sophistication and interpretive capacity. This is in no way to the discredit of these pioneers. Contemporary specialists on communist politics have available to them, in addition to these models and analytical schemes—what is at least as important—a rich collection of events and decisions of the later 1960s, 1970s, and 1980s on which to try them out.

Some of the best examples of contemporary state-of-the-art analysis of Soviet and communist political processes are to be found in the recent writings of Alexander Dallin and Archie Brown, the first reviewing our knowledge of Soviet political processes as they affect foreign policy, the second more broadly generalizing about pluralist, corporatist, and bureaucratic politics interpretations of European communist countries in general. Dallin concludes that "while the handicaps have been immense, a review of the record shows a formidable accumulation of instances supporting and illustrating the hypothesis of Soviet political conflict and, in spite of a frequent sense of frustration (and a number of false starts) on the part of many observers, a remarkable increase over time in insight and sophistication in analysis and interpretation."[179] His chapter on domestic sources of Soviet foreign policy in the Seweryn Bialer volume is a subtle and analytically sharp review and synthesis of the literature, reflecting the three-decade-long experimentation with the bureaucratic, interest group, and issue network models.

Archie Brown's summary of the state of knowledge with respect to interest groups in the politics of communist countries tells the story without exaggerating its theoretical implications.

> If scholars are better aware than they used to be that within the Soviet Union institutional rivalries are tacitly accepted, that certain party and state institutions may have common interests which differ from those of other party and state institutions, that departmentalism and localism exist, that there is covert competition for political office on the basis of what the Czech reformists called "Cabinet politics," that federation provides an institutional base for a limited amount of ethnic diversity and promotion of "national interests" on the part of those ethnic groupings within the party, within the intelligentsia and

> within the wider society, then this body of work has been of value not only for its general corrective to the totalitarian interpretation, but for the concrete details of political life that it has adduced in areas that did not attract much attention from proponents of the view that the Soviet Union was totalitarian. Yet, for all that it does not constitute pluralism.[180]

But even if the case has not been made for pluralism in the Soviet Union, students of communist politics, including Brown, view Yugoslavia and other Eastern European countries as having corporatist tendencies. Valerie Bunce argues a plausible case for corporatist phases in the Soviet development process, and Brown concedes that there may be such a potentiality. The pluralist polemic, and the polemics over the other models we have discussed have enabled us to ask more and better questions about communist politics. Systematic knowledge grows through the accumulation of evidence, but the very definition of what is evidence, and the orderly accumulation of evidence, depends on the kinds of questions we ask and the way we go about seeking answers. And here we come to the nub of our argument, that new models generate new questions, and stir up new polemics. And these polemics and the empirical research they stimulate are the lifeblood of creative scholarship.

Our comments would be incomplete if we did not draw some inferences from this review of the literature that might bear on future studies of communist politics. The use of theoretically informed case studies is already well established in the field. Perhaps a more systematic use of case studies is to be recommended, a more deliberate effort to sample communist politics-cum-policy reality. The ultimate reality of any political system consists of a universe or a population of policy decisions and implementations. It is a "stratified" universe or population. We know that the principal cause of stratification in the policy universe is the substance of issues—"different issues, different politics" as Dahl and Lowi have taught us. The next steps in the development of rigor in communism studies will consist of more systematic research programs—multiple case study research designs intended to sample the variety of communist policy processes—foreign and security policy, fiscal and economic policy, education, health, family, and welfare policy.

Notes

1. Giovanni Sartori, "Concept Misformation in Comparative Politics," *American Political Science Review* 64: 3 (December 1970), p. 1034.
2. Leonard Binder, "The Natural History of Development Theory," *Comparative Studies in Society and History* 28: 1 (January 1986), p. 3.

3. Giovanni Sartori (ed.) *Social Science Concepts: A Systematic Analysis* (Beverly Hills, CA: Sage, 1984).
4. Karl Deutsch, *The Nerves of Government* (New York: Free Press, 1966).
5. Robert Orr, "Reflections on Totalitarianism, Leading to Reflections on Two Ways of Theorizing," *Political Studies* 21: 4 (December 1973), p. 481; also see Abbott Gleason, "Totalitarianism in 1984," *Russian Review* 43: 2 (April 1984), pp. 145–60, for a review of the origins of the concept.
6. Carlton J.H. Hayes, "The Novelty of Totalitarianism in the History of Western Civilization," *Proceedings of the American Philosophical Society* (Philadelphia, 1940).
7. Hannah Arendt, *The Origins of Totalitarianism* (New York: Harcourt, Brace, 1951, 1966); and Carl J. Friedrich and Zbigniew Brzezinski, *Totalitarian Dictatorship and Autocracy* (Cambridge, MA: Harvard University Press, 1956, 1965).
8. Arendt, pp. 393ff.
9. Merle Fainsod, *How Russia Is Ruled* (Cambridge, MA: Harvard University Press, 1953); Leonard Schapiro. *The Communist Party of the Soviet Union* (New York: Vintage, 1960); J. L. Talmon, *Political Messianism: The Romantic Phase* (New York: Praeger, 1960); Belram D. Wolfe, *Three Who Made a Revolution* (Boston: Beacon Press, 1948); Zbigniew Brzezinski, *The Permanent Purge: Politics in Soviet Totalitarianism* (Cambridge, MA: Harvard University Press, 1956); John A. Armstrong, *Ideology, Politics and Government in the Soviet Union* (New York: Praeger, 1962).
10. Allen Kassof, "The Administered Society: Totalitarianism Without Terror," *World Politics* 16: 4 (July 1964), p. 559.
11. Carl J. Friedrich and Zbigniew Brzezinski, *Totalitarian Dictatorship and Autocracy* (Cambridge, MA: Harvard University Press, 1956); Hannah Arendt, *The Origins of Totalitarianism* (New York: Harcourt, Brace, 1966).
12. Frederic J. Fleron, Jr., "Soviet Area Studies and the Social Sciences: Some Methodological Problems in Communist Studies," in Fleron, *Communist Studies and the Social Sciences: Essays in Methodology and Empirical Theory* (Chicago: Rand McNally, 1965); Benjamin Barber, "Conceptual Foundations of Totalitarianism," in C. J. Friedrich (ed.) *Totalitarianism in Perspective* (New York: Praeger, 1969); Jeremy Azrael, "Varieties of Destalinization," in Chalmers Johnson (ed.) *Change in Communist Systems* (Stanford, CA: Stanford University Press, 1970); Juan J. Linz, "Totalitarian and Authoritarian Regimes," in Greenstein and Polsby (eds.) *Handbook of Political Science* (Reading, MA: Addison-Wesley, 1975), vol. 3.
13. Zbigniew Brzezinski, *The Soviet Bloc: Unity and Conflict* (Cambridge, MA: Harvard University Press, 1960).
14. James R. Townsend, *Politics in China* (Boston: Little, Brown, 1974).
15. Lucian Pye (ed.) *Political Science and Area Studies* (Bloomington: Indiana University Press, 1975).
16. George Breslauer, *Five Images of the Soviet Future* (Berkeley, CA: Institute of International Studies, 1978).
17. Ibid., p. 6.
18. Abbott Gleason, "Totalitarianism in 1984," p. 158.
19. Barrington Moore, *Terror and Progress, USSR* (Cambridge, MA: Harvard University Press, 1954).
20. Daniel Bell, "Ten Theories in Search of Reality: The Prediction of Soviet Behavior in the Social Sciences," *World Politics* 10: 3 (April 1958), pp. 327–65.

21. Alex Inkeles, "Models and Issues in the Analysis of Soviet Society," *Survey* 60 (July 1968), pp. 3–17.
22. Gleason, p. 154.
23. Ernest A. Menze (ed.) *Totalitarianism Reconsidered* (Port Washington, NY: Kennikat, 1981); and Stephen J. Whitfield, *Into the Dark: Hannah Arendt and Totalitarianism* (Philadelphia: Temple University Press, 1980).
24. Frederick C. Barghoorn, *Politics in the USSR* (Boston: Little, Brown, 1966, 1972); Frederick C. Barghoorn and Thomas F. Remington, *Politics in the USSR* (Boston: Little, Brown, 1986), pp. 18–19; Jerry Hough and Merle Fainsod, *How the Soviet Union Is Governed* (Cambridge, MA: Harvard University Press, 1979), p. 518; and James R. Townsend, *Politics in China* (Boston: Little, Brown, 1974, 1980, 1986), pp. 191–95.
25. Leonard Schapiro, *Totalitarianism* (New York: Praeger, 1972).
26. Juan J. Linz, "Totalitarianism and Authoritarian Regimes," in Greenstein and Polsby (eds.) *Handbook of Political Science* (Reading, MA: Addison-Wesley, 1975), vol. 3.
27. Fainsod, *How Russia Is Ruled*; Merle Fainsod, *How Russia Is Ruled*, rev. ed. (Cambridge, MA: Harvard University Press, 1963).
28. Barrington Moore, *Soviet Politics: The Dilemma of Power* (Cambridge, MA: Harvard University Press, 1950).
29. John Hazard, *The Soviet System of Government* (Chicago: University of Chicago Press, 1957); and John A. Armstrong, *Ideology, Politics and Government in the Soviet Union* (New York: Praeger, 1962); Adam Ulam, *The New Face of Soviet Totalitarianism* (Cambridge, MA: Harvard University Press, 1963).
30. David Easton, *The Political System* (Chicago: University of Chicago Press, 1953); H. D. Lasswell, *The Decision Process* (Bureau of Governmental Research, University of Maryland, 1956); and Gabriel A. Almond, "Comparative Political Systems," *Journal of Politics* 18: 3 (August 1956), pp. 391–409.
31. James R. Townsend, *Politics in China* (Boston: Little, Brown, 1974, 1980, 1986).
32. Hough and Fainsod, *How the Soviet Union Is Governed*, p. vii.
33. Mary McAuley, *Politics and the Soviet Union* (New York: Penguin, 1977).
34. David Lane, *Politics and Society in the USSR* (New York: New York University Press, 1978), p. xiii.
35. David Lane, *State and Politics in the USSR* (New York: New York University Press, 1985).
36. Stephen White et al., *Communist Political Systems* (New York: St. Martin's Press, 1982).
37. Georg Brunner, *Politische Soziologie der USSR* (Wiesbaden: Akademische Gesellschaft, 1977).
38. Daniel Tarschys, *The Soviet Political Agenda: Problems and Priorities, 1950–1970* (White Plains, NY: M. E. Sharpe, 1979).
39. T. H. Rigby, *Communist Party Membership in the USSR, 1917–1967* (Princeton, NJ: Princeton University Press, 1968).
40. Gabriel A. Almond and G. Bingham Powell, Jr., *Comparative Politics: System, Process and Policy*, 2nd ed. (Boston: Little, Brown, 1978); Judith May and Aaron Wildavsky *The Policy Cycle* (Beverly Hills, CA: Sage, 1978).
41. Arnold Horelick, Ross A. Johnson, and John D. Steinbruner, *The Study of Soviet Foreign Policy: Decision Theory Related Approaches* (Beverly Hills, CA: Sage, 1975).
42. William Potter, "Sources of Foreign Policy Change: Insights from the Policy Sciences,"

Conference on the Domestic Sources of Soviet Foreign Policy, UCLA Project on Politics and War, 11 October 1985.

43. Vernon V. Aspaturian, "The Soviet Decision-makers: Where, How, and by Whom Decisions Are Made," UCLA Project on Politics and War, 10–11 October 1985.
44. Richard Fagen, *The Transformation of Political Culture in Cuba* (Stanford, CA: Stanford University Press, 1969).
45. Robert Tucker, "Culture, Political Culture, and Communist Society," *Political Science Quarterly* 88: 2 (June 1973), pp. 173–90; and Stephen White, *Political Culture in Soviet Politics* (London: Macmillan, 1979).
46. Archie Brown, "Conclusions," in Archie Brown (ed.) *Political Culture and Communist Studies* (Armonk, NY: M. E. Sharpe, 1985), p. 154.
47. Richard Fagen, *The Transformation of Political Culture in Cuba* (Stanford, CA: Stanford University Press, 1969); Robert C. Tucker, "Culture, Political Culture, and Communist Society"; Archie Brown and Jack Gray, *Political Culture and Political Change in Communist States*, 2nd ed. (New York: Holmes & Meier, 1979); Archie Brown, *Political Culture and Communist Studies* (Armonk, NY: M. E. Sharpe, 1985); Jack Gray, "Conclusions," in Brown and Gray (eds.) *Political Culture and Political Change in Communist States*; Mary McAuley, "Political Culture and Communist Politics: One Step Forward, Two Steps Back," in Brown (ed.) *Political Culture and Communist Studies*; Stephen White, "Political Culture in Communist States: Some Problems of Theory and Method," *Comparative Politics* 16: 3 (April 1984), pp. 351–65; and Gabriel A. Almond, "Communism and Political Culture Theory," *Comparative Politics* 15: 2 (January 1983), pp. 127–38.
48. White, "Political Culture in Communist States."
49. Barghoorn, *Politics in the USSR*.
50. White, *Political Culture in Soviet Politics*.
51. Barghoorn and Remington, *Politics in the USSR* (1986); and Theodore Friedgut, *Political Participation in the USSR* (Princeton, NJ: Princeton University Press, 1979).
52. Wayne Di Franceisco and Zvi Gitelman, "Soviet Political Culture and 'Covert Participation' in Policy Implementation," *American Political Science Review* 78: 3 (September 1984), pp. 603–21; and Sidney Verba and Norman Nie, *Participation in America* (New York: Harper & Row, 1972).
53. Brown and Gray, *Political Culture and Political Change in Communist States*; Brown (ed.) *Political Culture and Communist Studies*.
54. David A. Dyker, "Yugoslavia: Unity out of Diversity?" in Brown and Gray (eds.) *Political Culture and Political Change in Communist States*.
55. Archie Brown, "Soviet Political Culture through Soviet Eyes," in Brown (ed.) *Political Culture and Communist Studies*, pp. 100–14.
56. Moore, *Terror and Progress, USSR*; Inkeles, "Models and Issues in the Analysis of Soviet Society."
57. Zbigniew Brzezinski and Samuel P. Huntington, *Political Power, USA/USSR* (New York: Viking, 1965).
58. Karl Deutsch, "Social Mobilization and Political Development," *American Political Science Review* 55: 3 (September 1961), pp. 493–514; Seymour Martin Lipset, "Some Social Requisites of Democracy: Economic Development and Political Legitimacy," *American Political Science Review* 53: 1 (January 1959), pp. 69–105; James Coleman, "Conclusion: The Political Systems of the Developing Areas," in Gabriel A. Almond and James Coleman (eds.) *The Politics of the Developing Areas* (Princeton, NJ: Princeton Univer-

sity Press, 1960); and Alex Inkeles and David Smith, *Becoming Modern* (Cambridge, MA: Harvard University Press, 1974).

59. Jan F. Triska and Paul M. Cocks (eds.) *Political Development in Eastern Europe* (New York: Praeger, 1977).
60. Paul M. Johnson, "Modernization as an Explanation of Political Change in East European States," in Triska and Cocks (eds.) *Political Development in Eastern Europe*.
61. Samuel P. Huntington, "Social and Institutional Dynamics of One-Party Systems," in Samuel Huntington and Clement Moore, *Authoritarian Politics in Modern Society* (New York: Basic Books, 1970), pp. 3–47.
62. Richard Lowenthal, "Development vs. Utopia in Communist Policy," in Chalmers Johnson (ed.) *Change in Communist Systems* (Stanford, CA: Stanford University Press, 1970), p. 112.
63. Kenneth Jowitt, *The Leninist Response to National Dependency* (Berkeley, CA: Institute of International Studies, 1978).
64. Kenneth Jowitt, "Soviet Neotraditionalism," *Soviet Studies* 35: 3 (July 1983), pp. 275–97.
65. Andrew Janos, *Politics and Paradigms* (Stanford, CA: Stanford University Press, 1986), p. 155.
66. Ibid., p. 155.
67. Otto Hintze, *Staat und Verfassung* (Gottingen: Vandenhoeck & Ruprecht, 1962); and Charles Tilly, *The Formation of National States in Western Europe* (Princeton, NJ: Princeton University Press, 1975).
68. Hugh Heclo, *Modern Social Politics in Britain and Sweden* (New Haven, CT: Yale University Press, 1974); and Peter Flora and Arnold Heidenheimer (eds.) *The Development of Welfare States in Europe and America* (New Brunswick, NJ: Transaction Books, 1981).
69. Janos, *Politics and Paradigms*, p. 60.
70. George Breslauer, *Five Images of the Soviet Future* (Berkeley, CA: Institute of International Studies, 1978).
71. Robert A. Dahl, *Polyarchy* (New Haven, CT: Yale University Press, 1970).
72. Otto Gierke, *Political Theories of the Middle Ages* (Cambridge: Cambridge University Press, 1900); John Neville Figgis, *The Churches in the Modern State* (London, 1913); Leon Duguit, *Traite de Droit Constitutionnel* (Paris: Boccard, 1925); Harold Laski, *Studies in the Problem of Sovereignty* (New Haven, CT: Yale University Press, 1917); Ernest Barker, *Political Thought in England from Herbert Spencer to the Present Day* (London: Williams & Norgate, 1915).
73. Arthur Bentley, *The Process of Government* (Chicago: University of Chicago Press, 1908); and Mary Parker Follett, *The New State, Group Organization and the Solution of Popular Government* (New York: Longmans, Green, 1918).
74. Suzanne Berger (ed.) *Organizing Interests in Western Europe* (Cambridge, MA: Harvard University Press, 1957); John Manley, "Neopluralism: A Class Analysis of Pluralism I and Pluralism II," *American Political Science Review* 77: 2 (June 1983), pp. 368–83; and Stephen Krasner, "Approaches to the State: Alternative Conceptions and Historical Dynamics," *Comparative Politics* 16: 2 (January 1984), pp. 223–46.
75. Charles E. Merriam and Harold F. Gosnell, *The American Party System* (New York: Macmillan, 1933); Elmer E. Schattschneider, *Party Government* (New York: Farrar & Rhinehart, 1942).
76. Samuel Huntington, *American Politics: The Promise of Disharmony* (Cambridge, MA: Belknap Press of Harvard University Press, 1981).

77. Charles Beard, *The Economic Basis of Politics* (New York: Knopf, 1922); Vernon Parrington, *Main Currents in American Thought*, 3 vols. (New York: Harcourt, Brace, 1927–30); and Frederick Jackson Turner, *The Frontier in American History* (New York: Henry Holt, 1920).
78. Pendleton Herring, *The Politics of Democracy* (New York: Norton, 1940); David Truman, *The Governmental Process* (New York: Knopf, 1951).
79. Manley, "Neo-Pluralism: A Class Analysis of Pluralism I and Pluralism II."
80. Charles E. Lindblom, *Politics and Markets* (New York: Basic Books, 1977); Robert A. Dahl, *Dilemmas of Democratic Pluralism* (New Haven, CT: Yale University Press, 1981).
81. Pendleton Herring, *Public Administration and the Public Interest* (New York: McGraw-Hill, 1936); *Presidential Leadership: The Political Relations of Congress and the Chief Executive* (New York: Farrar & Rhinehart, 1940).
82. V. O. Key Jr., *The Administration of Federal Grants in Aid to the States* (Chicago: Public Administration Services, 1937); and David Truman, *Administrative Decentralization* (Chicago: University of Chicago Press, 1941).
83. Henry Ehrmann, "Interest Groups," vol. XII, *International Encyclopedia of the Social Sciences* (New York: Macmillan, 1968), pp. 241ff.; Gabriel A. Almond, "Corporatism, Pluralism, and Professional Memory," *World Politics* 35: 2 (January 1983), pp. 245–60; Alfred Stepan, *The State and Society: Peru in Comparative Perspective* (Princeton, NJ: Princeton University Press, 1978); and Phillippe Schmitter, *Interest Conflict and Political Change in Brazil* (Stanford, CA: Stanford University Press, 1971).
84. H. Gordon Skilling, "Interest Groups and Communist Politics," *World Politics* 18: 3 (April 1966), pp. 435–51.
85. H. Gordon Skilling and Franklyn Griffiths (eds.) *Interest Groups in Soviet Politics* (Princeton, NJ: Princeton University Press, 1971).
86. Hough and Fainsod, *How the Soviet Union Is Governed*, p. 528.
87. William Odom, "A Dissenting View on the Group Approach to Soviet Politics," *World Politics* 28: 4 (July 1976), pp. 542–67; David Powell "In Pursuit of Interest Groups in the USSR," *Soviet Union/Union Sovietique* 6 (Part 1, 1979), pp. 99–124; Andrew Janos, "Interest Groups and the Structure of Power: Critiques and Comparisons," *Studies in Comparative Communism* 12: 1 (Spring 1979), pp. 6–20; and Andrew Janos, "Group Politics in Communist Society: A Second Look at the Pluralistic Model," in Huntington and Moore, *Authoritarian Politics in Modern Society*, pp. 437–50.
88. Joseph LaPalombara, "Monoliths or Plural Systems: Through Conceptual Lenses Darkly," *Studies in Comparative Communism* 8: 3 (Autumn 1975), pp. 305–32.
89. H. Gordon Skilling, "Interest Groups and Communist Politics Revisited," *World Politics* 36: 1 (October 1983), p. 5.
90. Franklyn Griffiths, "A Tendency Analysis of Soviet Policy-Making," in Skilling and Griffiths (eds.) *Interest Groups in Soviet Politics*.
91. Joel Schwartz and William Keech, "Group Influence and the Policy Process in the Soviet Union," *American Political Science Review* 62: 3 (September 1968), pp. 840–51; Philip D. Stewart, "Soviet Interest Groups and the Policy Process: The Repeal of Production Education," *World Politics* 22: 1 (October 1969), pp. 29–51; Peter Solomon, *Soviet Criminologists and Criminal Policy: Specialists in Policy Making* (New York: Columbia University Press, 1978); Thane Gustafson, *Reform in Soviet Politics; Lessons of Recent Policies on Land and Water* (Cambridge: Cambridge University Press, 1981).
92. Michel Oksenberg, "Occupational Groups in Chinese Society and the Cultural Revolu-

tion," *Chinese Studies* 2 (Ann Arbor: University of Michigan, Center for Chinese Studies, 1968); Alan Liu, *Communication and National Integration in China* (Berkeley: University of California Press, 1971); and J. Esmein, *The Chinese Cultural Revolution* (London: Deutsch, 1975).

93. Merle Goldman, *China's Intellectuals: Advise and Dissent* (Cambridge, MA: Harvard University Press, 1981); Lucian W. Pye, *Dynamics of Chinese Politics* (Cambridge, MA: Oelgeschlager, Gunn & Hain, 1981).
94. David S. Goodman (ed.) *Groups and Politics in the People's Republic of China* (Armonk, NY: M. E. Sharpe, 1984).
95. Ibid., p. 6.
96. Jan Triska and Charles Gati (eds.) *Blue Collar Workers In Eastern Europe* (London: Allen & Unwin, 1981).
97. Zvi Gitelman and Walter Connor (eds.) *Public Opinion in European Socialist Systems* (New York: Praeger, 1977).
98. Ibid., p. 5.
99. Archie Brown, "Pluralism, Power and the Soviet Political System: A Comparative Perspective," in Susan Gross Solomon (ed.) *Pluralism in the Soviet Union* (New York: St. Martin's Press, 1983), pp. 61–107.
100. G.D.H. Cole, *Guild Socialism* (London: Fabian Society, 1922).
101. Stein Rokkan, "Geography, Religion, and Social Class: Crosscutting Cleavages in Norwegian Politics," in Seymour Martin Lipset and Stein Rokkan, *Party Systems and Voter Alignments* (New York: Free Press, 1967); Robert Kvavik, *Interest Groups in Norwegian Politics* (Oslo: Universitetsforlaget, 1976).
102. Phillippe Schmitter, "Still the Century of Corporatism," in Phillippe Schmitter and Gerhard Lehmbruch, *Trends Toward Corporatist Intermediation* (Beverly Hills, CA: Sage, 1974), p. 100.
103. David Cameron, "Social Democracy: Corporatism, Labor Quiescence, and the Representation of Economic Interests in Advanced Capitalist Societies," in John Goldthorpe (ed.) *Order and Conflict in Contemporary Capitalism* (Cambridge: University of Cambridge Press, 1984).
104. Peter Katzenstein, *Small States in World Markets* (Ithaca, NY: Cornell University Press, 1985). See also Harold M. Wilensky, "Leftism, Catholicism, and Democratic Corporatism: The Role of Political Parties in Recent Welfare State Development," in Flora and Heidenheimer, *The Development of Welfare States in Europe and America*; and Phillippe Schmitter, "Interest Intermediation and Regime Governability in Contemporary Western Europe and North America," in Suzanne Berger (ed.) *Organizing Interests in Western Europe* (Cambridge: Cambridge University Press, 1981).
105. Valerie Bunce and John M. Echols, "Soviet Politics in the Brezhnev Era: Pluralism or Corporatism," in Donald R. Kelley, *Soviet Politics in the Brezhnev Era* (New York: Viking, 1980).
106. Valerie Bunce, "The Political Economy of the Brezhnev Era," *British Journal of Political Science* 13: 2 (April 1983), p. 131.
107. Ibid., p. 157.
108. Jerry F. Hough, "Pluralism, Corporatism and the Soviet Union," in Solomon (ed.) *Pluralism in the Soviet Union*, pp. 37–60.
109. H. Gordon Skilling, "Interest Groups and Communist Politics Revisited."
110. Archie Brown, "Political Power in the Soviet State," in Neil Harding (ed.) *The State in*

Society (Albany: State University of New York Press, 1984); Phillippe Schmitter, "Still the Century of Corporatism," in Schmitter and Lehmbruch, *Trends Toward Corporatist Intermediation*, pp. 99–100; Juan J. Linz, "Totalitarian and Authoritarian Regimes," in Greenstein and Polsby (eds.) *Handbook of Political Science*, vol. 3 (Reading, MA: Addison-Wesley, 1975), p. 312; and Alfred Stepan, *The State and Society: Peru in Comparative Perspective* (Princeton, NJ: Princeton University Press, 1978), p. 15.

111. Brown, "Political Power in the Soviet State," p. 68.
112. Robert A. Dahl, *Who Governs?* (New Haven, CT: Yale University Press, 1962).
113. Theodore Lowi, "American Business, Public Policy, Case Studies, and Political Theory," *World Politics* 16: 4 (July 1964), pp. 677–715.
114. J. Leiper Freeman, *The Political Process* (New York: Random House, 1965).
115. Hugh Heclo, "Issue Networks and the Executive Establishment," in Anthony King (ed.) *The New American Political System* (Washington, DC: American Enterprise Institute, 1978), pp. 87–124.
116. Ibid., p. 88.
117. John W. Kingdon, *Agendas, Alternatives, and Public Policies* (Boston: Little, Brown, 1984).
118. William Zimmerman, "Issue Area and Foreign-Policy Process: A Research Note in Search of a General Theory," *American Political Science Review* 67: 4 (December 1973), pp. 1204–12.
119. Nina Halpern, "Economic Specialists and the Making of Chinese Economic Policy, 1955–1983," Ph.D. dissertation, University of Michigan, 1985.
120. John W. Lewis, *Political Networks and the Chinese Policy Process* (Stanford, CA: Northeast Asia Forum on International Policy, 1986).
121. John Lowenhardt, *Decision Making in Soviet Politics* (New York: St. Martin's Press, 1981).
122. Hough and Fainsod, *How the Soviet Union Is Governed.*
123. Ibid., p. 525.
124. Alfred Meyer, *The Soviet Political System: An Interpretation* (New York: Random House, 1965), p. 468.
125. Allen Kassof, "The Administered Society: Totalitarianism Without Terror," *World Politics* 16: 4 (July 1964), pp. 558–75; T. H. Rigby, "Traditional, Market, and Organization Societies," *World Politics* 16: 4 (July 1964), pp. 539–57.
126. John A. Armstrong, "Sources of Administrative Behavior: Some Soviet and Western European Comparisons," *American Political Science Review* 59: 3 (September 1965), pp. 643–55.
127. Jerry Hough, *The Soviet Union and Social Science Theory* (Cambridge, MA: Harvard University Press, 1977).
128. Barghoorn, *Politics in the USSR* (1972), p. 202; see also Barghoorn and Remington, *Politics in the USSR* (1986), pp. 403–404.
129. David Granick, *Management of the Industrial Firm in the USSR* (New York: Columbia University Press, 1954); Joseph Berliner, *Factory and Manager in the USSR* (Cambridge, MA: Harvard University Press, 1957); and Jeremy Azrael, *Managerial Power and Soviet Politics* (Cambridge, MA: Harvard University Press, 1966).
130. Arnold Horelick, A. Ross Johnson, and John D. Steinbruner, *The Study of Soviet Foreign Policy: Decision Theory Related Approaches* (Beverly Hills, CA: Sage, 1975).
131. William Potter, "Sources of Foreign Policy Change: Insights from the Policy Sciences,"

Conference on the Domestic Sources of Soviet Foreign Policy, UCLA Project on Politics and War, 11 October 1985.

132. Ibid.
133. Jiri Valenta, "Soviet Decisionmaking and the Czechoslovak Crisis of 1968," *Studies in Comparative Communism* 8: 1 and 2 (Spring-Summer 1975), pp. 147–73.
134. Gail Lapidus, "The Making of Russia's China Policy: Domestic/Foreign Policy Linkages in Sino-Soviet Relations," UCLA Project on Politics and War, 11 October 1985.
135. Pye, *Dynamics of Chinese Politics*, p. 86.
136. Michel Oksenberg, "Methods of Communications Within the Chinese Bureaucracy," *China Quarterly* 57 (January-March 1974), pp. 1–39; Michel Oksenberg, "Economic Policy Making in China: Summer 1981," *China Quarterly* 90 (September 1982), pp. 165–94; Kenneth Lieberthal, *Central Documents and Politburo Politics in China* (Ann Arbor: University of Michigan, Chinese Studies, 1978).
137. Robert Conquest, *Power and Policy in the USSR* (London: Macmillan, 1961).
138. James C. Scott, "Political Clientelism: A Bibliographical Essay," in Steffen Schmidt et al., *Friends, Followers, and Factions* (Berkeley: University of California Press, 1977).
139. Carl Lande, *Leaders, Factions and Parties: The Structure of Philippine Politics* 6 (New Haven, CT: Yale Southeast Asia Monograph Series, 1965); Schmidt et al., *Friends, Followers, and Factions*, "Introduction," pp. 75–100 and pp. 506–10; James C. Scott, "Corruption, Machine Politics, and Political Change," *American Political Science Review* 63: 4 (December 1969), pp. 1142–58; and "Patron-Client Politics and Political Change in Southeast Asia," *American Political Science Review* 66: 1 (March 1972), pp. 91–113; Rene Lemarchand and Keith Legg, "Political Clientism and Development: A Preliminary Analysis," *Comparative Politics* 4: 2 (January 1972), pp. 149–78; and S. Eisenstadt and Rene Lemarchand, *Political Clientelism, Patronage, and Development* (Beverly Hills, CA: Sage, 1981).
140. Andrew Nathan, "A Factionalism Model for CCP Politics," *China Quarterly* 53 (January-March 1973), pp. 34–66.
141. Lande, *Leaders, Factions and Parties*; and Scott, "Patron-Client Politics and Change in Southeast Asia."
142. Nathan Leites, *On the Game of Politics in France* (Stanford, CA: Stanford University Press, 1959).
143. Andrew Nathan, "A Factionalism Model for CCP Politics," p. 396.
144. John W. Lewis, *Political Networks and the Chinese Policy Process* (Stanford, CA: Northeast Asia Forum on International Policy, 1986), p. 5.
145. Ibid. p. 7.
146. Ibid.
147. Ibid., p. 25.
148. Lucian W. Pye, *Asian Power and Politics* (Cambridge, MA: Belknap Press of the Harvard University Press, 1985), p. 27.
149. Ibid., p. 146.
150. Ibid., p. 177
151. "Clientelism," Symposium in *Studies in Comparative Communism* 12: 2 and 3 (Summer/Autumn 1979), pp. 159–211.
152. John Willerton, "Clientelism in the Soviet Union: An Initial Examination," *Studies in Comparative Communism* 12: 2 and 3 (Summer/Autumn 1979), pp. 159–83.
153. Zygmunt Bauman, "Comment on Eastern Europe," pp. 184–9.
154. John Burns, "Comment on China," pp. 190–4.

155. Nobutake Ike, "Comment on Japan," pp. 201–3.
156. T. H. Rigby, "The Need for Comparative Research," p. 207.
157. Ibid., p. 209.
158. T. H. Rigby and Bohdan Harasymiw, *Leadership Selection and Patron-Client Relations in the USSR and Yugoslavia* (London: Allen & Unwin, 1983).
159. Gyula Josza, "Political Seilschaften in the USSR," in Ibid., p. 169.
160. See n. 158, 144, and 148 above.
161. Erik P. Hoffmann, "Methodological Problems of Kremlinology," in Frederic J. Fleron, Jr. (ed.) *Communist Studies and the Social Sciences: Essays on Methodology and Empirical Theory* (Chicago: Rand McNally, 1969).
162. Ellen Mickiewicz, "Managing Public Opinion and International News in the Soviet Union," in *Domestic Sources of Foreign and Defense Policy*, UCLA Project on Politics and War, 1985. Cf. Alex Inkeles, *Public Opinion in Soviet Russia* (Cambridge, MA: Harvard University Press, 1950).
163. William A. Welsh, "A Game-Theoretic Conceptualization of the Hungarian Revolt: Toward an Inductive Theory of Games," in Fleron (ed.) *Communist Studies and the Social Sciences*.
164. Robert Packenham, "The Changing Political Discourse in Brazil," in Wayne Selcher (ed.) *Political Liberalization in Brazil* (Boulder, CO: Westview, 1986).
165. Brown, "Soviet Political Culture through Soviet Eyes," in *Political Culture and Communist Studies*, pp. 106ff.
166. Archie Brown, "Political Power in the Soviet State," in Neil Harding (ed.) *The State in Society*, p. 75.
167. Ibid., p. 74.
168. Clifford Geertz, *The Interpretation of Cultures: Selected Essays* (New York: Basic Books, 1973).
169. Adam Przeworski and James Teune, *The Logic of Comparative Social Inquiry* (New York: John Wiley, 1970), p. 30.
170. Albert Hirschman, "The Search for Paradigms as a Hindrance to Understanding," *World Politics* 22: 3 (April 1970), pp. 329–43.
171. John Womack, *Zapata and the Mexican Revolution* (New York: Knopf, 1968); James Payne, *Patterns of Conflict in Colombia* (New Haven, CT: Yale University Press, 1968).
172. Hirschman, p. 338.
173. Ibid., p. 331.
174. Harry Eckstein, "Case Study and Theory in Political Science," in Greenstein and Polsby, *Handbook of Political Science*, vol. 3 (Reading, MA: Addison-Wesley, 1975).
175. Roberto Michels, *Political Parties: A Sociological Study of the Oligarchical Tendencies of Modern Democracy* (New York: Hearst International Library, 1915).
176. Ronald Amann, "Searching for an Appropriate Concept of Soviet Politics: The Politics of Hesitant Modernization?" *British Journal of Political Science* 16: 4 (October 1986), pp. 475–94.
177. Ibid., p. 492.
178. Brzezinski and Huntington, *Political Power: USA/USSR*.
179. Alexander Dallin, "The Domestic Sources of Soviet Foreign Policy," in Seweryn Bialer, *The Domestic Context of Soviet Foreign Policy* (Boulder, CO: Westview, 1981), p. 363.
180. Archie Brown, "Political Power in the Soviet State," in Harding (ed.) *The State in Society* p. 179.

4

Rational Choice Theory and the Social Sciences

The Prehistory of Rational Choice Theory

Since this volume honoring the thirtieth anniversary of the publication of Anthony Downs's *Economic Theory of Democracy* has sentimental as well as substantive aspects, I ask your indulgence if I reach back for a few appropriate memories. In 1956–57 I occupied study 14 at the Center for Advanced Study in the Behavioral Sciences. Bob Dahl had occupied that study the previous year, and either he had left me his copy of the dissertation of Anthony Downs or Kenneth Arrow, who was a fellow that same year, gave me a copy. It was in the form of a report to the Office of Naval Research, which had funded the study. Indeed, it was presented as a dissertation in the form of a report to the ONR. There was no other version. No changes were made in the manuscript from dissertation to report to published book. Kenneth Arrow chaired Downs's committee, and Robert Dahl and Charles Lindblom were instrumental in getting the dissertation published. I still own that cardboard-bound, mimeographed version of *An Economic Theory of Democracy*, which must now be a collector's item.

Downs's book was the first thing I read at the Center in California in 1956. I was then deep in political sociology and psychology, and reading Downs's spare formulations and claims of explanatory power was an astringent experience. But there were aspects of the work that were quite continuous with a literature with which I was quite familiar. Marketlike metaphors were in quite general use in the analysis of democratic and American politics. The 1950s was the era of the "decline of ideology." Political pragmatism was in

---

Author's Note: The original version of this chapter was presented at the Conference Honoring the Thirtieth Anniversary of Anthony Downs's *Economic Theory of Democracy*, University of California, Irvine, October 27–28, 1988.

the air. T. V. Smith, the homespun philosopher from the University of Chicago, a colleague of the Chicago philosophical pragmatists, and an Illinois state senator, had presented a picture of the successful democratic politician as a somewhat cynical, corruptible, but peaceful resolver of conflicts as early as the mid-1930s. Pendleton Herring (1940) quotes Smith's comparison of the politicians of dictatorship with those of democracy:

> It is precisely that outcome [violence] of intergroup conflicts which the democratic politicians shield us from. If they sometimes lie in the strenuous task, it is regrettable but understandable. If they sometimes truckle, that is despicable but tolerable. If they are sometimes bribed, that is more execrable but still not fatal. The vices of our politicians we must compare not with the virtues of the secluded individual but with the vices of dictators. In this context, almost beautiful things may be said of our politicians—by way of compensation, if not by way of extenuation, of whatever vices attend upon the arduous process of saving us from violence and murder. People elsewhere get killed in the conflicts of interest over which our politicians preside with vices short of crimes and with virtues not wholly unakin to magnanimity. (p.135)

On the eve of our involvement in World War II, Herring employed market metaphors in describing party politics in the United States:

> Much of our present expectation of governmental aid and relief is only traditionalism expressed in novel terms. There is no great alteration in fundamental attitudes. We had a politics of the handout—free land, mining concessions, shipping subsidies, tariff, and so on. A survey of the nineteenth century reveals continual demands for grants and subsidies. The demands of the little fellows can no longer be met by homesteads and similar concessions. A broader distribution is now demanded. The process, however, involves few niceties of theory or philosophy; it appears as opportunism faintly flavored with humanitarianism. We do not find the ideological conflict which aroused passions so hotly in European countries. In the United States social problems have seldom been related to systematic philosophies, nor has public policy been guided by an abstract formulation of values. Leaders of discontent talk in terms of concrete needs. (p. 175)

And again he argues:

> Since major party politicians are not bound by party discipline to follow a definite program, they have much freedom to bargain with interest groups. In this sense the fact that our major parties stand for so little makes minor parties all the more unnecessary. Through the formation of blocs in Congress sections and states

> win concessions from party leaders. Special interest organizations control votes that may affect the political life of Democrats or Republicans. (p. 187)

In addition, Herring anticipated Downs's forecast that, given a normal distribution of voters' ideological predispositions,

> there is a strong tendency for both parties to take the same stand. Once a winning program is discovered, it is equally attractive to both parties. This is well illustrated by the appeal of Senator Arthur Vandenburg during the high tide of Democratic party success. He urged a liberalization of Republican party policy through support of unemployment insurance, retirement pensions, and minimum wage laws. . . . Republicans will not let Democrats have a monopoly of farmers, workers, and the middle class. Democrats are divided about the wisdom of alienating business. What is good for one party is also good for the other, the differences lying chiefly in matters of personnel, emphasis, and tempo rather than substance. The rivalry really comes down to who is going to manage the rearrangement and fix the terms. (p. 193)

Two years later, economist Joseph Schumpeter (1942) employed the market metaphor more directly in his analysis of the realistic workings of democracies. Speaking of political leadership, he said:

> This concept presents similar difficulties as the concept of competition in the economic sphere, with which it may be usefully compared. In economic life competition is never completely lacking, but hardly ever is it perfect. Similarly in political life there is always some competition, though perhaps only a potential one, for the allegiance of the people. The justification for this is that democracy seems to imply a recognized method by which to conduct the competitive struggle, and that the electoral method is practically the only method available for communities of any size. But though this excludes many ways of securing leadership which should be excluded, such as competition by military insurrection, it does not exclude the cases that are strikingly analogous to the economic phenomena we label "unfair" or "fraudulent" competition or restraint of competition. And we cannot exclude them because if we did we should be left with a completely unrealistic ideal. Between this ideal case which does not exist and the cases in which all competition with the established leader is prevented by force, there is a continuous range of variation within which the democratic method of government shades off into the autocratic one by imperceptible steps. (p. 271)

Downs (1957) drew directly on Schumpeter for Adam Smith's "invisible hand" metaphor as well. He quotes this passage from the Harvard economist:

> Similarly, the social meaning or function of parliamentary activity is no doubt to turn out legislation and, in part, administrative measures. But in order to understand how democratic politics serve this social end, we must start from the competitive struggle for power and office and realize that the social function is fulfilled, as it were, incidentally—in the same sense as production is incidental to the making of profits. (p. 29)

The continuity of Downs's theory with the conventional wisdom of the 1950s is reflected in his acknowledgment of his debt to Schumpeter: "Schumpeter's profound analysis of democracy forms the inspiration and foundation for our whole thesis, and our debt and gratitude to him are great indeed" (p. 29). Other predecessors and contemporaries of Downs in employing these marketlike metaphors included V. O. Key (1942), whose leading text on political parties from its first edition stressed the notion of political leadership as involving bargaining and exchanges. Elmer Schattschneider (1960), also a leading interpreter of American parties and elections, repeats the Schumpeter metaphor of the politician as entrepreneur. The task of the citizen is "to learn how to compel his agents to define his options," and the problem for the political system as a whole is

> how to organize [the electoral process] so as to make the best possible use of the power of the public in view of its limitations. A popular decision bringing into focus the force of public support requires a tremendous effort to define the alternatives, to organize the discussion and mobilize opinion. The government and the political organizations are in the business of manufacturing . . . alternatives. (p. 139)

The market metaphor thus was one of the "literary" metaphors common among students of American politics. Voting was viewed as "like" exchanging votes for policies. And the activities of politicians were viewed as "like" those of entrepreneurs engaged in efforts to increase market share, by trading issue positions and combining resources in search of winning coalitions.

The Downs revolution consisted of converting this literary metaphor into an explicit formal model, with all the advantages that such explication conferred. It generated specific hypotheses about party systems that could be tested empirically, and it opened up the possibilities of rigorous scientific work involving mathematization and the use of sophisticated statistics. Since this "will to deductive and inductive rigor" dominated the social sciences of the 1950s and 1960s, it is not surprising that the rational choice and public choice literature flowered in the next decades and into the present, and became the cutting edge of "scientific" political science.

But Downs remembered, just as many of the scholars joining this school tended to forget, that there were costs attendant upon adopting the rational market model. In the pre-Downsian era of literary metaphor, the market metaphor was only one of four or five other metaphors found to be useful in the study of politics.

One of these metaphors was politics as religion, with conversion, prayer, and worship rather than buying and selling as the defining activities. Some aspects of French, Italian, Spanish, Latin American, German, and Middle Eastern politics can be captured by this metaphor. Or there was politics as warfare, with paramilitary formations, arms, and fighting for control of the streets. Lenin referred to the leading organs of the Communist party as the general staff of the revolution. The operating patterns of Nazism, Fascism, Falangism, and other authoritarian movements can also be partly captured by this military metaphor.

We are all familiar also with the metaphor of the "game of politics," in which participants become involved because of the fun and excitement, rather than because of the power and policy aspects of political activity. Or, as suggested recently by Clifford Geertz (1980), politics may largely take the form of playacting, in which the principal goal is edification deriving from the actors' symbolic affirmation of their powers and roles.

Since politics can take on aspects of a market, a game, a war, a church, a dramatic performance—and the history of the politics of individual societies shows how explanation over time may require some or all of them—opting for one of them as the realistic or the most realistic model is bound to have costs, to exaggerate some of the potentialities of politics at the expense of others and at the expense of the dynamic developmental perspective. This is the main argument in this chapter, that rational choice analysis may lead to empirical and normative distortions, unless it is used in combination with the historical, sociological, anthropological, and psychological sciences, which deal with the values and utilities of people, cross-culturally, cross-nationally, across the social strata, and over time.

Rational Choice Theory as a Scientific Revolution

At the time that rational choice theory began to spread out of its native habitat in economics in the late 1950s and early 1960s, the dominant approaches to explanation in the social sciences were sociological theory, culture and personality theory, and social psychological theory. The first, sociological theory, drew on the European tradition of Max Weber, Emile Durkheim, Vilfredo Pareto, and others. The second, culture and personality theory, drew on psychoanalytic and anthropological theory as in the work of Margaret Mead, Ruth Benedict, Ralph Linton, Harold Lasswell, Abram Kardiner, the Kluckhohns, et al., or on that of the "authoritarian personality" version. Social psychological theory, associated with survey research and small group experimental methodologies, was advanced by the work of Samuel Stouffer, Paul Lazarsfeld, Rensis Likert, Angus Campbell, Carl Hovland, Kurt Lewin, Dorwin Cartwright, and others.

Nineteenth- and early twentieth-century sociological theory, contra Marx, treated ideas, preferences, and values as of importance in the formation, maintenance, and breakdown of institutions. Norms and values were central to Durkheim's (1973) theories of social integration. Human beings were joined together in societies on the basis of a *conscience collective,* a set of common values and beliefs; suicide was a symptom of normlessness, of *anomie.* Weber (1930) traced the origins of capitalism to the worldly asceticism of the Protestant sects. The will to order one's life, save and accumulate capital, and invest was based upon the religious view that salvation was somehow associated with success in one's worldly endeavors. For Talcott Parsons, social action was explained by feelings, beliefs, and values, and social institutions were maintained by socialization processes inculcating these orientations (see Parsons & Shils, 1951). Culture and personality theory, as in the work of Ruth Benedict (1934), explained the social structure, the politics, and the public policy of different societies in terms of "national character," cultural themes, modal personality, and the like – mixes of beliefs about authority and human relations – that result in part from the ways in which members of these societies were inducted into their adult roles. And social psychological theory treated attitudes and beliefs as important explanatory variables in electoral behavior (Lazarsfeld & Berelson, 1955), in the morale of the military (Shils & Janowitz, 1948), in responses to propaganda (Hovland, 1950), in prejudiced attitudes (Adorno, Frenkel-Brunswik, Levinson, & Sanford, 1950), and so on.

The mental, moral, and attitudinal dimensions were very much in the center of social science discourse in the 1950s and 1960s. This mental and moral world was assumed to be quite complex, dynamic, and generative and not simply reflective. It was a central argument of these literatures that attitudes and values varied substantially, cross-nationally and historically, and that they had substantial explanatory power.

The rational choice literature avoided this complexity. For economists, their intellectual tradition assumed a homogeneous material interest "utility" function. For the generation of political scientists who adopted the rational choice approach in the 1960s and 1970s there was a deliberate turning toward economics and turning away from the other social sciences. While one encounters occasional citations of social science literature in such early works as Anthony Downs's (1957) study celebrated in this volume, Riker's (1962) study of coalitions, and the early book of Buchanan and Tullock (1962)—occasional references to Parsons, Durkheim, Lazarsfeld, Campbell, Horney, Dahl, Easton, and the like—there is a clear break with the intellectual tradition of the social sciences of the 1950s and 1960s.

There is also a self-conscious adoption of the deductive strategy of economics in the analysis of political phenomena. Government and politics are assumed to be similar to markets. Officials, politicians, and voters are short-term material self-interest maximizers, seeking benefits in the form of power, legislative and administrative decisions, votes, and the like. Starting with these assumptions, the pioneers in this approach quickly established its power and parsimony in explaining aspects of party systems, constitutional arrangements, and political coalitions. The movement looks so much like the scientific revolution described by Thomas Kuhn (1962)—with its abrupt adoption of a new paradigm, noncumulative with previous scientific work, and with its prompt shift to the puzzle solving of a new "normal public choice science"—one is tempted to conclude that they had deliberately adopted a Kuhnian strategy. The dates of publication, however, rule out such a possibility.

Core Rational Choice Theory

Rational choice theory is a deductive strategy, purely such, for example, in the work of Downs, Riker, Buchanan and Tullock, and others, or deductive in combination with empirical testing of logically derived hypotheses as in the work of Fiorina (1981), Ferejohn (1987), Shepsle and Fiorina (1988), and others. It proceeds from assumptions, or axioms, about human motives and behavior, and draws the logical institutional and policy implications from those axioms. One aspect of this metamethodological approach is "methodological individualism," which argues that all social phenomena are derivable from, or can be factored into, the properties and behaviors of individuals. A second aspect is that political actors—voters, politicians, bureaucrats—are assumed to be material interest maximizers, seeking benefits in the form of votes, offices, power, and so on, at least cost.

There are a variety of positions taken in the rational choice literature on the nature of these assumptions. Some scholars attribute substantial or "sufficient" realism to the material self-interest assumption. Others argue that the question of realism is secondary, as long as the predictions generated from these assumptions are substantiated. Still others treat the method in purely heuristic terms, as an efficient way of generating hypotheses, starting with simple assumptions, and then complicating them in a controlled effort to increase explanatory power. Some of these scholars have argued more than one position over time.

Milton Friedman (1953), in his early book on "positive economics," tells us,

> The relevant question to ask about the "assumptions" of a theory is not whether they are descriptively "realistic," for they never are, but whether they are sufficiently good approximations for the purpose in hand. And this question can be answered only by seeing whether the theory works, which means whether it yields sufficiently accurate predictions. (p. 40)

And again, he argues that it is not necessary to establish the complete realism of

> any assumption of such theories. . . . A meaningful scientific hypothesis or theory typically asserts that certain forces are, and other forces are not, important in understanding a particular class of phenomena. It is frequently convenient to present such a hypothesis by stating that the phenomena it is desired to predict behave in the world of observation as if they occurred in a hypothetical and highly simplified world containing only the forces that the hypothesis asserts to be important. . . . Complete "realism" is clearly unattainable, and the question whether it is realistic "enough" can be settled only by seeing whether it yields predictions that are good enough for the purpose at hand or that are better than predictions from alternative theories. (p. 42)

Friedman attributes a limited realism to the economic-market model, and draws policy implications from it. He also recognizes cultural differences in a limited way. Thus he qualifies his view that price theory was the most robust theory of modern economics, stating that it deserved "much confidence *for the kind of economic system that characterizes Western nations*" (p. 42; emphasis added).

Buchanan and Tullock, in *The Calculus of Consent* (1962), take a position similar to that of Friedman:

> The ultimate defense of the economic-individualist behavioral assumption must be empirical. . . . Fundamentally, the only test for "realism" of the assumption lies in the applicability of the conclusions. (pp. 28–29)

But while Buchanan and Tullock stop short of adopting the "individual self-interest norm" as the only "realistic" one, they make a strong argument for its appropriateness in the analysis of politics:

> We know that one interpretation of human activity suggests that men do, in fact, seek to maximize individual utilities when they participate in political decisions and that individual utility functions differ. . . . [and] so long as some part of all individual behavior in collective choice-making is, in fact, motivated by utility maximization, and so long as the identification of the individual with the group does not extend to the point of making all individual utility functions identical, an economic-individualism model of political activity should be of some positive worth. (p. 30)

In his *Theory of Political Coalitions*, Riker (1962) defends the realism of the rational self-interest assumption. He argues that while individual behavior may deviate from the self-interest assumption, fiduciary behavior is client centered. The trustee is obligated to act in the material interest of the client. And since much of politics (e.g., the politician-voter/citizen relation) is based on a fiduciary relationship, the self-interest assumption is applicable to a large part of political action.

In later work, Riker defends the assumption on simple metamethodological grounds:

> The rationality assumption asserts that there is something about people that makes them behave (usually) in a regular way, just as in physical science the mechanical assumption is made that there is something about things that assures us they will (usually) move regularly. In both cases there is an assumption that things behave in regular ways. (Riker & Ordeshook, 1973, p. 11)

Riker and Ordeshook go on to argue

> that the notion of rationality plays a fundamental role in social science. It is one of the ways by which we arrive at the regularity necessary for generalization. Whether or not it is better than simple observation is currently the subject of some discussion in political science, being a particular form of the old debate between inductive and deductive methods or between radical empiri-

> cism and theoretical science. As is apparent, we side with deductive methods and postulated regularity, largely because we believe them more efficient than their alternative. . . . the method of postulated regularity is positively more efficient because it permits the easy generation of hypotheses and offers a single parsimonious explanation of behavior. As against this efficiency, the method of observed regularity is ad hoc. . . . Even if catalogued into hypotheses, behavior appears extraordinarily complex, while with a simplifying and coordinating theory much of the complexity disappears. On the practical grounds of efficiency, therefore, we prefer postulated regularity. (p. 12)

Riker appears to have dropped the issue of realism. The self-interest assumption has become an assumption of goal-oriented regularity.

Anthony Downs, in his *An Economic Theory of Democracy* (1957), qualifies the rational self-interest assumption:

> In reality, men are not always selfish, even in politics. They frequently do what appears to be individually irrational because they believe it is socially rational. . . . In every field, no account of human behavior is complete without mention of such altruism; its possessors are among the heroes men rightly admire. Nevertheless, general theories of social action always rely heavily on the self-interest maxim . . . because it tends to be realistic. (p. 9)

In later work, Downs (1988) adopts a more sociological-historical-philosophical approach to the individual utility problem and assimilates his economic model of democracy into it. He describes his early trailblazing work as involving

> a relatively abstract theoretical model of voter and party behavior . . . gradually introducing certain realistic elements into it, such as the cost of information. . . . It assumed that all individual preferences were given at the outset. I believe that approach provided an interesting and fruitful way to look at democratic politics. But it was not meant to be either comprehensive or fully realistic.

Morris Fiorina (1981) quotes from the early Downs approvingly, but adopts the contemporary version of rational choice in economic theory, where, he states,

> the assumption of "rational" behavior means no more than the notion that individuals engage in "maximizing" behavior. In any situation the alternatives open to an individual lead to various benefits (typically in some probabilistic

> fashion). These alternatives entail various costs. The individual chooses so as to maximize the difference between expected benefits and costs, where there are wide varieties of theories about how to calculate those expectations. This is the contemporary generalization of Downs's argument, and, I hope, the perspective of election studies of the future. (p. 198)

There is thus some ambiguity as to the claims being made for the realism of the rational self-interest assumption. There seem to be at least two different versions. The first is that it is "partly" realistic or "sufficiently realistic," or that its "realism doesn't make all that much difference" as long as it generates useful or valid predictions. The second version sets aside the material self-interest assumption and replaces it with a rational maximizing assumption in relation to any kinds of goals. But this later version of the assumption is not always adhered to. If we look at the policy-oriented work of Buchanan and Tullock, and Riker, for example, it is clear that policy recommendations tend to be made on the basis of the first version, the one that imputes some degree of realism to the rational self-interest assumption. It also may involve the introduction of other supporting assumptions, the realism of which is affirmed without being demonstrated, as suggested below.

Peripheral Rational Choice Theorists

The theorists whose views on the realism of the rational self-interest assumption have been described above might be called *core* rational choice theorists. They include the founders and leaders of the Rochester and Virginia schools of public choice theory (see below). Others of these schools are not on record as to their views on these methodological questions. There are a number of scholars, such as Terry Moe, Douglas North, Samuel Popkin, and Robert Bates, who might be described as *peripheral* members of the rational choice school, who use the economic model heuristically, employing it in combination with other models.

Thus Terry Moe (1979) argues that rational models may be taken as "pretheories, which provide a systematic basis for progress toward the goal of explaining certain social behaviors. In this capacity, they operate as intermediate mechanisms that aid in conceptualization, facilitate analysis through their simplicity and deductive power, point to relevant relationships, and thereby contribute to the development of empirical laws" (p. 237). Douglas North (1981), in his interpretation of the economic history of Western civilization, systematically applies the models of neoclassical economic theory to such political questions as the emergence of the state and its role in enhancing and inhibiting economic growth. He describes this as a heuristic undertaking, stating, "We must, of course, be cautious about the limits of neoclassical theory. Public choice theory—economics applied to politics—has at best had only a modest success in explaining political decision making" (p. 21).

Third World development theorists such as Popkin and Bates apply rational choice economic models again quite self-consciously as models. Thus Popkin (1979) weighs the alternative rational choice and moral economy models in his study of the Vietnamese peasantry:

> I have modified the two views of peasant society. A free-market economics approach, even when amended to take account of peasant aversion to risk, cannot explain the patterns of stratification and production in the precolonial, colonial, and revolutionary eras in Vietnam without considering collective goods and leadership, political coalitions that shape markets, and the infrastructure of the economic system, including taxes, courts, land titles, law and order, and insurance. The moral economy approach, while fully cognizant of the risks and dangers of markets and the importance of villages and patron-client relations for peasant survival, requires modification as well to take account of the ways in which aversion to risk, conflicts between public and private forms of investment, and conflicts among the peasantry limit the quality and extent of insurance and welfare embedded in peasant institutions. (p. 267)

Robert Bates (1987a), who has done exemplary work on African and Third World political economy, rejects the two major forms of political economy, conventional microeconomics and the "standard" radical or Marxist approaches. He points out:

> The study of agrarian politics reveals the limited relevance of voluntary exchange; economic coercion is a fact of everyday life. The study of rural communities reveals as well the significance of institutions other than markets. And the study of agricultural policy making demonstrates that consideration of objectives other than economic efficiency drives the selection of policies and forms of policy intervention. Clearly, then, conventional economics provides a weak foundation for the study of agrarian political economy. Radical political economy does little better. Consideration of the fate of the peasantry demonstrates that effective class action is problematic. And the analysis of public policy reveals that a theory of politics cannot rest on the presumption of historical materialism; political intervention as frequently retards the growth of productive forces as it promotes it. (p. 185)

Bates recommends a collective choice approach reconciled with culture theory in his most recent work. He recounts his intellectual history, saying that he began his work on the peasantry of the Third World

> by shouldering aside, as it were, the contribution of cultural studies. But now at the end, I want to return to this scholarly tradition. For having ventured into the field of political economy, scholars have acquired new tools; and it may now be time for them to return with these tools in hand to analyze the significance of distinctive values and institutions. Who can fail to appreciate the opportunity offered by contemporary game theory to provide a formal structure for kinds of symbolic displays analyzed by Goffman or Geertz, for example? Work on games of imperfect information offer grounds for analyzing their powerful insights into the subjective side of influence and power. And who can fail to appreciate the significance of models of collective choice for the analysis of such institutions as lineage systems, village councils, or systems of traditional authority? Already some scholars have recognized the value of applying these tools. One can hope that the contributions represent but a beginning of a new tradition of research into the properties of significant institutions. . . .
>
> In the early years of political economy, "rational choicers" posed as revolutionaries, attacking their sociologically minded brethren. Now it may be time to promote the synthesis and re-integration of these traditions. Because they work in cultures possessing distinctive beliefs, values, and institutions, those studying the developing areas may be best placed to take this important step. (pp. 55, 56)

The Case of Riker's Theory of Coalitions

It may be instructive to examine coalition theory as exemplified in the work of William Riker (1962), as an example both of the productivity of the rational choice approach and of its limitations in a general strategy of social explanation. Riker, in reviewing the empirical fate of the size, or minimal winning coalition principle, concludes that while the theory is deductively sound, "its empirical validity is somewhat less certain." He acknowledges that empirical studies of European cabinet formation have shown that many coalitions have been larger (or smaller) than minimal. Abram de Swaan (1973) and Lawrence Dodd (1976) have demonstrated that ideological similarity has been important in European coalition formation, and that this has resulted in many deviations from the "minimal winning" expectation. But Riker then goes on to say that when cabinets are examined according to their duration, it has been found that the oversized and undersized coalitions have not lasted as long on the average as the minimal ones, so that the size principle has indeed been supported empirically.

Indeed, Dodd found that of all the cabinets formed in Western Europe during the period 1918–1974, 31% were minimal winning coalitions and 69% were either over- or undersized. Thus the size principle failed on the percentage of tosses of the coin, so to speak; but it predicted better on the question of the duration of cabinets. Dodd found that, on the average, minimal winning coalitions lasted 58 months, while undersized cabinets lasted on the average of 9 to 20 months, depending on how far they fell short of a majority; oversized cabinets lasted 13 to 29 months, again depending on the extent to which they exceeded a majority.

There is thus something to the size principle. There is an underlying propensity for coalitions to oscillate around minimal winning size. But this theory misses a lot of what is going on in the world of cabinet coalitions. To understand cabinet formation we need more theoretical tools than Riker provides for us. Let me review two recent studies that began with Riker's size principle, introduced additional assumptions, and ended up with validated theories of different aspects of European government and cabinet formation.

Gregory Luebbert (1986), in a study of government formation in Europe and Israel, demonstrates a relationship between the structure and culture of political systems and the kinds of coalitions typically formed in them. Luebbert divides contemporary democracies into four types based upon their degree of legitimacy and consensuality—consensual, competitive, unconsolidated, and conflictual. Consensual democracies are those in which the regime enjoys high legitimacy and the opposition is supportive and cooperative; competitive democracies are characterized by high legitimacy, but the opposition parties are consistently competitive; conflictual democracies are lacking in widespread legitimacy, and the opposition is uncooperative; and unconsolidated democracies are those in which there is low legitimacy, but in which the parties tend to consensual practices. Luebbert finds that the size principle is sustained only in undominated competitive democracies, that is to say, among those democracies in which there is high legitimacy, in which no party is consistently in the majority, and in which the opposition is consistently competitive. In competitive democracies in which there is one dominant majority party (e.g., Israel, 1950–74; Belgium, 1973–80; the Netherlands, 1945–66), there is a strong tendency for oversized coalitions to form. Consensual and legitimate democracies such as Norway, Sweden, and Denmark have frequently been governed by undersized or minority coalitions, while in conflictual democracies such as the Fourth French Republic, the Weimar Republic, and Italy there has been an equal probability of minority and majority government. Thus Luebbert has established that rational self-interest might lead to consistently oversized and undersized coalitions under differing conditions of partisanship and legitimacy. He concludes:

> The limited relevance of this assumption should now be apparent; it is only in undominated-competitive systems that one finds the need for majorities that is absent in consensual systems; the ability to create them that is absent in conflictual systems; and the urgency that is missing in dominated-competitive systems, where dominance makes creation of majority governments virtually assured. (p. 84)

Kaare Strom (1983), in a study of minority government in post-World War II Europe, shows that minority coalitions "may form as the results of rational choices made by party leaders under certain structural constraints." Strom isolates two major species of minority governments – those that arise in consensual political systems in which the cost-benefit ratio of remaining outside the government is more favorable for a possible majority-making coalition partner or partners than the cost-benefit ratio of membership in the governing coalition, and those in which the costs of tolerating a minority government are lower than the systemic costs of opposing it. Strom analyzes coalition formation in Norway and Italy as exemplars of the two types. Both can be explained in terms of rational self-interest varying according to different structural-cultural constraints.

The implication of the work of Luebbert and Strom is that coalition theory in its pure game-theoretic size-principle form has to be supplemented by comparative political party theory if it is to explain coalition behavior in the real world. Thus as far as cabinet formation theory is concerned Riker's size principle turns out to have valuable payoffs. It set in motion a productive research program that led to a more rigorous theory of government formation in parliamentary democracies. The intellectual history of coalition theory with special reference to European cabinet formation is reviewed systematically and comprehensively in the recent work of Michael Laver and Norman Schofield (1989).

In an effort to adapt coalition theory to the analysis of political crises and change, Almond, Flanagan, and Mundt (1973) made a number of historical case studies using a common framework of analysis. The historical studies included the British Reform Act of 1832, the formation of the French Third Republic in the 1870s, the formation of the Weimar Republic after World

War I, the Meiji Restoration in Japan in the mid-1860s, and the Cardenas phase in the Mexican Revolution in the 1930s, among others. What is of relevance to the discussion here is that in order to use coalition theory in these historical studies we had to trace the transformation of political actors, their utilities, and resources as they were affected by changes in the international context and the domestic social structure and culture. From our estimates of these changes we could generate the logically possible coalitions, their policy and resource properties, and the probability of their occurrence at different stages in the development of these crises. The successful coalitions in these historical episodes were not necessarily the most probable ones by strict coalition-theoretic measures. Leadership—as measured by skill in resource mobilization and/or facility in manipulating, combining, or compromising issues—had to be factored in, in order to explain the Cardenas victory in Mexico and the Meiji Restoration in Japan, and to explain the failures of leadership (i.e., missed coalition opportunities) in the Ramsay MacDonald failure in the British Crisis of 1931, the Social Democratic failure in the formation of the Weimar Republic, and the like. Thus coalition theory has a role in the historical problems of the rise and fall of kings and republics, but a relatively modest one. It must be viewed in relation to the often dramatic macrochanges in international and domestic strategic, political, economic, and social structure, changing the rules and issues of the political game, the identity of the players, and the value of their resources. Even at the micro level, coalition theory will not take us all the way, by any means. It is a useful device that enables us to spell out coalition options under different assumptions, and their resource and utility properties. But the properties of utilities and resources cannot be captured fully in hard numbers. They have plastic possibilities that a strong will, insight and imagination, and a good sense of timing can enhance, reduce, or otherwise transform.

It is not only the case that rational choice scholars may fudge a bit on the question of the content and realism of their assumptions; in much of their work their inferences turn out to be based more on unacknowledged side assumptions. Thus Herbert Simon (1985), in his comparison of rational choice theory with cognitive "bounded rational choice" theory, comes to the conclusion that

> actors in the political drama do appear to behave in a rational manner—they have reasons for what they do, and a clever researcher can usually obtain data that give good clues as to what those reasons are. But this is very different from claiming that we can predict the behavior of these rational actors by application of the objective rationality principle to the situations in which they

> find themselves. Such prediction is impossible . . . because it depends on their representation of the world in which they live, what they attend to in that world, and what beliefs they have about its nature. (p. 300)

Simon makes the point that rational choice and game-theoretic studies of political phenomena typically rely on assumptions "not derivable from the principle of objective rationality" (p. 298). These assumptions usually have to do with the utility functions of the voters or political actors—their political beliefs, expectations, and calculations—which have to be ascertained empirically.

In a paper titled "Three Fallacies Concerning Majorities, Minorities, and Democratic Politics," Ian Shapiro (1989) makes an argument similar to that made by Herbert Simon. He criticizes the part of the public choice literature that proposes changes in the American Constitution to restrict the scope of governmental power or to require extraordinary majorities before government is able to act. Much of the public choice literature, and particularly that part of it associated with the work of James Buchanan and William Riker, makes additional assumptions regarding the distribution of political resources, as well as transaction costs, that are not factored into their policy conclusions (for example, see Buchanan, 1978; Wagner, 1977; Riker & Weingast, 1986). Thus the argument advanced by Tullock and others that justifies the requirement of extraordinary majorities in order to limit encroachments on private economic concentration is based on erroneous or complacent assumptions as to the distribution of political resources and as to the transaction costs of mobilizing extraordinary majorities. Shapiro attributes a central weakness to the failure of this literature

> to deal with the problem of resources, and we can now see that in so doing it ignores most of what politics is really about. For the sense of powerlessness that sometimes motivates political action, and at other times motivates our intuition that political action is warranted, is exactly the lack of resources of individuals and groups to achieve goods and limit harms on their own. . . . While the public choice theorists are persuasive that there is no reason to expect majority rule to produce fair or just outcomes, this does not supply a rationale for what is often a utilitarian jurisprudence geared toward wealth maximization. (p. 39)

Thus the public choice or rational choice literature may be faulted on the grounds that it often introduces supporting assumptions that are outside the logic of objective rationality, and that it often fails to acknowledge assumptions that are important for their policy conclusions, which may be of doubtful validity. These, of course, are serious criticisms if the rational choice assumption serves as a basis for policy conclusions. Where such an assumption is used heuristically, and where policy implications are related to empirical tests of actual human values and behavior, the rational choice model may play an important constructive role.

Concluding Reflections

There are many examples of the productivity of the rational choice approach. Scholars employing its insights and methods have illuminated aspects of democratic party and electoral systems, legislative organization and process, aspects of peasant politics in the Third World, problems of state building and revolution, and problems of international security and diplomacy. But though rational self-interest is a kind of culture, a kind of approach to valuation, rational choice theory has tended to resist drawing on the knowledge and insights of the social sciences that deal in detail with values and culture. I am not the first to make this observation. In recent years Aaron Wildavsky (1987), Lucian Pye (1987), Ronald Inglehart (1988), and others have argued the same point. One does encounter anthropological, sociological, and psychological propositions and insights among the peripheral rational choice theorists, such as Douglas North, Robert Bates, and Samuel Popkin. Along with this goes a more complex explanatory structure, including cultural and institutional differences.

The failure to relate this economic model of rationality in any way to the sociological, psychological, and anthropological literatures and particularly to the work of Max Weber, whose great theoretical accomplishment was an analysis of modern civilization and culture in terms of rationality and rationalization, is the most striking consequence of the almost complete "economism" of the rational choice literature. One of the major parts of Weber's sociology dealt with the "economic ethics of the world religions." In this careful, systematic comparison of the economic ethics of Buddhism, Confucianism, Hinduism, Islam, Judaism, and Christianity, he explained the origins of modern capitalism by the particular way the Protestant sects associated divine grace and salvation with material success. This theory of the cultural religious origins of "rational self-interest" is alive and kicking today in efforts to explain in part the rapid economic growth of the East Asian NICs (newly industrializing countries) in terms of their Confucian culture.

It was in this connection that Max Weber provided us with a typology of goal-oriented behavior that included—along with the rational self-interest variety, which he called *Zweckrationalitat*, or instrumental behavior—*Wertrationalitat*, or absolute value-oriented behavior, traditional or habitual behavior, and impulsive behavior. From this perspective we can see what a small part of the reality we, as social scientists, want to explain is captured by the rational choice model. In situations where absolute values come into play, where habit and tradition are important, or where affect and emotion are controlling, hardly rare occurrences, a simple rational choice forecast is going to mislead us.

The rational choice school offers us the alternative view of the self-interest assumption that it is simply a rational maximizing assumption, and that it does not have a particular substantive content. As the blank tile in Scrabble can take on the value of any letter, so the rational choice assumption, they seem to be assuring us, can take on the value of any utility imputed to it. Given this viewpoint it is difficult to defend their neglect of the social science literatures that display the variety of values, preferences, and goals in time and space—in different historical periods, in different cultures and societies, and among different social groupings. Though they make a most convincing case for including the "micro level" in the analysis of social and political institutions and processes, and the value of the deductive approach in generating hypotheses explicitly and efficiently, they leave out the disciplines that could specify the content of the utilities that operate at the micro level in different times and places. This failure of rational choice theorists to confront these literatures directly, except in a few recent cases, leaves them with theories that cannot travel very far in space and time, and cannot deal effectively with political change.

References

Adorno, Theodor, Frenkel-Brunswick, Else, Levinson, D. H., & Sanford, Nevitt. (1950). *The authoritarian personality*. New York: Harper & Row.

Almond, Gabriel A., Flanagan, Scott C., & Mundt, Robert. (Eds.). (1973). *Crisis, choice, and change*. Boston: Little, Brown.

Bates, Robert. (1987a). Agrarian politics. In Myron Weiner & Samuel Huntington (Eds.), *Understanding political development*. Boston: Little, Brown.

Bates, Robert. (1987b). *Macro political economy in the field of development* (Working Paper No. 40). Durham, NC: Duke University Program in International Political Economy.

Benedict, Ruth. (1934). *Patterns of culture*. Boston: Houghton Mufflin.

Buchanan, James. (1978). *The economics of politics*. West Sussex: Institute of Economic Affairs.

Buchanan, James, & Tullock, Gordon. (1962). *The calculus of consent.* Ann Arbor: University of Michigan Press.

Buchanan, James, & Wagner, Richard. (1977). *Democracy in deficit.* New York: Academic Press.

de Swann, Abram. (1973). *Coalition theories and cabinet formation.* San Francisco: Jossey-Bass.

Dodd, Lawrence. (1976). *Coalitions in parliamentary government.* Princeton, NJ: Princeton University Press.

Downs, Anthony. (1957). *An economic theory of democracy.* New York: Harper & Row.

Downs, Anthony. (1988). *The evolution of modern democracy.* Unpublished manuscript, Brookings Institution, Washington, DC.

Durkheim, Emile. (1973). *On morality and society.* Chicago: University of Chicago Press.

Ferejohn, John, Cain, Bruce, & Fiorina, Morris. (1987). *The personal vote.* Cambridge, MA: Harvard University Press.

Fiorina, Morris. (1981). *Retrospective voting in American national elections.* New Haven, CT: Yale University Press.

Friedman, Milton. (1953). *Essays in positive economics.* Chicago: University of Chicago Press.

Geertz, Clifford. (1980). *Megara.* Princeton, NJ: Princeton University Press.

Herring, E. P. (1940). *The politics of democracy.* New York: W. W. Norton.

Hovland, Carl. (1953). *Communication and persuasion.* New Haven, CT: Yale University Press.

Inglehart, Ronald. (1988). The renaissance of political culture. *American Political Science Review, 82* (4), 1203–1230.

Key, V. O., Jr. (1942). *Politics, parties and pressure groups.* New York: Crowell.

Kuhn, Thomas. (1962). The structure of scientific revolutions. Chicago: University of Chicago Press.

Laver, Michael, & Schofield, Norman. (1989). *The politics of coalitions in Europe.* New York: Oxford University Press.

Lazarfeld, Paul, & Berelson, Bernard. (1955). *Voting.* Chicago: University of Chicago Press.

Luebbert, Gregory. (1986). *Comparative democracy.* New York: Columbia University Press.

Moe, Terry. (1979). On the scientific status of rational choice theory. *American Journal of Political Science, 23* (1).

North, Douglas. (1981). *Structure and change in economic history.* New York: W. W. Norton.

Parsons, Talcott, & Shils, Edward. (1951). *Toward a general theory of action.* Cambridge, MA: Harvard University Press.

Popkin, Samuel. (1979). *The rational peasant.* Berkeley: University of California Press.

Pye, Lucian. (1987). *The mandarin and the cadre.* Ann Arbor: University of Michigan Press.

Riker, William. (1962). *The theory of coalitions.* New Haven, CT: Yale University Press.

Riker, William, & Ordeshook, Peter. (1973). *An introduction to positive political theory.* Engelwood Cliffs, NJ: Prentice-Hall.

Riker, William, & Weingast, Barry. (1986). *Constitutional regulation of legislative choice: The political consequences of judicial deference to legislatures.* Stanford, CA: Hoover Institution, Stanford University.

Schattschneider, Elmer E. (1960). *The semisovereign people.* New York: Holt, Rinehart & Winston.

Schumpeter, Joseph. (1942). *Capitalism, socialism, and democracy.* New York: Harper & Brothers.

Shapiro, Ian. (1989). Three fallacies concerning majorities, minorities, and democratic politics. In John Chapman & Alan Wertheimer (Eds.), *Majorities and minorities: Political and philosophical perspectives.* New York: New York University Press.

Shepsle, Kenneth, & Fiorina, Morris. (1988). *Is negative voting an artifact?* Stanford, CA: Stanford University, Graduate School of Business.

Shils, Edward, & Janowitz, Morris. (1948). Cohesion and disintegration in the Wehrmacht in World War II. *Public Opinion Quarterly, 12,* 280–315.

Simon, Herbert. (1985). Human nature in politics. *American Political Science Review, 79* (2).

Strom, Kaare. (1983). *Minority government and majority rule.* Unpublished doctoral dissertation, Stanford University, Department of Political Science.

Weber, Max. (1930). *The Protestant ethic and the spirit of modern capitalism.* London: Allen & Unwin.

Weber, Max. (1978). *Economy and society* (Vol. 1, Gunther Roth & Claus Wittich, Eds.). Berkeley: University of California Press.

Wildavsky, Aaron. (1987). Choosing preferences by constructing institutions. *American Political Science Review, 81* (1).

5

The Study of Political Culture

The Prehistory of Political Culture Theory

The effort to explain politics and public policy by political culture theory goes back to the very origins of political science. The Greek and Roman historians, poets, and dramatists comment on the ways in war and peace of the Spartans, Athenians, Corinthians, Parthians, Caledonians, Judeans, and the like. The concepts and categories we use in the analysis of political culture–subculture, elite political culture, political socialization, and culture change–are also implied in ancient and classic writings. The great families and tribes of Athens and Rome had their founder deities, their sacred fires, their traditions, and their civic-political propensities. In the ancient kingdom of Israel at least four elite political cultures were in conflict: the relatively cosmopolitan royal court engaged in war and diplomacy, pitted against the prophets and their supporters affirming and perfecting the Sinaitic revelations and covenant; and the Jerusalem priesthood and temple officialdom pitted against the surviving local cult leaders of the "high places."

The notion of political culture change is one of the most powerful themes of classical literature. Each Greek city-state had its memory of an austere Solonic or Lycurgan past by which to measure the corrupt present. The Catos were celebrators of the frugal, martial, and civic virtues of the early Roman republic. The Greeks had a cyclical theory of political change, and explained the rise and fall of political constitutions in social psychological terms.

Plato (n.d.), in *The Republic*, argues that "governments vary as the dispositions of men vary, and that there must be as many of the one as there are of the other. For we cannot suppose that States are made of 'oak and rock' and not out of the human natures which are in them" (p. 445). There is no stronger argument for the importance of the process of political socialization than Plato's: "Of all animals the boy is the most unmanageable, inasmuch as he has the fountain of reason in him not yet regulated; he is the most insidious, sharp witted, and insubordinate of animals. Wherefore he must be bound by many bridles." Mothers and nurses, fathers, tutors, and political officials all have the obligation to guide and coerce the incorrigible animal into the path of civic virtue.

Aristotle is a more modern and scientific political culturalist than Plato, since he not only imputes importance to political cultural variables, but explicitly treats their relationship to social stratification variables on the one hand and to political structural and performance variables on the other. He argues that the best attainable form of government is the mixed aristocratic-democratic form in a society in which the middle classes predominate. He says:

> The middle amount of all the good things of fortune is the best amount to possess. For this degree of wealth is the readiest to obey reason. . . . And the middle class are the least inclined to shun office and to covet office, and both of these tendencies are injurious to states. . . . those who have an excess of fortune's goods, strength, wealth, friends, and the like, are not willing to be governed. . . . they have acquired this quality even in their boyhood from their homelife, which was so luxurious that they have not gotten used to submitting to authority even in schools, while those who are excessively in need of these things are too humble.

A society in which the middle class is small produces a state "consisting of slaves and masters, not of free men, and of one class envious and another contemptuous of their fellows. This condition is very far removed from friendliness, and from political partnership," which Aristotle (1932) believed to be the cultural basis of the best and most lasting form of government (pp. 329–331).

Plutarch (n.d.), in his biography of Lycurgus, reports how the Spartan lawmaker proposed the engineering of the Spartan character from the moment of birth, so to speak, counseling the women to bathe their newborn sons in wine rather than in water, in order to temper their bodies. The nurses of Sparta used "no swaddling bands; the children grew up free and unconstrained in limb and form, and not dainty or fanciful about their food; not afraid in the dark, or of being left alone; and without peevishness, or ill-humour, or crying" (p. 62).

Machiavelli, Montesquieu, and Rousseau, among others of the later political theorists, contribute to the political culture tradition. Machiavelli and Montesquieu draw lessons from Roman history on the importance of moral and religious values and upbringing for the formation of the Roman character, which in turn explained the steadfast course and remarkable performance in war and in peace of the Republic. With expansion and riches, and the admixture of other cultural strains, came the debasement and collapse of this great empire. But both of these scholars, while emphasizing political cultural and socialization themes, tended to treat them anecdotally and illustratively rather than analytically, as did Plato and Aristotle.

The terms that Rousseau (n.d.) used to identify political culture are *morality, custom*, and *opinion*. He treats these as a kind of law more important than law properly speaking, a kind of law that is

> engraved on the hearts of the citizens. This forms the real constitution of the State, takes on every day new powers, when other laws decay or die out . . . keeps a people in the ways it was meant to go and insensibly replaces authority by the force of habit. I am speaking of morality, of custom, above all of public opinion. (p. 41)

Tocqueville's analysis of American democracy and of the origins of the French Revolution are among the most sophisticated treatments of these themes. In *Democracy in America* (1945) he points out:

> The manners of the people may be considered as one of the great general causes to which the maintenance of a democratic republic in the United States is attributable. I here use the word customs with the meaning which the ancients attached to the word *mores*; for I apply it not only to manners properly so called—that is, to what might be termed the *habits of the heart*—but to the various notions and opinions current among men and the mass of those ideas which constitute their character of mind. I comprise under this term, therefore, the whole moral and intellectual condition of a people. (I, p. 299)

Tocqueville had a similarly keen sense of political subculture. His analysis of the political attitudes of the French peasantry, bourgeoisie, and aristocracy on the eve of the revolution is a similar masterpiece of political culture analysis (see Tocqueville, 1955).

The Enlightenment, Liberalism, and Marxism

If the notion of political culture has in some sense always been with us, how do we explain its sudden popularity in the 1960s and the proliferation of research dealing with it in recent decades? We suggest that the failure of enlightenment and liberal expectations as they related to political development and political culture set the explanatory problem to which political culture research was a response, and the development of social theory in the nineteenth and twentieth centuries, and of social science methodology after World War II (particularly survey methodology), provided the opportunity for solving this problem. The intellectual challenge plus the theoretical developments and methodological inventions explain the emergence of this field of inquiry in its modern form.

By the second half of the nineteenth century these beliefs in intellectual, material, and moral progress, stimulated by the Industrial Revolution, strengthened by the success of political and social reforms in Britain and by the American example, and fortified by the development of evolutionary ideas in biology, took on a sense of inevitability. For liberalism the study of political culture was pointless since all the indicators pointed to the rise of educated, civically oriented, participant societies. Political culture was not problematic. Similarly, for Marxism political culture was not problematic. Marx was surely in the tradition of the enlightenment, save that he arranged the theoretical variables differently and viewed the historical process in dialectic rather than incremental terms. Instead of intellectual improvement pressing forward material and political-moral progress in a benign sequence, material improvement produces three political subcultures: an exploitative and ever concentrating capitalist class; an exploited, propagandized, and coerced working class; and an enlightened organization of revolutionaries. The end result is a universal enlightenment culture and society of mass welfare, rationality, and creativity.

There was, of course, a skeptical and cynical school—Mosca, Pareto, Michels, and others—that attacked both the Marxist and liberal varieties of enlightenment expectations, picturing in their stead a future of permanent elitist exploitation and authoritarian rule based on a different set of psychological and sociological premises. While in England and the United States the more sanguine enlightenment view predominated, there were scholars and publicists such as Graham Wallas (1921) and Walter Lippman (1922) who also challenged the easy assumption of growing mass rationality. But in the decades from the mid-nineteenth century until World War I the processes of enlightenment seemed to be going forward, and the concern with cultural patterns seemed to be in abeyance.

The Rise of Modern Political Culture Research

The enormity and irrationality of World War I, the rise of fascism, more particularly the rise of Nazism, and the climactic destructiveness of World

War II thoroughly shattered these complacent expectations. The effort to find an intellectual solution to these tragic historical puzzles – both the theories and the methods – came primarily out of American social science in the first decades after World War II. In the aftermath of the war, social science was primarily an American enterprise. It had been enriched by German and Italian scholarly refugees who brought with them their sociological, social psychological, and psychoanthropological traditions. We ought not to forget this strong European and particularly German influence on political culture research.

There were three intellectual components that fed into political culture research: the sociological tradition of Weber, Durkheim, Mannheim, Parsons, and others; the social psychological tradition of Graham Wallas, Walter Lippman, William McDougall, E. L. Thorndike, Paul Lazarsfeld, and others; and the psychoanthropological tradition stemming originally from Freud and including Theodore Adorno, Max Horkheimer, Else Fraenkel-Brunswik, Nevitt Sanford, Ruth Benedict, Margaret Mead, Harold Lasswell, Alex Inkeles, Daniel Levinson, and many others.

But most important in the rise of modern political culture research was the development of survey research methodology and technology. As is often the case in the history of science, progress is stimulated more by the development of new technical and empirical capabilities than by substantive theories and hypotheses. Theories remain speculations unless there are rigorous methods of validating them. The revolution in survey research technology had four main components: (1) the development of increasingly precise sampling methods, making it feasible to gather representative data on large populations; (2) the increasing sophistication of interviewing methods to assure greater reliability in the data derived by these methods; (3) the development of scoring and scaling techniques, making it possible to sort out and organize responses in homogeneous dimensions and relate them to theoretical variables; and (4) the increasing sophistication of methods of statistical analysis and inference, moving from simple descriptive statistics to bivariate, multivariate, regression, and causal path analysis of the relations among contextual, attitudinal, and behavioral variables. The invention of survey research technology may be compared to the invention of the microscope, making possible a strongly increased and accurate resolution of biological data in the one, and of social, psychological, and political data in the other.

Three decades after these early developments it is clear that political culture has found its way into the conceptual vocabulary of political science. It is part of the explanatory strategy of political science. It is the occasion for a persisting polemic in the discipline—not as prolific as the pluralism polemic, but quite respectable in the quantitative sense. There are perhaps some 35 or 40 book-length treatments of political culture of an empirical and theoretical sort, perhaps 100 article-length treatments in journals and symposia, and more than 1,000 citations in the literature.

A respectable part of the talent of the profession has been involved in these polemics, including Samuel Beer, Samuel Barnes, Brian Barry, Archie Brown, Dirk Berg-Schlosser, Harry Eckstein, Richard Fagen, Ronald Inglehart, Max Kaase, Dennis Kavanagh, Joseph LaPalombara, Robert Lane, S. M. Lipset, Herbert McCloskey, Carole Pateman, Robert Putnam, Lucian Pye, Irwin Scheuch, Robert Tucker, Aaron Wildavsky, and Stephen White. The broad theme that runs through this literature is the importance of values, feelings, and beliefs in the explanation of political behavior. Political values, feelings, and beliefs are not the simple reflections of social and political structure; nor are they reducible to rational choice individualism. The political content of the minds of citizens and political elites is more complex, more persistent, and autonomous than Marxism, liberalism, and rational choice theory would suggest.

The first social science response to the "German problem" was a psychocultural one. The phenomena of German politics seemed to invite the sciences of the irrational and the nonrational to join forces in efforts to explain them. There is a shelf full of books and journal articles interpreting National Socialism and the "German problem" in psychocultural terms. Psychocultural theory interprets German politics (and Japanese, American, Russian, French, and British politics) in terms of family structure and childhood socialization. It was the German patriarchal, authoritarian family that explained the mix of servile obedience and externalized hostility that produced German nationalism, ethnocentrism, and anti-Semitism. There was little room in this psychocultural interpretation of German politics for adult experience, for the impact of history, and for autonomous cognitive processes.

In this extreme form the psychocultural approach was soon discredited and rejected. We do not read Schaffner's *Fatherland.* (1948) and Rodnick's *Post-War Germans* (1948) anymore. But its stress on the importance of subjective factors in political explanation survives in two research "programs"—leadership studies that continue to emphasize personality factors, and political culture research that is concerned with group propensities and that is based to a substantial extent, though not entirely, on survey research.

Political culture theory defines political culture in this fourfold way: (1)

It consists of the set of subjective orientations to politics in a national population or subset of a national population. (2) It has cognitive, affective, and evaluative components; it includes knowledge and beliefs about political reality, feelings with respect to politics, and commitments to political values. (3) The content of political culture is the result of childhood socialization, education, media exposure, and adult experiences with governmental, social, and economic performance. (4) Political culture affects political and governmental structure and performance—constrains it, but surely does not determine it. The causal arrows between culture and structure and performance go both ways.

Critiques of Political Culture Theory

Political culture theory has been attacked from some four different perspectives. One line of argument, advanced by Brian Barry (1970, pp. 47ff.), and Carole Pateman (1980), attributes to political theory a determinist thrust, assuming that political socialization produces political attitudes, which in turn cause political behavior and underlie political structure. Barry and Pateman make the case that causality can and does work the other way—that institutions and performance influence attitudes. The early advocates of political culture explanation also recognized that causality worked both ways, that attitudes influenced structure and behavior, and that structure and performance in turn influenced attitudes. This was essentially a straw-man polemic.

The Marxist critique, reflected in the work of Jerzy Wiatr (1980) and others, holds that attitude change results from economic and social structural change; in other words, the causal logic works from class structure to political attitudes, political behavior, and structure. Political attitudes have a structurally necessary content, and hence have little independent or autonomous explanatory power. This argument is no longer seriously advanced by contemporary Marxists, who have discovered in recent decades that politics and the state have a degree of autonomy, and that ethnicity, nationality, and religion do not easily give way to resocialization.

A third line of criticism, stemming mainly from students of communism—Richard Fagen (1969), Robert Tucker (1973), Stephen White (1979, 1984), and others—suggests that it is inadmissible to separate political attitudes from behavior. To restrict the concept of political culture to its psychological aspect amounts to a radical "subjectification" of the phenomenon. Such a separation gives a conservative propensity to political culture theory.

It understates the malleability of attitudes in response to structural change. In contrast to the first and second arguments, this point of view preserves the political culture concept, but modifies its content to include behavior. What is overlooked in this critique is the fact that separating the psychological dimension from the behavioral one enables us to ascertain what these relationships really are. Failure to separate them prevents us from exploring the complexities of the relation between political thought and political action.

A fourth line of criticism was advanced by the rational choice or "methodological individualist" school of thought. Ronald Rogowski (1974) and Samuel Popkin (1979) argue that political structure and behavior can be explained by the short-run material interest calculations of political actors. In some versions of this theoretical approach there is no place for values, norms, feelings, and more complex cognitive components. History, memory, and cultural context have no explanatory power. A simple plugging in of rational choice in any political situation gives one all the explanatory power one needs. Others in this school employ the rational choice assumption simply as a heuristic device, as a way of deriving hypotheses systematically and cumulatively, and recognize the explanatory power of cultural and sociological variables.

Persistence and Change in Political Culture

The literature of contemporary political culture scholarship is focused on the experience of three regions: (1) the political culture of advanced industrial societies; (2) the role of political culture in the development of communist societies; and (3) the role of political, economic, and religious culture in the modernization of Asian countries. The first theme really consists of two parts: (a) a literature dealing with findings related to *The Civic Culture* (Almond & Verba, 1963), and a literature dealing with the theme of changing political culture in advanced industrial societies associated primarily with the work of Ronald Inglehart and Samuel Barnes.

Since the publication of *The Civic Culture* in 1963 there have been a substantial number of follow-up studies of political attitudes in the United States, Britain, West Germany, and Italy. Indeed, there have been more than two decades of surveys. Some of these data are included in *The Civic Culture Revisited* (Almond & Verba, 1980). From these and other sources we can get some kind of impression of how stable political culture is, and of the factors that may transform it.

Recent studies of American political culture—including Lipset and Schneider's *The Confidence Gap* (1983), based on several hundred opinion surveys conducted in the United States since the 1940s—show a serious decline in trust and confidence in American political, economic, and social leadership and institutions. The high confidence and legitimacy reported in *The Civic Culture* seem to have been replaced by skepticism as to the effectiveness and integrity of American political, military, economic, and other leaderships. While none of this evidence supports a crisis of legitimacy, surely the United States in the 1980s no longer has the confident civic culture of the early 1960s. And, suggesting how volatile these indicators of trust are, after several years of the Reagan administration, a follow-up study (1985) showed that economic improvement and better leadership morale had reduced this alienation and distrust significantly.

As far as Britain is concerned, Dennis Kavanagh (1980), in *The Civic Culture Revisited*, speaks of a "decline in the deferential and supportive elements" in British political culture in the period from 1960 to 1980. But he points out that there is more dissatisfaction with performance than with the system as a whole. He says that "recent years of slow economic growth have led to greater social tensions, group rivalries, and growing dissatisfaction with incumbent authorities" and that "traditional bonds of social class, party, and common nationality are waning, and with them the old restraints of hierarchy and deference" (p. 170).

Kendall Baker, Russell Dalton, and Kai Hildebrandt (1981), in their analysis of German survey data from the 1950s through the 1970s, document a thorough transformation of German political culture from the apolitical passive pattern pictured in *The Civic Culture*, to the prodemocratic, politicized, and participation-oriented culture of the 1970s and 1980s. Thus the declining civic culture in the United States and Britain and the emerging civic culture in West Germany show political culture to be a relatively soft variable, significantly influenced by historical experience and by governmental and political structure and performance. The trauma of National Socialism, a cunningly engineered governmental and political structure, and an effective economy seem to have produced a stable democracy in Germany. On the other hand, the Vietnam War, the counterculture, and Watergate have seriously undermined the civic culture in the United States; poor economic performance and declining international prestige have also reduced the legitimacy of British political institutions.

The plasticity of political culture in the advanced industrial societies is also suggested by the empirical studies of Ronald Inglehart (1975, 1989), Samuel Barnes and Max Kaase (1979), and their collaborators. Inglehart demonstrates, from a set of surveys he administered in Europe and the United States over a period of more than a decade in the 1970s and early 1980s, that generational changes in the advanced industrial democracies have transformed the policy or issue cultures of these democracies, and that these new issues have begun to modify their party systems. In its first version, Inglehart's theory held that the generations born in Europe and the United States in the post-World War II period up to the mid-1970s had experienced continued peace, rapid economic growth, rising educational opportunities, and increased media exposure. This political socialization tended to downplay the salience of the older issues of economic, political, and military security that had influenced the attitudes of previous generations, and gave salience to a new set of participatory, quality-of-life, and environmental issues. Later, Inglehart's and other surveys during the "stagflation" years of the later 1970s and early 1980s reported a return of economic anxiety, but the newer quality-of-life attitudes survived as well. Barnes and Kaase (1979), in their five-country study of attitudes toward political action, pursuing Inglehart's lead, demonstrate that this new political culture of advanced industrial societies also includes changes in attitudes toward political action—the readiness to resort to unconventional modes of political participation such as demonstrations, marches, sit-ins, and the like, in addition to the conventional modes of political participation. Thus a combination of historical experience and changed political socialization patterns—generational and period effects—have significantly altered the political culture of the advanced democracies.

In his most recent book, Inglehart (1989) draws a balance between continuity and change in the development of European values and attitudes, based on a longitudinal series of surveys extending over more than 15 years:

> Surveys carried out repeatedly over many years show enduring cross-national differences in levels of overall life satisfaction, happiness, political satisfaction, interpersonal trust, and support for the existing social order. These attributes are part of a coherent syndrome, with given nationalities consistently ranking relatively high (or relatively low) on all of them. High or low scores on this syndrome have important consequences for the political and social behavior of given peoples, shaping the prospects for viable democracy, among other things. As we have seen, large cross-cultural differences in this syndrome of attitudes persisted throughout the period from 1973 through 1988; and fragmentary additional evidence suggests that these differences can be traced back into the 1950s. (chap. 13, p. 1)

Inglehart then goes on to point out that there have also been remarkable changes in European attitudes. Thus attitudes in Italy show less distrust than has been true of the past. And he points to the remarkable changes in German political attitudes in the last two decades, associated with rising standards of living and good governmental performance.

If these recent studies of political culture in Europe and the United States suggest that it can change relatively quickly in response to changed circumstances and experience, studies of political attitudes in communist countries suggest the persistence of certain aspects of political culture in the face of very powerful transformative efforts (see, e.g., Almond, 1983; Brown, 1984; Brown & Gray, 1977; White, 1979, 1984). Unfortunately, there is little good survey research available on the political culture of the communist countries, but there is some; and there are other kinds of data from which students of communist countries are able to draw inferences. This literature argues that despite the systematic efforts of communist movements to penetrate, manipulate, organize, indoctrinate, and coerce over a period of several decades, nothing like "socialist man" has emerged. Nationalist feelings have survived in substantial strength; cultural and religious identities persist with great vitality. In countries like Czechoslovakia, which at an earlier time had democratic traditions, these traditions seem to persist, ready to pop out, whenever history makes this possible. In Poland there may very well be stronger liberal currents today than existed in the years of its independence. The communist experience with political culture approximates a set of "crucial case studies" in Eckstein's (1975) sense. If a monopoly control of the media of communication, a monopoly or near monopoly of organization, penetrative police controls, and the like cannot transform values and attitudes, then some explanatory power must be assigned to political culture and the socialization processes that maintain it.

A third set of historical developments – the extraordinary rate of economic growth of the East Asian Confucian countries in contrast with other Asian countries influenced by Islam and Hinduism – also suggests the importance of culture in the shaping of economic and political behavior. Hofheinz and Calder (1982) make the argument that the emphasis on loyalty, education, mutuality, and respect for authority in these areas rests on the norms of Confucianism. Spengler (1980) attributes a market-oriented entrepreneurialism in Japan to Confucian social thought. Bellah (1957) argues that the religious values of the Tokugawa period affected the economic takeoff of the Meiji restoration era. Winston Davis (1987) summarizes some of this literature, offering a modified version of Weber's theory of the relation between the economic ethics of religions and economic growth.

Rather than viewing religious ethics as necessary conditions of economic growth, Davis argues that they may influence economic growth, either by facilitating or tolerating it or by obstructing the development of attitudes and values conducive to economic discipline and performance. The questions we ought to ask, according to Davis, are not of the either/or sort; rather, we should ask, "Has religion motivated economic change? Has it tolerated change? Has it promoted a quiescent acceptance of the social costs imposed by development?" (p. 226). Davis makes a qualified case for the contribution of Confucianism to the strong economic growth propensities of the East Asian countries.

Lucian Pye (1985), in a wide-ranging and imaginative study of culture and politics in Asia, shows how Confucianism, Hinduism, and Islam contribute, though in different ways, to paternalistic, "familistic," consensual, and clientelistic political patterns throughout East, Southeast, and South Asia. He argues that the Asian area may have its own patterns of modernization, that education and economic growth need not necessarily lead to democratization, or, if they do, then it might have these paternalistic, consensual, and clientelistic propensities. The unanticipated reversal of modernization and the emergence of populistic Islamic fundamentalism in Iran and elsewhere in the Middle East similarly argues the strength of traditional political culture and socialization variables.

The Present State of Political Culture Theory

The historical record at first glance would seem to be ambiguous. Political culture on the one hand can change relatively quickly; on the other hand it would seem to be able to take quite a pounding without changing very much. What can we learn from these historical experiences, and from the research that has accumulated in the last several decades, about two of the fundamental questions raised by political culture theory: first, the stability of political culture, its persistence and autonomy, and hence its explanatory significance in political explanation; and second, the relative importance of the factors affecting political culture, in particular the relative importance of early childhood, adult workplace, community, and media experience, and direct experience of political and governmental performance?

On the stability or persistence of political culture, the data we now have suggest that political moods, such as trust in political incumbents and confidence in political and social institutions, seem to be quite changeable, varying with the effectiveness of the performance of these leaders, officers, and agencies. Basic political beliefs and political values are more resistant, though still subject to change. Thus in the United States and Britain in the 1960s and 1970s trust in leaders and confidence in political, economic, and social elites declined sharply. But the evidence did not show any serious attrition in the basic legitimacy of American and British political and social institutions, despite the poor economic and governmental performance experienced in both countries.

The transformation of basic German political attitudes seems to have been accomplished as a consequence of three major causes: (1) the most powerful historical experiences affecting people directly (military collapse, bombing, occupation, partition, forced migration, international humiliation); (2) imaginative constitutional engineering (an electoral system biased in favor of the larger political parties, the constructive vote of nonconfidence, federalism); and (3) a remarkable political and policy performance producing a "miracle" of reconstruction and growth. It is impossible to separate out and assign a specific weight to the role played by changes in basic cultural patterns produced by changes in family structure, childhood socialization, and adult resocialization. All that we can say is that these factors together have produced a changed political culture in West Germany, characterized by democratic and regime legitimacy and a participant political culture.

In the United States the decline of trust and confidence and of consensual politics seems also to have been overdetermined by a costly and demoralizing defeat in the decade-long Vietnam War, by racial conflict on a major scale, by major changes in American social and cultural norms brought about in part by the "counterculture," and by the demoralizing scandals of the Nixon administration. But these powerful impacts have not significantly undermined the legitimacy of American institutions–governmental, political, and economic.

Thus our evidence shows that basic political beliefs such as regime legitimacy have considerable stability. Only catastrophes seem to be able to affect these attitudes in short periods of time; otherwise the rate of change is relatively slow.

Finally, most resistant to change are attitudes, identities, and value commitments associated with ethnicity, nationality, and religion. These are primordial values and commitments that seem to be almost indestructible. It is these primordial values and commitments, and the socialization processes that maintain them, that explain the failure of the Soviet Russian and communist efforts to transform the political cultures of the Eastern European countries, and even in Russia, particularly outside the Great Russian area. But the resistance of political cultures in Eastern Europe is not limited to national, ethnolinguistic, and religious identities. It is argued that in Czechoslovakia liberal political attitudes persist in even greater strength than in the precommunist period; and in Poland it seems that liberal political attitudes are now widespread where there were none before. Political learning cannot be reduced to simple reactivity.

The theory of political socialization has made some progress in the last decades. Generally speaking, there is evidence that family authority has changed in a participatory direction. It is difficult to determine how much of an independent contribution such changes as these may have made to the democratization of political culture in industrial societies, since so many other influences were operative in the same direction during those decades. The evidence also shows that increasing educational levels in advanced industrial societies have raised the proportion of politically efficacious citizens, and transformed the political cultures of advanced industrial societies in a participatory direction (Hyman, 1975).

One of the most significant changes in the political socialization process is the emergence of the electronic media, particularly television. Studies of voting behavior in the United States in the late 1940s and 1950s produced the "two-step flow of communications" theory of Katz and Lazarsfeld (1955). This theory held that the impact of the mass media on attitudes and behavior was mediated by opinion elites—trusted individuals, clergymen, teachers, older family members, and the like. The messages transmitted by the media were interpreted by these opinion leaders, and it was presumed that ordinary people were protected from mass manipulation.

Television has weakened the hold of opinion leaders and has accentuated the importance of the mass media in the shaping of values and attitudes. The greater access that television has to the senses and the rise of influential television commentators and interpreters, according to Austin Ranney (1983), have eroded the importance of the intimate, face-to-face opinion leader, with important consequences for family, community, interest group, and political party cohesion. Sidney Verba and his collaborators (1988), in their recent study of attitudes of elites in the United States, Sweden, and Japan, demonstrate that in all three of these countries the various leading groups of politicians, bureaucrats, business leaders, labor leaders, and the like describe the media as being at the very highest level of political influence. In Verba and Orren's (1985) earlier study of elite attitudes in America, the media were viewed by other elites not only as influential, but as *too* influential. Thus the changing character of the media seems to have changed the relationship between political elites and publics in advanced industrial societies. The amount of discretion accorded to leaders has been reduced; political styles and skills have been transformed.

It is also apparent from German and French political experience that constitutional and political-structural engineering may have significant effects on political culture. German constitutional arrangements have ensured that Bonn was not a repeat of Weimar. Surely German political stability over more than three decades, which is in substantial part attributable to constitutional arrangements, has made an important contribution to the legitimacy of the German system. Similarly, the French experiments with mixed "presidential-parliamentary government" and its electoral system have made an important contribution to the stability and effectiveness of the Fifth Republic, and have reduced French political cynicism and alienation.

Thus the political culture theory that survives today is not the familistic, childhood, and "unconscious"-dominated set of ideas of the 1940s, but rather a theory that emphasizes the cognitive-level attitudes and expectations influenced by the structure and performance of the political system and the economy. But if much of it is fluid and plastic, there are persistent and stable components, such as basic political beliefs and value commitments, and primordial attachments that affect and constrain our political behavior and our public policy.

A System, Process, and Policy Approach to Political Culture

There have been a number of polemics about the content of political culture. What are its components, and how do they relate one to the other? The Fagen-Tucker-White thesis would move us away from conceptual disaggregation, toward a more inclusive concept. Lowell Dittmer (1977) attacks the prevailing definition of political culture as the "subjective perception of an objective political reality" as a blurred conception not distinguished from "political structure on the one hand and political psychology on the other" (p. 581). He proposes a sharper focus for the definition of political culture within the framework of a semiological systems approach. But he acknowledges that the theoretical superiority of such an approach has still to be demonstrated.

In my work with G. Bingham Powell, we have argued that if political culture is the subjective dimension of the political system, then it must be a divisible set of orientations toward the various structures and aspects of the political system (Almond & Powell, 1978). Members of the political system have knowledge of these various parts and structures; they have feelings toward them, and they judge or evaluate them according to various norms. Thus from the separation of the political system into the three levels of system, process, and policy, it follows that every political system has a system, process, and policy culture. System culture consists of knowledge, feelings, and evaluations vis-a-vis the political authorities, the role incumbents; knowledge, feelings, and evaluations toward the regime, that is, the institutional structure; and knowledge, feelings, and evaluations toward the nation. Thus when we talk about the legitimacy of a political system we have to specify whether we are talking about the leaders and the officialdom, the regime, the nation, or some combination of these.

Process culture consists of the knowledge, feelings, and evaluations members of the political system have toward the self as political actor, and toward other political actors, including other political groupings such as parties and interest groups, and specific political and governmental elites. Policy culture consists of the knowledge, feelings, and evaluations members of the political system have toward the outputs of the system – its internal policies (extractive, regulative, and distributive) and its external policies (military, diplomatic, economic).

Disaggregating political culture in these systemic terms enables us to explore the logical or interactive structure of political culture. It may lead us to remedy some of the conceptual shortcomings spelled out by Lowell Dittmer, on the one hand, and at the same time to avoid some of the turgidity of semiology, on the other. It is clear that these three levels of political culture are closely related. At one relatively simpleminded level, it is clear that dissatisfaction with policy outputs is likely to lead to dissatisfaction with the political authorities responsible for those outputs. Dissatisfaction with the political process is likely to lead to dissatisfaction with the regime. Sustained dissatisfaction with policy outputs may, in some kinds of political systems, lead to a change in the political authorities, just as sustained dissatisfaction with the political process may lead to regime or structural change. Deteriorating performance either at the process or the policy level, in countries that include separate ethnic components, may over time lead to a decline in national legitimacy and the rise of autonomy and secessionist movements as in Great Britain, Canada, Spain, and other countries in recent years.

On the other hand, satisfactory and responsive policy and process performance may over time increase the legitimacy of political authorities, of regimes, and of nations. There is something like a process of capital accumulation and depletion in this interaction between process and policy performance and system legitimacy.

Treating political culture in terms of these three levels illuminates some aspects of political strategy. Threats to a regime by virtue of process dissatisfaction may be dealt with directly, as was the case in the process of democratization in Britain in the nineteenth century. The bargaining process turned not on the either/or question of universal suffrage, but rather on limited enfranchisements, step by step, that were responsive to the most mobilized sections of the population. The Bismarck strategy in Germany bought off popular demands for full enfranchisement on the part of the middle and working classes by shrewd policy inducements – welfare policy for the working class, trade policy for the industrialists and large landowners, and an aggressive foreign policy for everyone. This Bismarckian strategy of using distributive policy as a way of mitigating and containing demands for participation has been followed in a number of contemporary Third World countries – in particular South Korea and Taiwan.

A systemic approach to political culture research, along such lines as these, has the virtue of keeping it firmly grounded in the structure and performance of the political system. It lends itself to formal, logical analysis, and generates interesting hypotheses on important aspects of politics.

References

Almond, Gabriel A. (1983) "Communism and Political Culture Theory." *Comparative Politics* 13 (January).

Almond, Gabriel A., and G. Bingham Powell (1978) *Comparative Politics: System, Process, Policy*. Boston: Little, Brown.

Almond, Gabriel A., and Sidney Verba, eds. (1963) *The Civic Culture*. Princeton, NJ: Princeton University Press.

Almond, Gabriel A., and Sidney Verba, eds. (1980) *The Civic Culture Revisited*. Boston: Little, Brown.

Aristotle (1932) *Politics* (H. Rackham, trans.). London: Heineman.

Baker, Kendall, Russell Dalton, and Kai Hildebrandt (1981) *Germany Transformed*. Cambridge, MA: Harvard University Press.

Barnes, Samuel, and Max Kaase (1979) *Political Action: Mass Participation in Five Western Democracies*. Beverly Hills, CA: Sage.

Barry, Brian (1970) *Sociologists, Economists and Democracy*. London: Macmillan.

Bellah, Robert N. (1957) *Tokugawa Religion*. Boston: Beacon.

Brown, Archie, ed. (1984) *Political Culture and Communist Studies*. New York: M. E. Sharpe.

Brown, Archie, and Jack Gray, eds. (1977) *Political Culture and Political Change in Communist States*. New York: Holmes & Meier.

Davis, Winston (1987) "Religion and Development: Weber and the East Asian Experience." In

Myron Weiner and Samuel Huntington, eds., *Understanding Political Development*. Boston: Little, Brown.

Dittmer, Lowell (1977) "Political Culture and Political Symbolism." *World Politics* 30 (July).

Eckstein, Harry (1975) "Case Studies in Political Explanation." In Fred I. Greenstein and Nelson W. Polsby, eds., *Handbook of Political Science* (Vol. 7). Reading, MA: Addison-Wesley.

Fagen, Richard (1969) *The Transformation of Political Culture in Cuba*. Stanford, CA: Stanford University Press.

Hofheinz, Roy, and Kent Calder (1982) *The East-Asia Edge*. New York: Basic Books.

Hyman, Herbert (1975) *The Enduring Effects of Education*. Chicago: University of Chicago Press.

Inglehart, Ronald (1975) *The Silent Revolution: Changing Values and Political Style Among Western Publics*. Princeton, NJ: Princeton University Press.

Inglehart, Ronald (1989) *Changing Culture*. Princeton, NJ: Princeton University Press.

Katz, Elihu, and Paul Lazarsfeld (1955) *Personal Influence: The Part Played by People in the Flow of Mass Communications*. Glencoe, IL: Free Press.

Kavanagh, Dennis (1980) "Political Culture in Britain: The Decline of the Civic Culture." In Gabriel A. Almond and Sidney Verba, eds., *The Civic Culture Revisited*. Boston: Little, Brown.

Lipset, S. M. (1985) "The Confidence Gap: Down But Not Out." Unpublished manuscript.

Lipset, S. M., and William Schneider (1983) *The Confidence Gap*. New York: Free Press.

Pateman, Carole (1980) "The Civic Culture: A Philosophical Critique." In Gabriel A. Almond and Sidney Verba, eds., *The Civic Culture Revisited*. Boston: Little, Brown.

Plato (n.d.) *The Works of Plato* (Jowett, trans.). New York: Dial.

Plutarch (n.d.) *The Lives of the Ancient Greeks and Romans* (John Dryden, trans.). New York: Random House.

Popkin, Samuel (1979) *The Rational Peasant*. Berkeley: University of California Press.

Pye, Lucian W. (1985) *Asian Power and Politics: The Cultural Dimensions of Authority*. Cambridge, MA: Belknap Press of Harvard University Press.

Ranney, Austin (1983) *Channels of Power*. New York: Basic Books.

Rodnick, David (1948) *Post-War Germans*. New Haven, CT: Yale University Press.

Rogowski, Ronald (1974) *Rational Legitimacy*. Princeton, NJ: Princeton University Press.

Rousseau, Jean Jacques (n.d.) *The Social Contract*. New York: Carlton House.

Schaffner, Bertram (1948) *Fatherland: A Study of Authoritarianism in the German Family*. New York: Columbia University Press.

Spengler, Joseph (1980) *Origins of Economic Thought and Justice*. Carbondale: Illinois University Press.

Tocqueville, Alexis de (1945) *Democracy in America*. New York: Knopf.

Tocqueville, Alexis de (1955) *The Old Regime and the French Revolution*. Garden City, NY: Doubleday.

Tucker, Robert C. (1973) "Culture, Political Culture, and Communist Society." *Political Science Quarterly* (June).

Verba, Sidney (1965) "Germany: The Remaking of Political Culture." In Lucian Pye and Sidney

Verba, *Political Culture and Political Development*. Princeton, NJ: Princeton University Press.

Verba, Sidney (1988) *Elites and the Idea of Equality*. Cambridge, MA: Harvard University Press.

Verba, Sidney, and Gary Orren (1985) *Equality in America: The View from the Top*. Cambridge, MA: Harvard University Press.

Wallas, Graham (1921) *Human Nature in Politics*. New York: Knopf.

White, Stephen (1979) *Political Culture and Soviet Politics*. London: Macmillan.

White, Stephen (1984) "Political Culture in Communist States." *Comparative Politics* 14 (April).

Wiatr, Jerzy (1980) "The Civic Culture from a Marxist Sociological Perspective." In Gabriel A. Almond and Sidney Verba, eds., *The Civic Culture Revisited*. Boston: Little, Brown.

6

Communism and Political Culture Theory

A Test of Political Culture Theory

The success or failure of communist regimes in transforming the attitudes and behavior of populations may constitute a test of the explanatory power of political culture theory.[1] We may view communist regimes as "natural experiments" in attitude change. Such regimes seek and usually succeed in establishing organization and communication media monopolies, as well as penetrative police and internal intelligence systems. Ideological conformity is rewarded; deviation is heavily penalized. Communities and neighborhoods come under the surveillance of party activists. Children of all ages are organized in party-related formations, and school instruction places emphasis on appropriate ideological indoctrination. In addition to this powerful array of institutional and communication controls, the communist movement has a clear-cut, explicit set of attitudes, beliefs, values, and feelings that it seeks to inculcate.

Political culture theory imputes some importance to political attitudes, beliefs, values, and emotions in the explanation of political, structural, and behavioral phenomena—national cohesion, patterns of political cleavage, modes of dealing with political conflict, the extent and the character of participation in politics, and compliance with authority. Political culture has never seriously been advanced as the unidirectional "cause" of political structure and behavior, although political culture theorists have been represented as taking such a position by some critics.[2] The relaxed version of political culture theory—the one presented by most of its advocates—is that the relation between political structure and culture is interactive, that one cannot explain cultural propensities without reference to historical experi-

---

From Gabriel A. Almond, "Communism and Political Culture Theory," *Comparative Politics*, Vol. 13, No. 1.

ence and contemporary structural constraints and opportunities, and that, in turn, a prior set of attitudinal patterns will tend to persist in some form and degree and for a significant period of time, despite efforts to transform it. All these qualifications and claims are parts of political culture theory. The argument would be that however powerful the effort, however repressive the structure, however monopolistic and persuasive the media, however tempting the incentive system, political culture would impose significant constraints on effective behavioral and structural change because underlying attitudes would tend to persist to a significant degree and for a significant period of time. This is all that we need to demonstrate in order to make a place for political culture theory in the pantheon of the explanatory variables of politics.

The communist experience is particularly important as an approach to testing political culture theory because from one point of view it represents a genuine effort to "falsify" it. The attitudes that communist movements encounter in countries where they take power are viewed as false consciousness—whether they be nationalism, religious beliefs, liberal-pluralistic views, ethnic subcultural propensities, or attitudes toward economic interests. These attitudes are viewed as the consequences of preexisting class structure and the underlying mode of production, as transmitted by associated agents of indoctrination. Communist movements either eliminate or seek to undermine the legitimacy of these preexisting structures and processes and replace them with a quite new and thoroughly penetrative set. If they succeed in some reasonable length of time—let us say, a generation—in transforming attitudes in the desired direction, we might conclude that political culture theory has been falsified, that it is a weak variable at best.

Surely communist takeovers are the best historical experiments we have for these purposes. In addition, there are quite a few of them; they have occurred in different cultural-developmental settings; and most of them have been in operation for a generation. The principal problem with this approach to testing theory is that it leaves much to be desired as an experimental test. The "laboratories" are not open to investigators; the data are spotty and in large part inferential. And finally the scale and the intensity of the efforts undertaken to change attitudes have varied from one country to another. The experiences of Poland, Hungary, and Czechoslovakia are quite different from those of the Soviet Union, Cuba, and Yugoslavia.

One further intriguing point about this topic is that it represents a good illustration of a payoff for theory derived from area case studies. From this point of view the reader should not expect a contribution to the depth of knowledge about an area but an exploitation of findings in an effort to develop theory.

Political Culture Theory in Marxism and Leninism

This utilization of communist experience to test political culture theory fits congenially into the great themes of Marxist and Leninist ideology. The term has come into increasing usage in Soviet and East European social science. Stephen White notes that Lenin employed the term and that Brezhnev used it also.[3] Georgi Shaknazarov, the president of the Soviet Political Science Association, in an article published in *Pravda* on January 17, 1979, announcing the meeting of the International Political Science Association in Moscow, listed political culture as one of the three major subjects of political science. He defined political culture as "the participation of diverse social opinions in politics, the political culture of the people and political culture training, the regulation of social-political attitudes." He presented this topic as being at the same level of importance as the study of the state and the political system and the study of foreign policy and international relations.

Aside from such indications of terminological receptivity, the phenomena of political culture have been accorded an important place in communist theory, although the terms employed by Marx, Lenin, and contemporary communist scholars are *ideology, consciousness, spontaneity, economism*, and the like. In the works of Marx and Engels, political culture phenomena are important intervening variables; in Leninist theory political culture – in particular, elite political culture – is the independent variable. Indeed, an elite possessed of a particular political culture in the sense of an indoctrinated communist party and an "objective revolutionary situation" very broadly defined are the necessary and sufficient conditions of communist revolution. No one can read Lenin's organizational text, *What Is to Be Done*, without becoming aware of how much importance he attached to the proper indoctrination of the communist party, the unambiguous explication of beliefs, procedures, and appropriate affective modalities.

For Marx, a changed political consciousness was a consequence of underlying structural alterations – it developed gradually at first and changed its cognitive content and affective tone as the means of production and class characteristics and relations changed. Marx predicted that at certain points in the historical process, for example, at the point of extreme proletarian "immiseration," the cultural transformation would be more rapid. Although the concepts of political socialization and elite political culture are present in Marxism, they are not well developed. According to Marx, capitalist ideology gradually loses its force as its deviation from reality becomes increasingly plain. Men are rational actors; the leaders "catch on" first, the followers soon after. The transformation of political culture occurs in bursts and is congruent with major structural changes – the dictatorship of the proletariat, the introduction of socialism and of communism. The learning process may be slow, but it is sure.

Marxism is thus a structural theory. Marx would probably have sided with Brian Barry, Carole Pateman, and Ronald Rogowski about the priority of structure in the causal interaction with attitude, belief, and feeling. Changes in culture follow inevitably from changes in structure; cultural properties have a consequential relation to structure. Attitudinal variables explain *lead* and *lag* in the processes of historical change and hence may be viewed as intervening rather than independent variables.

It is clear from the Leninist strategy of elite and mass political socialization that Lenin understood the interactive character of structural-cultural relationships. He believed in the possibility of indoctrinating a revolutionary elite, in other words, transforming its political culture. But he did not believe that the revolutionary indoctrination of the masses was possible. Ordinary workers and peasants had to be manipulated into revolution through appeals to their immediate values and interests; that is, the revolutionary elite would have to adapt their revolutionary tactics to the cultures of the masses. Lenin expected that once a revolution had been attained these subcultural tendencies among the workers, peasants, and ethnic and religious groups would persist for some unknown length of time until the communist millennium, which would be brought about by fundamental structural changes.

In the Marxism-Leninism currently explicated in the theoretical and "social science" literature of socialist countries, the full conceptual framework of political culture theory is employed. It is easy to see why the term has been adopted by socialist social scientists. Although the term *subculture* was not employed until recently, it has always been assumed that each class under capitalism has its own subculture, which, in turn, imposes a constraint on communist strategy and tactics. The peasantry under capitalism can be mobilized for land reform but not for socialism. Even under socialism, residual peasant proprietary attitudes persist and impose limits on policy. The working class is inclined toward "bread-and-butter" economic goals, not socialist ones, and the persistence of such residual attitudes under socialism affects productivity and public policy. An incentive system inconsistent with the egalitarian values of communism must be continued to take account of these propensities. Professionals and technical specialists continue to be seduced by the values and special interests of their professions; these cultural propensities persist under socialism and explain the continuous struggles between the party and various specialists in the bureaucracy and the society.

Ethnicity as an ineradicable basis of subculture manifests itself, according to Marxist-Leninist doctrine, in secessionist and autonomist tendencies. Under capitalism, ethnicity can be mobilized in the form of liberation movements affiliated with or led by indoctrinated communists. Under socialism, ethnicity persists, justifying federal governmental arrangements. Ethnic subcultural identities as expressed in linguistic, literary, and cultural forms, as well as cuisine, costumes, festivals, and the like, are acknowledged as legitimate and reconcilable with socialist universalism. Religious subcultures are viewed as basically reactionary formations fostering vestigial attitude patterns. Accommodations to religious communities under socialism, in contrast to ethnicity, are expedient and are entered into only on tactical political grounds.

The theme of political culture change is a powerful one in Leninist theory. Certain attitudinal changes are assumed to occur in the transition from feudal forms of the political economy to capitalist forms and from early capitalist forms to later ones. After a communist revolution takes place, certain attitude changes are supposed to accompany the shift from the period of the proletarian dictatorship to the period of socialism, and a set of related structural and cultural changes is assumed to be associated with the shift from socialism to communism.

Marxist-Leninist theory has well-articulated views on the agents and the processes of political socialization. All the agents of socialization treated in the Western socialization literature are to be found in the socialist literature. Family, church, school, workplace, interest group, political party, the media of communication, local government, and government output and performance are all recognized as having some impact on political attitudes and culture. The principal distinction made in Leninist theory is between those agents of socialization that foster traditional patterns of political culture and those that foster rational and appropriate ones. Families, religious bodies, ethnic communities, professional groups, and face-to-face communication media outside the Communist party and related organizations tend to foster residual cultural tendencies, whereas schools, the Communist party and related organizations, and the mass media of communication are the principal agents of appropriate political socialization.

Political Culture in Communist Reality

If we turn from ideological formulations to the political reality of Eastern Europe, the picture we get of political attitudes and values is a complex and varied one. We may perhaps distinguish three versions of political culture in communist countries: (1) the official or ideological political culture that is a mix of exhortation and imputation, (2) the operational political culture or what the regime is prepared to tolerate and believes it has succeeded in attaining, and (3) the real political culture based on the evidence such as opinion surveys and other kinds of research or on inferences drawn from the media or official statements. The distinctions among these three versions of political culture need to be elaborated. All communist regimes have some version of the Leninist ideological culture, although in those countries that made their own revolutions (e.g., Yugoslavia, China, and Cuba), the political culture may deviate from the ideal model, from the Soviet version, and from the versions in those countries dominated by the Soviet Union. The operational political culture consists of values, attitudes, and feelings that the regime is prepared to tolerate at least in the short run, given the universal shortfall from the ideological model in all communist countries. This operational model may encompass the extreme of Hungary, where Kadar's slogan of the 1960s, "He who is not against us is with us," represents a substantial admission of defeat in efforts undertaken to produce positive culture transformation, to the situation in the Soviet Union, where the operational expectations are a good deal more positive and are in part supported by reality.

The difference between what is sometimes called the operational political culture and the real political culture is defined in a sense by the battleground between the regimes' immediate campaigns and efforts to change attitudes, behavior, beliefs, and the affective tone of the population. From this point of view we can argue that Kadar's slogan is an acknowledgment that the Communist party of Hungary had failed to falsify political culture theory or that the "Czech Spring" is dramatic evidence of a similar sort that a score of years of organizational and media monopoly, repression and terror, and powerful incentives had failed to alter in any significant degree the civic propensities of the Czechoslovak population. Insofar as the operational political culture itself acknowledges the resistance it is encountering and in the degree that it has lowered its sights from some reasonable approximation of a Marxist-Leninist culture, we can argue that political culture theory survives unfalsified. If in addition evidence of a direct sort points to the fact that attitudes and beliefs among the population fall significantly short of this official operational political culture, then we have even stronger confirmation of the validity of political culture theory.

The ideological political culture in every communist country posits an ideal communist man who is both the builder of the new society and a product of its institutions and practices. The fullest elaboration of the qualities of this ideal communist man is to be found in the Program of the Communist party of the Soviet Union adopted by the 22nd Congress in 1961, in a section entitled "The Moral Code of the Builder of Communism." Some version of this moral code (or something very similar in the values and qualities stressed) is to be found in a central place in the most important ideological formulations, training manuals, schoolbooks, and the like of all the communist countries. The qualities stressed include "dedication to the Communist cause; love for the socialist motherland and other socialist countries; conscientious labor for the good of society; a high consciousness of social duty; collectivism and comradely mutual assistance and respect; moral integrity in public and private life; intolerance of injustice, dishonesty or careerism; friendship and brotherhood with the other peoples of the USSR, and solidarity with the workers and peoples of other countries; and firm opposition to the enemies of communism, peace and freedom."[4]

The evidence does not suggest that any of the communist regimes has succeeded in inculcating these values among significant parts of the population. Even in the Soviet Union, where the regime has been in substantial control of the population for two full generations and where the revolution was led by an indigenous elite, the extent of success in remodeling man has been relatively modest. Samuel Huntington's claim that the Soviet Union is a dramatically successful case of planned political culture change would seem to be exaggerated.[5] This is not to argue that there have been no positive accomplishments in culture change. The Soviet regime has widespread legitimacy; its centralized, penetrating, and relatively unlimited institutions are accepted. A diffuse notion of socialism has widespread validity, and the acceptance of the obligation of sociopolitical activism in the sense of participating in campaigns has strong and widespread support. But these limited successes in the center of the communist world hardly extend into the countryside, into the blue-collar, relatively uneducated working class, or into the non-European parts of Russia. It can be argued that particularly in Asiatic Russia, where traditional religious attitudes and ethnic nationalism display considerable staying power, Soviet indoctrinators have had to come to terms with stubborn traditionalism of various kinds.[6] Much of the legitimacy of the Soviet regime, one writer argues, results from the fact that the structure of the Soviet system is very much like the preexisting Tsarist one in the sense of centralization, the extensive scope of government, and its arbitrariness. The acceptance of socialism as well as the obligation of sociopolitical activism is the success story of communist political socialization, but these attitudes tend to be concentrated in the European center and among the educated, professional, and white-collar strata of the population.[7] Political activism in this context should not be confused with civic and political participation; instead, it takes the form of mobilized activity and voluntary public service. One writer has described Soviet participation in the following terms: "The many political and administrative activities in which Soviet citizens participate take place within a dual framework of control. The hierarchical structure of the Soviets, and of the Soviet political system in general, serves to coordinate the agenda and priorities of the participatory organs at any given moment, concentrating them on centrally determined goals, while the supervision of Communist party organs provides control of staffing, leadership selection, and auditing of the quality of activities."[8]

This contrast between the ideological and the operational political culture creates a certain tension among communist ideologists and students of public opinion and the media of communication. With the introduction of public opinion research in the Soviet Union and Eastern Europe in the 1960s, the problem of opinion and attitude differences had to be confronted, for it produced a polemic of modest proportions among "monists" and "pluralists." A. K. Uledov, a Soviet interpreter of public opinion who presents a monist point of view, argued that deviations in opinion from the ideological model reflect a lag between the old and the new, between progressive and backward forces. Proponents of a pluralist point of view, reflected in the writing of Grushin and to a much greater extent in the work of Polish, Czechoslovak, and Yugoslav scholars, argue that under socialism, nonconforming opinion may contribute to social progress. Thus the pluralist attempt to legitimate oppositional and critical tendencies, thereby reducing the tensions among the ideological, the operational, and the real political cultures, tends to reduce the ideological model to that of a credo by adopting an operative normative model more reconcilable with reality. This treatment of pluralism as legitimate, however, is distinctly a minor theme in the more conservative communist regimes, having surfaced primarily in such countries as Poland, Czechoslovakia, and Yugoslavia.[9]

In testing political culture theory in communist countries it is useful to sort them into three categories: (1) the Soviet Union itself, where the communist "experiment" began and was carried through by an indigenous communist elite; (2) other countries such as Yugoslavia, China, Cuba, and

Vietnam, where the communist revolution was imported and carried out by indigenous elites; and (3) countries such as Poland, Hungary, Czechoslovakia, Romania, and East Germany, where communist regimes were imposed from the outside. For our purposes in this chapter we will examine briefly the experience of (1) the Soviet Union, (2) Yugoslavia and Cuba, and (3) Poland, Hungary, and Czechoslovakia. If political culture theory is to be falsified, we would expect to see major change in political culture in the desired direction in all three categories and to a larger degree in the case of the Soviet Union because its revolution was indigenous and has been in operation more than sixty years; to a substantial degree in Yugoslavia and Cuba because their revolutions were made by indigenous elites; and to a lesser in Poland, Hungary, and Czechoslovakia because their communist regimes, which have been in existence for only a single generation, were imposed on them from the outside and have been maintained by the threat or the actuality of Soviet military occupation.

Political Culture in Yugoslavia and Cuba

In the case of Yugoslavia it may be inappropriate to speak of three versions of political culture. The Leninist ideological version is not seriously propagated. The operational version is a relatively loosely formulated set of norms and expectations that on the basis of empirical evidence are not too far from the reality of opinion and attitude. These norms include an acceptance of ethnic identity and of political autonomy of the various ethnic components, an acceptance of private landownership among the peasantry, and of religious freedom. The two new elements in Yugoslav political culture are political activism and participation and enterprise self-management, which ideologically is supposed to represent the fulfillment of the ideal of participation and the essence of Yugoslav democratic socialism. Here one can distinguish a difference between the official political culture and the real political culture. The official political culture sanctions "classlessness" in participatory patterns; but much evidence that has been gathered from studies of political recruitment and opinion surveys demonstrates that political participation in the sense of officeholding and other forms of activism is biased toward the upper social and economic groupings in the population and is dominated by members of the League of Communists. Enterprise self-management appears to be effective. It involves all levels of workers in matters having to do with wages, hours, conditions of labor, and similar trade union issues but not in production and other management decisions.[10]

Thus the political leadership of Yugoslavia has settled for a set of operational political cultural norms that accommodate prerevolutionary ethnic, religious, and economic propensities and the socialization agencies that tend to perpetuate them. The novel elements of participation and decentralized socialism have been accepted in a limited way, particularly among the educated, advantaged, and politically mobilized strata of the population.

In contrast to Yugoslavia, another country that made its own revolution – Cuba – has been subjected to concentrated indoctrination designed to produce a new "Cuban socialist man." This ideological political culture differs from the Leninist one in its lack of emphasis on the "party" and its greater emphasis on heroism, selflessness, *personalismo*, and the propaganda of the deed. It appears to draw on a Latin American revolutionary tradition as much as on specifically Leninist ideological norms. In two decades of Cuban communism, these ideals have been propagated in connection with major campaigns of mobilization for purposes of defense, literacy, sugar cane harvesting, and revolutionary-military activities abroad. Such evidence as we have from reports and surveys of one kind or another suggests that these campaigns have had moderate success in creating regime legitimacy, the acceptance of the norm of activism in the implementation of goals, and the acceptance of socialism in the diffuse sense of that term. In recent years there is evidence of growing bureaucratization, less stress on utopian ideals and mass mobilization, and more stress on efficiency and regimentation. A pattern similar to that in the Soviet Union, in which the utopian culture of the socialist man takes on the proportions of an eschatology and the operational political culture stresses compliance with the regime's policies and programs, may emerge. Real popular values and attitudes may increasingly take the form of adaptations to constraints and incentives as well as according legitimacy to the new institutions.[11]

Thus our three cases of indigenous communist revolutions – the Soviet Union, Yugoslavia, and Cuba – fail to falsify political culture theory. The revolutionary aims of creating a "socialist man" have been practically given up in the Soviet Union and Cuba and were never seriously pursued in Yugoslavia. The Soviet Union has settled for popular legitimacy, a general belief in socialism, and a willingness to participate in campaigns initiated by the regime. The Yugoslav political elite has tended to accommodate itself to powerful ethnic commitments, peasant proprietary values, and religious beliefs and has successfully inculcated a sense of legitimacy, an acceptance of decentralized socialism, and an obligation to participate.

In the case of Cuba, a personalist version of Leninism seems to be giving way to a more bureaucratic, apathetic relationship between elite and mass, with positive culture changes taking such forms as regime legitimacy, a belief in "socialism," and an acceptance in some sense of the obligation to take part in campaigns.

The changes that have taken place under these relatively favorable circumstances are of a limited sort, not of sufficient magnitude and character to falsify political culture theory and accord validity to a structural one.

The Cases of Poland, Hungary, and Czechoslovakia

The communist experiences in Poland, Hungary, and Czechoslovakia offer even stronger supports for political culture theory. Communist parties have been in control in all three countries for over thirty years, and Soviet troop deployments and the Brezhnev Doctrine impose constraints on their policies. Despite these penetrative pressures and external threats and constraints, prerevolutionary nationalist, religious, economic, and political attitudes have persisted and have resulted in the renunciation of sanguine expectations of fundamental attitude change. Were the Soviet threat to be neutralized, there is little doubt that liberal regimes, even ones initiated by the communist parties (as was the case in Czechoslovakia in 1967–68), would be established. Communist efforts at resocialization might have been counterproductive in the sense of having created strong liberal propensities in countries such as Poland and Hungary where those orientations were relatively weak in the prerevolutionary era.

In Poland after thirty years of revolutionary experience, something like a legitimate pluralist regime emerged in 1981, which allowed the new Solidarity union, the Catholic church, and the army to engage in bargaining relations with the Communist party. As of this writing it is not clear which arrangements will survive the martial-law regime. On the positive side, there is evidence of an acceptance of a diffuse egalitarian socialism among a large proportion of the Polish population. But the evidence is overwhelming that the Polish working class continues to be passionately Polish, Catholic, and "bread and butter" oriented.[12]

In Hungary, peasant proprietary attitudes, reflected in surveys showing that private garden plots and household improvements are the preoccupations of most of the agricultural population, remain strong. Similarly, religious attitudes remain strong even among young people. Hungarian nationalism shows no signs of abating. One writer described the legitimacy of the communist regime in Hungary in the following terms: "The current standoff in Hungary between elites and potential publics is tenuous, but it appears as if everyone fears the hazards of questioning the situation too closely."[13] Although most Hungarians accept an egalitarian socialism, there is little acceptance of Marxism-Leninism among the population. In Hungary, the reaction to ideological indoctrination takes the form of a thoroughgoing depoliticization.[14]

Of all the communist cases, that of Czechoslovakia presents the strongest support for political culture theory. As one writer observed of the period after 1948, "Neither the new economic base nor the new institutional structures succeeded in changing the political cultures of Czechs and Slovaks in the direction which the holders of institutional power desired. If anything, the opposite happened. The old values and beliefs were reinforced . . . If a Czech 'new man' had been created by 1968, he was, ironically, one more firmly devoted to social democratic and libertarian values than the Czech of 1946. In the interactions between structures and cultures it would appear that the dominant Czech political culture came much closer to changing Czechoslovak Communism than Czechoslovak Communism came to procuring acceptance of its official culture."[15]

What the scholarship of comparative communism has been telling us is that political cultures are not easily transformed. A sophisticated political movement ready to manipulate, penetrate, organize, indoctrinate, and coerce and given an opportunity to do so for a generation or longer ends up as much or more transformed than transforming. But we have to be clear about what kind of a case we are making for political culture theory. We are not arguing at all that political structure, historical experience, and deliberate efforts to change attitudes have no effect on political culture. Such an argument would be manifest foolishness. Major scholarly efforts such as those of Alex Inkeles and David H. Smith and Herbert Hyman demonstrate the powerful and homogenizing effects of education, the introduction of the mass media, and factory employment in very different cultural contexts.[16] There is a major literature of experimental studies on some of the conditions and possibilities of attitude change. What all this seems to demonstrate is that man is a complex animal who is tractable in some respects and intractable in others. Both the successes and the failures of our communist cases suggest that there is a pattern to this tractability-intractability behavior, that liberty once experienced is not quickly forgotten, and that equity and equality of some kind resonate in the human spirit.

Notes

1. This is a position argued by a number of British specialists on communist countries. See Archie Brown and Jack Gray, *Political Culture and Political Change in Communist States*

(New York: Holmes & Meier, 1977); also, Stephen White, *Political Culture and Soviet Politics* (London: Macmillan, 1979). We have benefited greatly from these studies and conclusions.

2. See inter al. Brian M. Barry, *Sociologists, Economists, and Democracy* (London: Collier-Macmillan, 1970), 48ff.; Carole Pateman, "The Civic Culture: A Philosophical Critique" in Gabriel A. Almond and Sidney Verba (eds.), *The Civic Culture Revisited* (Boston, MA: Little, Brown, 1980); and Ronald Rogowski, *A Rational Theory of Legitimacy* (Princeton, NJ: Princeton University Press, 1976).
3. Brown and Gray, *Political Culture and Political Change*, 58. See also White's book-length treatment of this subject, *Political Culture and Soviet Politics.*
4. Stephen White, in Brown and Gray, *Political Culture and Political Change*, 35–36.
5. See White, *Political Culture and Soviet Politics*, 114ff.
6. Ibid., 95; see also Gregory J. Massell, *The Surrogate Proletariat: Moslem Women and Revolutionary Strategies in Soviet Central Asia, 1919–1929* (Princeton, NJ: Princeton University Press, 1974), 322ff.
7. White, *Political Culture and Soviet Politics*, chaps. 3 and 4. For a detailed analysis of participation in the Soviet Union, see Theodore H. Friedgut, *Political Participation in the USSR* (Princeton, NJ: Princeton University Press, 1979), chap. 1 and pp. 307ff.
8. Ibid., 49. The Soviet regime has succeeded in inculcating a sense of "participatory-subject competence," particularly among the educated strata of the society. See Gabriel A. Almond and Sidney Verba (eds.), *The Civic Culture* (Princeton, NJ: Princeton University Press, 1963), and citations and discussions in Friedgut, *Political Participation*, 319ff.
9. Walter D. Connor and Zvi Gitelman, *Public Opinion in European Socialist Systems* (New York: Praeger, 1977), chap. 1.
10. David Dyker in Brown and Gray, *Political Culture and Political Change*, chap. 3; Jan Triska and Paul M. Cocks (eds.), *Political Development in Eastern Europe* (New York: Praeger, 1977), 158ff.
11. See Richard R. Fagen, *The Transformation of Political Culture in Cuba* (Stanford, CA: Stanford University Press, 1969); Jorge I. Dominguez, *Cuba: Order and Revolution* (Cambridge, MA: Belknap Press of Harvard University Press, 1978), chap. 12; Francis Lambert, "Cuba: Communist State in Personal Dictatorship," in Brown and Gray, *Political Culture and Political Change*, chap. 8.
12. See Connor and Gitelman, *Public Opinion*, chap. 2 and pp. 184ff; Brown and Gray, Political Culture and Political Change, chap. 4; Triska and Cocks, *Political Development*, chap. 5.
13. Gitelman, in Connor and Gitelman, *Public Opinion*, 161.
14. See also Brown and Gray, *Political Culture and Political Change*, chap. 5; Triska and Cocks, *Political Development*.
15. Archie Brown and Gordon Wightman, "Czechoslovakia: Revival and Retreat," in Brown and Gray, *Political Culture and Political Change*, 189; see also Connor and Gitelman, *Public Opinion*, 178.
16. Alex Inkeles and David H. Smith, *Becoming Modern: Individual Change in Six Developing Countries* (Cambridge, MA: Harvard University Press, 1974); and Herbert Hyman, *The Enduring Effects of Education* (Chicago: University of Chicago Press, 1975).

PART II

Generations and Professional Memory

7

Pluralism, Corporatism, and Professional Memory

The current wave of "interest group" studies, to which the book under review belongs, is the third such wave since the beginning of professional political science at the turn of the century.

I

The first wave was part of a larger antiformalist movement, which in its beginnings emphasized the political party, the "boss," and the machine. It was a reaction against the theory of sovereignty; its ideology was libertarian and pluralist, and its methodology realistic and "processual." Arthur F. Bentley, often cited as the father of interest group theory, might perhaps be more appropriately viewed as an uncle rather than a direct antecedent,[1] for Bentley considered the group as the fundamental "particle" of politics operating under the institutional cover of administrative agencies, courts, legislative bodies, and political parties, as well as organized interest groups. It was a sociological revolt against legal formalism: group interaction constituted the reality of political life operating behind the formal legal-institutional disguises of society and the state.

Properly speaking, the first wave of interest group studies began in the late 1920s with the publication of Odegard's study of the prohibition movement and Herring's book on interest groups and the Congress. Over the next two decades, more than a dozen major monographic interest group studies

From Gabriel A. Almond, "Pluralism, Corporatism, and Professional Memory" (review of Suzanne Berger, ed., *Organizing Interests in Western Europe: Pluralism, Corporatism, and the Transformation of Politics*. New York: Cambridge University Press, 1981), *World Politics*, Vol. 35, No. 2.

appeared, including the work of Pollock, Childs, Schattschneider, Rutherford, Brooks, Zeller, McKean, Garceau, Leiserson, Latham, and Blaisdell.[2] These studies, and particularly those of Herring, Odegard, and Schattschneider, nourished a generation of political scientists in the 1930s and 1940s. Finally, David Truman brought this movement to its theoretical fruition.[3]

This, then, was an extremely visible and consequential political science movement.[4] It was empirically and theoretically variegated. It drew on European sociological and political theory—German and French, as well as British.[5] The researchers who contributed to this literature had either themselves studied abroad or had taken their Ph.D.s at universities where the faculty had at least in part been European trained.

The second wave of interest group studies was continuous with the first. It was initiated under the auspices of the Social Science Research Council at the time its presidency was held by Pendleton Herring and the chairmanship of the Committee on Political Behavior was held by David Truman. Within a year or two, a similar program was begun under the auspices of the International Political Science Association under the presidency of James K. Pollock.

These two related impulses sought to spread the word of empirical political science research and to encourage an escape from formalism and ideologism in European and Third World political studies. The program of grants for the study of political groups offered by the Committee on Comparative Politics of the SSRC gave support to the work of some 25 American specialists on European, Latin American, Middle Eastern, and Southeast Asian politics. Since this research program and that of the IPSA are summarized in Suzanne Berger's introduction to the book under review, it may be useful to illustrate the variety of the publications produced or supported by them. Among the works to which the SSRC Committee contributed its support are Edward Banfield's *Moral Basis of a Backward Society*,[6] Samuel Beer's *British Politics in the Collectivist Age*,[7] Henry Ehrmann's "Interest Groups and Bureaucracy in Western Democracies,"[8] Carl Lande's *Leaders, Factions and Parties: The Structure of Philippine Politics*,[9] Joseph LaPalombara's *Interest Groups in Italian Politics*,[10] Juan Linz's "An Authoritarian Regime: Spain,"[11] Seymour M. Lipset's *Political Man*,[12] Val Lorwin's "Labor Organizations and Politics in Belgium and France,"[13] Fred Riggs's "Interest and Clientele Groups in Thailand,"[14] and Myron Weiner's *The Politics of Scarcity: Public Pressure and Political Response in India*.[15]

Other contributions to this literature were stimulated by the IPSA program described in Henry Ehrmann's *Interest Groups on Four Continents*,[16] which included papers by Lavau, Hirsch-Weber, Finer, Tsuji, Heckscher, and Djordjevic on French, German, British, Japanese, Swedish, and Yugoslavian interest groups. Other work on European pressure groups appearing in this same quite substantial body of research included studies by Ehrmann, LaPalombara, Meynaud, W.J.M. MacKenzie, Finer, Eckstein, Wootton, and Kaiser—on trade unions, business associations, professional societies, and interest groups in general in France, Britain, Germany, and Italy.[17] These interest group studies covered many countries and all the continents except Africa and Antarctica. The SSRC and IPSA programs were viewed as ways of enriching the data base of politics and generating hypotheses about the conditions and consequences of different forms of government-society interactions in which interest groups played important roles.

The third wave of interest group studies began in the early 1970s, largely in response to the difficulties that Keynesian economic policies and pluralist politics had encountered in grappling with the economic and political problems of the 1970s. The combination of inflation, slowdown of growth, and rising unemployment in advanced industrial societies—along with the declining capacity of the pluralist apparatus of political parties and interest groups to form stable coalitions and generate effective policies—produced a crisis mood in political science and political sociology. In this context, both neoconservative and neocorporatist diagnoses and remedies proliferated.

The neocorporatist literature focused on the interaction of the major economic interest groupings with the appropriate components of government (particularly bureaucracy) in a bargaining process over the central problems of wages, prices, social policy, and investment. Philippe Schmitter points out that in 1974, three essays on corporatist themes appeared almost simultaneously; the authors were the German sociologist Gerhard Lehmbruch, the British sociologists Ray Pahl and Jack Winkler, and Schmitter himself, a political scientist at the University of Chicago.[18] A few years later, Schmitter and Lehmbruch joined forces in editing a volume dealing with this theme, which drew on the collaborative efforts of half a dozen or more American, European, and Japanese social scientists.[19]

Their overall research program is in its early stages and has not as yet solved its conceptual problems or reported much progress in the accomplishment of its objectives. Schmitter defines corporatism institutionally or structurally, as "a system of interest representation in which the constituent units are organized into a limited number of singular, compulsory, noncompetitive, hierarchically ordered, and functionally differentiated categories, recognized or licensed (if not created) by the state, and granted a deliberate representational monopoly within their respective categories in exchange for observing certain controls on their selection of leaders and articulation of demands and supports."[20] In another context, Harold Wilensky presents a definition that separates structural properties from output or policy properties: "By democratic corporatism I mean the capacity of strongly organized central economic interest groups interacting under government auspices within a quasi-public framework to produce peak bargains involving social policy, fiscal and monetary policy and incomes policies – the major interrelated issues of modern political economy."[21]

The contemporary crisis of political economy in advanced industrial societies is the challenge to which this corporatist body of interest group studies is a response. It is a research program of importance, and promises to enrich political theory and to contribute to public policy. It is still at the stage of conceptual groping and hypothesis formulation. Schmitter presents us with a threefold classification scheme of corporatism, pluralism, and syndicalism. Corporatism is a system of comprehensive, compulsory, monopolistic associations, licensed by the state; pluralism is a system of spontaneously forming, nonlegal, competitive associations interacting in informal and unregulated ways with each other and the state; while in syndicalism, the associations interact with each other without reference to or interference from the state. Lehmbruch offers a historical-sociological classification scheme consisting of liberal corporatism (e.g., the kind operating in the democratic industrial countries), statist corporatism (e.g., the fascist, authoritarian, and clerico-authoritarian variety), and traditional corporatism (e.g., the guild systems of the medieval cities).[22] In his contribution to the book under review, Schmitter seems to have adopted Lehmbruch's classification (Chapter 10: "Interest Mediation and Regime Governability in Contemporary Western Europe and North America"). Charles Maier, drawing on the work of the late Stein Rokkan, speaks of "corporate pluralism" (Chapter 1: "Fictitious Bonds of Wealth and Law: On the Theory and Practice of Interest Representation"). Robert Kvavik, also in part drawing on Rokkan's work, proposes a classification consisting of competitive pluralism, corporate pluralism, and statist pluralism – an analytical scheme that suggests that all differentiated societies and political systems are pluralistic in some measure and form, and vary in the extent of integration and the centralization of control.[23] Kvavik's scheme would protect us from the theoretical embarrassment of a Polish, Yugoslavian, or Spanish type of authoritarian pluralism that arises in societies in which, according to Schmitter's scheme, such phenomena ought not to arise at all.

But the important problem confronting the corporatist research agenda is its effectiveness in discriminating among the components of the crisis of contemporary political economy. How do corporatist solutions—whether structural changes, policy changes, or both—cope with the interactions of wages, prices, employment, and savings and investment? The classification of types of corporatism-pluralism should enable us to relate these institutional and/or bargaining patterns to the various elements of public policy and political behavior. We are at the beginning of research efforts of this kind. Schmitter's paper in the book under review examines the relationship between corporatist arrangements and regime governability in Western Europe and North America, Wilensky deals with the relationship between corporatism and "welfare backlash."[24] In an unpublished paper, Peter Lange explores the relationships among economic conditions, trade union militancy, and the propensity of trade unions to adopt corporatist-type bargaining solutions.[25]

This third wave of interest group studies flows in continuity with the second wave, which, in the work of Beer, Rokkan, LaPalombara, Ehrmann, Linz, and others, included discussions of European corporate pluralism. It did not escape the attention of these scholars that corporatist arrangements and designs had played important roles in British, Scandinavian, Italian, French, and Spanish politicoeconomic development.[26] What distinguishes the contemporary concern for corporatism is its centrality in a growing polemic over the causes of and remedies for the economic and political crises in advanced industrial societies. In the Europe of the 1950s, the crises consisted of problems of democratic stabilization and economic recovery after the devastation of World War II, the cultural-political demoralization of Nazi rule and occupation, and the division of Europe during the cold war. In that context, political parties and interest groups constituted the battleground for the ideological future of Europe. It was not accidental then—just as it is not accidental today—that research focused on the particular aspect of the political process associated with the historical crisis. In the 1950s, the emergence of pragmatic, bargaining trade unions in a growing economy was essential to the process of democratization. In the 1970s and 1980s, the plagues of inflation, retardation of growth, unemployment, and the declining legitimacy of democratic government seem to call for a changed relationship among interest groups, as well as between interest groups, parties, and bureaucracy, in order to contain these threatening tendencies. Thus the questions we ask about interest groups are different at different historical junctures. But interest group theory ought to be sufficiently versatile to be able to grapple with differing historical contexts. We do not need a new theory whenever things seem to go awry. Perhaps, before we declare them obsolete, we need to know, and to understand a bit better, the theories we have. When Schmitter proclaimed that the century of corporatism was still with us, our knowledge was already such as to suggest that some degree of pluralism was built into modern differentiated societies, whether authoritarian or democratic. Thus corporatism is a variety of pluralism—to be distinguished from a more disaggregated competitive variety of pluralism at one extreme, and from a state-controlled variety at the other.

II

In her summary of the characteristics of the research program of the Committee on Comparative Politics and the "pluralist" literature supported by this program or otherwise generated in the 1950s and 1960s, Suzanne Berger acknowledges that this review oversimplifies "and perhaps also overstresses the elements of unity and theoretical coherence of this body of research" (p. 4). She cites only two programmatic statements, leaving the larger theoretical and monographic literature unmentioned; consequently, it is not clear whether she is generalizing about the literature supported by the SSRC Committee on Comparative Politics in the late 1950s and 1960s, the program of the International Political Science Association in the late 1950s, or the larger literature of the 1950s and 1960s dealing with interest groups and pluralist themes—of which the first two were simply parts.

From the point of view of accepted scholarly standards, Berger and her associates should, of course, have conducted a search of the earlier literature. It is a matter of some concern that many of the authors of the chapters on individual countries fail to cite previous monographic studies—by either Europeans or Americans—dealing with interest groups in those countries, and that Berger does not seem to have benefited from a reading of a number of important codifications of interest group theory,[27] to say nothing of the more extensive formulations of Pendleton Herring, V. O. Key, Jr., and David Truman.

The casualness of the search of the earlier literature and the distortion of its contents are serious weaknesses in an otherwise important contribution to the interest group literature. If this professional amnesia were peculiar to Berger's undertaking, it would warrant a sharper judgment. But the impairment of professional memory has become common in political science and helps to explain its fragmented and faddish character. The behavioral movement buried the memory of the institutionalists, only to have a "statist" counterrevolution take place in the last year or two. The "dependency" movement in comparative politics vilified and buried the modernization and pluralist theories, and now has to come to terms with its own exaggerations and distortions. *Organizing Interests in Western Europe* misses an opportunity to cumulate its work with a rich literature; it thereby loses valuable comparative perspectives, and theoretical insights.

In her summary, Berger argues that in the pluralist literature, "there is no general theory – as there is in Marxism – of the ranking, or relations of dominance and subordination in the potentially infinite array of interests that industrial society generates" (p. 5). She attributes to this literature the view that crosscutting cleavages, overlapping memberships, and social mobility "create a fluidity in the relations among various organized interests and . . . undermine the bases on which a situation of permanent domination could be constructed" (p. 5). This interpretation of the position of pluralistic interest group studies on economic inequality hardly does justice to the work of Pendleton Herring, David Truman, Robert Dahl, Henry Ehrmann, and Joseph LaPalombara.[28] Indeed, one of the most powerful findings to come out of the political science literature of the post-World War II era – in interest group studies and survey research, replicated over and over again – is that political elites, organization leaders, members, political activists, and political participants are drawn substantially from the higher socioeconomic strata, whatever the country or ideological system. This general proposition about the universality of the relationship of socioeconomic and political inequality is not inconsistent with the pluralist view that interest group organization can enhance the political power of poorer groups and increase their share of income and opportunity.[29]

Berger contends that the pluralist literature assigns too great a weight to socioeconomic determinants of interest, in contrast to historical experience, governmental policy, and intraorganizational factors. She attributes to it the view that "interest groups form as spontaneous emanations of society. The boundaries between them correspond to what may be regarded as the 'natural' divisions of society, that is, those generated by different roles in the economy and statuses in the society" (p. 5). A literature that draws so heavily on Tocqueville; that includes monographic studies of civic groups, issue groups, and church groups; and that chronicles the formation of trade associations, trade unions, and professional societies in reaction to governmental policy, or the formation and splitting of trade unions as a consequence of revolutions,[30] can hardly be characterized as overstressing economic modernization and industrialization as a cause of interest group formation, and as neglecting cultural and governmental variables.

Berger depicts this literature as being ahistorical, almost mechanical in its approach to the formation of interest groups. The earlier studies are described as not having appreciated "the various routes that Western nations followed to modernization and industrialization, the specificities of national traditions and values" (p. 6). Surely this description fails to do justice to the historical richness of the work of a Beer, an Ehrmann, or a Lorwin, and the explicit historical hypotheses in my own work dealing with the differences in the characteristics of interest groups in Britain, France, and Germany.[31]

Berger maintains that the sole explanation offered in the pluralist literature for differences in interest group structure and functioning is the form taken by the relation between interest groups and political parties: "Conditions in some countries made it possible for interests to emerge and organize freely and in other countries to subordinate interest group formation to ideological politics, thereby deforming the expression of the pragmatic needs, the 'real' interests of society" (p. 6). She could have arrived at such a conclusion only by taking my report of a 1957 SSRC Conference as representing the theoretical content of this literature. No doubt an examination of the many items contained in it would have revealed considerable richness and variety of explanatory hypotheses for the interest group patterns encountered in the European, Latin American, and Asian countries covered by that research program.

"The previous literature," argues Berger, "saw interest groups in advanced industrial societies as formulating social demands and channeling them into the political process" (p. 18). More broadly, she implies that it was dominated by a model of a stable division of functions among structures, while the contributors to her volume employ a model in which the functioning of the state, political parties, and interest groups varies with changes in society and economy. Surely, the pluralist and functional literature avoided this attribution of special functions to special structures; rather, it presented the notion of multifunctionality as a property of all political structures. Thus the classification of interest groups included institutional interest groups (bureaucratic entities), nonassociational groups (informal factional and clientelist groups), and anomic groups (mobs, riots, etc.). It was this very substitutability in the political division of labor that gave definition to the varieties of political process.

Berger also states that "the studies of interest groups in various countries that the Committee sponsored devoted relatively little attention to relations between leaders and followers or to conflicts within the group over objectives. . . . The question of representation was reformulated as a problem of survey research. . . . Thus surveys were to answer the questions of whom interest groups represented and of whether the interests defended by the organized were the same as those of the unorganized" (p. 8). Joseph LaPalombara devoted a substantial part of his book on interest groups in Italy to internal organization and its significance for Italian politics and society.[32] Similarly, Samuel Beer's study of British political groups dealt with internal organization and interest representation in ways that are quite discriminating and backed up by great empirical detail.[33] Myron Weiner's book on Indian interest groups dealt with the problem of interest representation and organization in anything but bland and optimistic terms.[34] If Berger had gone back to the earlier literature, she would have found discussions of internal organization in cornucopian quantities. Harwood Childs, for instance, entitled Part II of his *Labor and Capital* "The Representative Character of Group Agency."[35] Oliver Garceau paid substantial attention to the internal politics of the American Medical Association.[36] In David Truman's study of interest groups, an entire part, "Group Organizations and Problems of Leadership," dealt with these issues and the question of representativeness.[37]

Berger's comment that a proposal was made at the 1957 SSRC Conference to employ survey research in investigating the representativeness of the demands of organized interest groups seems to imply that there is something obviously mistaken about this methodological suggestion. But one is led to ask, why not? Banfield's penetrating study of attitudes toward group affiliation in southern Italy was based in part on Thematic Apperception Tests administered in southern and northern Italy (as well as in Utah). The Civic Culture study, then in an early planning stage, was soon to compare organizational affiliation and attitudes toward organizations in a number of European countries; its results had considerable bearing on interest group theory.

While this literature has been criticized for shortcomings it did not have, it has been credited with achieving something to which it only aspired. It was the hope of the Committee in embarking on this program that it would culminate in a number of empirical-theoretical contributions. There are no distinctive theoretical products that fulfill these aspirations, and the focus on interest groups in comparative politics continued in a lower key. Two doctoral dissertations stimulated by this movement provided continuity between the second and third wave of interest group studies: Philippe Schmitter's study of Brazilian groups,[38] and Robert Kvavik's work on Norway.[39] If the second wave failed to produce interest group theory, the third wave still may.

III

The differences between the interest group literature of the 1950s and 1960s and the collection of essays in *Organizing Interests in Western Europe* are not attributable only to disparities in the historical situation and related problems of political economy. They were produced by a new disciplinary and cultural mix. The literature of the 1950s and 1960s was dominated by American political scientists. Indeed, though pluralism as a political theory was European in inspiration, empirical interest group research was strictly an American enterprise until after World War II. It was not unusual in those years for European scholars to remark that pressure groups and the lobby were political phenomena peculiar to the United States.[40] European Marxists or socialists tended to reduce lobbying and associational activity to "class realities," while conservative European political scientists viewed interest groups as phenomena subversive of legitimacy and authority, and hence appropriate for study only as pathologies.

The studies of European interest groups carried out in the 1950s and 1960s by American (and some European) political scientists were part of a larger process of the "Americanization of Europe"—particularly in the social sciences—after World War II. The present volume, to quote from Gerald Feldman's essay, reflects in some measure "the Europeanization of America" (p. 161). It is no longer possible to point to the United States as a model of an effectively functioning competitive pluralism that Europeans should adopt in order to clean up their political acts and "modernize." The United States has begun to suffer those crises of authority, confidence, and stability that were previously assumed to be uniquely European.

From this point of view, the fact that almost half of the contributors to Suzanne Berger's volume are holders of European chairs brings a needed balance to the cultural-historical perspective of interest group studies. But it is also noteworthy that the team consists mostly of historians, economic historians, and sociologists, in contrast to the greater number of political scientists who produced the literature of the 1950s and 1960s. It is therefore not surprising that the search of the literature the contributors to this volume undertook (with one or two exceptions) did not include or make use of the large and variegated body of work on interest groups that had been produced between the late 1920s and the mid-1960s.

The twelve essays that make up the body of *Organizing Interests* are on the whole of good quality. All of them are historically literate; and if, as Suzanne Berger suggests, some of them come out of a Marxist historical tradition, hardly a proposition is advanced here that would not be assimilable in an eclectic codification of interest group theory.

Perhaps the most interesting theoretical essays are those by Charles Maier, Jurgen Kocka, Claus Offe, Charles Sabel, Alessandro Pizzorno, Gerald Feldman, and Philippe Schmitter. In an elegant, data-and-bibliography-rich chapter, Charles Maier places the study of interest groups in the historical perspective of an earlier "estatist" stratum, in which those parts of the society having the "right to interest" were directly represented; he proceeds to a second stage of oligarchic individualism (the "liberal parenthesis" of mid-nineteenth-century England), and then a third stage, the age of collectivism and associationism. His impressive erudition makes it possible for him to compare and contrast the historical experiences and corporatist propensities of Britain, France, Germany, the Scandinavian, and the Low Countries. This essay should quickly become recognized as the best available introduction to the topic of interest groups.

Jurgen Kocka's analysis of the "white-collar" class in Germany is of unusual interest; it demonstrates the ways in which early German bureaucratization on the one hand, and the radicalization of the working class on the other, conditioned the values and organizational propensities of salaried employees. Here is a case in which interest organization influenced class structure and culture rather than the other way around. Claus Offe's analysis of corporatist trends in Germany is of particular value, though his definition of corporatism as having a heavy statist component does – like Schmitter's earlier definition – limit the usefulness of the concept in analyzing the relation between varieties of corporate organizations and corporate policies. His analytical elaboration of degrees and types of corporatism is an important contribution to theoretical work in the field. And his arguments as to the inherent inequalities among interest groups, and the decline in the responsiveness of interest group elites to interest group members as the elites are co-opted by government, are points that call for attention.

Charles Sabel's comparative analysis of the internal politics of trade unions in Germany and Italy reflects a shrewd ability to combine rational choice analysis with good case studies. His thesis that corporatist arrangements are inherently unstable – because interest group elites are caught between the demands of the rank and file and the pressure of bureaucrats and bargaining partners – is an important proposition that will have to be tested through empirical studies.

Alessandro Pizzorno's essay on interest groups and political parties in pluralist systems contains an excellent treatment of the emergence of pluralist ideas in the nineteenth century, in the work of Tocqueville, Gierke, Maitland, Leo XIII's *Rerum Novarum,* Durkheim, Harold Laski, and G.D.H. Cole. Pizzorno is better on the historical-sociological origins than on the historical operation of the pluralist system.

Gerald Feldman, in his study of interest groups in Germany during World War I and the inflation of the 1920s, shows how corporatist institutions can become overloaded when they seek to back up failing bureaucratic and parliamentary institutions. The "unloading" of parliament and bureaucracy on interest groups may lead to the collapse of the corporatist apparatus. Feldman poses the problem as one of discovering the optimal arrangement of the triangular relationships among labor, business, and government.

Aside from Schmitter's chapter, which will be discussed below, the remaining essays are good case study contributions to the larger literature of interest groups. They will have to await a codifier of interest group theory to draw out their implications. Suzanne Berger, in a first-rate study of the traditional middle class of France, demonstrates how an obsolescent and volatile social stratum can delay its demise indefinitely through unconventional political action. Hernes and Selvik point out that developed corporatist systems have a local level as well as a national one. John Keeler's paper on the French agricultural federation provides a useful case study of a well-developed corporatist enclave in the French political economy; the federation is a device that quite obviously accords privilege and power to corporate elites in exchange for their willingness to sacrifice the interests of the smaller, marginal peasants. Michele Salvati's comparison of the political crises of 1968 and 1969 in France and Italy, while interesting, is difficult to relate to the larger themes of the book. Juan Linz's detailed and lengthy analysis of interest groups in Spanish politics over the course of the nineteenth and twentieth centuries is part of his own continuing program of ever deepening and illuminating explorations into Spanish history, society, and culture.

Despite Berger's disavowal of coherent and theoretical aspirations, it is not correct to represent this volume as having no coherent theme or theoretical import. In her introduction, Berger herself spells out the principal theoretical issues that are advanced in the book. They all have to do with the role of corporatist "intermediation" in the solution of the crises of contemporary political economy. That seven out of the twelve essays are important contributions to the corporatist debate is to the credit of the editor and her associates.

From this point of view, the most ambitious essay in the volume is Philippe Schmitter's "Interest Intermediation and Regime Governability in Contemporary Western Europe and North America." Schmitter aims at the very center of the corporatism target. In effect, he asks the question: Is corporatism the solution to the headaches and heartaches of our contemporary lives – the decay of governmental effectiveness and legitimacy as democracies confront the intractable problems of inflation, declining growth, unemployment, and poverty?

The chapter operationalizes these concepts and tests the relationships empirically with data from 15 advanced industrial democracies. This paper, which consists mostly of tables accompanied by analysis, stands in sharp contrast with the rest of the book, which contains no statistical tables at all.

Schmitter tells us that his data answer his question positively; that is, corporatism does seem to reduce "ungovernability"; but when we look more closely at how he has operationalized corporatism and ungovernability, we are left with the feeling that he has done a great service to the profession by making, in the sense of Pareto, a series of creative mistakes quickly. Schmitter's criteria for corporatism are the proportion of workers affiliated in trade unions and the degree of centralization of trade union organization. His dependent variable of "ungovernability" is operationalized by three indicators: unruliness in the sense of degree of collective protest, internal war, and strike violence; instability in the sense of cabinet changes and party fractionalization; and fiscal ineffectiveness in the sense of increasing governmental revenue, reliance on direct taxation, and government borrowing.

But it is evident that Schmitter has not really properly operationalized his theoretical independent and dependent variables. Corporatism is facilitated by the density of trade union membership and the centralization and unity of the union movement; but this is not all there is to corporatism. Schmitter would be the first to argue that corporatism is a form of interest intermediation—i.e., a kind of relationship and bargaining process with other interest groups and governmental agencies. He does not get at these properties directly even though he has a small "*n*" and could have coded them with relative accuracy. On the dependent side of the theory, Schmitter gives us the three aspects of ungovernability to which we have already referred. Why are there no measures of corporatist policy bargains (e.g., wage restraints, price controls, tax exemptions)? Indeed, Schmitter should have demonstrated that such agreements and measures were fashioned in more or less formalized tripartite institutional settings. In other words, we have associations between aspects of interest group organization, social violence, and governmental instability and aspects of fiscal policy, but the corporatist schema of structure and policy is present only by inference, and rather indirect inference at that.

Despite these critical comments, *Organizing Interests in Western Europe* is an important book, and Schmitter's paper is a substantial, if somewhat faulty, effort at moving from hypotheses and speculations toward tested theory. All of the essays can be mined for significant hypotheses bearing on the issue of corporatist solutions to problems of political economy, and Schmitter's approach to operationalization can be improved in efforts at testing these hypotheses.

Notes

1. Arthur F. Bentley, *The Process of Government* (Chicago: University of Chicago Press, 1900).
2. James K. Pollock, "Regulation of Lobbying," *American Political Science Review*, XXI (May 1927), 335–41; Peter H. Odegard, *Pressure Politics: The Story of the Anti-Saloon League* (New York: Columbia University Press, 1928); E. Pendleton Herring, *Group Representation Before Congress* (Washington, DC: Brookings Institution, 1929); Herring, *Public Administration and the Public Interest* (New York: McGraw-Hill, 1936); Herring, *The Politics of Democracy* (New York: Norton, 1940); Harwood L. Childs, *Labor and Capital in National Politics* (Columbus: Ohio University Press, 1930); E. E. Schattschneider, *Politics, Pressures, and the Tariff* (New York: Prentice-Hall, 1935); M. Louise Rutherford, *The Influence of the American Bar Association on Public Opinion and Legislation* (Philadelphia: Foundation Press, 1937); Robert R.R. Brooks, *When Labor Organizes* (New Haven: Yale University Press, 1937); Belle Zeller, *Pressure Politics in New York* (New York: Prentice-Hall, 1937); Dayton McKean, *Pressures on the Legislature of New Jersey* (New York: Columbia University Press, 1938); Oliver Garceau, *The Political Life of the American Medical Association* (Cambridge, MA: Harvard University Press, 1941); Avery Leiserson, *Administrative Regulation: A Study in Representation of Interests* (Chicago: University of Chicago Press, 1942); Earl Latham, *The Group Basis of Politics* (Ithaca, NY: Cornell University Press, 1952); Donald C. Blaisdell, *Economic Power and Political Pressures* (Washington, DC: Temporary National Economic Committee Monograph 26, 1949).
3. David Truman, *The Governmental Process* (New York: Knopf, 1951).
4. The contributors to this interest group literature included seven presidents of the American Political Science Association and one president of the International Political Science Association.
5. See, among others, Alexis de Tocqueville, *Democracy in America* (New York: Knopf, 1945), Vol. I, p. 191; Vol. II, p. 106; and throughout; F. W. Maitland's "Introduction" to his translation of Otto Gierke, *Political Theories of the Middle Ages* (Cambridge: Cambridge University Press, 1900); G.D.H. Cole, *Guild Socialism; A Plan for Economic Democracy* (London: L. Parsons, 1920); Leon Duguit, *Traite de droit constitutionnel* (Paris: Boccard, 1925), Vol. V; Harold Laski, *The Problem of Sovereignty* (London: Oxford University Press, 1947); Emile Durkheim, *Les regles de la methode sociologique* (Paris: Presses Universitaires de France, 1950), 100ff.
6. Edward Banfield, *Moral Basis of a Backward Society* (Glencoe, IL: Free Press, 1958).
7. Samuel Beer, *British Politics in the Collectivist Age* (New York: Knopf, 1965).
8. Henry Ehrmann, "Interest Groups and Bureaucracy in Western Democracies," in Reinhard Bendix, ed., *The State and Society* (Boston: Little, Brown, 1968).
9. Carl Lande, *Leaders, Factions and Parties: The Structure of Philippine Politics*, Yale Southeast Asia Monographs No. 6 (New Haven: Yale University Press, 1969).
10. Joseph LaPalombara, *Interest Groups in Italian Politics* (Princeton: Princeton University Press, 1964).
11. Juan Linz, "An Authoritarian Regime: Spain," in Erik Allardt and Yrjo Littunen, eds., *Cleavages, Ideologies, and Party Systems* (Helsinki: Westermarck Society, 1964).
12. Seymour M. Lipset, *Political Man* (Garden City, NY: Doubleday, 1960).

13. Val Lorwin, "Labor Organizations and Politics in Belgium and France," in E. M. Kassalow, ed., *National Labor Movements in the Post-War World* (Evanston, IL: Northwestern University Press, 1963).
14. Fred Riggs, "Interest and Clientele Groups in Thailand," in Joseph L. Sutton, ed., *Problems of Politics and Administration in Thailand* (Bloomington, IN: Institute of Training for the Public Service, 1962).
15. Myron Weiner, *The Politics of Scarcity: Public Pressure and Political Response in India* (Princeton: Princeton University Press, 1962).
16. Henry Ehrmann, *Interest Groups on Four Continents* (Pittsburgh, PA: University of Pittsburgh Press, 1958).
17. Henry Ehrmann, *Organized Business in France* (Princeton: Princeton University Press, 1957); Joseph LaPalombara, *The Italian Labor Movement* (Ithaca, NY: Cornell University Press, 1957); Jean Meynaud, *Les groupes de pression en France* (Paris: Librairie Armand Colin, 1958); W.J.M. MacKenzie, "Pressure Groups: The Conceptual Framework," *Political Studies*, III (3, 1955), 247ff.; Samuel Finer, *Anonymous Empire: A Study of the Lobby in Great Britain* (London: Pall Mall Press, 1958); Harry Eckstein, *Pressure Group Politics: The Case of the British Medical Association* (Stanford, CA: Stanford University Press, 1960); Graham Wootton, *The Politics of Influence: British Ex-Servicemen, Cabinet Decisions and Cultural Change, 1917–1957* (Cambridge, MA: Harvard University Press, 1963); Joseph H. Kaiser, *Die Reprsentation organisierter Interessen* (Berlin: Duncker & Humblot, 1956).
18. Gerhard Lehmbruch, "Consociational Democracy, Class Conflict, and the New Corporatism," *IPSA Round Table* (September 1974); Ray Pahl and Jack Winkler, "The Coming Corporatism," *New Society*, XXX (October 10, 1974), 72ff.; Philippe Schmitter, "Still the Century of Corporatism?" *Review of Politics*, XXXVI (January 1974), 85ff.
19. Philippe Schmitter and Gerhard Lehmbruch, *Trends Toward Corporatist Intermediation* (Beverly Hills, CA: Sage, 1979).
20. *Ibid.*, 13.
21. Harold Wilensky, "Leftism, Catholicism, and Democratic Corporatism: The Role of Political Parties in Recent Welfare State Development," in Peter Flora and Arnold Heidenheimer, eds., *The Development of Welfare States in Europe and America* (New Brunswick, NJ: Transaction Books, 1981), 345ff.
22. Schmitter and Lehmbruch (fn. 19), 15ff.
23. Robert Kvavik, *Interest Groups in Norwegian Politics* (Oslo: Universitetsforlaget, 1976), 20ff.
24. Wilensky (fn. 21).
25. Peter Lange, "The Conjunctural Conditions for Consensual Wage Regulations; An Initial Examination of Some Hypotheses." Paper presented at meeting of the American Political Science Association, New York, September 1981.
26. See, for example, Beer (fn. 7), chaps. 1 and 2, p. 330; Stein Rokkan, "Numerical Democracy and Corporate Pluralism," in Robert A. Dahl, ed., *Political Oppositions in Western Democracies* (New Haven: Yale University Press, 1966), chap. 4; LaPalombara (fn. 10), 227–31, 383–84; Ehrmann (fn. 17), part 1; Linz (fn. 11), 270.
27. See, among others, David B. Truman, "Political Group Analysis," in David Sills, *International Encyclopedia of the Social Sciences* (New York: Macmillan, 1968), XII, 241ff.; Henry Kariel, "Pluralism," *ibid.*, 164ff.; Henry Ehrmann, "Interest Groups," *ibid.*, VII, 486ff.; J. David Greenstone, "Group Theories," in Fred Greenstein and Nelson Polsby, *Handbook of Political Science* (Reading, MA: Addison-Wesley, 1975), II, 243–318; and Robert H. Salisbury, "Interest Groups," *ibid.*, IV, 171–228.

28. Herring (fn. 1, 1940), chap. 29; Truman (fn. 3), chap. 16, esp. 522ff.; Dahl (fn. 26), 367ff., and *Polyarchy: Participation and Opposition* (New Haven: Yale University Press, 1971), chap. 6; LaPalombara (fn. 17), chap. 1; LaPalombara (fn. 10), 42ff. and 394ff.; Ehrmann (fn. 17), chap. 9.
29. See, among others, Norman H. Nie, G. Bingham Powell, and Kenneth Prewitt, "Social Structure and Political Participation," *American Political Science Review*, 63 (June and December 1969), 361–78, 808–32; Sidney Verba and Norman H. Nie, *Participation in America: Political Democracy and Social Equality* (New York: Harper & Row, 1972); Sidney Verba, Norman H. Nie, and Jae-on Kim, *Participation and Political Equality* (New York: Cambridge University Press, 1978), chap. 14; Kay L. Schlozman and Sidney Verba, *Injury to Insult: Unemployment, Class, and Political Response* (Cambridge, MA: Harvard University Press, 1979).
30. See, for example, Truman (fn. 3), 56ff., on interest groups and government; on varieties of interest groups, pp. 63ff.; and on the origins of interest groups and government, pp. 74ff. Also, LaPalombara (fn. 17), on the effect of war and revolution on the trade union movement; Ehrmann (fn. 17), on the impact of war and fascism on French business organization.
31. For emphasis on the importance of historical experience in the formation of interest groups, see particularly the first chapters of Beer (fn. 7), Ehrmann (fn. 17), and LaPalombara (fn. 10). Also, Gabriel A. Almond and G. Bingham Powell, *Comparative Politics: A Developmental Approach* (Boston: Little, Brown, 1966), 314ff.
32. LaPalombara (fn. 10), 161ff.
33. Beer (fn. 7), chap. 4 and throughout.
34. Weiner (fn. 15), chap. 2.
35. Childs (fn. 2), chap. 4.
36. Garceau (fn. 2).
37. Truman (fn. 3), chaps. 5, 6, 7.
38. Schmitter, *Interest Conflict and Political Change in Brazil* (Stanford, CA: Stanford University Press, 1971).
39. Kvavik (fn. 23).
40. See E. Pendleton Herring, "The British Have Lobbies Too," *Virginia Quarterly Review*, VI (July 1930), 342ff.

8

The Return to the State

Arguments for a return to the concept of the state have been made intermittently ever since Frederick Watkins (1968) prematurely solemnized its burial 20 years ago. The writers who have advocated a return to the state have had different goals and agendas. In the cases of Nettl (1968), Stepan (1978), and Nordlinger (1981), the argument seems to be one of emphasis. The campaign carried on under the auspices of the Committee on States and Social Structures of the Social Science Research Council to "bring the state back in" speaks of "paradigmatic shifts" (Evans, Rueschemeyer, and Skocpol 1985). The "pluralist-functionalist" and Marxist paradigms, which are described as the waning paradigms of contemporary political science, are said to be societally reductionist, according no autonomy to state structures and politics and hence fundamentally lacking in explanatory power. The statist paradigm remedies this defect and will replace these earlier approaches.

I respond to three questions raised by this polemic. First, are the pluralist, structural functionalist, Marxist, and other literatures of political science societally reductionist? Second, does the "statist paradigm" remedy these defects? Third, regardless of the substantive merits of these arguments, are there heuristic benefits flowing from this critique of the literature?

Arguments for a Return to the State

I propose to review these criticisms and make a search of the literature to determine the extent to which this view of "mainstream" political science is sustained by evidence. I cover ground similar to that covered by G. David Garson (1974) in an article published more than 10 years ago and in a subse-

---

quent book (1978). He provided a review of the history of interest group theory, using as his data base all of the articles and reviews that had appeared in the *American Political Science Review* since it began publishing in 1906. He also included some 20 frequently cited books dealing with group theory. His principal conclusion was that political science "grows" largely reactively, in response to outside stimuli: "the rise of economic groups, the tides of progressivism and disillusion, the birth and excitement of modern psychology," and the like (1974, 1519), rather than through the self-conscious testing of analytical models.

Using group theory as exemplifying this disciplinary propensity, he pointed to the early polemic between the "classic" sovereignty and "classic" pluralist theorists. The classic theory of sovereignty overstated its case, although if one looks carefully at this nineteenth-century literature one will find careful qualifiers of the plenary power of the state. The assertion of the absolute authority of the state ran into the anomalies of the empirical and normative limits on state authority—both the conservative ones of religion and property and the liberal ones of the rights of association, assembly, petition, and the like. Classic pluralism similarly overstated its case, rejecting the very notion of state sovereignty, and characterizing the state as one association among many. By denying any sovereignty whatever to the state, Laski (1917) and the other early pluralists deprived themselves of an agency capable of remedying injustice and providing basic security. Garson points out that the history of political science would have been quite different if these alternatives had been formulated as analytical models, as ideal types, rather than assuming that they modeled reality or that reality ought to be made to conform to them. The contemporary statists in their posing of the pluralist and statist alternatives make a similar mistake.

In a more recent article Andrew McFarland (1987) reviews the history of interest group theory in the period since World War II. Prior to the mid-1960s, he points out, "the work of Dahl, Truman, Lindblom, and others provided a coherent and convincing theory of power in America. Dahl's polyarchy and the implicit 'economic theory of democracy' provided a theory of elections. Truman's description of American institutions and politics as a complex texture of decentralized bargaining among a myriad of interest groups was readily assimilated into Dahl's pluralist discussion of power. Lindblom's theory of incremental decision making showed why policies emerging from decentralized bargaining within a polyarchy might be both more effective and representative than policies emerging from central government direction" (p. 129).

The disillusionment and demoralization in U.S. politics in the 1960s and

1970s shook the credibility of this model; in its place a "plural-elitist" model, developed in the work of Lowi (1969) and others, came to be an influential view in the discipline. In this model special interests captured particular areas of public policy, forming "iron triangles" or "subgovernments," not subject to popular control. This pluralist revisionism of the 1970s and 1980s reacted only to the interest group theory of the 1950s and 1960s, and as I shall suggest it failed to register the fact that its pessimism was similar to the pluralist pessimism of the 1930s, which was based on a many-times replicated appreciation of the fact that the power of business interests was substantially more equal than other interests.

A third model, associated with the work of James Q. Wilson (1980), McFarland calls the "triadic model." In this model the policy process is viewed as specialized by issue areas. Normally, interest groups mobilizing to lobby the government in a particular direction are opposed by countervailing groups, and "state agencies are normally assumed to have a significant degree of autonomy . . . as well as a capacity to give some coherence and continuity to the system" (p. 141). The triad consists of the two interest group camps and an autonomous set of state agencies, varying across issue areas.

The important point made by Garson and McFarland from the perspective of the present statism-pluralism polemic is that with the exception of the classic pluralism interlude of the turn-of-the-century period and a few formulations in the 1950s and 1960s (Latham 1952; Golembiewski 1960), the various versions of interest group theory have operated with some measure and form of governmental autonomy.

The intellectual history that I shall review is readily accessible. In an article titled "The State," published in the original *Encyclopedia of the Social Sciences*, the political theorist George Sabine complained a bit about the concept. "The word commonly denotes no class of objects that can be identified exactly, and for the same reason it signifies no list of attributes which bears the sanction of common usage. The word must be defined more or less arbitrarily to meet the exigencies of the system of jurisprudence or political philosophy in which it occurs" (1934, 328). Thirty-four years later in the successor compendium of social science knowledge, *The International Encyclopedia of the Social Sciences*, Frederick Watkins observed that the complexity of the interaction of government and people is such that "political scientists prefer to use other terms in describing the phenomena that once was subsumed under the concept 'state' " (1968, 156).

Watkins acknowledges that the concepts of the state and sovereignty made sense in the century and a half between the Treaty of Westphalia and the French Revolution, during the Age of Absolutism, when Louis XIV could say "l'Etat c'est moi," and Frederick II could speak of himself as "der erste Diener des Staates." Democratization led to a devaluation of the normative concept of the state. In a democratic society it is hard to distinguish the state from the citizens in whose name its authority is being exercised: "Sovereignty thus conceived is little more than a bloodless legal fiction. Attention shifts from the state to the government, which though it makes no claim to sovereignty, does all the actual ruling" (p. 153).

If there is any point in the use of the concept, according to Watkins, it is in the Weberian sense "that the distinctive feature of the state, as compared with other associations, is its attempt to monopolize coercive power within its own territory. . . . From the standpoint of a purely descriptive political science it is sufficient, therefore, to define the state in terms of the limit, and to study the conditions that accompany the greater or lesser degrees of monopoly that have been achieved in particular times and places. The difficulty is that it places excessive emphasis on the coercive aspects of political life" (pp. 153–54).

As the state concept fell into disuse in mainstream political science it was replaced by such terms as *government*, and later by *political system*. The tendency to abandon the state concept and replace it by other concepts was attributable to the enormous political mobilization that took place in the Western world in the nineteenth and twentieth centuries and the proliferation of new political institutions—political parties, pressure groups, the mass media, and the like—that accompanied it. The concept of the political system included the phenomena of the state—the legally empowered and legitimately coercive institutions—but it also included these new extralegal and paralegal institutions of political parties, interest groups, media of communication, as well as social institutions such as family, school, and church, insofar as they affected political processes. Political system theory and structural functionalism were not reductionist of the state and governmental institutions. They grew out of a realism that recognized the processual character of politics, and examined institutions—legal, paralegal, and informal—in terms of what they actually did. Structural functionalism was just that; and system theory was a formal acknowledgment that the political process was a set of interdependent subprocesses.

For the Marxists and neo-Marxists, however, the state continued to be a central concept, the instrumentality through which the capitalist class dominated the social order. For the Marxists the assimilation of the state into the political system and its disaggregation into a host of interacting phenomena in mainstream political science represented a fudging of the reality of class struggle. As I shall suggest, for the Marxist intellectual tradition the relation of the state to class struggle continues to the present day to be a central polemical issue. And Skocpol's notion of the autonomy of the state has to be seen in the context of that Marxist, neo-Marxist, and post-Marxist polemic.

The first major assault on this abandonment of the state concept in mainstream political science was that of J. P. Nettl, whose article "The State as a Conceptual Variable" (1968) appeared in the same year as the publication of Watkins's encyclopedia article. Nettl explained the neglect of the concept of the state in Britain and the United States, and particularly in the United States, by the fact that the phenomena of "stateness" are weak in those countries. But the general point made by Nettl regarding the differing salience of the state in the United States and in continental Europe has been appreciated at least since Tocqueville and has been part of the conventional wisdom of comparative government and politics. Though he advocates a return to the state concept, he does not effectively deal with Sabine's and Watkins's uneasiness about the ambiguity of the term.

He offers a definition of the state with four components. First, "it is a collectivity that summates a set of functions and structures in order to generalize their applicability" (1968, 562). It is not clear which structures and which functions Nettl includes in this collectivity, although he refers to bureaucracies, parliaments, and even political parties. Second, the state is a unit in international relations; all independent nations, whether having strong or weak states, have this unified international aspect. Third, the state is autonomous; it is a distinct sector of society. And fourth, the state is a sociocultural phenomena, by which Nettl means that the individual members of the state have a generalized cognition and perception of it.

"Stateness," according to Nettl, is a quantitative variable, and the strength and weakness of the state in individual societies can be compared through functional analysis. Nettl includes among these functions that of central administration, which varies in strength and scope across countries. Thus Anglo-American central administration is weaker than the continental European pattern. Law enforcement patterns differ in strong and weak states; thus in Britain and the United States law and law enforcement have more autonomy than is the case in continental Europe. The legal professions are more clearly independent of government. He also suggests the hypothesis that the strength and the weakness of central administration are related to the strength and weakness of party systems.

Nettl's contribution is an argument to go beyond the mainstream Anglo-American view of the state as the "general area of central government in contradistinction to society" (p. 591) and to examine the proposition that "more or less stateness is a useful variable for comparing western societies, and that the absence or presence of a well-developed concept of state relates to and identifies important empirical differences in these societies" (p. 592).

When all is said and done, Nettl has disaggregated the state into a variety of components, which he treats as quantifiable and measurable variables. The all-important question for his thesis, how the state concept relates, aggregates, summates, integrates—and so on—such phenomena as bureaucracies, courts, armies, parliaments, parties, interest groups, media of communication, and public opinion is not answered by Nettl. What political phenomena does it include? What does it exclude? How should one weight these components? Like Sabine and Watkins, Nettl is telling us that to measure stateness it is necessary to operationalize and disaggregate the concept. What the state is depends on which operational measures one decides to use. Nettl's argument that nations vary in their degree of stateness, by which he means the scope and extent of governmental power and authority, was similar to the arguments then being made by political scientists using other terms such as *public, policy, governmental output*, and *governmental performance*. Lowi's threefold classification of policy areas—regulative, distributive, and redistributive—had already been on the table for four years at the time of Nettl's writing and was soon to be used by the former in cross-national comparison. The comparative historical and econometric public policy movements were getting under way in the middle and late 1960s, and they would successfully bring to earth those cross-national contrasts that Nettl was emphasizing in his notion of "stateness."

Another predecessor claimed by the contemporary statist movement is Alfred Stepan, whose *State and Society: Peru in Comparative Perspective* appeared in 1978. Stepan is also critical of the "reductionism" of the liberal-pluralist and classic Marxist approaches to the state and politics. But he does not go quite as far as the more recent statists. While his area specialty is Latin America, his reductionist critique is addressed to comparative politics generally. The particular point he makes with respect to Latin American studies is that there is an alternative body of theory—the organic-statist-corporatist theoretical tradition—that is more appropriate for the analysis of Latin American and Ibero-European politics, since this theoretical tradition developed in response to the institutional traditions and characteristics of these areas. He describes the liberal-pluralist approach to the state as integrally individualist and as fully committed to the doctrine that there can be no "general good" other than that which flows from the pursuit of the interests of individuals: "A methodological and normative assumption among both political and economic thinkers in the liberal pluralist tradition is that it is undesirable to use the concept of the general good" (p. 7). Stepan also argues that liberal-pluralism treats the state as a dependent variable, that such theories tend systematically to draw attention away from viewing the state as an autonomous agency. This distortion of liberal-pluralism in Stepan's work is shared with the contemporary statist movement, and I will return to this question of the place of the general welfare, the state, and the government in pluralist theory and research. It should, however, be pointed out that Stepan's book reflects a more substantial search of the literature than the later work in the new statist tradition.

It is not clear where to locate Eric Nordlinger in this polemic (1981). He stops short of unfurling a new paradigmatic banner (1987). He is empirical and "positivist" to the core. In asserting the autonomy of the state he by no means excludes the power of societal factors. Rather, he attributes a societal reductionism to his mainstream colleagues and represents his own work as an important effort to carve out a place for the initiative of governmental officials in the making of public policy. If one corrects for his misreading of the pluralist tradition, there is no change of paradigm here, but rather a research program of considerable promise intended to distinguish among polities according to the degree to which state (governmental) personnel take the initiative in the making of public policy and the factors and conditions that explain these differences in degree. I do not believe that a research program of this kind would strike the typical political science practitioner as a revolutionary departure from mainstream research designs, which, as I shall show, typically accord quite substantial policy initiative and autonomy to political executives, high-level bureaucrats, legislative committees and leaders, and the like.

Nordlinger avoids vague and amorphous formulations. Unlike the statists, he offers a definition of the state in operational terms: "The definition of the state must refer to individuals rather than to some other kinds of phenomena, such as 'institutional arrangements' or the legal normative order. Since we are primarily concerned with the making of public policy, a conception of the state that does not have individuals at its core could lead directly into the anthropomorphic and reification fallacies. . . . Only individuals have preferences and engage in actions that make for their realization. And only by making individuals central to the definition can Hegelian implications (substantive and metaphysical) be avoided when referring to the state's preferences" (1981, 9).

Nordlinger has three other components of a definition of the state. The state should be defined to include not only the government and the bureaucratic agencies that derive their authority from it, "it should include all public officials—elective and appointive—at high and low levels—who are involved in the making of public policy" (1981, 10). It should avoid all characterizations that may vary from case to case, such as legitimacy and sovereignty. Finally, a definition should seek neutrality; it should avoid attributing specific functions and purposes to all states, such as the preservation of stability or the reproduction of capitalism.

With this carefully empirical set of defining characteristics, Nordlinger attacks what he alleges to be the "near unanimity . . . of all variants of liberal and Marxist writing on democratic politics" on the question of the dominance of societal constraints on the making of public policy. He refutes these imputed theoretical positions by asserting that there are three levels of state autonomy in policy-making and then illustrates them through an analysis of the secondary literature. The lowest level of state autonomy (type 3) refers to situations in which state and society preferences do not diverge and the state acts on its own preferences; that is to say, the particular policy adopted is the one preferred by state officials even though it does not encounter opposition from society. The second level of autonomy is one in which society's preferences differ from the state's preferences, but state officials persuade society to adopt state preferences. The third and highest level (type 1) is represented in situations in which the preferences of state and society diverge; but the state nevertheless enacts a policy consistent with its preferences. This extreme case, crucial to the support of Nordlinger's theory of state autonomy, is illustrated by analysis of the various ways in which the state can play on social division and employ the formidable powers of government. In a later paper (1987), Nordlinger offers a fourfold classification of state-society relations in terms of high and low state autonomy and societal support that has interesting research possibilities. Though Nordlinger fails to—and indeed cannot—document his characterization of liberal scholarship as societally reductionist, there is no doubt that he has made an important contribution to empirical theory. His analysis is rigorous and heuristic, full of interesting research leads.

Pluralism as Theory and in Empirical Research

The view associated with the Committee on States and Social Structures of the Social Science Research Council (SSRC) is a more integral critique of the so-called waning orthodoxies or paradigms of contemporary political science. These orthodoxies are "pluralism-structural functionalism" and

Marxism. They are said to treat the state as a dependent variable; its actions are explained by the interplay of interest groups or of social classes. Thus Theda Skocpol, in her introduction to the first book published under the auspices of this committee, states that the previously dominant pluralist-functionalist approaches viewed government "primarily as an arena within which economic interest groups or normative social movements contended or allied with one another to shape the making of public policy decisions. Those decisions were understood to be allocations of benefits among demanding groups. Research centered on the societal 'inputs' to government and on the distributive effects of governmental outputs. Government itself was not taken very seriously as an independent actor, and in comparative research variations in governmental organization were deemed less significant than the general functions shared by the political systems of all societies" (Evans, Rueschemeyer, and Skocpol 1985, 4; cf. Skocpol 1982).

This attribution of society-centeredness to the earlier literature is repeated at other points in this first book of the SSRC Committee (Evans, Rueschemeyer, and Skocpol 1985, chaps. 4, 10). Stephen Krasner, another committee member, comments along these same lines in a review article: "Pure interest group versions of pluralism virtually ignore public actors and institutions. The government is seen as a cash register that totals up and then averages the preferences and political power of societal actors. Government may thus be seen as an arena within which societal actors struggle to insure the success of their own particular preferences. The major function of public officials is to make sure that the game is played fairly. If public institutions are viewed as figurative cash registers or as literal referees, there is no room for anything that could be designated as a state as actor with autonomous preferences capable of manipulating and even restructuring its own society" (1984, 226). According to Krasner, where pluralists do recognize the initiating role of political leaders, they reduce state institutions to "individuals acting in roles" not restrained by institutional "imperatives and restraints." This is a more complex version of the reductionist argument; for Krasner it is an individualist as well as a societal reductionism.

In making the case for this reductionist treatment of the state and government in pluralism and structural functionalism, neither Skocpol nor Krasner provides us with a literature search commensurate with the scope and variety of the political science literature about which they are generalizing. They seem to claim that the literature of political science may be subsumed under these two categories of pluralism-structural functionalism and Marxism. Would they include the substantial literature on Communist countries?

Surely this literature, even that part of it that experimented with pluralist models, took governmental actors seriously, and dealt with the coercive, extractive, and regulative powers of government in addition to the allocative. Would an examination of the comparative government and politics literature and the country studies of Britain, France, Germany, Italy, and so on, with their emphasis on the power of political executives and bureaucracies, sustain Skocpol's complaint regarding the neglect of state agencies in mainstream political science? In U.S. studies how would they deal with the substantial literature on the presidency, the Congress, and the courts? How would they dispose of the flurry of publications on military regimes in Third World countries that appeared in the 1960s and 1970s?

If we look at the larger specifically pluralist literature, can we sustain this statist critique? Suppose we examine the ideas of the original statists in order to put both pluralism and statism into historical perspective. And then let us look at the empirical research done by the pluralists. Does it indeed conform to the society-centered reductionist pattern presented by Skocpol, Krasner, and their collaborators? Does it conform to the on-the-whole similar portraits presented by Nettl, Stepan, and Nordlinger?

It is sobering that although their central theme is the affirmation of statism as an alternative to pluralism, neither Skocpol nor Krasner nor the other antipluralists cited here seem to have looked into the original confrontation of statism and pluralism at the end of the nineteenth century and in the early decades of the twentieth. And although their argument for a return to the state rests on the claim that the pluralist empirical literature reduced the state and government to an arena and treated the government as a dependent variable (to the extent that it treated it at all), they simply fail to cite or to discuss the very substantial pluralist "interest group" literature of the last three quarters of a century.

It would not have taken a major search to raise serious questions about the validity of these statist characterizations. There are excellent reviews of the early statist and pluralist literature in the two encyclopedias of the social sciences—articles on the state by George Sabine (1934) and Frederick Watkins (1968) and articles on pluralism by Francis Coker (1934) and Henry Kariel (1968), all political theorists of repute. Sabine traces the emergence of the state concept from Machiavelli's *il stato* in *The Prince* and the first adoption of the term *secretary of state* for ministerial offices in the reign of Elizabeth. Its usage spread with the rise and diffusion of absolutism. And the notion of sovereignty developed along with it. The emergence of the state in the course of the sixteenth to nineteenth centuries was associated with expansion, aggression, and war making. As a process, the Western European state arose out of a logic of aggression or defense against aggression. It was a consequence of the growth of armies and the recruitment and training of civil bureaucracies concerned with the extraction of resources, the procurement of supplies, and the regulation of behavior—all primarily in relation to this military-defense-expansion set of goals. The potential progressiveness of the state resulted from this concentration of power and its separation from the person of the ruler or rulers. Compared with the complicated dynastic, sacred, and secular particularisms that preceded it, it had the potential for providing greater personal security, a larger internal market, and perhaps improved systems of law and justice.

The notion of state sovereignty survived the crises of the democratic revolutions. What happened was that the "people" became sovereign or "parliament" became sovereign. But the state was conceived as unitary, as above society, and as legitimately penetrative of the entire territory and population under its jurisdiction.

It was this conception of the centralized, superimposed absolute state, embodied in the sovereign and the agencies of the "crown," that was the target of the pluralists of the late nineteenth and early twentieth centuries. Opposition to this all-powerful notion of state sovereignty came from both the Right and the Left. From the conservative side, J. Neville Figgis (1914) affirmed the autonomous rights of churches and neighborhood communities. From the Center and the Left, Ernest Barker (1930), A. D. Lindsay (1929), and Harold Laski (1919) affirmed the autonomy of economic and professional groups and trade unions. The English theorists drew on German and French authorities—Otto Gierke (1900), Emile Durkheim (1950), and Leon Duguit (1919)—for authority for their antimonism. What is crucial for the argument of the contemporary statists is Francis Coker's (1934) unequivocal statement:

> Neither the pluralists nor their theoretical forerunners, however, really make the groups independent of the state. Gierke maintained that the state is sovereign—supreme in legal and moral right—where general interests require the exertion of organized social power for their maintenance. Paul Boncour regarded the state as the sole organ of national solidarity, with a duty to prevent any group from acting oppressively toward the public, other groups or its own members. Durkheim ascribed to the state the function of defining general policies, leaving to the several associations only the task of diversifying, under state supervision, the application of the policies according to the special requirements of the several associations. Figgis described the state as the *communitas communitatem* and assigned to it distinctive tasks and a superior authority as the chief agency of social adjustment and coordina-

> tion. . . . Barker warns against carrying the recent pluralist trends too far; the state as the most embracing scheme of social life must be allowed to adjust the relations of associations to one another and to their members in order to preserve the equality of associations, and protect the individual from the possible tyranny of his own group. (p. 172)

Laski—the most extreme of the antimonists—goes far toward recommending a powerful state that would own monopolistic industries; regulate the rest of the economy; set basic standards for hours, wages, and working conditions; and fix prices for necessities. Coker concludes:

> It appears then that when the pluralists set forth their abstract theory they deny the sovereign power of the state or else characterize the power of something which is properly only ultimate and reserved; but when they devise the specific institutional arrangements to carry out their theory they assign to the state numerous tasks, in laying down general policies and seeing that they are observed, which obviously require, not an ultimate and reserved, but a very direct and constantly exercised power. . . . They would retain the state but deprive it of sovereignty. It appears, however, that they accomplish this compromise only in words. They allow the state to secure its funds through compulsory taxation, retain the whole traditional system of a compulsory allegiance applied to all members of the community and assign to this comprehensive and coercive association extensive duties in directing the economic and social life of the community. (1934, 173)

In the *International Encyclopedia of the Social Sciences* (1968) Henry Kariel gives a version of pluralist theory somewhat more supportive of the reductionist government-as-arena model. But here he is referring to the earlier formulations of the theorists of pluralism. He reports that by the 1930s "it appeared necessary to some of the pluralists to reintroduce what they had previously banished; a unified purpose above and beyond the will of a plurality of groups. . . . They had rejected such ideas as common good, community interests, and general will. Yet they found it scarcely possible to conceive of the political process without the purposeful, helpful hand of the state, especially as domestic group competition, and foreign threats endangered the viability of a pluralistic political order. Thus both Laski and Cole were finally driven to recognize needs more fundamental than a vibrant group life. They were to argue for both leadership to give expression to these needs and a state equipped to satisfy them" (p. 507). Kariel insists, however, that a latent integral pluralism persists in some unspecified part of mainstream political science.

The pluralist writings that are viewed as coming closest to the portraits presented by the statists are those of Arthur Bentley (1908, 1967), David Truman (1951), and Earl Latham (1952). Bentley's *Process of Government* received almost no attention for the several decades between its publication in 1908 and the appearance of Truman's book in 1951. In his introduction to the 1967 edition of Bentley's book, Peter Odegard remarks on the fact that Bentley provides few empirical data on interest group activity, despite the fact that pressure groups and the lobby were high-salience issues at the turn of the century. His book was essentially theoretical; it came close to presenting a formal model, an analytical reduction of institutions to observable behavior with interest groups the all-powerful explanatory variable. Peter Odegard argues that had the book been more balanced as between modeling and empirical data and had the model been presented as a model rather than as an abstraction of reality, Bentley might not have been so long neglected by scholars. Thus the large U.S. pressure group literature that appeared in the 1920s to 1940s was not influenced by his work; and the pressure group literature of the 1950s and 1960s sometimes cited Bentley, but it did not adopt his group reductionist and behaviorist model. The empirical pressure group research of the first decades of the twentieth century originated in the muckraking tradition of the turn-of-the-century period.

David Truman, the leading group theorist of recent political science, utilized Bentley as an analytical model but devoted almost half of his trail-breaking book to the interactions of interest groups and governmental processes. Though governmental institutions are treated from a group perspective, there is clear recognition of their autonomous decision-making capacity. Thus in his chapter on the executive, he points out that

> the importance of the executive branch, however, does not derive simply from its size or from the variety of its activities. It is of far greater significance that the operation of these activities necessitates choices among alternate lines of action, the exercise of discretion. . . . Both the newer and the expanded older functions of government create the necessity for a large measure of administrative discretion, and the tendency is toward the widening of such powers rather than toward their restriction. . . . The obligation to remain minimally accessible to all legitimate interests in the society can supply him with a measure of independence and a persuasive power that effectively supplements his formal authority. . . . Access to the governor or president is not sought by interest groups simply out of habit; the means of leadership in the hands of these officials are not negligible. The president's roles as chief executive, chief legislator, chief of state, and commander of the armed forces are real, not nominal. (1951, 396, 427)

It is not possible save through distortion to describe these several chapters depicting the interaction of groups and government as simply reflecting the arena or the cash register model. Executives, congressmen, and judges have both authority and discretion.

In his article "Political Group Analysis" in the *International Encyclopedia of the Social Sciences*, Truman refers to this "referee" model of governmental processes as an oversimplification leading "to the error of treating a limiting case as if it were the norm. This obvious error occurs with great frequency in the literature, despite the fact that even our rough knowledge of the distribution of cases of the relation between interest group and government demonstrates that this oversimplification fails to square with the evidence concerning a vast range of instances" (1968, 243–44).

Earl Latham (1952) does present an integral group theory of U.S. government. He does this by characterizing governmental institutions as groups themselves, and argues the case for a group politics equilibrium model of the policy-making process. But he runs into problems with governmental agencies as groups. He finds that there is a unilateral, asymmetrical quality about government as groups. The policeman can stop traffic; drivers cannot stop the policeman. He gropes in an effort to accommodate the peculiar properties of officials. He rejects Krasner's metaphor of the pluralist state as a cash register more than 30 years before Krasner uses it: "In these adjustments of group interest, the legislature does not play the part of inert cash register, ringing up the additions and withdrawals of strength; it is not a mindless balance pointing to and marking the weight and distribution of power among the contending groups" (p. 391). Thus both houses of Congress are groups with senses of identity and with their own interests. Executives, legislators, and judges are "officials"; if they are members of groups, their groups are not of the same order as nonofficial groups. He writes, "The groups so privileged collectively make up the instrumentalities of the state, and such groups are distinguished from others only in their possession of the characteristics of officiality" (p. 389).

The reductionist model, while applicable to the work of Bentley and Latham, can be applied to that of Truman only with difficulty. And it completely fails to capture the empirical interest group research of the 1920s to 1960s, the very literature described as society-centered by the neostatists. In demonstrating that this literature operated with a very lively sense of the autonomy and discretion of government, both empirically and normatively, I shall cite a selection of Americanists—in particular Pendleton Herring, Elmer Schattschneider, V. O. Key, Jr., Robert Dahl, and Bauer, Pool, and Dexter—

and Harry Eckstein, Henry Ehrmann, and Joseph LaPalombara among the Europeanists. On the question of societal reductionism more broadly in the political science literature of the 1960s and 1970s, I shall review briefly some of the U.S. and comparative government text literature of this period.

One of the most influential political science studies of the 1930s was Pendleton Herring's *Public Administration and the Public Interest* (1936). His principal question was how administrative organization in a democracy could resist the onslaught of particularistic groups and its own conservative propensities and contribute to the general welfare. In the light of the conflicts of the New Deal period, he points out that the democratic state must somehow deal with the conflict between capital and labor. "It cannot afford to await the survival of the fittest. The exigencies of the age demand positive state activity in order that democracy itself may continue" (p. 379). He continues, "Unless we are to rest resigned with this situation upon the supposition that this is the inherent nature of the democratic state, there is need for promoting a purpose of the state over and above the purposes of the medley of interests that compose it" (p. 380).

On the autonomy of the state and the need for increasing this autonomy, Herring writes, "The need of attempting to formulate an official program in the public interest by a responsible administrative agency arises from the experienced strength of minority groups in pressing their case by propaganda and organized agitation. . . . The offering of positive proposals by a responsible administration is then the first goal to seek. . . . The increased power of the president means, of course, an increase in the importance of the bureaucracy. . . . If the existence of the democratic regime rests upon the assumption that the state exists not for the welfare of any one class but for the benefit of the people as a whole, this great and growing bureaucracy must be guarded from domination by economic groups or social classes" (pp. 383–84). This whole concluding chapter of Pendleton Herring's work of the mid-1930s might well serve as a bible for the contemporary state autonomy movement, even to the point of the use of the same vocabulary.

Elmer Schattschneider, a leading authority on U.S. politics and pressure groups of the 1930s and 1940s, describes the U.S. presidency as the principal rallying point for the great public interest of the nation, the point at which the issues of public policy are discovered and exploited (1942).

V. O. Key, Jr.—the leading U.S. theorist of parties, elections, public opinion, and pressure groups—whose views are crucial for the statist critique of pluralism, has a long concluding chapter, "Pressure Groups and the General

Welfare," in his text on political parties, first published in 1948 and appearing until well into the 1960s. He argues that public officials and political leaders "can frequently obtain acceptance of a policy more nearly reflecting the general interest by going over the heads of pressure group leaders to workers, businessmen, to farmers who have ordinarily a greater sense of community responsibility than do their hired men in the offices of pressure societies" (1952, 174). To illustrate the capacity of government to resist special interests, Key cites major statutes regulating the interests of powerful groups in the 1930s – among them the Public Utility Holding Company Act, and the Food, Drug, and Cosmetic Act – where powerful organized interests were present and actively lobbying against the legislation and where there were no organized groups representing the ordinary citizens whose interests were protected by these acts. These last two examples would come close to representing Nordlinger's type 1 cases of state autonomy.

The two classic political process studies of the 1960s – Dahl's *Who Governs?* (1961) and Bauer, Pool, and Dexter's *American Business and Public Policy* (1963) – both reported results reflecting the autonomy of governmental officials and governmental agencies. In their conclusions on the relative importance of "societal" and governmental agencies in the enactment of the Reciprocal Trade Agreements Act of 1954–55, Bauer, Pool, and Dexter point out that "a Republican administration"– normally most susceptible to the pressure of business interests for protection from foreign competition – "felt free to adopt as the most cherished item of its legislative program a Roosevelt measure which transferred tariff making from the legislative to the executive branch" (1963, 466), where, it should be pointed out, tariff making would be less exposed to group pressures. Indeed, their study of business interests and tariff policy in the post-World War II period records the attenuation of "societal" influences and the attainment of "state autonomy" with respect to this field of foreign economic policy. Dahl's study of redevelopment policy-making in New Haven in the 1960s has the well-deserved reputation of having moved the study of policy-making forward by demonstrating the strong relationship between political structure and process and the substance of public policy. Rather than being societally reductionist, Dahl's study was directed against the community power model of C. Wright Mills, Floyd Hunter, and others, which was reductionist, attributing generalized and dominant political influence to the upper business and professional interests. Dahl demonstrated that New Haven had a number of different policy processes that were triggered by different kinds of issues. In the case of redevelopment in New Haven, he shows that Mayor Lee initiated this policy long before there was any interest group or popular movement favoring urban renewal. Krasner (1984) acknowledges that this was the case, but insists the Dahl has reduced "state institutions" to "individuals and roles," failing to take into account the constraints of institutions. I will deal with this version of the reductionist thesis in the context of how statists define state autonomy.

In an authoritative work on governmental regulation in the United States, James Q. Wilson (1980) writes in his introduction, "Today the federal government is active with respect to virtually the full range of human affairs, much of its power is exercised, and many of its purposes are defined, by a large bureaucratic apparatus" (p. vii). In his concluding discussion of the origins of regulation, he shows how neither a societal nor a statal "paradigm" would capture reality: "The Civil Aeronautics Board (CAB) was created to help business, but the Occupational Safety and Health Administration (OSHA) was formed over the objections of business. The laws administered by the Environmental Protection Agency (EPA) were enacted over the opposition of those segments of the economy to be regulated. . . . The Shipping Act that was to be administered by what later became known as the Federal Maritime Commission (FMC) was passed over the opposition of the shipowners whom it was to regulate, but with the support of shippers it was supposed to help. Though the Sherman Antitrust Act did not have to overcome well-organized business opposition, neither was the chief impetus for its passage the demand of business" (p. 364).

During the 1920s and 1930s, at a time when U.S. pressure group studies were already thriving, European scholars viewed pressure groups in reductionist and normative terms. The political scientists of the Left tended to reduce pressure groups to class phenomena. Conservative European political scientists viewed pressure groups as political pathologies. Only the state and the bureaucracy had legitimate power and were capable of acting in the general interest.

After World War II, a number of empirical studies of interest groups in Britain, France, Germany, Italy, and other countries began to appear. For the purposes of our argument here it may be sufficient to review three exemplars of this literature: Harry Eckstein's study of the British Medical Association (1960), Henry Ehrmann's study of organized business in France (1957), and Joseph LaPalombara's (1964) study of Italian interest groups.

In the introduction to his study of the British Medical Association, Eckstein points out:

> Pressure is concentrated upon the executive in Britain, first because of the logic of cabinet government in a political system having two highly disciplined

> parties; such a system precludes any consistently successful exertion of influence through members of Parliament, or, less obviously perhaps, through the political parties. Secondly, pressure is focussed on the executive because the broad scope and technical character of contemporary social and economic policies has led to a considerable shift of functions to the bureaucracy. . . .
>
> The predominance of skeletal legislation is not due solely to circumstance (e.g., technical legislation) but also reflects the power of the executive which likes to have a relatively free hand. (1960, 18, 20)

He points out that pressure groups are anxious not to get on the wrong side of the government because of the crucial powers that they enjoy over their affairs. Commenting on Bentley's one-sided interpretation of group influence, Eckstein observes, "The state in Britain today disposes directly of 40 percent of the national income, and that fact speaks for itself. We may regard political systems as amalgams of potential and actual pressure groups, groups which from a political standpoint are merely 'categoric' groups, and groups which have actually been drawn into politics, chiefly through the impact of public policies, either policies actually adopted or policies which are threatened. In short, we can usefully stand Bentley on his head to supplement Bentley right side up; if interaction among politically active groups produces policy, policy in turn creates politically active groups" (p. 27).

According to Eckstein, the influence and effectiveness of pressure groups is substantially dependent on governmental policy and organization. His approach is neither societally reductionist nor statist reductionist. Like almost all of his pluralist colleagues, he sees the policy process as a set of interactions between state and society.

Ehrmann's (1957) study of business groups in France emphasizes the tradition of central administrative power. He notes the importance of the nationalized industries under the Fourth Republic, the control of money and credit, exports, and convertability, governmental price fixing, and the like. He describes the transformations of the Fifth Republic as shifting power from the parties and parliament to the executive and bureaucracy. In language that would gratify the most "statist" of the neostatists Ehrmann catalogs the major triumphs of President de Gaulle in battles with organized interests:

> In regard to major decisions, e.g. the Algerian or the European policies, the liquidation of the African Community, or the preparations for an atomic striking force, the interested lobbies (some of them solidly organized and amply financed) were generally ignored by the Elysee and had difficulties in obtain-

> ing a hearing in the offices of the Prime Minister. . . . In two thirds of his most resounding conflicts with the National Assembly the President of the Republic wanted it to be known that he denied to the deputies the exercise of rights granted to them by the wording of the constitution because the parliament was in fact obeying the injunction of the agricultural lobby. Such affirmations of the regime's fundamental hostility towards intermediaries standing between 'le pouvoir' and 'le peuple' were designed to dramatize its intentionally authoritarian style. (1963, 278).

To similar effect LaPalombara (1964) in his study of Italian interest groups has a whole chapter dealing with the factors that enable the Italian bureaucracy to resist the pressure groups. Among these factor is the culture of the bureaucracy, the sense that the official has of the general or the public interest as he encounters the overtures, blandishments, and threats of pressure organizations: "The typical bureaucrat recognizes that he is involved in a highly politicized process and that the concept of public interest is one of the few meaningful weapons he can utilize in order to assert a bureaucratic decision that is not tied to narrow, particularistic interest group considerations" (p. 384). The socialization of the bureaucrat in the administrative organization also contributes to the capacity to resist the pressure of special interests. La Palombara concludes from his interviews of Italian officials that "when bureaucrats in large number define their role as requiring the objective application of the law, they generally do so with pride and with a sense of having to protect the bureaucracy—and therefore the nation—against the irrational and particularistic forces at large in the country" (p. 388).

The literature that we have reviewed on pluralist theory, group theory, and the activities of interest groups in the United States and Europe gives the statist polemic the best chance of being sustained. It is after all this literature that has been arguing the case for the influence of "societal" organizations in the making of public policy. Though this literature does by and large stress the importance of interest and pressure groups in policy-making, it clearly does not support the reductionist thesis. Autonomous government agencies are present and important throughout this literature. The pluralist "paradigm" is not the one-sided one of Skocpol, Krasner, and others but rather a two-directional one with the state influencing the society as well as the society influencing the state.

If the statist polemicists cannot be sustained with respect to that literature most likely to support their thesis, how does it fare with respect to the more general political science literature of the pluralist era, for example in the U.S. and comparative government text books of the 1950s and 1960s? A few examples may make the point. The two leading U.S. textbooks of the 1940s to 1960s, written by William Anderson and the perennial (Frederick) Ogg and (P. Orman) Ray, give great stress to the powers of the U.S. presidency. Anderson speaks of the U.S. executive as "the government in a very real sense." He has "the power to formulate programs of action" (Anderson and Weidner 1953, 578). Ogg and Ray speak of the U.S. president as "the most powerful elected executive in the world. He is at once the chief formulator of public policy as embodied in legislation, leader of a major political party boasting thousands of functionaries and millions of adherents, chief architect of U.S. foreign policy, . . . director of one of the most gigantic administrative machines ever created, . . . commander in chief of more than two million men in uniform," and so on (p. 258).

Austin Ranney in a text of the 1960s describes the president as making a great deal of law: "He is generally regarded as our 'chief legislator,' . . . mainly because he has taken over most of the initiative in the nation's statute-making process" (1966, 442). In the 1963 edition of another leading text on U.S. government, Burns and Peltason's *Government by the People*, the authors also speak of the president as the chief legislator (pp. 424–25). Indeed, without exception, the texts of the pluralist era in U.S. political science refer to the president as the chief legislator and policymaker of the nation.

The texts in comparative government during these decades gave similar stress to the importance of the political executive. Carter and Herz (1972) speak of the political executive in democracies as laying down "the essential lines of policy in every field of domestic and foreign affairs; he must coordinate the innumerable agencies of what, in most modern countries, has become the biggest business establishment"–"the executive branch of government. . . . he must deal with a vast variety of interest groups and be able to resist their often powerful pressures" (p. 152). And in the Samuel Beer and Adam Ulam text edition of 1964, the chapter on Britain describes the British cabinet as the very center of power and the higher civil service as the initiator and drafter of almost all legislation (p. 103).

The conventional wisdom of the political science literature of this period emphasized the importance not only of the political executive but of the bureaucracy. Thus Robert Putnam exclaimed, "Public bureaucracies, staffed largely by permanent civil servants, are responsible for the vast majority of policy initiatives taken by governments. Discretion not merely for deciding individual cases, but for crafting the content of most legislation has passed from the legislature to the executive. Bureaucrats, monopolizing as they do much of the available information of shortcomings of existing policies, as well as much of technical expertise necessary to design practical alternatives, have gained a predominant influence over the evolution of the agenda for decisions" (1973, 17).

It might be expected that the political sociologists would be more likely to manifest the society-centeredness that the statists have attributed to the pluralists and the structural functionalists. Since sociologists specialize in social structure and processes, it might be expected that they would incline toward explaining the state and politics in terms of society. In a series of papers on the scope and content of political sociology going back to the 1950s, S. M. Lipset and William Schneider trace the history of this debate from the state-centeredness of the Hegelians to the society-centeredness of Proudhon and Marx. In Max Weber and the later political sociologists the causal arrows go both ways, and both concepts—state and society—are disaggregated into their component parts. Lipset and Schneider argue, "Political sociology can be defined as the study of the interrelationship between society and polity, between social structures and political institutions. It is important to note that this definition does not assign causal priority to society over polity; political sociology is not solely the study of the social factors that condition the political order. Indeed political institutions are themselves social structures, and hence are often the independent (that is) causal factors that affect nonpolitical social structure" (1973, 400–401).

A Note on Marxism and Structural Functionalism

The evidence on the pluralist literature, both theoretical and empirical, clearly cannot support the neostatist critique of society-centeredness. But the neostatists also included structural functionalism and Marxism in their polemic against society-centeredness. With respect to Marxism, they are without question correct. Skocpol argues that "at the theoretical level, virtually all neo-Marxist writers on the state have retained deeply imbedded society-centered assumptions, not allowing themselves to doubt that, at base, states are inherently shaped by classes or class struggles and function to preserve and expand modes of production" (Evans, Rueschemeyer, and Skocpol 1985, 5). Martin Carnoy's review (1984) of neo-Marxist theories of the state—from Gramsci to Althusser to Poulantzas and Offe—by and large supports Skocpol's (1982) summary.

Indeed, David Easton (1981) characterizes the entire "return-to-the-state" movement as arising out of a contemporary revival of Marxism. He speaks of three Marxist "comings." The first coming occurred at the time of the origins of the Marxist movement, which touched the United States only superficially in the 1880s and 1890s. The second coming occurred in the Great Depression of the 1930s. This impingement affected U.S. academic life and political science more deeply. The whole, now older, generation of political science was affected by this second wave and by the disillusionments of the late 1930s and 1940s. The third coming of Marxism had taken the form of this neostatist movement—more complex than the first two visitations, but presenting some of the same difficulties.

The polemic against structural functionalism is the least developed theme in the neostatist movement. It is said to be societally reductionist, but no attention is given to the "structural" part of structural functionalism, which after all deals with state agencies and institutions. "Functionalism" developed out of the realist recognition that legal or customary norms defining the powers of the various institutions usually failed to capture their performance. Often they were quite misleading. Hence the properties of institutions were not taken as normatively given but as something to be researched empirically. And particularly if one wanted to compare political systems across cultures, one had to examine functions as well as normative and legal structures. Structural functionalism is as old in some ways as political science itself. Separation of powers—a structural functional theory—has been a central theme of political theory at least since Montesquieu.

Neostatist Definitions of the State

I promised to analyze the statist movement on three levels of validity and utility. The first of these was the strong statist position that pluralism-structural functionalism and Marxism were societally reductionist, that they did not attribute autonomy to the state, and hence were inadequate approaches to political explanation. Our analysis of the evidence suggests that this characterization of pluralism both in theory and in empirical research is incorrect. Overwhelmingly, the pluralist literature has been shown to be one in which governmental autonomy is recognized; in which the explanatory logic goes in both directions, from society to the state and from the state to the society. Neostatism seems to be a polemic internal to Marxism, since this intellectual movement has in the past decades operated from a social class reductionist set of assumptions.

If the critique by the neostatists of the mainstream literature of political science has not been supported by evidence, it may still be that the statist approach is significantly superior to pluralism-structural functionalism as an approach to explanation, that it specifies the elements and variables of analysis better, that its causal logic is more powerful, and the like. The writers in this genre may have been careless and mistaken in their search of the literature, but their approach to research design may be superior.

The shift from institutionalism to realism in the political science of the late nineteenth and early twentieth centuries was enormously productive. It gave birth to the work of Vilfredo Pareto, Max Weber, Emile Durkheim, Woodrow Wilson, James Bryce, Moissaye Ostrogorski, Roberto Michels, Graham Wallas, George Catlin, Charles Merriam, Harold Lasswell, and Harold Gosnell, among others; to the large empirical literature on political parties and pressure groups; and to realistic studies of governmental institutions and processes. This movement of "realism" assumed that by "unpacking" and disaggregating general and diffuse concepts it was possible to reach a firmer grasp of the reality scholars were seeking to understand, interpret, and explain. We understand liberty, justice, equality, obligation better by spelling out their varieties and their component parts. Similarly, as a part of this movement of realism, legal-institutional concepts such as the state were disaggregated. One spoke of government or of the political system and its various legal-institutional components—executives, bureaucracies, legislatures, and courts—and of agencies and institutions of a paralegal and nonlegal sort, such as political parties, interest groups, and media of communication.

The neostatist movement wants to reverse this trend and return to large and relatively loosely defined concepts such as the state and society. They write about "strong and weak states" and "strong and weak societies," but it is not clear what they mean by strength and weakness. So many dimensions are conflated here that they cannot expect this approach to research to be taken seriously. Indeed, it is an irony of the statist movement that this central concept either is not clearly specified or, when it is specified, is very like the definitions of *government, political system,* and other terms denoting the totality of political phenomena employed in the mainstream literature.

Theda Skocpol approximates a definition of the state in her earlier work on revolutions, where she sets aside the neo-Marxist efforts of Miliband, Poulantzas, Anderson, Therborn, and Offe because they fall short of acknowledging the possibility of state autonomy. She writes:

> We can make sense of social revolutionary transformations only if we take the state seriously as a macro-structure. The state properly conceived is no mere arena in which socio-economic struggles are fought out. It is rather a set of administrative, policing, and military organizations headed, and more or less

> coordinated by, an executive authority. Any state first and fundamentally extracts resources from society and deploys these resources to create and support coercive and administrative organizations. Of course, these basic state organizations are built up and must operate within the context of class-divided socioeconomic relations as well as within the context of national and international dynamics. Moreover, coercive and administrative organizations are only parts of overall political systems. These systems also may contain institutions through which social interests are represented in state policy-making as well as institutions through which nonstate actors are mobilized to participate in policy implementation. Nevertheless, the administrative and coercive organizations are the basis of state power as such. (1979, 29)

Skocpol is struggling here to free herself from the class determinism of Marxism. She even adopts the system metaphor to accommodate important aspects of politics not easily reducible to coercive and administrative organizations. But in her later work she comes back to a concept the limits and content of which are unspecified. Thus in her more recent formulation (Evans, Rueschemeyer, and Skocpol 1985) she skirts the question of defining the state. What she does after critiquing the Marxist and pluralist-structural functionalist approaches to the state is to cite favorably more "state-centered" types of research, such as the work of Nettl, Stepan, and others. For more remote ancestors of the statist approach she cites Max Weber and Otto Hintze. Because her approach is through illustration rather than specification, it is difficult to distinguish the extent to which and the ways in which her state-centered approach would differ from the treatment of the state and government in the work of Herring, V. O. Key, Eckstein, Ehrmann, the text writers in U.S. and comparative government. It is also impossible to determine how it differs from the treatment in structural functionalism of executives, bureaucracies, courts, legislatures, parties, pressure groups; or how it compares with the enormous literature of the 1960s and 1970s that could not properly be subsumed under either of these approaches.

In a later chapter in the SSRC volume (Evans, Rueschemeyer, and Skocpol 1985), in collaboration with Margaret Weir, Skocpol presents a number of diagrams of the policy process. She rejects two that begin the policy process with "socially rooted demands" or "authoritative intellectual developments" in favor of the third one, which presents the starting point of policy explanation as "state structures and policy legacies," and in which the activities of politicians and officials and the demands of social groups are treated as intervening variables. She is clearly insisting here on a "state-centered" explanation of the policy process. I suggest that the important contrast here is between the state-society interaction model of mainstream political science and this state-centered one.

In Chapter 2 of the same volume, Dietrich Rueschemeyer and Peter Evans adopt the Weberian definition of the state as the agency that seeks and maintains a monopoly of legitimate violence in a given territory. This is not substantially different from mainstream efforts to define government and the political system (e.g., Almond and Coleman 1960, 6, 7). And if one reads the fine print in the statist literature it is clear that their definitions are quite similar to mainstream definitions. Leaving aside the neo-Marxist vocabulary, the conclusions of Rueschemeyer and Evans as to the complexity and diversity of state phenomena comparatively considered are really quite eclectic and mainstream: "We recognize that across a range of historical circumstances—in ways that vary substantially—the state tends to be an expression of pacts of domination, to act coherently as a corporate unit, to become an arena of social conflict, and to present itself as the guardian of universal interests" (Evans, Rueschemeyer, and Skocpol 1985, 48).

Stephen Skowronek's *Building a New American State* (1984), often represented as the exemplar of the new statist paradigm, does not offer a definition of the state. The narrative of this important contribution to U.S. administrative and political history is carried not by the "state" but by the "government," the "administration," or the "bureaucracy" or by particular agencies of government like Congress, courts, and political parties.

Stephen Krasner goes a great deal further in specifying the essence of the statist approach. He attributes five characteristics to the recent statist literature "that distinguish it from orientations associated with the behavioral revolution" (1984, 224). Echoing a criticism of Theda Skocpol, Krasner states that the statist approach views politics more in terms of rule and control than of allocation. Krasner does not seem to be aware here of the political science literature on regulatory policy and agencies, on the emphasis in the structural functionalist literature on extractive and regulative, as well as the distributive, aspects of politics. The early and influential theoretical work of Lowi (1964), whose threefold classification of types of public policy—the regulative, distributive, and redistributive—has had such great influence in empirical political science research, is also unmentioned by Krasner.

A second characteristic of the literature is the argument that the state is an actor in its own right. "It cannot be understood as a reflection of societal characteristics or preferences" (p. 225). Here Krasner is simply repeating the myth of the societal reductionism of pluralism.

Krasner's third point is that statist studies place more emphasis on institutional constraints on individual behavior. Statists, according to Krasner, accord only a very small scope of discretion and initiative at the individual level: "Actors in the political system, whether individuals or groups, are bound within these structures, which limit, even determine, their conceptions of their own interest and their political resources" (p. 225). On this point Krasner is probably correct. Most mainstream political scientists would draw back from a thoroughgoing determinist position.

Krasner's fourth contrast has to do with viewing political phenomena in a longitudinal and historical perspective. He makes much of the tree model of historical choice points, the argument that a particular choice tends to preclude other options. This decision tree model is, of course, a contribution from behavioral social science. The importance of the longitudinal, historical dimension has long been recognized by behavioral political science, in public opinion and election studies, in the political psychobiographical literature, and in structural functional analysis. More recently, behaviorist students of the Congress such as Polsby (1968), Lawrence Dodd (1986a, 1986b), and Cooper and Brady (1981) have exploited the possibilities of the historical approach.

Krasner's fifth and final point is that behavioral political science tends to view political phenomena in equilibrium, process, and compatibility terms and fails to appreciate the importance of conflict and stress. This is difficult to square with the history of pluralism. Pluralism as a normative theory was born out of the struggle of economic, religious, and ethnic groups against the overpowering sovereign state, as well as the effort to conquer the state in order to use its coercive powers to benefit the interests of exploited groups and classes. The pressure group struggle described by Herring, Odegard, Schattschneider, Key, and others hardly took the form of a smoothly purring machine. Political culture research, consociational theory, corporatist theory, and development and modernization theory all treat conflict as central themes.

Thus with the exception of determinism in the structural sense, Krasner has listed a set of properties that do not demarcate statist studies from the main body of political science literature.

Some Concluding Reflections

Thus on two of the three grounds named, the statist movement is in error. Its attribution of societal reductionism to the pluralist-structural functionalist approaches is not supported by the preponderance of evidence. Its assertion that a statist approach is both different from prevailing views in mainstream political science research and a distinctly improved approach to political explanation also fails to convince. Either it is diffuse or allusive in its formulation of what statism is or its definitions are indistinguishable from "behavioral" or structural functionalist definitions of things political. More telling, perhaps, is the fact that in pressing their critique of older political science approaches to political explanation, the statists have fallen into the trap of neglecting nonstatal variables, such as political parties, interest groups, and the media of communication. From this point of view it is a distinctly inferior model of political explanation to the models they criticize.

If statism fails in its polemic against pluralist reductionism and if its positive formulations do not convince, there still is a third ground on which to give it positive marks—the "heuristic" ground. It is surely the case in the history of scholarship that "stirring things up," even in the absence of substantive merit in a particular intellectual initiative, often proves to have been useful in the net and balance. Scholarly disciplines have a way of settling into ruts, becoming repetitive and endlessly replicatory or concerned with trifling modification and emendation of argument. A scholarly tantrum may have the effect of stirring the senses and alerting the mind to new possibilities.

Aside from generally capturing attention and provoking semantic adaptations on the part of many scholars, it may be argued that statism has drawn attention to institutional and particularly administrative history as a focus for political science research. This is all to the good. But if this, indeed, is the positive achievement of this intellectual episode, then one has to question why the literature of institutional and administrative history was not searched. Why are there no references to the four volumes of L. D. White's administrative history of the United States: *The Federalists* (1956), *The Jeffersonians* (1951), *The Jacksonians* (1954), and *The Republican Era, 1868–1901* (1958)? Why no reference to White's *Trends in Public Administration* (1933)? More recently, why no reference to LaPalombara's *Bureaucracy and Political Development* (1963), Ezra Suleiman's *Elites in French Society* (1978), John Armstrong's *European Administrative Elite* (1973), or Robert Putnam's *Comparative Study of Political Elites* (1976)?

If there is something basically at fault with this literature—and I am sure that the statists, coming from their primarily neo-Marxist and international relationist backgrounds, have something novel to contribute to the tradition of institutional history—it is still a fundamental rule of scholarship that one searches the literature before venturing to improve on it. Nevertheless, on this quite limited ground it may be argued that the statist movement has performed a constructive role.

But at what exorbitant and unnecessary cost! A generation of young scholars has been encouraged to reject much of its scholarly ancestry with little more than a paradigmatic farewell. And they have been urged to adopt ambiguous phraseology in the place of a hard-won tradition of operational rigor.

References

Almond, Gabriel A., and James S. Coleman. 1960. *The Politics of the Developing Areas.* Princeton: Princeton University Press.

Anderson, William, and Edward Weidner. 1953. *American Government.* 4th ed. New York: Henry Holt.

Armstrong, John A. 1973. *The European Administrative Elite.* Princeton: Princeton University Press.

Barker, Ernest. 1930. *Church, State, and Study: Essays by Ernest Barker.* London: Methuen.

Bauer, Raymond, Ithiel Pool, and Lewis Dexter. 1963. *American Business and Public Policy.* New York: Atherton.

Beer, Samuel, and Adam Ulam. 1964. *Comparative Government.* New York: Random House.

Bentley, Arthur F. 1908. *The Process of Government.* Chicago: University of Chicago Press.

Bentley, Arthur F. 1967. *The Process of Government.* Ed. Peter Odegard. Cambridge, MA: Harvard University Press.

Burns, James M., and J. W. Peltason. 1963. *Government by the People.* Englewood Cliffs, NJ: Prentice-Hall.

Carnoy, Martin. 1984. *The State and Political Theory.* Princeton: Princeton University Press.

Carter, Gwendolyn, and John Herz. 1972. *Government and Politics in the Twentieth Century.* New York: Praeger.

Coker, Francis. 1934. Pluralism. *Encyclopedia of the Social Sciences.* New York: Macmillan.

Cooper, Joseph, and David Brady. 1981. Toward a Diachronic Analysis of Change. *American Political Science Review* 75: 998–1006.

Dahl, Robert A. 1961. *Who Governs?* New Haven: Yale University Press.

Dodd, Lawrence. 1986a. The Cycles of Legislative Change: Building a Dynamic Theory. In *Political Science,* ed. Herbert Weissberg. New York: Agathon.

Dodd, Lawrence. 1986b. A Theory of Legislative Cycles. In *Congress and Policy Change,* ed. Gerald Wright, Leroy Riesselbach, and Lawrence Dodd. New York: Agathon.

Duguit, Leon. 1919. *Law in the Modern State.* Trans. H. J. Laski. New York: Huebsch.

Durkheim, Emile. 1950. *Les Regles de la methode sociologique.* Paris: Presses universitaires de France.

Easton, David. 1981. The Political System Besieged by the State. *Political Theory* 9: 303–25.

Eckstein, Harry. 1960. *Pressure Group Politics: The Case of the British Medical Association.* Stanford: Stanford University Press.

Ehrmann, Henry. 1957. *Organized Business in France.* Princeton: Princeton University Press.

Ehrmann, Henry. 1963. Bureaucracy and Interest Groups in Fifth Republic France. In *Faktoren der Politischen Entscheidung,* ed. Ernst Fraenkel. Berlin: Gruyter.

Evans, Peter, Dietrich Rueschemeyer, and Theda Skocpol, eds. 1985. *Bringing the State Back In.* Cambridge: Cambridge University Press.

Figgis, John Neville. 1914. *Churches in the Modern State.* London: Longmans.

Garson, G. David. 1974. On the Origins of Interest-Group Theory: A Critique of a Process. *American Political Science Review* 68: 1505–19.

Garson, G. David. 1978. *Group Theories of Politics.* Beverly Hills: Sage.

Gierke, Otto. 1900. *Political Theory of the Middle Ages.* Cambridge: Cambridge University Press.

Golembiewski, Robert J. 1960. The Group Basis of Politics: Notes on Analysis and Development. *American Political Science Review* 54: 962–71.

Herring, Edward Pendleton. 1936. *Public Administration and the Public Interest.* New York: McGraw-Hill.

Kariel, Henry. 1968. Pluralism, *International Encyclopedia of the Social Sciences.* New York: Macmillan.

Key, Vladimir O., Jr. 1952. *Politics, Parties, and Pressure Groups.* New York: Crowell.

Krasner, Stephen. 1984. Approaches to the State: Alternative Conceptions and Historical Dynamics. *Comparative Politics* 16: 223–46.

LaPalombara, Joseph. 1963. *Bureaucracy and Political Development.* Princeton: Princeton University Press.

LaPalombara, Joseph. 1964. *Interest Groups in Italian Politics.* Princeton: Princeton University Press.

Laski, Harold. 1917. *Studies in the Problem of Sovereignty.* New Haven: Yale University Press.

Laski, Harold. 1919. *Authority in the Modern State.* New Haven: Yale University Press.

Latham, Earl. 1952. The Group Basis of Politics: Notes for a Theory. *American Political Science Review* 46: 376–97.

Lindsay, Alexander D. 1929. *The Essentials of Democracy.* Philadelphia: University of Pennsylvania Press.

Lipset, Seymour Martin, and William Schneider. 1973. Political Sociology. In *Sociology: An Introduction,* ed. Neil Smelser. New York: John Wiley.

Lowi, Theodore. 1964. American Business, Public Policy, Case-Studies, and Political Theory. *World Politics* 16: 677–715.

Lowi, Theodore J. 1969. *The End of Liberalism: Ideology, Policy, and the Crisis of Public Authority.* New York: W. W. Norton.

McFarland, Andrew. 1987. Interest Groups and Theories of Power in America. *British Journal of Political Science* 17: 129–47.

Nettl, J. P. 1968. The State as Conceptual Variable. *World Politics* 20: 559–92.

Nordlinger, Eric. 1981. *On the Autonomy of the Democratic State.* Cambridge, MA: Harvard University Press.

Nordlinger, Eric. 1987. Taking the State Seriously. In *Understanding Political Development*, ed. Myron Weiner and Samuel Huntington. Boston: Little, Brown.

Ogg, Frederick, and P. Orman Ray. 1959. *Essentials of American Government.* 8th ed. Ed. William Young. New York: Appleton-Century-Crofts.

Polsby, Nelson W. 1968. The Institutionalization of the U.S. House of Representatives. *American Political Science Review* 62: 144–68.

Putnam, Robert. 1973. The Political Attitudes of Senior Civil Servants in Western Europe. *British Journal of Political Science* 3: 257–97.

Putnam, Robert. 1976. *The Comparative Study of Political Elites.* Englewood Cliffs, NJ: Prentice-Hall.

Ranney, Austin. 1966. *The Governing of Men.* New York: Holt & Rinehart.

Sabine, George. 1934. The State. *Encyclopedia of the Social Sciences.* New York: Macmillan.

Schattschneider, Elmer. 1942. *Party Government.* New York: Farrar & Rinehart.

Skocpol, Theda. 1979. *States and Social Revolutions: A Comparative Analysis of France, Russia and China.* Cambridge: Cambridge University Press.

Skocpol, Theda. 1982. Bringing the State Back In. In *Items*, vol. 36. New York: Social Science Research Council.

Skowronek, Stephen. 1984. *Building a New American State.* Cambridge: Cambridge University Press.

Stepan, Alfred. 1978. *State and Society: Peru in Comparative Perspective.* Princeton: Princeton University Press.

Suleiman, Ezra. 1978. *Elites in French Society.* Princeton: Princeton University Press.

Truman, David. 1951. *The Governmental Process.* New York: Knopf.

Truman, David. 1968. Political Group Analysis. *International Encyclopedia of the Social Sciences.* New York: Macmillan.

Watkins, Frederick. 1968. *International Encyclopedia of the Social Sciences.* New York: Macmillan.

White, Leonard D. 1933. *Trends in Public Administration.* New York: McGraw-Hill.

White, Leonard D. 1951. *The Jeffersonians.* New York: Macmillan.

White, Leonard D. 1954. *The Jacksonians.* New York: Macmillan.

White, Leonard D. 1956. *The Federalists.* New York: Macmillan.

White, Leonard D. 1958. *The Republican Era, 1868–1901.* New York: Macmillan.

Wilson, James Q., ed. 1980. *The Politics of Regulation.* Chicago: University of Chicago Press.

9

The Development of Political Development

During the two decades between the mid-1940s and the mid-1960s, comparative politics and development studies were growth industries. Based primarily in the United States and taking off at the same time that important developments were occurring in the social sciences, these studies sought to make sense out of the reconstruction of governments and economies in post-war Europe and the explosion of nations and the search for modernization in the Third World.

Development Studies

Development studies of the Third World enlisted the efforts and made the reputations of a whole generation of political scientists, economists, sociologists, anthropologists, and other social scientists. An early research wave in the 1950s and 1960s swept into the new nations of Africa and Asia. It consisted of young Ph.D. candidates and postdoctoral researchers—David Apter (1955, 1961), Leonard Binder (1961, 1962), Henry Bienen (1967), James Coleman (1958), Lucian Pye (1956, 1962), Dankwart Rustow (1957), Richard Sklar (1963), Robert Ward, Richard Beardsley, and John Hall (1959), Crawford Young (1965), Myron Weiner (1957, 1962), Aristide Zolberg (1963), and many others. These then-young scholars gave us our first theoretically informed monographic studies of Ghana, Uganda, Nigeria, the Ivory Coast, the Congo, Tanzania, Turkey, Iran, India, Pakistan, Japan, Malaya, and Burma, to list some of the more important ones.

During this same period, a group of political sociologists and quantitatively inclined political scientists, working with statistical data on contem-

---

porary nations, developed and tested hypotheses regarding the relationship between aspects of modernization such as industrialization, urbanization, education, and the spread of the mass media, on the one hand, and political mobilization and democratization, on the other. These included Daniel Lerner (1958), Seymour Martin Lipset (1959), James Coleman (1960), and Karl Deutsch (1961), who presented these "social mobilization" hypotheses in a number of versions in the late 1950s, followed by Philips Cutright (1963), Deane Neubauer (1967), Donald McCrone and Charles Cnudde, (1967), and others, who brought precision and statistical sophistication to bear on these relationships.

Economic historians and economists were especially challenged by Third World problems and prospects and produced a substantial literature, including studies by Alexander Gerschenkron (1953, 1962), Simon Kuznets (1955, 1959), Bert Hoselitz (1952), Max Millikan (1967; see also Millikan and Blackmer 1961), Edward Mason (1958), W. A. Lewis (1955), Hollis Chenery (1955), Gerald Meier (1964; see also Meier and Baldwin 1957), Walt W. Rostow (1960), Albert Hirschman (1958), Everett Hagen (1962, 1968), and others. The economic historians were concerned with the implications of Western experience with industrialization for Third World development, while the economists dealt with questions of development strategy and planning, international trade and development, the problems of technology transfer, the economics of agricultural development, entrepreneurship in the Third World, and the like.

The "new," the "emerging," the "underdeveloped" or "developing" nations, as they were variously called, challenged the classificatory talents and theoretical imaginations of Western social scientists. They brought to this effort to illuminate the prospects of the Third World the ideas and concepts of the enlightenment and nineteenth- and early twentieth-century social theory, which had sought to make sense out of European and American modernization. The "progress" promised by the enlightenment—the spread of knowledge, the development of technology, the attainment of higher standards of material welfare, the emergence of lawful, humane, and liberal polities, and the perfection of the human spirit—now beckoned the Third World, newly freed from colonialism and exploitation, and straining against its own parochialisms. The challenging question confronting the scholars of the 1950s and 1960s was how these new and developing nations would find their way into the modern world.

The social and political theorists who contributed to this literature included sanguine Condorcets and skeptical Voltaires. Some thought, as Robert Packenham (1973) put it, that all good things go together, that science, technology, industry, and democracy were part of a seamless web, while others like Hirschman (1958), Samuel Huntington (1965), S. N. Eisenstadt (1964), and Packenham himself anticipated disequilibria, decay and breakdown, and a long groping process. The insights, the hypotheses, the analytic categories that these theorists brought to their work came from Karl Marx, Sir Henry Maine (1883), Max Weber (1918/1979), Ferdinand Toennies (1887/1957), Emile Durkheim (1893/1933), and other nineteenth- and early twentieth-century writers. A group of students of development followed in the historical sociological tradition of Weber, emphasizing structural specialization and cultural secularization. These included Eisenstadt (1964), Reinhard Bendix (1964), and Gunther Roth (1971).

Talcott Parsons as a codifier of much of this literature was influential in the conceptual efforts of development theorists (1937; Parsons and Shils 1951). His grandiose plans for the unification of the social sciences, his conceptions of system and function, of the interaction of culture and personality, and his categories of orientation to action entered into the work of both micro and macro development theorists. Some of these writers gave special emphasis to psychological factors in modernization processes—attitudes, values, and personality characteristics. These included David McClelland and his students (1953, 1961), Pye (1962; Pye and Verba 1965), Hagen (1962), Lerner (1958), and, more recently, Alex Inkeles and David Horton Smith (1974). Others stressed the importance of institutions in development processes, either specific institutions such as bureaucracy (Braibanti 1966; Eisenstadt 1962) or interactions among institutions (Sutton 1954; Riggs 1957; Shils 1960; Almond 1956; Almond and Coleman 1960; Almond and Verba 1963; Apter 1965). Though these writers may have stressed the macro or the micro aspect of development and modernization, most acknowledged the importance of both levels.

Some writers proposed and tested specific development hypotheses, such as Huntington's (1968) "mobilization-institutionalization" explanation of political order and breakdown (1968), Rustow's (1967, 1970) theory of historical transitions to democracy, Robert Dahl's (1971) theory of the conditions of polyarchy, and Robert Holt and John Turner's (1966) explanation of economic growth in England and Japan in contrast to France and China, in terms of the counterproductive economic consequences of powerful regulatory states in the latter two countries. A group of writers presented linear theories of economic and political modernization. Walt W. Rostow was the pioneer in this genre with *The Stages of Economic Growth* (1960), followed by the socioeconomic-political "phases of modernization" schema of Cyril Black (1966) and by A.F.K. Organski's *The Stages of Political Development*

(1965). Rostow (1971) published a later expanded version of his argument that included the political preconditions of economic growth. Most of these various approaches to political development are well summarized in a paper by Samuel Huntington and Jorge Dominguez (1975).

In an appraisal of the intellectual productivity of these decades, Francis X. Sutton (1982), an officer of the Ford Foundation since 1954, spoke of "the exciting expansion of international scholarship that has been one of the academic glories of our time." As a result of these efforts, he stated, "the academic world has become a great storehouse of what had hitherto been rather scattered pockets of expertise throughout this country, and a great flowering of intellectual effort on far places has resulted."

The Political Development Series

In midcourse of this outpouring of creative work, the Committee on Comparative Politics of the Social Science Research Council (SSRC) embarked on a program of conferences and publications designed to bring together existing knowledge and expertise on development problems and patterns. The planning of this series grew out of the conviction that development in the Third World called not only for a mix of economic policies but for political institutions with the capacity for mobilizing and upgrading human and material resources. Political variables were viewed as being as important as economic ones; indeed, it was the assumption of the committee's program that there could be no economic development without political development. The first program in this series was on communications media and processes and political development. It began with a conference directed by Lucian Pye in 1961 and culminated in the first volume of the Political Development Series (Pye 1963). This book contained theoretical discussions of the relationships of communications and political development, as well as case studies of communications patterns in Japan, Turkey, Iran, Thailand, and Mainland China. Among the themes developed in the volume were the role of the mass media in transforming attitudes, communications patterns in Third World areas, and the role of intellectuals in modernizing processes.

The second volume, edited by Joseph LaPalombara (1963), treated the place of bureaucracy in modernization and development, containing theoretical, historical, regional, and country chapters. The themes covered included the tensions between bureaucratization and democratization, the place of bureaucracy in European political development, and Third World experience in the recruitment and training of government personnel. The third volume, edited by Robert Ward and Dankwart Rustow (1964), took two relatively successful cases of development outside of the European-North American area—Japan and Turkey—and compared them historically, institutionally, and culturally. The fourth volume, edited by James Coleman (1965), dealt with the central process of modernization—education—examining its significance for economic and political development in various types of societies pursuing different educational and developmental strategies.

The fifth volume, edited by Lucian Pye and Sidney Verba (1965), focused on political culture and political development, comparing the attitude patterns of some ten European and Third World nations and considering the consequences of these cultural patterns for industrial development and democratization. The sixth volume, edited by LaPalombara and Myron Weiner (1966), dealt with political parties, party systems, and interest groups in Western Europe, the United States, and some Third World countries, exploring the role and potentialities of political groups in economic and political developmental processes.

The goals of these first six volumes were modest: simply to draw on available knowledge and expertise in the United States and abroad and to present a "state-of-the-art" analysis of the role of these political institutions and processes in developed and developing societies. For students of comparative politics and political development in the 1960s and 1970s, these volumes became the authoritative, world-scale codifications of knowledge on comparative institutions—bureaucracy, parties, political culture, and educational and communications institutions and processes.

The last three volumes of the committee series had more ambitious purposes. Two of them—Volumes 7 and 9—were parts of a theoretical project intended to present and test a particular theory of political development. Volume 7, *Crises and Sequences in Political Development* (1971), was written by six of the then committee members: Leonard Binder, James Coleman, Joseph LaPalombara, Lucian Pye, Sidney Verba, and Myron Weiner. This group proposed that developmental patterns could be explained by the way in which nations and societies encountered and solved a common set of state- and nation-building problems. The form that these problems and challenges took, and the sequence in which these "crises" occurred, would constrain, if not determine, the structural and cultural development of political systems. The five problems, or "developmental crises," as they came to be called, were national identity, legitimacy, participation, penetration, and distribution. The central chapters of Volume 7 treated these individual crises, drawing on historical and contemporary experience to elaborate them. In addition, there were three more general chapters (contributed by Binder, Coleman, and Verba) presenting, analyzing, and evaluating the "crisis and sequence" hypothesis from a number of perspectives.

Volume 9 contained the work of some ten historians who were asked to test the crisis and sequence hypothesis against the historical experience of most of the countries of Europe as well as the United States (Grew 1978). Given the methodological differences between historians and political scientists, Volume 9 of the committee series must be considered an unusually successful interdisciplinary experiment. The historians who participated included distinguished practitioners of their craft. They took their obligations seriously and produced an unusual volume on comparative state and nation building, concluding that the theoretical framework presented in Volume 7 was illuminating and useful in describing the historical developmental patterns of the nations or groups of nations that they analyzed. In a lucid introductory essay, Raymond Grew summarized and reformulated the "crisis and sequence" approach and suggested a research agenda growing out of this enterprise. The notion of a sequential order in these crises had to be rejected, a proposition that had already been questioned in Volume 7.

Volume 8 approached the theme of political development from an empirical historical perspective (Tilly 1975). Since Third World countries were in most cases involved in the process of seeking to create centralized states out of congeries of tribal and traditional structures, the European historical experience with state building might serve to illuminate these contemporary problems and processes. A historian-cum-sociologist, Charles Tilly, was commissioned to lead this undertaking with the support of a number of European historians and social scientists. As in Volumes 7 and 9, state building was seen as the consequence of historical efforts to cope with a series of critical problems, such as defense against external aggression, the maintenance of internal order, the supply of food and other essential goods, and the extraction of resources for these and other purposes. The building of the state apparatus through the recruitment and training of civilian and military personnel, and their organization into bureaucracies, grew out of efforts to cope with these problems of defense, domestic order, revenue extraction, and expenditure control. The way in which these problems were encountered and dealt with helped explain the differences among political institutions in Britain, France, Germany, Italy, Spain, and other countries treated in the volume. The authors of Volume 8 concluded that European historical experience may illuminate some aspects of Third World state-building prospects and that state building tends to be a generic process requiring the concentration of extractive, regulative, and distributive capacities. In Europe these developments occurred in the context of almost continuous civil and international warfare—with coercive power requiring resource extraction and the regulation of behavior, and these in turn requiring trained personnel and bureaucratic organizations.

Political Development Research as Ideology

This substantial literature did not lend itself easily to simple characterizations. It was methodologically variegated, including Weberian historical sociological studies as in Eisenstadt (1962), Bendix (1964), and Roth (1971); Parsonian analysis as in Sutton (1954) and Riggs (1957); statistical methods as in Neubauer (1967) and McCrone and Cnudde (1967); psychological methods as in McClelland et al. (1953); and rational choice modeling as in Harsanyi (1969) and much later as in Popkin (1947/1979). Politically it included scholars with relatively naive expectations of democratization in the Third World, as well as skeptics and pessimists who foresaw authoritarian regimes. It included "hawks" and "doves" as the Vietnam War divided American academic circles. Over time, as the new and developing nations encountered difficulties and turned largely to authoritarian and military regimes, the optimism and hopefulness faded, and interest, productivity, and creativity abated.

In the mid-1960s an attack on development research began that assimilated mainstream social science and comparative politics to American imperialism and neocolonialism. It was described as an inhumane "positivist" literature, as a Cold War literature, as an ideology that could not be separated from Vietnam. The political standpoint of the critics varied from that of a Mark Kesselman with a moderate left perspective to the more principled Marxism of Suzanne Bodenheimer (now Jonas), to the "dependency" theorists, Fernando Cardoso, Andre Gunder Frank, and others.

In a review article appearing in 1973, Mark Kesselman described the political development literature of comparative politics as preoccupied with order and stability and as predicting an ethnocentric American pattern of economic growth, democratization, and de-ideologization in the new nations of the Third World. Kesselman reviewed Huntington's *Political Order in Changing Societies* (1968) and Binder et al.'s *Crises and Sequences in Political Development* (1971), of the SSRC series, as major exemplars of these propensities. But he included the much larger literature of political development. He stated that "one approach (with many variations) has dominated comparative politics; the search for order" (p. 153).

In a much more sweeping critique, Suzanne Bodenheimer (1970) wrote of the "ideology of developmentalism" that suffused the literature of comparative politics, sociological theory, and behavioral political science. She attributed to the political development literature four epistemological sins leading it to four errors in theory. The epistemological sins were the beliefs (1) in the possibility of an objective social science free of ideology, (2) in the cumulativeness of knowledge, and (3) in universal laws of social science, and the belief that (4) these versions of social science were exportable to Third World countries. These epistemological sins led to the theoretical errors of belief in incremental and continuous development, the possibility of stable and orderly change, the diffusion of development from the West to Third World areas, and the decline of revolutionary ideology and the spread of pragmatic and scientific thinking.

This characterization of the development literature as ethnocentric, projective, quietistic, and unilinear and as the intellectual handmaiden of capitalism and imperialism stemmed from the work of Marxist theorists, mostly in Latin America. In an article that appeared in the mid-1960s titled "The Sociology of Development and the Underdevelopment of Sociology," Andre Gunder Frank (1969) reviews the American development literature from Weber through Parsons, Hoselitz, Rostow, McClelland, and many others. Frank "examines the North American emperor's social scientific clothes and exposes the scientific nakedness behind his ideological sham" (p. xi). It is a theory, he alleges, that imputes a set of modern properties to the West and bases Third World modernization on the diffusion of these characteristics to the non-West; "one part of the system, Western Europe and Northern America, diffuses and helps the other part, Asia, Africa, and South America, to develop" (p. 76).

Cardoso and Faleto (1979) argue that "in almost all theories of modernization it is assumed that the course taken by political, social, and economic systems of Western Europe and the United States, foretells the future for the underdeveloped countries. The 'development process' would consist in completing and even reproducing the various stages that characterized the social transformation of these countries" (p. 11).

This characterization of modernization theory is repeated in the writings of American students of Latin American development. Thus Ronald Chilcote and Joel Edelstein (1974) describe the "diffusionist model" of the American literature as depicting a process in which "progress will come about through the spread of modernism to backward, archaic, and traditional areas. Through the diffusion of technology and capital, these areas will inescapably evolve from a traditional toward a modern state" (p. 3). And Samuel and Arturo Valenzuela (1978) in a recent article impute to the development literature the view that "in the process of modernization all societies will undergo by and large similar changes" and that "the history of the presently modern nations is taken as the source of universally useful conceptualizations" (p. 538). This view of the political development literature of these earlier decades as simplemindedly ethnocentric is canonized in a paper by Joel Migdal (1983) on the state of the art in political development studies. Again, in a recent article Tony Smith (1985) characterizes the developmentalist paradigm "as 'unilinear' or 'ethnocentric' in its concept of change; that is, it projected a relatively inflexible path or continuum of development in which social and political forms would tend to converge, so that the developmental path of the West might well serve as a model from which to shed light on transformations occurring in the South" (p. 537).

The claim that the primarily American literature presented a monolithic and unilinear model of political development and projected Anglo-American and capitalist values on the outside world cannot survive an even casual reading. Confining ourselves to the Political Development Series, which was one of the most visible products of this literature, it is instructive that in the first volume of the series, and in the first effort to specify the content of modernization and development, Pye (1963) presented a most circumspect treatment, which bears repeating in the light of the "ethnocentric-unilinear" image presented by these critics:

> In recent years there has been a conspicuous and uneasy search for satisfactory words to identify and describe the nonindustrialized societies of the world which have now become or are shortly to become sovereign nations. We have sought to use, but with only varying degrees of satisfaction, such terms as "backward," "non-Western," "underdeveloped," "developing," and "emerging." In large measure the problem, of course, stems from our concern over possibly offending those being identified. But it also arises from our own uncertainty as to the nature of these societies, their future prospects, and the appropriateness of our even suggesting that possibly they should change their character to be more in accord with the industrially advanced societies. A generation of instruction in cultural relativism has had its influence, and social thinkers are no longer comfortable with any concept which might suggest a belief in "progress" or "stages of civilization." In the meantime, however, as the West has gradually learned to appreciate and sympathize with cultural differences, many of the spokesmen for the non-Western world have become increasingly impatient with their own traditions and have insisted that

it is their right and duty to change their societies to make them more like the industrial world. Yet there is a note of qualification in even the most insistent of these calls for change, for there is the realization that more respect is to be gained from being distinctive than from being an inferior version of a foreign culture. Everyone seems to sense that some forms of difference are acceptable while others are not. (p. 14)

LaPalombara (1963) in that same year speaks in the most unqualified terms of the dangers of applying a unilinear Anglo-American model to the analysis of Third World developments:

It is apparent, for example, that rapid economic change leading to industrialization can be effected without conformance to the social and institutional patterns that we might ascribe to the Anglo-American model. Indeed, it may very well be that rapid change in the economic sector is much more meaningfully related to what we might call an undemocratic pattern of social and political organization. In any event, if any kind of clarity is to emerge from our use of such concepts as modernization and development, it will be vitally necessary to specify what we mean by the concepts and to indicate explicitly when a shift in meaning occurs. Failure to do this is certain to encumber our discussions of political change with confusion and with culturally limited and deterministic baggage. (p. 10)

And Ward and Rustow (1964), in their comparative study of Japan and Turkey, state unequivocally:

Democracy and representative government are not implied in our definition of modernization. Czar Peter of Russia, Sultan Mahmud of Turkey, and Emperor Meiji of Japan were modernizers, but decidedly not democrats or conscious forerunners of democracy. Germany was more modern in the 1930's than in the 1880's, though its government was less representative and less liberal. Classical Marxists believed that all societies move along a single path, though not at equal pace, toward one preordained goal. This artless and simplistic notion does not gain in validity as we change the sign at the finish line from "Communism" to "Democracy."

There are nonetheless certain definite political characteristics that modernizing societies share. Commonly modernization begins under autocracy or oligarchy and proceeds toward some form of mass society—democratic or authoritarian. Under whatever regime, the hallmarks of the modern state are a vastly expanded set of functions and demands. Public services come to include education, social security, and public works while civic duties involve new forms of loyalty, tax payment and, in a world of warring states, military

> service. The very concepts of public service and civic duty, indeed, are among the vital prerequisites of modern politics. (p. 5)

In a similar mood, Coleman (1965) tells us that the dangers of "ethnocentrism, teleological bias, and the absence of a single objective measuring rod complicate the conceptualization of 'political development'" (p. 15). He proposes that modernization is an open-ended process consisting of trends toward increasing structural differentiation leading to increased governmental capacity and trends toward equality in the legal, participatory, and distributive senses. The movement might be in a liberal democratic direction, but it might with equal probability be in an authoritarian direction. In my own work I argue explicitly against the simple diffusionist notion of unilinearity in the early 1960s (Almond 1970, chaps. 5, 6). Huntington (1968) argues the improbability of democratic outcomes in Third World political systems (see also Huntington and Moore 1970). And Dahl (1971) takes a similarly pessimistic view.

The attribution of the view to mainstream comparative politics that the modernization of the Third World implied a capitalist and democratic outcome simply cannot be sustained by evidence. The great theorist of modernization, Max Weber, was most pessimistic about the prospects of democracy and capitalism and foresaw a future dominated by bureaucracy. Alexander Gerschenkron (1962), a leading European economic historian, emphasized that the later the industrialization, the greater the probability of a major role for state authority. Recognizing the fragility and superficiality of democratic institutions in Third World countries, Edward Shils (1960), in one of the early and influential classifications of Third World politics, spoke of "tutelary democracies" and "modernizing oligarchies" as being the most common forms that Third World political development was taking at the time that he was writing. Whether and how soon genuine democratization would occur depended on fundamental changes in social structure and culture, processes drawn out in time and uncertain in outcome. LaPalombara and Weiner (1966), in their conclusions as to the role of political parties in modernizing processes, are quite skeptical about the prospects of competitive party systems in Third World nations (pp. 433ff.).

The Dependency Movement

The unanimity of dependency writers – North American as well as Latin American – in this egregious misrepresentation of mainstream comparative politics, and the acceptance of this view on the part of others, looks more like a conversion phenomenon than a genuine and critical literature search. Indeed, the dependency writers rarely cite the "modernization" literature in detail, and, when they do, they often quote out of context, exaggerate, and otherwise distort the literature. Peter Smith (1983) refers to some of this dependency literature as "guerrilla-intellectual work" and to the dependency movement as an "ambush." The dependency literature in this sense has to be seen as a political-intellectual activity, as scholarship in the support of political goals. Indeed, dependency writing rests on the Marxist theory of knowledge, the view that political knowledge above all is essentially class struggle based, is inextricably ideological. Thus the modernization and development literature cannot escape its association with capitalism and imperialism; it is a defense of capitalism and imperialism. The dependency perspective, on the other hand, is a defense of the interests of the exploited peasants and workers on the periphery of the capitalist world. With the intellectual choice formulated in these terms, with the aspiration to social science and objectivity denigrated as an inhumane status quo supporting "positivism," scholars are excused from serious searches of the literature. The social science of capitalism is procapitalist by necessity; the only alternative is a prosocialist social science. The dependency school could fortify its position by drawing on Thomas Kuhn's (1960) theory of scientific revolutions, a philosophy of science that rejected the assumption of scientific cumulation in favor of a discontinuous conception of paradigm change. This became the epistemological position for many social scientists in the 1960s, and it gave their metamethodological discussions a certain philosophy of science chic.

How can we explain this intellectual ambush, this intellectual-guerrilla movement? For the Latin American scholars who led this movement, there was for the most part no special change in viewpoint. They were Marxist intellectuals who in the mid-1960s acquired much greater resonance as expectations of increased growth and welfare were disappointed and as repressive military and authoritarian regimes replaced the populist ones of the 1950s and early 1960s.

The American *dependencistas,* on the other hand, came largely from a generation of Ph.D.s in Latin American politics or history in the mid-1960s. Their formative years as intellectuals were overshadowed by the black rebellion, the Vietnam War, Watergate, and the campus-based cultural revolution of the 1960s. Their views were also shaped by the failure of development hopes in the Third World and particularly in Latin America. These American Latin Americanists adopted the Marxist framework of their Latin American colleagues at a time when the bona fides of American civilization and American scholarship were widely questioned. In doing so, however, they cut their ties with the tradition of neutral social science scholarship even as an aspiration. For while it may be said that full objectivity, full detachment from one's social and cultural biases, is an impossibility, the constant search for ways of minimizing ideological and cultural bias, of bringing them under control, is very much alive. The American *dependencistas* had given up the injunction of Thomas Huxley to "sit down before fact as a little child, be prepared to give up every preconceived notion, follow humbly wherever and to whatever abysses nature leads, or you shall learn nothing." It was this scholarly norm of aspiration toward value-free social science that these then-young scholars rejected.

Dependency theory, elaborated in the work of Fernando Henrique Cardoso and Enzo Faletto (1969), Andre Gunder Frank (1969), Osvaldo Sunkel (1973), Theotonio Dos Santos (1970), and others, came out of the Marxist-Leninist intellectual tradition. It was Marxist in its emphasis on class struggle in political-economic explanation; it was Leninist in its emphasis on imperialism. The analytic structure of dependency theory is relatively simple and straightforward. World capitalism consists of four interrelated classes – the capitalist center (the capitalist classes in the United States, Western Europe, Japan, etc.); the periphery of the center (the exploited underclasses of the advanced capitalist world); the center of the periphery (the dependent bourgeoisie in Latin American, African, and other Third World countries); and the periphery of the periphery (the rural peasant and Indian populations, the *favela* dwellers, and the like in Latin American and other Third World countries). Capitalist political economy creates and maintains a coercively exploitative and extractive process, drawing resources from the periphery to the center and condemning the periphery to a state of underdevelopment or distorted development. This vicious circle can be broken only by fundamental change in the periphery and the center, the elimination of capitalism, and the introduction of socialism.

By comparison with Marxism and Leninism, dependency theory is incomplete and inconclusive. While it speaks of revolution and socialism as alternatives to the capitalist world system, the strategy, whether Marxist, Leninist, or some other, is left to implication. Marxist and Leninist theories are predictive theories. In Marx the dialectic of class struggle leads to the dictatorship of the proletariat by an economic-sociological-psychological logic; in Lenin mature capitalism leads to imperialism and war, and these in turn give way to the dictatorship of the proletarian vanguard as social breakdown occurs and an increasingly disciplined revolutionary vanguard seizes power.

The *dependencistas* tell us only part of the story. In the place of the allegedly complacent notions of the modernization theorists, they affirm as political reality this fourfold exploitative scheme. From the dependency point of view, all the work of the development economists, political scientists, sociologists, social psychologists, and anthropologists was elaborate window dressing concealing the underlying stark confrontations of exploiter and exploited in the capitalist center, in the periphery of the center, in the dependently developed periphery, and in the underdeveloped periphery of the periphery.

The most authoritative version of this schema was first presented by Cardoso and Faletto in the first edition of their book *Dependency and Development in Latin America* (1969). A later writing of Cardoso (1973) takes into account the extraordinary growth rates in Latin America in the late 1960s and early 1970s by describing this growth as "associated dependent" development. "Associated dependent" development refers to Third World economies in the age of the multinationals, when there is economic growth in dependent countries, a form of growth that is distorted, which redounds to the benefit of the exploiting classes, particularly in the capitalist metropole; the condition of the peripheral lower classes is left unimproved or worsened. In later writings Cardoso (1979; Cardoso and Faletto 1979) seems to be backing off a bit from this extreme pessimism and its revolutionary implications. But only a socialist *transformation* can eliminate dependency, as Cardoso and Faletto (1979) spell it out in the concluding paragraphs of the most recent edition of their book. They explicitly exempt socialist societies from dependency theory. They write: "Although there are forms of dependent relationships between socialist countries, the structural context that permits an understanding of these is quite different from that within capitalist countries and requires specific analyses" (p. xxiv).

Dependency theory is not very good Marxism (or very good Leninism). Marx was far too good a historian and social scientist to have treated the world political economy as divisible into four class formations. The social periphery of metropolitan capitalism would not qualify as a Marxist proletariat, nor would the peripheral social groups of the dependent countries. A Marxist revolution would have to occur in the capitalist industrialized world, and not in the backward, predominantly rural, agricultural periphery. That part of the world would have to wait its turn, its own capitalist, industrial maturation.

Dependency theory is not very good Leninism, in that for Lenin imperialism and war were necessary conditions for proletarian revolution, but the development of a conscious, disciplined communist party was the *sufficient* condition, and dependency theory has no category for internal political variables. The internal politics and policies of hegemonic and dependent nations have no explanatory power, except by implication. The entire historical process, from the dependency perspective, is driven by hegemonic capitalism, its agents, the multinationals and the dependent indigenous bourgeoisies, motivated by an unremitting appetite for profits and capital accumulation. Internal politics is present either in the passive mood of a politics dominated by the imperialist hegemon or by implication in the active revolutionary socialist mood.

The dependency approach can best be characterized as a propaganda fragment of an ideology, a polemic against mainstream development theory. Having attributed a simpleminded interpretation of Third World development to the social sciences of the advanced capitalist countries, the *dependencistas* proposed an alternative, almost reciprocal interpretation of Third World development. If, as alleged, capitalist social science posited a benign, tutelary relationship between the First and the Third worlds, the dependency interpretation posited a malign, exploitative relationship. If, as alleged, capitalist social science posited the effective diffusion of capitalist and democratic institutions and processes from the First to the Third World, the dependency writers posited penetrated and distorted economies, and suppressive political institutions doing the dirty work of the hegemonic classes.

Dependency as a Research Agenda

The test of any research approach is its productivity. Does it generate novel ways of looking at the subject matter? Does it increase our knowledge and make it more reliable? Are its concepts and theories open to modification by experience? What impact has dependency theory had on Third World and particularly Latin American studies? A number of points have to be made in this connection. First, Latin American social science studies in the United States were in their infancy at the time that the dependency approach became popular. There was rapid growth in the number of Third World and particularly Latin American specialists in the 1950s and 1960s, but Latin American area studies had not had sufficient time to develop traditions and professional norms. Second, conditions of research in Latin America (and in Africa and Asia as well) changed in the 1960s and the early 1970s. The collapse of popular regimes in much of Latin America made research access much more difficult for both American and indigenous scholars. Third, the wave of repression in Latin America and other Third World areas tended to radicalize the indigenous intellectuals. Indeed, it was this situation of repressive military regimes, more or less supported by the United States, that made the dependency scenario plausible. Hence, along with the restrictions on research freedom characteristic of authoritarian regimes, the climate for research became heavily politicized in Latin America and among American students of Latin America (Dominguez 1982).

These circumstances may explain the fact that a substantial proportion of the students of Latin America in the United States adopted the dependency perspective, abjuring "positivist" social science and its separation of the study of politics from its conduct. Surely not all of the Latin Americanist profession moved in this direction. Some converted to it; some flirted with it. But all of the Latin Americanists had to take this approach seriously since it had such powerful and influential advocates in the countries where they did their research.

We should not blink the fact that the adoption of a dependency perspective was a backward step, a movement away from the hard-won rule of evidence and inference in social studies. It gave up the battle for science in the study of society on the grounds that a complete victory could never be won. It involved the adoption of unfalsifiable concepts of the state as a pact of class domination, of politics as struggle and that alone, and of society as a complex of exploiting and exploited economic classes.

But if the dependency portrait of American development research was distorted, and if the dependency approach in itself was flawed, as we suggest that it was, there are still two questions to be considered that, positively answered, might result in some favorable evaluation of the consequences of the dependency movement. First, was there any merit at all in the critique of modernization research? And second, did the dependency perspective produce creative research itself, and did it have a constructive impact on mainstream political science?

With regard to the first question we would have to acknowledge that dependency theory stressed variables that development theory in its earlier stages tended to neglect. The dependency approach is based on two causal propositions: (1) economics in the sense of the structure of production and the associated economic class structure causes politics and (2) the hegemonic capitalist nations cause the "underdevelopment" of the dependent nations. Mainstream political development theory in the 1950s tended to confine itself to national and political variables. It focused on the internal politics of the nation-state, neglecting the international context.

These were biases that grew out of the world situation that development research sought to capture in the years after World War II. Eastern and Western Europe were in the throes of boundary changes and constitutional transformations. There were new governmental institutions, new electoral arrangements, new party and interest group systems taking shape against a background of political catastrophe and destruction. In the Middle East, Africa, and Asia new nations were emerging by the dozens. Comparative politics of the 1950s and 1960s was a massive, enthusiastic, primarily American effort to encompass this novel and heterogeneous reality. That it tended to be synchronic rather than diachronic, that it was concerned with order and a low-cost approach to social change, were the consequences of the political reality and intellectual challenges confronting us in those years. The big political story in those decades was the emergence of political order out of the conflictual disorder of war and the collapse of empires. It is true that the view of development and change was one that stressed cost. No group of scholars coming out of the background of the 1930s and 1940s could minimize the issue of cost in human life and material destruction of violent and revolutionary change. It is also true that there tended to be a pluralist bias in these development theories. But this again calls for no apology in view of the tormented search for the reintroduction of pluralism in those societies that have sought to eliminate it. The hope for a low-cost and pluralist approach did not blind this generation of scholars. We have already pointed out that the notion of an incremental, low-cost developmental future for Third World countries was sharply challenged in early work of Huntington (1965) and by Eisenstadt (1964), Packenham (1966, 1973), and many others. Indeed, this naivete was more characteristic of politicians than it was of academics. It was part of the packaging accompanying requests for appropriations for foreign aid programs.

Systematic account of the role of international variables in national development was already being taken in the 1960s, and the best of this work does not draw at all from the dependency literature. A number of papers (including one by Karl Deutsch) in Harry Eckstein's (1963) collection on "internal war" dealt explicitly with the role of international factors in civil and guerrilla wars. James Rosenau edited a volume appearing in 1964 that dealt with international aspects of civil strife. The contributions included papers by Rosenau himself, Morton Kaplan, George Modelski, Andrew Scott, Karl Deutsch, and Richard Falk. Later work of Rosenau (1980) dealt with national-international linkages in more general terms. An early article of this writer's placed national development in the context of international interaction (Almond 1970, chap. 6). This was elaborated in a later article that examined the ways in which national political development influenced the international system in which the international environment affected national development (Almond 1971). A later book treated the role of international variables in national development theoretically and through a set of historical case studies (Almond 1973). Several of the chapters in Volumes 8 and 9 of the SSRC Political Development Series (Tilly 1975; Grew 1978) emphasized the importance of international events for political development; in particular, see Samuel Finer's chapter on the role of war and the military in Volume 8 and Tilly's introduction and conclusion to that volume. More recently, Gourevitch (1977) has done interesting research on the internal political consequences in Europe and America of international economic crises such as the depressions of 1870–90 and the 1930s. Peter Katzenstein's recent book *Small States and World Markets* (1985) is a most significant analysis of the interaction of national and international variables in the explanation of political-economic development.

One may argue that more theoretical and empirical work is necessary on the national-international linkage. But it is doubtful that the dependency view of these relationships, which reduces them to class concepts, is a constructive way out of this neglect. Similarly, the "world system" treatment of the national-international relationship, like the dependency approach, offers a spurious solution to the problem by denying causal significance to internal national variables (see Thompson 1983, passim).

From the very beginning of development research, the interaction of politics and economics was stressed. Lerner (1958), Lipset (1959), Coleman (1960), and Deutsch (1961) all emphasized the political consequences of industrialization. Industrialization, associated with the spread of education and the emergence of the mass media, resulted in political mobilization. An earlier, somewhat naive version of this hypothesis related industrialization to democratization. But by the mid-1960s the sober view was that industrialization and the other components of social mobilization produced political mobilization that might constrain development in an authoritarian populist direction *or* in a democratic direction. Thus mainstream political development studies tested Marxist and other hypotheses as open propositions regarding the relations among changing organization and control of production, changing class structure, and changing political tendencies. As evidence accumulated, a more complex and finely grained theory of the relation between economics and politics supplanted the earlier cruder and simpler ones.

The economists and economic historians dealt with aspects of economic and political interaction from other perspectives as well. As we have already suggested, Alexander Gerschenkron (1953) at a quite early time pointed out that the later the industrialization, the greater the likelihood of strong state intervention. Simon Kuznets (1955) in early work showed that in the first stages of industrial growth there was a tendency toward increasing income inequality. At higher levels of industrialization there is greater equality. The Kuznets or "U-shaped curve" hypothesis has been tested and elaborated a number of times in the last few decades (Adelman and Morris 1967; Chenery et al. 1974; Chenery 1979).

Thus it is not correct to say that the "dependency" emphasis on political economy and on international variables had significant impact on mainstream development studies. The movement toward the inclusion of international variables and in the direction of political-economic analysis was internally generated in both international relations and comparative politics studies, and was not the result of the dependency polemic. The best of this recent work in international political economy shows little evidence of having been influenced by the dependency literature. At most we may say that the dependency critique gave some accent to already strong tendencies in mainstream research.

While the "dependency" perspective may in some sense have become the most salient perspective in Latin American and African studies, there has been a lively polemic over its merits among students of the Third World, and the balance now seems to be moving toward its critics. Robert Packenham (1976, 1983) from the beginning has been critical of dependency theory as being based on a set of unfalsifiable assumptions. Recognizing the importance of international interaction in constraining the choices of developing countries, Packenham suggests that dependency ideas be viewed as hypotheses to be tested against data on political and economic exchanges between the advanced capitalist countries and the developing ones. He calls this "analytic" dependency, by contrast with the "holistic" dependency of Cardoso and others of the dependency school. Tony Smith (1979, 1981a, 1981b) views the development literature from the perspective of his important study of the variety of different historical imperialisms and their consequences for postimperialist development. He sharply criticizes dependency theory on the ground that it denies explanatory power to the specific characteristics and experiences of individual countries.

James Caporaso (1978), in a special issue of *International Organization* titled "Dependence and Dependency in International Relations," concludes his comments on a critical note:

> With respect to dependency I am both less certain and more cautious about fruitful directions to take. Our impulses to quantify and test are so strong that we often miss nuance and complexity, which I am afraid we have already done in our premature efforts to test dependency theory. These dangers are all the

> more real because semantic precision and syntactical clarity are not the strong points of dependency theory. Instead of measurement and testing, I would expect that a sober assessment of the kinds of knowledge claims made by dependency theory would be a first order of business. If dependency theory can be expressed as a body of testable propositions, the next steps would be similar to those outlined for dependence. I suspect there will be great controversy at this first stage and that severe disagreement will exist between those who want to move dependency theory in the direction of verifiable theory along positivist lines and those who see it as an interpretive device. At this juncture, different scholars may have to part company and go different ways. (p. 43)

In a later review article, Caporaso (1980) gives unqualifiedly favorable treatment to two dependency publications (Cardoso and Faletto 1979; Evans 1979). At the end of his review, however, he gently chides the dependency writers for their resistance to the notion that there can be degrees of dependency. Caporaso cannot quite swallow the Cardoso argument that dependency is an all-or-nothing situation. He wonders why Cardoso and Faletto present so little evidence to support their conclusions, relying rather on assertions backed up by illustrative examples. Caporaso applauds Cardoso and Evans for their stress on political economy and international variables, without questioning the determinist ways in which politics and economics are related and in which the international arena is portrayed with its remarkable omission of the "Second World."

Efforts to test the validity of dependency propositions include cross-national statistical studies and case studies of various kinds. It should be pointed out that the moment empirical testing is adopted as a standard for validating or invalidating dependency propositions, we are in mainstream social science territory. Thus Bruce Russett (1983), in his report on statistical efforts to test dependency propositions, is careful to describe the ideas of such writers as Cardoso, Dos Santos, and Gunder Frank as the "dependency perspective," reserving the term "dependency theory" to describe the findings of scholars using "quantitative statistical methods to create rigorous theories and sub-theories that are derived from the conceptualizations of the dependency perspective" (p. 562).

Russett summarizes the quantitative literature dealing with two of the principal themes of the dependency perspective, the negative effect of penetration of foreign capital on rates of growth in peripheral countries and the effect of such penetration on patterns of inequality. Russett finds, on examining almost a dozen cross-national statistical studies carried out in the 1970s and early 1980s, that there is almost unanimous agreement that short-term penetration by foreign capital is associated with higher rates of GNP per capita growth. For the longer term, the relationship between growth and capitalist penetration is less clear. Some writers find a deteriorating rate of growth. Other more recent work, including Russett's own research, suggests a positive relationship. The view of some *dependencistas* that the effect of capitalist penetration is negative on growth has not survived these empirical tests. The relationship would seem to be complex, positive in some times and places and negative in others, with local conditions, size, resources, and historical experience having substantial impact.

The larger empirical study from which Russett reported some results presents an unconvincing defense of dependency theory (Sylvan et al. 1983). It demonstrates that the greater the capitalist penetration, the greater the degree of concentration on a few export commodities. There also seems to be a tendency to concentrate trade with a few trade partners. Beyond this the findings of this statistical study of Third World trade and cultural exchange patterns are inconclusive. The effects of foreign penetration on patterns of growth and distributive tendencies vary widely according to specific circumstances. To quote the report: "We refute relatively simplistic formulations of *dependencia* theory and reinforce the arguments of those noted theorists, steeped in the experience of their own countries and regions, who have consistently emphasized the importance of contextual variables and have resisted broad brush generalizing" (p. 106).

The general relationship between economic growth and equality is described by the Kuznets U-shaped curve. Studies summarized in Chenery (1979, chap. 11) now show that the original insight of Kuznets (1955) based on European experience—to the effect that inequality increases in the early stages of economic development and then declines at higher levels—has been substantially confirmed. The dependency perspective would suggest that given these larger trends, the more penetrated a less developed country by foreign capitalism, the greater the inequality in income distribution. Russett's review (1983) of the research testing this hypothesis is inconclusive. But the dependency argument that this deterioration in income equality is an inevitable consequence of capitalism—built in, so to speak—does not survive the counterexamples of such countries as South Korea, Taiwan, Malaysia, Singapore, and Thailand, where income distribution has improved along with growth. Deliberate development policies involving the introduction of labor-intensive industries, infrastructure improvements, manpower training, land distribution, and agricultural policies may mitigate the negative impact of growth on distribution. In other words, the Kuznets curve may be mitigated by deliberate development policy choices.

One of the most sophisticated dependency studies so far produced is Peter Evans's (1979) analysis of the "triple alliance" of multinational corporations, elite, local capital, and what he calls the "state bourgeoisie" in Brazil. By the indigenous private business elite he does not mean to include the entire bourgeoisie, but only that part that is involved in the larger and more modern economic enterprises. And by the "state bourgeoisie" he refers to that part of the bureaucracy that manages public enterprises and oversees the economy. He acknowledges that in "semi-peripheral" dependent countries such as Brazil, where industrialization has already taken root, economic growth even of substantial proportions is possible. In addition, the relation between the multinationals and the private and state bourgeoisie is not hierarchic, but pluralistic, a relationship that can be and is modified by bargaining. But this domestication of the multinationals is capable of only one kind of redistribution, according to Evans: "redistribution from the mass of the population to the state bourgeoisie, the multinationals, and elite local capital. The maintenance of the delicate balance among the three partners militates against any possibility of dealing seriously with questions of income redistribution, even if members of the elite express support for income redistribution in principle" (p. 288).

Though Evans claims to be dealing with Brazilian politics and public policy, he barely touches on political forces outside of the "triple alliance" such as the military, the Church, the industrial working class, and the larger part of the middle class not included in "elite local capital." His "triple-alliance-semi-periphery" model (which he extends from the Brazilian case to include countries at economic levels or with potentials like that of Brazil—for example, Mexico and Nigeria) is dependent for its effectiveness on the economic, political, and military support of the capitalist powers (principally the United States) and the support, tolerance, or passivity of those internal power groups not included in the "triple alliance." The Brazilian model, according to Evans, cannot survive without its allies from the center and without the support, ineffectiveness, and passivity of domestic political forces. Though he acknowledges the vulnerability of the triple-alliance model to external as well as internal power and to policy changes, Evans nevertheless asserts that "despite all that has changed, the essential features of imperialism as it was described by Hobson and Lenin remain" (p. 50).

The weakness in Evans's analysis lies in his ideological assumptions. The power structure of international capitalism and semiperipheral dependent development is vastly oversimplified, so that the only possible alternatives are the continuation of the triple alliance or its collapse as a consequence of internal or external transformations. For Evans as well as for Cardoso and other dependency writers there are no degrees of dependency. There is dependency or socialism.

Another theoretically sophisticated study in this broad tradition was Guillermo O'Donnell's (1973) work on "bureaucratic authoritarianism." In this study, O'Donnell sought to explain the trend toward authoritarianism in Latin American politics during the 1960s and 1970s by the dynamic of "dependent capitalist development." As dependent economies moved from import-substitution strategies to the introduction of capital goods industries and consumer durables – as these economies sought to "deepen" and industrialize under conditions of international dependency – the requirements for capital accumulation, investment, and the control of populist pressures called for a repressive and technically sophisticated state apparatus. Hence the alliance of the military and the economic technicians in bureaucratic authoritarian regimes.

The advantage of the O'Donnell formulation was that the proposition was presented as an empirically testable hypothesis. Unlike most dependency propositions it was not simply asserted and illustrated; it was asserted and tested tentatively by O'Donnell himself in the two cases of Brazil and Argentina. More important, it was tested in a volume edited by David Collier (1979) and published under the auspices of the Social Science Research Council. The volume included contributions from O'Donnell and Cardoso as well as a number of other Latin American and American scholars. The results of this test by and large were a rejection of the purely economic explanation or "industrial deepening" theory of bureaucratic authoritarianism. Albert Hirschman questions whether such a monocausal theory should ever have been seriously entertained (Collier 1979, chap. 3). Julio Cotler challenges the hypothesis from the perspective of a number of country experiences (chap. 6). Neither O'Donnell (chap. 7) nor Cardoso (chap. 2) seriously defends the theory. James Kurth, in an impressive examination of European historical experience, demonstrates the looseness of the connection between industrialization and authoritarian political institutions in the Europe of the late nineteenth and early twentieth centuries (chap. 8). Collier, in an excellent summary chapter, disaggregates the concept of bureaucratic authoritarianism and points out the direction for more productive research on Latin American political economy. What is constructive about this "bureaucratic authoritarianism" intellectual episode is that through simply following the rule of scientific evidence and inference, we have succeeded in escaping from a sterile polemic and have moved into solid and productive research on the interaction of political and economic variables in development processes.

In addition to statistical and country studies, there have been a number of specific industrial case studies intended to exemplify dependency or to test the validity of its propositions. Among these, two very recent case studies make serious claims to having tested the dependency approach. Gary Gereffi (1983), in an analysis of the pharmaceutical industry in Mexico, argues that he has made a crucial case study testing the validity of the dependency argument. By a "crucial case study," in Harry Eckstein's (1975) sense, Gereffi means that a demonstration of the validity of dependency propositions in the case of pharmaceuticals in Mexico would constitute proof of their general validity, since Mexican pharmaceuticals constitute a "least likely case" for dependency. That is, as Gereffi puts it, in Mexico after World War II, conditions were most favorable for the indigenous development of world leadership of a dynamic and technologically sophisticated segment (steroid technology) of the pharmaceutical industry. Mexico had exclusive access to the most efficient raw material, and a local firm (Syntex) was a world leader in steroid technology, with a high volume of output. Even given these favorable conditions, multinational pharmaceutical corporations invaded and largely took over the Mexican industry, with two consequences supportive of the dependency approach: indigenous growth in Mexico was distorted by "an inequitable distribution of industry benefits favoring the central capitalist economies and the transnational corporations (TNCs) more than Mexico, and by a restriction of Mexico's choices in pursuing its development options" (p. 155).

These are not, properly speaking, the principal dependency propositions on growth and distribution. Dependency propositions are global, not industry specific. Even if Gereffi had proven these propositions in the Mexican pharmaceuticals case, they could not be generalized across economies and across nations. There are far too many variables and too much variation to be captured in a single case. By his own claims, Gereffi has not proven the dependency argument. The third phase of his case study describes the efforts of the Mexican state after 1975 to protect Mexican interests vis-a-vis the multinational corporations by the establishment of a state corporation to control the production, pricing, and supply of the steroid raw material. While the maximum program of this state corporation failed to be fulfilled, the program was able to increase the price paid for the raw material and the rate of return to Mexican farmers. Furthermore, Gereffi views the entrance of the state into the pharmaceuticals picture in Mexico as a relatively open and potentially productive one from the point of view of domestic interests. In other words, he does not exclude the possibility of a reversal of dependency trends through state decisions in Mexico and other Third World countries. In the second part of his book Gereffi examines the pharmaceutical industry cross-nationally and comes to conclusions in conflict with Evans's "triple-alliance" thesis. Thus he finds private pharmaceutical companies capable of acting in support of societal goals, and state pharmaceutical companies and governmental regulators in some Third World countries intervening effectively in the interest of a more equitable distribution of access to pharmaceuticals.

As we have just seen, Gereffi (1983) does not claim to validate the dependency perspective as advanced by such writers as Cardoso and Evans. It is an open, varied, and changing phenomenon that he describes. And, in contrast to the pessimism of Cardoso, Evans, and others, he concludes, "The continuing dilemmas of development most be understood, then, as generating not just constraints, but also opportunities for national actors" (p. 253).

In his case study of the mining industry of Peru, David Becker (1983), employing a more classical Marxist social democratic approach, views the emergence of a national bourgeoisie out of the development of the Peruvian mineral industries in progressive terms. The corporate national bourgeoisie, in his judgment, is not simply a creature of the multinational corporations. It pursues a more progressive social, economic, and political policy than the old oligarchy. It has been responsible for growth and greater distributive equity and enjoys substantial legitimacy. Becker argues that given the present situation in Peru a socialist alternative does not exist: "The ascent of the corporate national bourgeoisie has not arrested what would otherwise have been a broadly based movement of popular liberation and has led to some noteworthy gains for the popular sectors" (p. 334).

Becker also points out that the state in Peru, while substantially influenced by the corporate national bourgeoisie, is not its creature. It has autonomy and can act in the interests of other sectors of society. The Peruvian trade union movement is relatively robust and supportive of the bourgeois democratic regime. This picture of power and policy in Peru is in contrast to Evans's "triple-alliance" model of Brazil. Becker gives short shrift to the dependency ideas of such theorists as Cardoso, on the grounds that empirical investigation "consistently fails to verify them" (p. 341). These are his concluding comments:

> Deficient in explanatory power and unable to stand up to empirical tests, the "theory" of dependency as a systemic outcome of relations with international capitalism is, in reality, an ideology. Dependencista ideology has been useful to political and economic elites striving to free themselves and their nations from subjugation to neocolonialism. That goal has been largely attained. Now

> the task is to focus on the national basis of elitism and domination—which an ideology that blames all evil in the Third World on the metropoli cannot do. The ideology depreciates the drive to institute local participatory democracy (a step forward even in its less-than-perfect bourgeois incarnation) and to extend it beyond formal politics; one searches in vain for a dependencista appreciation that democracy is the only meaningful check on elite power. Accordingly, dependencismo no longer furthers, as it once did, the cause of general human liberation. It is time, therefore, for progressives to lay it to rest. (p. 342)

When we deal with case studies like that of Becker or even Gereffi, or with the statistical tests summarized by Russett, we are really beyond the dependency approach. We are back in mainstream social science and political science research, where we are governed by professional criteria of evidence and inference.

The Productivity of Mainstream Comparative Politics

While Third World research continues on a substantial scale, it no longer is the "growth industry" it was in the 1950s and 1960s. This is in part a consequence of restricted access for research in repressive regimes, but it is also a consequence of an abated excitement. Development has turned out to be a brutal, slogging process. There have been more economic growth successes than democratization ones. Nevertheless, the integral pessimism of the late 1960s and early 1970s has turned out to be inappropriate. The relationship between politics and economic development turns out to be more complex than expected. The authoritarian regimes of Brazil, Argentina, Uruguay, and others seem to have run their course and have given way, or are giving way, to popular regimes favoring "turning the rascals out," just as popular regimes were turned out in these countries in earlier decades. Development and modernization seem to produce enough disappointments to discredit both popular and authoritarian regimes in turn.

The accomplishments of area studies in the last decade have been substantial. Aside from the distortions produced by the dependency movement, primarily in Latin American and African studies, much good work has been done. It would not be an exaggeration to claim that area studies have come to interact creatively with one another and have both drawn upon and contributed to political theory in the last few decades. The concept of "clientelism" has proven to be particularly fruitful in Third World area studies. The recognition of the importance of patron-client relations in politics has roots in sociological and anthropological theory. The earliest contribution to this literature was that of Carl Lande (1965), who interpreted Philippine politics almost entirely in terms of a factionalism based on patron-client relations. Within a few years, applications of the patron-client concept appeared in Keith Legg's (1969) study of Greek politics, James C. Scott's (1972) studies of Southeast Asian politics, and Rene Lemarchand's (1972) work on African politics. Jackson and Rosberg (1984) make effective use of the patron-client concept in their recent study of personal rule in Black Africa. Clientelism has also proven to be a useful concept for the analysis of Middle Eastern political processes, as is suggested in the work of James Bill and Carl Leiden (1979) and of Robert Springborg (1982). The general theoretical implications of patron-client relations and their intellectual history are treated in an excellent symposium edited by Steffan Schmidt et al. (1977). Eisenstadt and Lemarchand (1981) have also drawn together a cross-area collection of patron-client studies, and Eisenstadt (1984) more recently has presented a sociological theory of clientelism.

Despite the difficulties of access to field research, communism studies have produced distinguished work in recent years. The application of analytic models and concepts from comparative politics and political sociology has illuminated communist politics in important ways. The polemic among Gordon Skilling (1983; Skilling and Griffiths 1971), T. H. Rigby (1980), Jerry Hough (1983), and others over the applicability of interest group theory and pluralism to communist political processes has been unusually productive of insight. Similarly, Rigby and his associates have made good use of the concepts of legitimacy and patron-client relations in analyzing Soviet and communist politics (see Rigby and Feher 1982; Rigby and Harasymiw 1983). The concepts of bureaucratic politics (Dawisha et al. 1980), political participation (Friedgut 1979), and political culture (Brown and Gray 1977; White 1979) have also been applied in Soviet and communism studies. Jan Triska has pioneered in utilizing political development and political sociology concepts in Eastern European studies (see Triska and Cocks 1977; Triska and Gati 1981).

There has been a similar effort to illuminate Chinese politics through the application of Western social science notions. Harry Harding (1984), in a review of Chinese political studies, divides Chinese political science scholarship in the post-World War II period into three generations. The first generation of studies was primarily descriptive of the emerging institutions and processes. The second generation, based primarily on materials brought to light in the Cultural Revolution, was a more specialized literature dealing with such themes as the bureaucracy, various areas of public policy, and geographic regions. More recently, Western social science concepts and models have been applied to Chinese data. Thus there are applications of factional models, interest group models, bureaucratic politics models, belief system models, and generational models. Harding concludes his analysis by projecting the prospects of future work on China, based on, at least for the moment, more accessible data. He sees great promise in this combination of more open access for field research and a closer integration of Chinese studies into comparative politics.

The significance of this three-decade-long interaction between political theory and area studies has not been fully appreciated. Giovanni Sartori (1970), in his celebrated "concept misformation" article, and some of the contributors to the Robert Ward and Lucian Pye (1975) symposium on political science and area studies would seem to have missed the point of this intellectual experience when they criticize it for "concept stretching" or ethnocentrism. Surely Hugh Skilling, T. H. Rigby, and Jerry Hough when they debated about interest groups in communist political systems were not so naive as to believe that they would discover chambers of commerce, farm bureaus, Leagues of Women Voters, and the like in the Soviet Union, Poland, Hungary, and so on. They were dissatisfied with the totalitarian model and tried the interest group model for fit. What came out of this exercise was a sharper delineation of the power-policy structure in communist political systems. The same might be said of the patron-client model, the bureaucratic politics model, the issue network and "iron triangle" model, and the other conceptual models taken primarily from American political studies that have proven so useful in bringing out the similarities and differences among First, Second, and Third World countries. Creative model fitting has been the essence of the game. The critique of this work as ethnocentric or as violating methodological rules stems from an ideological bias or from an extreme ideographic methodological position.

In the 1970s, there was a renewed interest in Western Europe. In the "new nation" excitement of the 1950s and early 1960s, training and research in European studies had declined. In the 1970s, the advanced industrial societies (now including Japan) began to develop "interesting" problems – the environment and the "quality of life," a slowdown of growth, inflation, unemployment, party realignment and dealignment, and "ungovernability." There were interesting movements, issues, and solutions in the wind – tax rebellions, neocorporatism, neoeconomic classicism, neoconservatism. The accessibility of these countries for research and the availability of reliable quantitative data challenged the theoretically adventurous and methodologically sophisticated scholars in comparative politics.

There have been a number of solid accomplishments in comparative and development studies in the last decade or so.

(1) Political Economy Studies

The political economy of development continues to be a productive research field. Hollis Chenery (1979; Chenery et al. 1974) and his collaborators in World Bank-sponsored research continue to produce important studies illuminating the issues of growth, distribution, and public policy in Third World countries. Albert Fishlow and his collaborators (1978), as well as Howard Wriggins (1978), have made important contributions to our understanding of important Third World welfare and growth issues within the framework of the research program of the Council on Foreign Relations.

(2) Comparative Political History

The field of comparative political history has been particularly productive of insight into developmental patterns in the last decade. Over the longer time span this approach to history as a way of generating hypotheses about political development has been influenced by three intellectual currents: (1) Weberian political sociology, (2) neo-Marxist ideas, and (3) more general social scientific hypotheses and methods. The influence of Marx has been pervasive in comparative historical sociology. Since his work, no serious political scientist or sociologist can afford to neglect the role of economic forces in the explanation of social reality. The important difference has been between those who insist on a primacy for economic forces and class structure in historical explanations and those who attribute explanatory significance in addition to religion, ethnicity, political processes, personality, and the like.

Weber's sociology of religion was in some sense a polemic against the Marxist view of economic causality, though social class and status continue to play important explanatory roles in his sociological theory and research. In the postwar period there have been noteworthy contributions to comparative political history by Weberians, primarily in the earlier decades. Eisenstadt's *The Political Systems of Empires* (1963) was in direct continuity with Weber's theory of types of "domination." Eisenstadt's study of bureaucratic empires filled in a theoretical and empirical gap in Weber's monumental work, and his later work continued to develop Weberian themes. Reinhard Bendix in 1964 published his *Nation-Building and Citizenship,* which contrasted nation-state developments in Western Europe, Russia, Japan, and India utilizing Weber's political sociological concepts of rationality and traditionality, patrimonialism, bureaucratization, plebiscitarian democracy, and the like. Gunther Roth (1968) got significant explanatory mileage out of Weber's concept of patrimonialism in the analysis of Third World development.

The neo-Marxist trend (if one can still properly call it that) has been quite productive, beginning with Barrington Moore's *Social Origins of Dictatorship and Democracy* (1966), including Perry Anderson's *Lineages of the Absolutist State* (1974) and Immanuel Wallerstein's *The Modern World-System* (1974, 1980), and culminating in Theda Skocpol's *States and Revolutions* (1979). While all four of these writers would characterize themselves as in some sense drawing on Marxism, they display a wide variety of explanatory logics. Thus Wallerstein's world-system theory is a simple monocausal world capitalism logic with three actors—a capitalist core, a semiperiphery, and a periphery. Barrington Moore's *Social Origins* presents two causal logics—an explicit parsimonious "bourgeousie-rural social structure" explanation of the historical origins of capitalist democracy, fascism, and communism, embedded in a much more complex and dense series of historical case studies reflecting cultural and political as well as economic explanations. Anderson rejects a warfare theory of the origins of the European absolutist state and proposes a more orthodox Marxist logic of peasant-nobility class struggle in the late feudal period in Western Europe. Finally, Skocpol's study of the classic social revolutions in France, Russia, and China is related to Marxism mainly by self-characterization. Class structure and conflict are not Skocpol's powerful variables in explaining these great social revolutions. They are more in the nature of background factors, while serious military defeats and collapsing state structures are the sufficient causes. Skocpol refers to herself as a "structuralist," viewing history as largely explained by the interplay of international, social, and state structures, and with politics and leadership definitely soft-pedaled.

The more eclectic social science-influenced comparative historical current began in the early 1970s with the SSRC volumes edited by Binder et al. (1971), Tilly (1975), and Grew (1978), discussed earlier. Two symposia deal with the theme of the collapse and reinstitution of democracy in the last few decades. Juan Linz and Alfred Stepan (1978) attempted to distill generalizations from our historical experience with the collapse of democracies in Europe and Latin America in the last half century. Philippe Schmitter, Guillermo O'Donnell, and their collaborators (forthcoming) have attempted to codify more recent experience with transitions to democracy from authoritarian regimes in Europe and Latin America.

The international political economy school has produced a series of comparative historical studies linking politics and economics and national and international factors. This fruitful interdisciplinary work has produced, among others, such interesting studies as Gourevitch's (1977, 1984) two analyses of the consequences of major depressions—that of 1870–90 and that of the 1930s—for European and American political development; Kurth's analysis of the interaction of industrialization and democratization in Europe during the late nineteenth century (in Collier, 1979); Peter Katzenstein's symposium (1978) comparing and explaining the foreign economic policies of the major democratic capitalist nations; and Katzenstein's recent brilliant *Small States and World Markets* (1985).

(3) Comparative Survey Research

Comparative survey research has made major progress in the last few decades. Sidney Verba and his associates (1978), Ronald Inglehart (1975), Samuel Barnes and his associates (1979), and Robert Putnam (1973) and his collaborators (1981) have vastly improved our understanding of the structure, conditions, and consequences of political participation and of the political culture of mass and elite groups in advanced industrial societies. The cross-national accumulation of electoral results and of survey data on partisanship and attitudes on issues has made possible increasingly accurate analyses of political trends. Contributions such as Richard Rose's *Electoral Behavior: A Comparative Handbook* (1974) and Dalton, Flanagan, and Beck's *Electoral Change in Advanced Industrial Democracies* (1984) have provided us with more rigorous explanations of changing political behavior.

(4) Comparative Public Policy Studies

Comparative public policy has been established as an important field in political science under the leadership of Arnold Heidenheimer (see Heidenheimer, Heclo, and Adams 1983), Peter Flora (see Flora and Heidenheimer 1981), Hugh Heclo (1974), and Richard Rose (1984). It has generated a set of empirically validated propositions about the economic, political, and cultural conditions affecting differences in the public revenue and expenditure policies, and in income maintenance, health, and education policies in Europe and North America in the last century.

(5) Econometric Studies

In the econometric tradition, important statistical work has been done on the relationships among economic growth, the volume and composition of governmental revenue and expenditure, the ideological composition of governments, the level and structure of trade union organization, strike levels, inflation, and unemployment rates. This literature, in which the work of Douglas Hibbs (1977, 1978), David Cameron (1978, 1982), Roger Hollingsworth (1982), and James Alt and K. Alec Chrystal (1983) has been of particular importance, along with the comparative public policy literature and the historical political economy literature cited earlier, represents substantial responses to the challenge of a political economy of comparative politics.

(6) Comparative Interest Groups and Neocorporatist Studies

A comparative interest group and neocorporatist literature has developed in the past decade, contributed to by Philippe Schmitter and Gerhard Lehmbruch (1979), Suzanne Berger (1981), John Goldthorpe (1984), and others. This literature deals with the interesting problem of the interaction of interest groups and bureaucracies in the contemporary crises of political economy. A major investigation of trade associations and the political economy of advanced industrial societies is currently under way under the leadership of Schmitter.

(7) Comparative Political Party Studies

The classic tradition of comparative political party studies is being carried on by Giovanni Sartori (1976), Arend Lijphart (1977, 1984), and G. Bingham Powell (1982), among others. This work has brought our understanding of electoral engineering and of the conditions and consequences of different varieties of party systems to higher levels of rigor.

(8) Methodology

Finally, mainstream comparative politics has generated a useful methodological literature, dealing with problems of linguistic equivalence in cross-national research, setting standards in conceptualization, and exploring the explanatory power of different comparative strategies. Adam Przeworski and Henry Teune (1970), Robert Holt and John Turner (1970),

Sidney Verba (1967), Giovanni Sartori (1970, 1976), Arend Lijphart (1971), and Mattei Dogan and Dominique Pelassy (1984), among others, have all made important contributions to this literature.

The ideological battle has not had the "chilling" effect in studies of advanced democratic nations that it has had on Third World area studies, particularly Latin America. This is due to the fact that the intellectual tradition of European and American area studies is older and better established. The professional corps is larger; there are more publication outlets. The neo-Marxist literature of Europe and America is not as simplistic as the *dependencia* literature. Neo-Marxist and mainstream comparative studies meet in a common interest in social class and economic variables as explanatory of political phenomena. They move apart when class becomes the primum mobile of political explanation and when the concept of the state becomes a set of unspecified and unverified coercive relations among classes.

A new research thrust concerned with reaffirming the importance of the state in political explanation has still to prove its productivity. Eric Nordlinger's (1981) argument urging the importance of the state and government as initiating policy, as having autonomy even under great societal pressure, makes a useful contribution to research strategy. On the other hand, the concept of the state in the recent volume edited by Evans, Rueschemeyer, and Skocpol (1985) seems to have metaphysical overtones. This neostatist movement seems to have overlooked the fact that the pluralist and structural functional movements in political science were efforts, largely successful, to demystify the state concept, to disaggregate and operationalize it, so that it could be accurately observed and measured. It surely will serve no useful purpose to remystify the state concept, to reintroduce its Hegelian reification and ambiguity (Krasner 1984; Lentner 1984). In addition, these neostatists have not as yet done a good search of the literature. Though evangelists of a new comparative history, they caricature the historical background of the pluralist movement. Far from demeaning the state, the pluralists were powerful advocates of the mobilization of the less advantaged elements of the population in order to gain access to the state and to increase state power for welfare objectives. The pluralists were not only New Dealers; they were also engineers in the construction of what later became the "imperial presidency." Charles Merriam, Pendleton Herring, V. O. Key, and others all served apprenticeships in the work of the National Resources Planning Board, the President's Committee on Administrative Management, and the early Bureau of the Budget—all of which were concerned with strengthening the state. The allegation that the pluralists reduced the state and government to a simple arena where societal interests compete with one another simply does not bear close scrutiny. We must ask if the neostatists have ever examined the last chapters of Truman's *The Governmental Process* (1951), or E. Pendleton Herring's *Federal Commissioners* (1936) and *Presidential Leadership* (1940), or V. O. Key's *The Administration of Federal Grants to States* (1937) and *Politics, Parties, and Pressure Groups* (1949). Indeed, there are, in any university library, many shelves of books dealing with political and governmental institutions strongly influenced by pluralism that would challenge this caricature of the pluralist treatment of the state.

The neostatists do not make clear what they propose to pack into the state concept, but they seem to resist the thought of unpacking it for analytic and empirical research purposes. As this neostatist impulse takes tangible form in empirical studies of one kind or another, will it not lead to research on executives, bureaucracies, military institutions, parliaments, political parties, interest groups and electorates, or relations and interactions among them? Will it avoid studies of comparative public revenue and expenditure, comparative public policy, comparative political culture? Indeed, if this neostatism is more than semantic juggling, it will surely be disaggregated into these specific research themes. And it is difficult to see what new insight, what new research programs will have been stimulated by "bringing the state back in."

This account of comparative politics and political development studies in the last few decades makes the case that the field is not in "crisis," as some have argued. If there has been a crisis it has been a political rather than an intellectual one. This essay also makes the case that the characterization of the literature of comparative politics as an ideological defense of imperialism and capitalism simply is not borne out by evidence. The dependency writers who have been responsible for this portrayal of the field have failed to search the literature; where they cite it, they often misrepresent its content and meaning. The dependency research program has not made its case. Its principal propositions have failed to be confirmed or have been disconfirmed. Insofar as the dependency approach has become a serious research program involving rigorous case studies and quantitative tests of the relations between carefully operationalized variables, it has become part of mainstream comparative politics. The argument that the *dependencistas* directed our attention to the importance of the international environment for economic and political development and brought political economy perspectives to bear on these processes cannot be sustained. These tendencies were already present in the mainstream literature, and they continue with great vigor today. And if one examines the literature cited in these international and political economy studies, there is little evidence of impact of the dependency perspective. One cannot escape the conclusion that the dependency movement was a political movement, and that its net effect may have been intellectually counterproductive.

Mainstream comparative studies, rather than being in crisis, are richly and variedly productive. If there is no single paradigm today, it may be said that there never was one. In the four decades since World War II, the level of rigor has been significantly increased in quantitative, analytical, and historical-sociological work. It has not escaped cultural and ideological bias, but it aspires to and attains an ever greater honesty and detachment.

References

Adelman, Irma and Cynthia Taft Morris. 1967. *Society, Politics, and Economic Development: A Quantitative Approach*. Baltimore: Johns Hopkins University Press.

Almond, Gabriel A. 1956. "Comparative Political Systems." *Journal of Politics* 18, no. 3 (August).

Almond, Gabriel A. 1970. *Political Development: Essays in Heuristic Theory*. Boston: Little, Brown.

Almond, Gabriel A. 1971. "National Politics and International Politics." In *The Search for World Order*, edited by Albert Lapawsky et al. New York: Appleton-Century-Crofts.

Almond, Gabriel A. and James Coleman, eds. 1960. *The Politics of the Development Areas*. Princeton, NJ: Princeton University Press.

Almond, Gabriel A., with Scott Flanagan and Robert Mundt. 1973. *Crisis, Choice, and Change*. Boston: Little, Brown.

Almond, Gabriel A. and Sidney Verba. 1963. *The Civic Culture*. Princeton, NJ: Princeton University Press.

Alt, James E. and K. Alec Chrystal. 1983. *Political Economics*. Berkeley: University of California Press.

Anderson, Perry. 1974. *Lineages of the Absolutist State*. New York: Humanities Press.

Apter, David E. 1955. *The Gold Coast in Transition*. Princeton, NJ: Princeton University Press.

Apter, David E. 1961. *The Political Kingdom in Uganda: A Study in Bureaucratic Nationalism*. Princeton, NJ: Princeton University Press.

Apter, David E. 1965. *The Politics of Modernization*. Chicago: University of Chicago Press.

Barnes, Samuel H., Max Kaase, et al. 1979. *Political Action: Mass Participation in Five Western Democracies*. Beverly Hills, CA: Sage.

Becker, David. 1983. *The New Bourgeoisie and the Limits of Dependency*. Princeton, NJ: Princeton University Press.

Bendix, Reinhard. 1964. *Nation-Building and Citizenship: Studies of Our Changing Social Order.* New York: Wiley.

Berger, Suzanne D., ed. 1981. *Organizing Interests in Western Europe: Pluralism, Corporatism, and the Transformation of Politics.* New York: Cambridge University Press.

Bienen, Henry. 1967. *Tanzania: Party Transformation and Economic Development.* Princeton, NJ: Princeton University Press.

Bill, James A. and Carl Leiden. 1979. *Politics in the Middle East.* Boston: Little, Brown.

Binder, Leonard. 1961. *Religion and Politics in Pakistan.* Berkeley: University of California Press.

Binder, Leonard. 1962. *Iran: Political Development in a Changing Society.* Berkeley: University of California Press.

Binder, Leonard, James Coleman, Joseph LaPalombara, Lucian Pye, Sidney Verba, and Myron Weiner. 1971. *Crises and Sequences in Political Development.* Princeton, NJ: Princeton University Press.

Black, Cyril E. 1966. *The Dynamics of Modernization.* New York: Harper & Row.

Bodenheimer, Suzanne. 1970. "The Ideology of Developmentalism." *Berkeley Journal of Sociology* 95–137.

Braibanti, Ralph, ed. 1966. *Asian Bureaucratic Systems Emergent from the British Imperial System.* Durham, NC: Duke University Press.

Brown, Archie and Jack Gray, eds. 1977. *Political Culture and Political Change in Communist States.* New York: Holmes & Meier.

Cameron, David. 1978. "The Expansion of the Public Economy: A Comparative Analysis." *American Political Science Review* 72, no. 4 (December).

Cameron, David. 1982. "Social Democracy, Corporatism, and Labor Quiescence: The Representation of Economic Interest in Advanced Capitalist Society." In *Order and Conflict in Contemporary Capitalism: Studies in the Political Economy of Western European Nations,* edited by John J. Goldthorpe. Oxford: Oxford University Press.

Caporaso, James. 1978. "Dependence, Dependency, and Power in the Global System: A Structural and Behavioral Analysis." *International Organization* 32.

Caporaso, James. 1980. "Dependency Theory: Continuities and Discontinuities in Development Studies." *International Organization* 34, no. 3 (Autumn).

Cardoso, Fernando Henrique and Enzo Faletto. 1969, 1979. *Dependencia y desarrollo en America Latina* [Dependency and Development in Latin America]. Mexico City: Siglo Veininno Editores.

Cardoso, Fernando Henrique. 1973. "Associated Dependent Development: Theoretical and Practical Implications." *Authoritarian Brazil: Origins, Policies, and Future,* edited by Alfred Stepan. New Haven, CT: Yale University Press.

Cardoso, Fernando Henrique. 1979. "On the Characterization of Authoritarian Regimes in Latin America." In *The New Authoritarianism in Latin America,* edited by David Collier. Princeton, NJ: Princeton University Press.

Cardoso, Fernando Henrique and Enzo Faletto. 1979. *Dependency and Development in Latin America,* Berkeley: University of California Press.

Chenery, Hollis. 1955. "The Role of Industrialization in Development Programs." *American Economic Review Papers and Proceedings* 45 (May): 40–57.

Chenery, Hollis. 1979. *Structural Change and Development Policy*. New York: Oxford University Press.

Chenery, Hollis et al. 1974. *Redistribution with Growth*. New York: Oxford University Press.

Chilcote, Ronald and Joel C. Edelstein, eds. 1974. *Latin America: The Struggle with Dependency and Beyond*. Cambridge, MA: Schenkman.

Coleman, James S. 1958. *Nigeria: Background to Nationalism*. Berkeley: University of California Press.

Coleman, James S. 1960. "Conclusion: The Political Systems of the Developing Areas." In *The Politics of the Developing Areas*, edited by Gabriel A. Almond and James Coleman. Princeton, NJ: Princeton University Press.

Coleman, James S., ed. 1965. *Education and Political Development*. Princeton, NJ: Princeton University Press.

Collier, David, ed. 1979. *The New Authoritarianism in Latin America*. Princeton, NJ: Princeton University Press.

Collier, Ruth Berins and David Collier. 1979. "Inducements versus Constraints: Disaggregating 'Corporatism.'" *American Political Science Review* 73 (December).

Cutright, Philips. 1963. "National Political Development: Measurement and Analysis." *American Sociological Review* (April).

Dahl, Robert A. 1971. *Polyarchy: Participation and Opposition*. New Haven, CT: Yale University Press.

Dalton, Russell J., Scott C. Flanagan, and Paul Allen Beck, eds. 1984. *Electoral Change in Advanced Industrial Democracies*. Princeton, NJ: Princeton University Press.

Dawisha, Karen, Graham Allison, Fred Eidlin, and Jiri Valenta. 1980 *Studies in Comparative Communism* (Winter).

Deutsch, Karl W. 1961. "Social Mobilization and Political Development." *American Political Science Review* 55, no. 3 (September): 493–514.

Dogan, Mattei and Dominique Pelassy. 1984. *How to Compare Nations: Strategies in Comparative Politics*. Chatham, NJ: Chatham House.

Dominguez I. 1978. *Cuba: Order and Revolution*. Cambridge, MA: Harvard University Press.

Dominguez, Jorge I. 1980. *Insurrection or Loyalty: The Breakdown of the Spanish American Empire*. Cambridge, MA: Harvard University Press.

Dominguez, Jorge I. 1982. *LASA Newsletter* 13, no. 2 (Summer).

Doran, Charles F. and George Modelski, eds. 1983. *North-South Relations: Studies of Dependency Reversal*. New York: Praeger.

Dos Santos, Theotonio. 1970. "The Structure of Dependence." *American Economic Review* 60, no. 5: 235–46.

Durkheim, Emile. [1893] 1933. *The Division of Labor in Society*. New York: Macmillan.

Eckstein, Harry, ed. 1963. *Internal War*. Glencoe, IL: Free Press of Glencoe.

Eckstein, Harry. 1975. "Case Study and Theory in Political Science." In *Handbook of Political Science*, vol. 7, edited by Fred I. Greenstein and Nelson W. Polsby. Reading, MA: Addison-Wesley.

Eisenstadt, S. N. 1963. *The Political Systems of Empires*. Glencoe, IL: Free Press.

Eisenstadt, S. N. 1964. "Breakdowns of Modernization." *Economic Development and Cultural Change* 12, no. 4 (July): 345–67.

Eisenstadt, S. N. 1984. *Patrons, Clients, and Friends: Interpersonal Relations and the Structure of Trust in Society.* Cambridge: Cambridge University Press.

Eisenstadt, S. N. and Rene Lemarchand. 1981. *Political Clientelism, Patronage, and Development.* Beverly Hills, CA: Sage.

Evans, Peter. 1979. *Dependent Development: The Alliance of Multinational, State, and Local Capital in Brazil.* Princeton, NJ: Princeton University Press.

Evans, Peter B., Dietrich Rueschemeyer, and Theda Skocpol, eds. 1985. *Bringing the State Back In.* New York: Cambridge University Press.

Fishlow, Albert et al. 1978. *Rich and Poor Nations in the World Economy.* New York: McGraw-Hill.

Flora, Peter and Arnold J. Heidenheimer, eds. 1981. *The Development of Welfare States in Europe and America.* New Brunswick, NJ: Transaction.

Frank, Andre Gunder. 1969. *Latin America: Underdevelopment or Revolution.* New York: Monthly Review Press.

Friedgut, Theodore H. 1979. *Political Participation in the USSR.* Princeton, NJ: Princeton University Press.

Gereffi, Gary. 1983. *The Pharmaceutical Industry and Dependency in the Third World.* Princeton, NJ: Princeton University Press.

Gerschenkron, Alexander. 1953. "Social Attitudes, Entrepreneurship, and Economic Development." *Explorations in Entrepreneurial History* 6 (October).

Gerschenkron, Alexander. 1962. *Economic Backwardness in Historical Perspective: A Book of Essays.* Cambridge, MA: Harvard University Press.

Goldthorpe, John J., ed. 1984. *Order and Conflict in Contemporary Capitalism: Studies in the Political Economy of Western European Nations.* Oxford: Oxford University Press.

Gourevitch, Peter. 1977. "International Trade, Domestic Coalitions, and Liberty: Comparative Responses to the Crisis of 1873–1896." *Journal of Interdisciplinary History* 8: 281–313.

Gourevitch, Peter. 1984. "Breaking with Orthodoxy: The Politics of Economic Policy: Responses to the Depression of the 1930's." *International Organization* 38, no.1.

Grew, Raymond, ed. 1978. *Crises of Political Development in Europe and the United States.* Princeton, NJ: Princeton University Press.

Hagen, Everett E. 1962. *On the Theory of Social Change: How Economic Growth Begins.* Homewood, IL: Dorsey.

Hagen, Everett E. 1968. *The Economics of Development.* Homewood, IL: Richard D. Irwin.

Harding, Harry E. 1984. "The Study of Chinese Politics: Toward a Third Generation of Scholarship." *World Politics* 36, no. 2 (January): 284–307.

Harsanyi, John. 1969. "Rational-Choice Models of Political Behavior vs. Functionalist and Conformist Theories." *World Politics* 21, no. 4.

Heclo, Hugh. 1974. *Modern Social Politics in Britain and Sweden: From Relief to Income Maintenance.* New Haven, CT: Yale University Press.

Heidenheimer, Arnold J., Hugh Heclo, and Carolyn Adams. 1983. *Comparative Public Policy: The Politics of Social Choice in Europe and America.* New York: St. Martin's.

Herring, E. Pendleton. 1936. *Federal Commissioners.* Cambridge, MA: Harvard University Press.

Herring, E. Pendleton. 1940. *Presidential Leadership.* New York: Farrar & Rinehart.

Herz, John, ed. 1982. *From Dictatorship to Democracy: Coping with the Legacies of Authoritarianism and Totalitarianism.* Westport, CT: Greenwood.

Hibbs, Douglas. 1977. "Political Parties and Macroeconomic Policy." *American Political Science Review* 71 (December).

Hibbs, Douglas. 1978. "On the Political Economy of Long Run Trends in Strike Activity." *British Journal of Political Science* 8 (April): 165–66.

Hirschman, Albert O. 1958. *The Strategy of Economic Development.* New Haven, CT: Yale University Press.

Hirschman, Albert O. 1963. *Journeys Toward Progress: Studies of Economic Policy-Making in Latin America.* New York: Twentieth Century Fund.

Holt, Robert and John Turner, 1966. *The Political Basis of Economic Development.* Princeton, NJ: Van Nostrand.

Holt, Robert and John E. Turner, eds. 1970. *The Methodology of Comparative Research.* New York: Free Press.

Hollingsworth, Roger. 1982. "The Political-Structural Basis for Economic Performance." *Annals of the American Academy of Political and Social Science* (January).

Hoselitz, Bert F. 1952. *The Progress of Underdeveloped Areas.* Chicago: University of Chicago Press.

Hough, Jerry. 1983. "Pluralism, Corporatism and the Soviet Union." In *Pluralism in the Soviet Union,* edited by Susan Gross Soloman. London: Macmillan.

Huntington, Samuel P. 1965. "Political Development and Political Decay." *World Politics* 17, no. 3: 386–430.

Huntington, Samuel P. 1968. *Political Order in Changing Societies.* New Haven, CT: Yale University Press.

Huntington, Samuel. 1984. "Will More Countries Become Democratic?" *Political Science Quarterly* 99, no. 2.

Huntington, Samuel P. and Jorge I. Dominguez. 1975. "Political Development." In *Handbook of Political Science,* vol. 3, edited by Fred I. Greenstein and Nelson W. Polsby. Reading, MA: Addison-Wesley.

Huntington, Samuel P. and Clement H. Moore, eds. 1970. *Authoritarian Politics in Modern Society: The Dynamics of Established One-Party Systems.* New York: Basic Books.

Inglehart, Ronald. 1975. *The Silent Revolution: Changing Values and Political Style among Western Publics.* Princeton, NJ: Princeton University Press.

Inkeles, Alex and David Horton Smith. 1974. *Becoming Modern: Individual Change in Six Developing Countries.* Cambridge, MA: Harvard University Press.

Jackson, Robert H. and Carl G. Rosberg. 1984. *Personal Rule in Black Africa: Prince, Autocrat, Prophet, Tyrant.* Berkeley: University of California Press.

Katzenstein, Peter J. 1978. *Between Power and Plenty: Foreign Economic Policies of Advanced Industrial States.* Madison: University of Wisconsin Press.

Katzenstein, Peter. 1985. *Small States and World Markets.* Ithaca, NY: Cornell University Press.

Kesselman, Mark. 1973. "Order or Movement? The Literature of Political Development as Ideology." *World Politics* 26, no. 1.

Key, V. O., Jr. 1937. *The Administration of Federal Grants to States*. Chicago: Public Administration Service.

Key, V. O., Jr. 1949. *Politics, Parties, and Pressure Groups*. New York: Crowell.

Krasner, Stephen D. 1984. "Approaches to the State: Alternative Conceptions and Historical Dynamics." *Comparative Politics* 16, no. 2.

Kuhn, Thomas S. 1960. *A Theory of Scientific Revolution*. Princeton, NJ: Princeton University Press.

Kuznets, Simon. 1955. "Economic Growth and Income Equality." *American Economic Review* 4, no. 5.

Kuznets, Simon. 1959. *Six Lectures on Economic Growth*. New York: Free Press.

Lande, Carl H. 1965. *Leaders, Factions, and Parties: The Structure of Philippine Politics*. New Haven, CT: Southeast Asia Studies, Yale University Press.

LaPalombara, Joseph. 1963. *Bureaucracy and Political Development*. Princeton, NJ: Princeton University Press.

LaPalombara, Joseph and Myron Weiner, eds. 1966. *Political Parties and Political Development*. Princeton, NJ: Princeton University Press.

Legg, Keith, R. 1969. *Politics in Modern Greece*. Stanford, CA: Stanford University Press.

Lemarchand, Rene. 1972. "Political Clientelism and Ethnicity in Tropical Africa: Competing Solidarities in Nation-Building." *American Political Science Review* 66, no. 1.

Lentner, Howard H. 1984. "The Concept of the State: A Response to Stephen Krasner." *Comparative Politics* 16, no. 3.

Lerner, Daniel. 1958. *The Passing of Traditional Society: Modernizing the Middle East*. Glencoe, IL: Free Press.

Lewis, W. Arthur. 1955. *The Theory of Economic Growth*. London: George Allen & Unwin.

Lijphart, Arend. 1971. "Comparative Politics and Comparative Method." *American Political Science Review* 65, no. 3.

Lijphart, Arend. 1977. *Democracy in Plural Societies: A Comparative Exploration*. New Haven, CT: Yale University Press.

Lijphart, Arend. 1984. *Democracies: Patterns of Majoritarian and Consensus Government in Twenty-one Countries*. New Haven, CT: Yale University Press.

Lindblom, Charles E. 1977. *Politics and Markets*. New Haven, CT: Yale University Press.

Linz, Juan J. and Alfred Stepan, eds. 1978. *The Breakdown of Democratic Regimes*. Baltimore: Johns Hopkins University Press.

Lipset, S. M. 1959. "Some Social Requisites of Democracy." *American Political Science Review* 53: 69–105.

Maine, Henry. 1883. *Ancient Law*. New York: Holt.

Mason, Edward. 1958. *Economic Planning in Underdeveloped Areas*. New York: Fordham University Press.

McClelland, David C. 1961. *The Achieving Society*. Princeton, NJ: Van Nostrand.

McClelland, David C. et al. 1953. *The Achievement Motive*. New York: Appleton-Century-Crofts.

McCrone, Donald and Charles Cnudde. 1967. "Toward a Communication Theory of Democratic Political Development: A Causal Model." *American Political Science Review* 61, no. 3.

Meier, Gerald M. 1964. *Leading Issues in Development Economics: Selected Materials and Commentary*. New York: Oxford University Press.

Meier, Gerald M. and Robert E. Baldwin. 1957. *Economic Development: Theory, History, Policy*. New York: Wiley.

Migdal, Joel S. 1983. "Studying the Politics of Development and Change: The State of the Art." In *Political Science: The State of the Discipline*, edited by Ada Finifter. Washington, DC: American Political Science Association.

Millikan, Max F. 1967. *National Economic Planning*. New York: Columbia University Press.

Millikan, Max F. and Donald L.M. Blackmer. 1961. *The Emerging Nations: Their Growth and United States Policy*. Boston: Little, Brown.

Moore, Barrington, Jr. 1966. *Social Origins of Dictatorship and Democracy: Land and Peasant in the Making of the Modern World*. Cambridge, MA: Harvard University Press.

Nelson, Joan M. 1979. *Access to Power: Politics and the Urban Poor in Developing Nations*. Princeton, NJ: Princeton University Press.

Neubauer, Deane. 1967. "Some Conditions of Democracy." *American Political Science Review* 61, no. 4.

Nordlinger, Eric A. 1981. *On the Autonomy of the Democratic State*. Cambridge. MA: Harvard University Press.

O'Donnell, Guillermo A. 1973. *Modernization and Bureaucratic Authoritarianism: Studies in South American Politics*. Berkeley: Institute of International Studies, University of California.

Organski. A.F.K. 1965. *The Stages of Political Development*. New York: Knopf.

Packenham, Robert. 1966. "Political Development Doctrines in the American Foreign Aid Program," *World Politics* 18, no. 2.

Packenham, Robert A. 1973. *Liberal America and the Third World: Political Development Ideas in Foreign Aid and Social Science*. Princeton, NJ: Princeton University Press.

Packenham, Robert A. 1976. "Trends in Brazilian National Dependency Since 1984." In *Brazil in the Seventies*, edited by Riordan Rhett. Washington, DC: American Enterprise Institute.

Packenham, Robert A. 1983. "The Dependency Perspective and Analytical Dependency." In *North-South Relations*, edited by Charles F. Doran and George Modelski. New York: Praeger.

Parsons, Talcott. 1937. *The Structure of Social Action*. New York: McGraw-Hill.

Parsons, Talcott, and Edward A. Shils, eds. 1951. *Toward a General Theory of Action*. Cambridge, MA: Harvard University Press.

Popkin, Samuel. [1947] 1979. *The Rational Peasant*. Berkeley: University of California Press.

Powell, G. Bingham, Jr. 1982. *Contemporary Democracies: Participation, Stability, and Violence*. Cambridge, MA: Harvard University Press.

Przeworski, Adam and Henry Teune. 1970. *The Logic of Comparative Social Inquiry*. New York: Wiley.

Putnam, Robert D. 1973. *The Beliefs of Politicians: Ideology, Conflict, and Democracy in Britain and Italy*. New Haven, CT: Yale University Press.

Putnam, Robert D., Joel D. Aberbach, and Bert A. Rockman. 1981. *Bureaucrats and Politicians in Western Democracies*. Cambridge, MA: Harvard University Press.

Pye, Lucian W. 1956. *Guerrilla Communism in Malaya: Its Social and Political Meaning*. Princeton, NJ: Princeton University Press.

Pye, Lucian W. 1962. *Politics, Personality, and Nation Building: Burma's Search for Identity*. New Haven, CT: Yale University Press.

Pye, Lucian W., ed. 1963. *Communications and Political Development*. Princeton, NJ: Princeton University Press.

Pye, Lucian W. And Sidney Verba, eds. 1965. *Political Culture and Political Development*. Princeton, NJ: Princeton University Press.

Rigby, T. H., ed. 1980. *Authority, Power and Policy in the USSR*. New York: St. Martin's.

Rigby, T. H. and Ferenc Feher, eds. 1982. *Political Legitimation in Communist States*. New York: St. Martin's.

Rigby, T. H. and Bohdan Harasymiw, eds. 1983. *Leadership Selection and Patron-Client Relations in the USSR and Yugoslavia*. London: Allen & Unwin.

Riggs, Fred W. 1957. "Agraria and Industria." In *Toward a Comparative Study of Public Administration*, edited by W. J. Siffen. Bloomington: University of Indiana Press.

Rose, Richard. 1974. *Electoral Behavior: A Comparative Handbook*. New York: Free Press.

Rose, Richard. 1984. *Comparative Policy Analysis*. Glasgow: Centre for the Study of Public Policy, University of Strathclyde.

Rosenau, James N., ed. 1964. *International Aspects of Civil Strife*. Princeton, NJ: Princeton University Press.

Rosenau, James N. 1980. *The Study of Global Interpendence: Essays on the Transnationalization of World Affairs*. London: Frances Pinter.

Rostow, Walt W. 1956. "The Take-Off into Self Sustained Growth." *Economic Journal* 66: 25–48.

Rostow, Walt W. 1960. *The Stages of Economic Growth: A Non-Communist Manifesto*. Cambridge: Cambridge University Press.

Rostow, Walt W. 1971. *Politics and the Stages of Growth*. Cambridge: Cambridge University Press.

Roth, Gunther. 1968. "Personal Rulership, Patrimonialism, and Empire Building in the New States." *World Politics* (January).

Russett, Bruce. 1983. "International Interactions and Processes: The Internal vs. External Debate Revisited." In *Political Science: The State of the Discipline*, edited by Ada Finifter. Washington, DC: American Political Science Association.

Rustow, Dankwart A. 1957. "Politics and Islam in Turkey 1920–1955." *Islam and the West*, edited by Richard Frye. 'S-Gravenhage, Netherlands.

Rustow, Dankwart A. 1967. *A World of Nations: Problems of Political Modernization*. Washington, DC: Brookings Institution.

Rustow, Dankwart. 1970. "Transition to Democracy: Toward a Dynamic Model." *Comparative Politics* 2, no. 3.

Sartori, Giovanni. 1970. "Concept Misformation in Comparative Politics." *American Political Science Review* 64, no.4.

Sartori, Giovanni. 1976. *Parties and Party Systems: A Framework for Analysis*. Cambridge: Cambridge University Press.

Sartori, Giovanni, Fred W. Riggs, and Henry Teune. 1975. *Tower of Babel: On the Definition and Analysis of Concepts in the Social Sciences*. Pittsburgh, PA: International Studies Association.

Schmidt, Steffan W., James C. Scott, Carl Lande, and Laura Guasti, eds. 1977. *Friends, Followers and Factions: A Reader in Political Clientelism*. Berkeley: University of California Press.

Schmitter, Philippe and Gerhard Lehmbruch, eds. 1979. *Trends towards Corporatist Intermediation*. Beverly Hills, CA: Sage.

Schmitter, Philippe, Guillermo O'Donnell, and Laurence Whitehead, eds. Forthcoming. *Transitions from Authoritarian Rule: Southern Europe and Latin American*. Baltimore: Johns Hopkins University Press.

Scott, James C. 1972. "Patron-Client Politics and Political Change in Southeast Asia." *American Political Science Review* 66, no. 1.

Shils, E. A. 1960. *Political Development in the New States*. The Hague: Mouton.

Skilling, H. Gordon. 1983. "Interest Groups and Communist Politics Revisited." *World Politics* 36, no. 1 (October).

Skilling, H. Gordon and Franklyn Griffiths, eds. 1971. *Interest Groups in Soviet Politics*. Princeton, NJ: Princeton University Press.

Sklar, Richard. 1963. *Nigerian Political Parties: Power in an Emergent African Nation*. Princeton, NJ: Princeton University Press.

Skocpol, Theda. 1979. *States and Revolutions: A Comparative Analysis of France, Russia, and China*. Cambridge: Cambridge University Press.

Smith, Peter H. 1979. *Labyrinths of Power: Political Recruitment in Twentieth-Century Mexico*. Princeton, NJ: Princeton University Press.

Smith, Peter H. 1983. Unpublished discussion, Joint Seminar on Political Development, Harvard-MIT, Cambridge, MA.

Smith, Tony. 1979. "The Underdevelopment of Development Literature." *World Politics* 31, no. 2.

Smith, Tony. 1981a. "The Logic of Dependency Theory Revisited." *International Organization* (Autumn).

Smith, Tony. 1981b. *The Pattern of Imperialism: The United States, Great Britain, and the Late-Industrializing World since 1915*. New York: Cambridge University Press.

Smith, Tony. 1985. "Requiem or New Agenda for Third World Studies." *World Politics* (July): 537.

Springborg, Robert. 1982. *Family, Power and Politics in Egypt*. Philadelphia: University of Pennsylvania Press.

Stepan, Alfred. 1971. *The Military in Politics: Changing Patterns in Brazil*. Princeton, NJ: Princeton University Press.

Stepan, Alfred, ed. 1973. *Authoritarian Brazil: Origins, Policies, and Future*. New Haven, CT: Yale University Press.

Stepan, Alfred. 1978. *The State and Society: Peru in Comparative Perspective*. Princeton, NJ: Princeton University Press.

Sunkel, Osvaldo. 1973. "Transnational Capitalism and National Disintegration in Latin America." *Social and Economic Studies* 22: 132–36.

Sutton, Francis X. 1954. "Social Theory and Comparative Politics." Unpublished paper, Social Science Research Council Conference, Princeton University, June.

Sutton, Francis X. 1982. "Rationality, Development, and Scholarship." Social Science Research Council *Items* 36, no. 4.

Sylvan, David, Duncan Snidal, Bruce M. Russett, Steven Jackson, and Raymond Duvall. 1983. "The Peripheral Economies: Penetration and Economic Distortion, 1970–1975." In *Contending Approaches to World System Analysis*, edited by William Thompson. Beverly Hills, CA: Sage.

Thompson, William R., ed. 1983. *Contending Approaches to World System Analysis*. Beverly Hills, CA: Sage.

Tilly, Charles, ed. 1975. *The Formation of National States in Western Europe*. Princeton, NJ: Princeton University Press.

Toennies, Ferdinand. [1887] 1957. *Community and Society*. East Lansing: Michigan State University Press.

Triska, Jan F. and Paul Cocks, eds. 1977. *Political Development in Eastern Europe*. New York: Praeger.

Triska, Jan F. and Charles Gati, eds. 1981. *Blue-Collar Workers in Eastern Europe*. London: George Allen & Unwin.

Truman, David. 1951. *The Governmental Process*. New York: Knopf.

Valenzuela, Samuel and Arturo Valenzuela. 1978. "Modernization and Dependency." *Comparative Politics* (July).

Verba, Sidney. 1967. "Some Dilemmas in Comparative Research." *World Politics* 20, no. 1.

Verba, Sidney, Norman H. Nie, and Jae-on Kim. 1978. *Participation and Political Equality: A Seven-Nation Comparison*. London: Cambridge University Press.

Wallerstein, Immanuel. 1974, 1980. *The Modern World-System*. 2 vols. New York: Academic Press.

Ward, Robert and Dankwart Rustow, eds. 1964. *Political Development in Japan and Turkey*. Princeton, NJ: Princeton University Press.

Ward, Robert E., Richard Beardsley, and John W. Hall. 1959. *Village Japan*. Chicago: University of Chicago Press.

Weber, Max. [1918] 1979. *Economy and Society: An Outline of Interpretive Sociology*, edited by Gunther Roth and Claus Wittich. Berkeley: University of California Press.

Weiner, Myron. 1962. *The Politics of Scarcity: Public Pressure and Political Response in India*. Chicago: University of Chicago Press.

White, Stephen. 1979. *Political Culture in Soviet Politics*. London: Macmillan.

10

The International-National Connection

One of the positive contributions attributed to the "dependency" movement, by its defenders as well as many of its critics, is its stress on the importance of the international context in the explanation of internal politics and political development. The dependency writers rejected the development research of the 1950s and the 1960s on the grounds that it failed to consider the constraints imposed on Third World development by the context of international capitalism, which penetrated, controlled, and distorted the political economies of these countries. These constraints were viewed as so complete as to reduce internal variables to insignificance. The Third World was condemned to backwardness or distorted development by virtue of this international class system. This position is no longer seriously advanced, but in the net the dependency experience is credited with the large heuristic contribution of having turned development studies around by bringing the international dimension into the development picture.

Thus Theda Skocpol expresses a common contemporary point of view about the "national-society-centeredness" of contemporary development theory:

> The theoretical approaches that have been dominant until recently—structural-functional evolutionism, and unilineal Marxism—have generalized too specifically from the apparent logic of English development in the eighteenth and early nineteenth centuries. Essentially modernization has been conceived as a dynamic internal to a nation.[1]

And Atul Kohli commends the dependency approach for having drawn

---

From Gabriel A. Almond, "The International-National Connection," *British Journal of Political Science*, Vol. 19, Part I. Copyright © 1989 by Cambridge University Press. Reprinted by permission.

attention "to world economic conditions as constraints on contemporary developing countries."[2] Andrew Janos develops a similar argument in a review and critique of political-sociological theory of the nineteenth and present centuries:

> Another and perhaps still more crucial point of criticism arises out of what may be called the structural parochialism of conventional political sociology. This parochialism is expressed in a tendency to seek explanations for political phenomena solely within the structure and culture of the "underlying" society. In this mode of analysis French politics is explained by French culture, German politics by configurations among social classes in Germany, Russian politics by the mode of production in Russia, and so on.[3]

Tony Smith makes the same case, arguing that mainstream modernization and developmentalist theory must do penance for their parochialism: "Still another frank admission must be that these concerns are not limited to the field of comparative study, but involve international relations as well."[4]

I shall be arguing in this chapter that this characterization of the comparative politics literature as having neglected national-international interaction is an exaggeration. Peter Gourevitch, in a series of original papers that searched and evaluated this literature, comments in a more discriminating way:

> We all know about [international-national] interaction; we all understand that international politics and domestic structures affect each other. Having recently read, for a variety of purposes, much of the current literature which explores this interaction, I think the comparativist's perspective has been neglected, that is, the reasoning from the international system to domestic structure.[5]

Gourevitch is correct in pointing out that research on the international impact on national development has lagged, although there is more there than Gourevitch reports, and the pace has been picking up in recent decades. While the dominant paradigm of political sociology from Marx to Barrington Moore has stressed the importance of internal social structure and culture in the shaping of politics and the state, there is a minor tradition from Otto Hintze to Charles Tilly, Peter Gourevitch, and Peter Katzenstein that stresses the impact of international factors on internal political structure and process, a tradition quite independent of the dependency movement. It is this minor tradition that I present here.

It is relevant to point out that research on the impact of national factors on international politics was the first of these interdisciplinary genres to thrive. Since the interwar period there has been a preoccupation with the impact of national politics and policy on international relations among American diplomatic historians, political scientists, and international relationists, growing out of historical American isolationism—particularly by the between-the-world-wars experience, which was widely interpreted as leading to the diplomatic breakdown of the 1920s and 1930s, and to World War II. The struggle between President Wilson and Senator Lodge, culminating in the refusal of the U.S. Senate to ratify the Versailles Treaty, was the historical trauma that obsessed the scholars of the period between the wars. And for post-World War II scholarship the fear continued to nag and rankle that as the enthusiasm of World War II mobilization subsided, America would withdraw into its isolationist shell.

This scholarly mood coincided with the expansion and professionalization of political science; within a decade or two after World War II, a sizable literature had accumulated, dealing with domestic constraints on foreign policy and the Congress (Dahl),[6] the bureaucracy (Cohen),[7] interest groups and political parties (Bauer, Pool, and Dexter),[8] public opinion and political culture (Markel and Almond),[9],[10] and foreign policy decision making (Snyder, Bruck, and Sapin).[11] It is primarily an American literature, dealing with American foreign policy, though there are a few comparative items (Waltz, Hanrieder).[12] The studies included in this category vary in their explanatory strategy. Some are relatively specific in their definition of the consequences of domestic factors for international politics; others define the dependent variable more diffusely as international stability, cosmopolitanism-isolationism, cold war effectiveness, and the like. The more recent literature of this genre has been concerned with explaining foreign economic policy in terms of domestic constraints (Katzenstein).[13]

The movement in recent decades toward exploring the impact of the international environment on domestic politics primarily through historical study could have no better patron saints than John Robert Seeley, the Cambridge historian of the late nineteenth century, and Otto Hintze, the German constitutional historian of the Wilhelminian and Weimar period. Seeley cautioned his students:

> Never be content with looking at states purely from within; always remember that they have another aspect which is wholly different, their relation to foreign states. This is a rule which it is particularly necessary to impress upon English students, for there is no nation which has disregarded it so much as our own.

> We have an inveterate habit of regarding our own history as self-contained, and of assuming that whatever has happened in England can be explained by English causes. So much so, that I think the English history still remains to be written which shall do anything like justice to foreign or continental influences which have contributed to determine the course of English affairs.[14]

For Otto Hintze, remedying this neglect of international factors in the explanation of national development was almost an obsession. Out of more than fifty monographs, articles, and review articles reprinted in the three volumes of his *Collected Papers*, more than a dozen contain sharp–even passionate–criticisms of those political and sociological theorists who seek to explain the structure of states purely in terms of internal forces, social structure, religious tendencies, and the like.[15] Indeed, Hintze attacked the entire discipline and corpus of political theory from Aristotle through Machiavelli, Montesquieu to Marx, for this fixation on internal causes and constraints.

The turn of the nineteenth century was a fertile period for large-scale historical political demographies such as Woodrow Wilson's two-volume *The State*.[16] Seeley's *An Introduction to Political Science*, quoted above, was a pocket version of such a treatise. In a review article of the largest such compendium by Wilhelm Roscher, Hintze tells us that Roscher's theory of political development breaks down because

> it looks at the state essentially from an internal perspective, in relation to social development. He has not given enough consideration to the fundamental fact that the domestic life of individual states is in large part dependent on the relation of states with each other, on the push and pull amongst them, on the rise and collapse of neighbor states, on variations in international pressure, in brief what Ranke called the larger world context.[17]

In his first major essay on this theme published in 1902, translated as "The Formation of States and Constitutional Development," Hintze attacks Marx on the grounds that he fails to appreciate the importance of the development of the state in relation to its neighbors. He does not reject Marx out of hand. He attributes a "germ of truth" to the Marxist argument that a "people's political constitution is in effect shaped by its social structure." He faults it for wrenching the "single state from the context in which it was formed; the state is seen in isolation, exclusive in itself, without raising the question whether its peculiar character is co-determined by its relation to its surroundings."[18]

Hintze also takes a discriminating position on the issue of the importance of idealist and materialist forces in political explanation. It would be worthwhile for our structuralists to pay close attention to his "plague on the houses" of Hegel and Ranke on the one hand and Marx on the other, as he comments:

> It used to be thought that everything could be explained in terms of individual will power, planning and calculation; and nowadays it is equally widely held that the driving forces of history are to be found in the natural conditions of each country or in the relations of economic production. . . . The impact of the outside world must pass through an intellectual medium; and the only question is how strong is its refraction, to what extent it possesses independent vigor and can exert a counterweight. With this reservation we can—indeed, must—stress that in the life of peoples external events and conditions exercise a decisive influence upon the internal constitution. History does not permit progressive spiritual development, following its own laws, as was supposed by Hegel; there is rather a constant collaboration of the inner and outer world.[19]

Seeley's and Hintze's strictures had little resonance in political research until the nation-state explosion in the post-World War II decades posed with special urgency the question of how states "grow." And even then the dominant tradition of explaining state structure and process continued to stress domestic factors. In an article written some twenty years ago (1971), I forecast a movement away from what might be described as the biological model of the political system in which comparativists

> classify species of political structure, and attribute to them a degree of stability and a relationship to environment comparable to that of biological organisms. But political systems and societies are not organisms in relatively stable relationship to their environments. The exchanges between political systems and their environments may be massive, for the boundaries between them are highly porous, and both the structure of the system and its environments may undergo gross transformations quickly. . . . We are at the beginnings of significant curricular adaptations which will get us away from this biological model and enable us to deal more effectively with the interaction of the domestic society, the international environment, and the political system.[20]

A trailbreaking article by Peter Gourevitch published some ten years ago points out the "circular" character of causality in national-international interaction.[21] He argues that "in using domestic structure as a variable in explaining foreign policy," as we have done above, "we must explore the extent to which that structure itself derives from the exigencies of the international system." He then analyzes the ways in which domestic politics and policy are influenced principally by the international economic and international security environments. He refers to other aspects of the international environment, such as ideology and religion, but the burden of this section of his article treats the impact of war and trade on domestic politics in the sense of specific events or decisions, political regime characteristics, and coalition patterns. In a recent book as well as in earlier articles, he deals systematically and in detail with the impact of the international economy on domestic policy-cum-politics.[22] Gourevitch's work is the most rigorously formulated and well-researched treatment of the international-national relationship that has thus far been produced. Some of his findings on the international economy shall be reported below.

The Seeley-Hintze Law

It is a matter of some interest that the early formulations of Seeley and, particularly, Hintze anticipated the findings of the more recent literature dealing with the international impact on political development. Indeed, it is in Hintze's work that one first finds the relationship formulated as a theory, which he attributes to his Cambridge mentor, John Robert Seeley. As the Cambridge historian had put it:

> It is reasonable therefore to conjecture that the degree of government will be directly proportional, and that means that the degree of liberty will be inversely proportional, to the degree of pressure. In other words, given a community which lives at large, in easy conditions and furnished with abundant room, you may expect to find that community enjoying a large share of liberty; given a community which has to maintain itself against great difficulties and in the midst of great dangers, you may expect to find in it little liberty and a great deal of government.[23]

And at a later point and more succinctly, "We see that intense government is the reaction against intense pressure, and on the other hand liberty, or relaxed government, is the effect of relaxed pressure. This is the general rule; as a matter of course it will suffer many exceptions."[24]

Seeley briefly documents this proposition by reference to the "intensity of government" in France and Prussia-Germany by contrast to Britain and particularly the United States. But it is Hintze who takes Seeley's law and tests it against world political history. His first major essay on the subject (1902) argued that "all the great empires of ancient times and of the non-European world were despotic in their form of government. . . . free constitutions emerged only where a number of states existed next to each other on equal terms, the independence of each one being recognized by the others. . . . Such a society of states has always been the exception, if we look at the past of the human race . . . it is a phenomenon that emerges only once on a large scale – namely in the European system of states, which owes its rise to a wholly individual historical process."[25] Hintze attributes this unique historical development to the rivalry of Papacy and Empire in the middle ages, a rivalry that made it possible for individual nations to attain autonomy; and the common cultural and religious traditions in the European area, which fostered a comity of nations and a balance of power.

Hintze developed this theme of the effect of the external setting on the internal characteristics of states in connection with three major political organizations – the armed forces, ministerial government, and representative institutions. In each case he seeks to explain differences in these institutional patterns in terms of two sets of constraints "which conditioned the real organization of the state. These are first, the structure of social classes, and second, the external ordering of the states – their position relative to each other, and their over-all position in the world."[26]

He compares the military organization of Sparta, Rome, and on up to Prussia and England, demonstrating the complex interplay among social structure, military technology, political structure, foreign policy, and the international context. In a similarly rich analysis of the origins and variety of ministerial government, Hintze draws a sharp contrast between continental and particularly German patterns with the "cabinet responsible to parliament" of the British system. Writing in 1908, he expresses great pessimism about the prospects of a responsible parliament-cabinet system in Germany in view of her exposed strategic situation, which had historically required the development of a large and costly standing army, maintained and managed by a powerful and efficient bureaucracy within the framework of an authoritarian monarchy.[27]

In a series of four essays beginning on the eve of World War I and continuing during the lifetime of the Weimar Republic, Hintze sought to explain the differing development of political authority and representative institutions in the occident. It was self-conscious, comparative history informed by the methodological ideas of John Stuart Mill and Max Weber. In his 1913 essay "Power Politics and Governmental Constitutions" he poses the question, "How does it happen that England and America have a quite different kind of constitutional system than the continental European states; and France has a very different system than Germany and Prussia, or Austria-Hungary, and Russia?"[28] Attacking the exponents of race, national character, and socioeconomic structure as the principal explanation of constitutional differences, Hintze asks how it is possible for sociological and political theorists to advance such monocausal internal explanations of constitutional differences, not only in the light of the historical development of political institutions in the Christian West but in the light of the contemporary pulling and hauling of world politics. The reason, he argues, that sociological and political theorists overlook the influence of international power politics is that it is very difficult to grapple with these influences in terms of general laws. These connections tend to have a singular character, which historians are more likely to observe than political theorists, who tend to abstract particular states from their environment and context. He points to comparative history as the methodological approach likely to produce a more systematic treatment of international-national interaction in the development of the modern states.

In this essay and one that followed in 1914 titled "The Constitutional Life of Contemporary States," he presents a theory of European state formation that has not been excelled in its sharpness of formulation and the richness of the body of historical evidence presented in its elaboration and defense.[29] He points out that the systems of government of the major European powers consists of two types—the English and the continental European. Though there were important differences between England and the continental states already in the middle ages, by the mid-seventeenth century the state on the Continent took on the form of military absolutism with a strong bureaucratic administration, while in England monarchic authority was greatly diminished and a parliamentary regime had been instituted.

What caused this sharp differentiation in the historic European state-building process? He points out that there were autonomous local institutions and estate assemblies on the European continent quite similar to those in England. Why in the English case did they develop into a parliamentary and locally autonomous system, while on the Continent the estates and autonomous towns were set aside and destroyed through a process of bureaucratic centralization and local penetration? Similarly, there were aspiring monarchs in England (e.g., Henry VIII and Elizabeth) just as there were in France and Prussia. But the monarchic power was checked in England.

The explanation for this striking difference in governmental institutions lay in the geostrategic situations of England and the Continent. England could carry on an effective diplomatic-political role substantially by means of maritime power. Continental European countries, with their exposed frontiers, could survive and expand only through large standing armies, which called for large extractive and regulative powers and organizations. Hintze elaborates, "The whole history of the European state system is a chain of attempts of the one or the other powers to win supremacy, while the other powers sought to defend their independence or their very existence."[30] Out of this tense equilibrium extending through the seventeenth and eighteenth centuries emerged "the centralized great power, the military and official state. . . . The soul of this new state structure is the will to power, the backbone is the large standing army, in this form a previously unknown phenomenon. It is astonishing how this institution of the standing army transformed and determined the structure and life of the most remote organs and functions of the state."[31] England escaped this development and underwent a mostly gradual process of balancing monarchic, aristocratic, and bourgeois powers within a relatively decentralized administrative framework. And this was attributable to the fact that it could play a major international strategic role relying primarily on naval power.

This contrast between continental European and Anglo-American historical development and its significance is now a cliche of comparative politics. But its first sharp and explicit formulation is to be found in these pre-World War I essays of Hintze, elaborated in a comparative historical context that includes not only England, France, and Prussia-Germany, but Russia, Poland, Austria-Hungary, the Scandinavian countries, and the United States as well.

Hintze applies his thesis of the mutual interaction of international and domestic factors to the Polish case and to the situation of the Weimar Republic in the mid-1920s. He points to the Polish case as suggesting a corollary to Seeley's law, that if there is too much internal resistance to centralizing authoritarianism in a situation of external threat, then the state may be gobbled up by its neighbors. The Weimar Republic in the mid-1920s is another exception to Seeley's law. When the autonomy of a state is limited by foreign powers, the law loses its applicability. The state is unable to respond to external threat; through losing this capacity it loses much of its "stateness," and becomes an object of international politics. But these exceptions to Seeley's law lead Hintze to the more general law of politics of which Seeley's law is simply a special case. "This general law holds that the spirit and essence of internal politics is dependent on the external conditions of a state."[32] He points out that any government that carries out the terms of the Versailles Treaty and of the reparations agreements is bound to lose its legitimacy among its own people. In this case, external pressure and penetration result in the delegitimation and breakdown of authority. Hintze did not foresee the triumph of National Socialism in Germany and the ultimate confirmation of Seeley's insight, although he lived to experience it, and to withdraw from active academic life because of it.

Seeley's law and Hintze's corollaries are history-bound generalizations. They pertain to the European state-building processes of the sixteenth to nineteenth centuries. We can hardly explain the centralization and concentration of power in communist regimes, or the alternation of authoritarian and populist regimes in the Third World as simply attributable to the operations of the power-political dynamics of Seeley's law. External pressure conspired with internal pressure in Chile to produce an authoritarian regime. But external pressure contributed first to an authoritarian trend and later to a loosening and democratizing trend in Argentina, Brazil, the Philippines, Korea, Taiwan, and other countries. For today's world the simple dialectics of power politics of Seeley's law cannot explain political development. The contending powers have ideologies that direct the kind of influence they exert on the internal affairs of other powers. Thus the pressure of the Soviet Union on Eastern Europe has tended to perpetuate internal power concentration, but the counterpressure generated within these countries is pluralistic. American external pressure on other countries is often pluralistic in its internal consequences.

And yet there is something to be said for the Seeley-Hintze formulation as long as it is not taken to be the only explanation of internal power concentration or diffusion. The worldwide Great Depression of the 1930s produced power concentrations, but of substantially different kinds among the major powers. The two great wars of this century have been associated with power concentrations among the democracies, and it is a principal thesis regarding the prospects of reducing power concentration in the Soviet Union that international détente would have this effect.

The International Security Environment in Political Development Research

Our search of the literature uncovered a substantial number of research genres in the Seeley-Hintze tradition. These include a number of different approaches to the theme of war and state building, the international economic environment and national political development, the impact of the international environment on revolutions and political crises, and the influence of international politics and economics on the structure and process of democratic regimes, in particular consociationalism and neocorporatism.

War and State Building

Some three decades were to elapse after the work of Hintze before the theme of the impact of war and international pressure on state building was resumed in serious research terms. In the mid-1960s, the Committee on Comparative Politics of the Social Science Research Council initiated a research program on this topic, and some early hypotheses were formulated.[33] Charles Tilly's study of the formation of states in Western Europe, discussed below, was a major product of this program.

A year before the publication of the Tilly volume, Perry Anderson's two-volume study of the origins of the absolutist state system in Europe of the sixteenth and seventeenth centuries appeared.[34] Anderson also places great weight on international conflict and war in the state-building process, but as a Marxist he gives prior honors to class phenomena. He offers a two-stage theory of the causality of the European state system. The emergence of strong states in Western Europe was to be explained by the crisis of feudalism in the fourteenth and fifteenth centuries, particularly in such countries as Spain, France, and England.[35] In these early stages of state building, the centralization of authority in monarchies and the development of powerful bureaucracies and armies are explained by an aristocracy no longer capable of coping with a mutinous peasantry without centralization and concentration of power. Once these instrumentalities—armies and bureaucracies—had been constructed, the more developed states proceeded to threaten and invade the less developed societies of Eastern Europe. The development of modern state organizations and standing armies in such countries as Prussia and Austria was in reaction to this aggressive pressure primarily from Spain, France, and Sweden.[36] Though Anderson concedes the importance of international conflict and warfare in the development of the Western European states, his principal argument is the priority of internal conflict between aristocrats and peasants as the triggering mechanism of the whole sequence of state-building developments of the seventeenth and eighteenth centuries.

In this respect, Anderson's analysis differs from the approach of Charles Tilly and his collaborators, who produced the major contemporary study of European state building.[37] While Hintze stressed the institutional aspects of the development of the Western European state system, Tilly and his associates focused on the substantive problem areas and challenges confronting the state builders of the sixteenth and seventeenth centuries, the successful surmounting of which resulted in the great nation-state system of the eighteenth and nineteenth centuries. These challenges were to develop military instrumentalities capable of countering external threat, to extract the resources required for these security needs, to cope with problems of internal order and supply, and to recruit, train, and organize the personnel required for these tasks. The historical contributions to this volume included Samuel Finer's comparative study of the growth of armed forces in France, Britain, and Prussia-Germany; Gabriel Ardant's and Rudolf Braun's studies of the development of tax policy in France, England, and Brandenburg-Prussia; David Bayley on internal order and policing in Western Europe; Tilly's own study of the regulation of the food supply; and Wolfram Fischer and Peter Lundgreen on the recruitment and training of administrative personnel.

In his effort to draw together a coherent logic of state building from these and other researchers, Tilly proposes a sequence more elaborate than, though consistent with, Seeley's law. Tilly writes that, under the pressure of international conflict, "recurrently we find a chain of causation running from (1) change or expansion in land armies to (2) new efforts to extract resources from the subject populations to (3) the development of new bureaucracies and administrative innovations to (4) resistance from the subject population to (5) renewed coercion to (6) durable increases in the bulk and extractiveness of the state."[38]

War and Public Expenditures

A number of political econometricians have dealt with the relation between the incidence of war and state building, operationalizing state building according to the level of public revenue and expenditure. The English economists Peacock and Wiseman were the first to challenge the conventional wisdom that governmental activities would expand in roughly linear response to the emergence of social problems stemming out of economic growth and industrialization. The most influential theory of this sort, advanced at the turn of the century by the German economist Adolph Wagner – referred to as "Wagner's Law" – asserted that governmental expenditures in industrial societies will grow at a more rapid rate than national economic product.[39] Wagner explained this tendency toward increasing state activity by the pressure of social progress and the values of modern industrial societies. Peacock and Wiseman, in a study of public expenditure in the United Kingdom in the nineteenth and present centuries, challenge this proposition, showing that the growth of public expenditure in England was not a linear, incremental process, but rather was sharply influenced by the impact of war.[40] They argue that national crises, particularly war, changed public expectations about the legitimacy of levels of taxation. Government found popular uses for these increased revenues, and thus public expenditures, having been ratcheted up by costly wars, never returned to their prewar levels.

A more recent quantitative analysis of this relationship between war and state building by Karen Rasler and William R. Thompson reviews the historical-statistical record of British, American, French, and Japanese revenues and expenditures, and concludes that war, and particularly global war, "must be considered one of the more important sources of the growth and expansion of the modern state."[41] If we view this war and public expenditures literature along with the historical state-building literature, we may attribute a central role to warfare in both the original state-building process in the sixteenth-eighteenth centuries and the continued rapid growth of the state in the nineteenth and twentieth centuries.

Wars and Occupations

Warfare has usually been associated with boundary changes, annexations, limitations on the autonomy of the defeated states, the levying of tribute, reparations, and the like. In some cases it has involved religious penetration and conversion; in the last centuries it has resulted in changes in internal political organization. Thus the advancing Napoleonic armies carried revolutionary constitutions and legal codes along with them. And the armies of the "Holy Alliance" reestablished legitimate constitutions as they advanced. The wars of the nineteenth century and World War I were largely limited to boundary changes, national unification, and the like; although the Allied occupation of Germany after World War I was intended not only to guarantee reparations but to assure an acceptable German regimė. During and after World War II the advances of Nazi armies, Soviet armies, and Western armies were all associated with political changes of the most significant sort. The Eastern European countries were Sovietized; the Nazi-occupied territories were "Nazified"; in the postwar period the German and Japanese constitutions were in considerable part drafted by American authorities.

There is little comparative literature on occupations; most of the work is in the form of monographic, single-country studies. Two symposia deal with some of these themes. One, edited by Robert Wolfe, compares German and

Japanese experience.[42] A second, edited by John Herz, examines the transformation of the political systems of Germany, Italy, Japan, France, and Austria, and the role of occupations in these transformations.[43]

The phenomena of military conquest, occupation, and the direct introduction of political institutions, constitutions and legal codes, social policies, and so on by the victors is, of course, a different form of international penetration than that contemplated in Seeley's physics-like rule of pressure intensity. It suggests the limitation of Seeley's metaphor. The variety and forms of intervention by foreign actors in the internal affairs of states cannot be captured by this simple model. Hintze's historical treatment of these themes extracts the heuristic value of the metaphor without being limited by it.

The International Economy and National Political Development

The Timing of Industrialization

The impact of the international economic environment on national political development is treated in a number of research genres. Historical timing in industrialization as a factor affecting internal political-economic tendencies is treated in the work of the European economic historian Alexander Gerschenkron, in the work of Albert Hirschman, which stresses Latin American experience, and more generally in the work of the economic development theorists.

Gerschenkron, in his historical accounts of industrial development in Europe, points out that the later developers in Europe confronted international competitive conditions that were different from those found by the earlier developers.[44] Only through protectionist measures, greater economic concentration, and a more important role for the state were they able to develop industries and compete in international markets. Thus the uneven development of the world economy offers part of the explanation of differences in the scope and depth of governmental penetration of the society and economy in the later developers.

Albert Hirschman compares Latin American experience with Gerschenkron's picture of "late" development in Europe, particularly that of Germany, Italy, and Russia. The "late, late" industrializing Latin American countries also resorted to government power in protecting indigenous industries supplying capital, controlling consumption, and providing entrepreneurial guidance. Three collections of Hirschman's essays contain analyses and evaluations of various governmental development projects and approaches undertaken in a number of Latin American countries.[45]

The foreign aid and development experience of the last decades has generated a large literature of country studies, and studies of specific economic sectors and projects, as well as a theoretical literature of both an analytical and prescriptive variety. The history of economic development ideas in the last half century is told in a collection of retrospective lectures by the development theory pioneers, edited by Gerald Meier and Dudley Seers,[46] and in a small book on the history of development ideas and approaches by Meier.[47] Meier, in agreement with Gerschenkron and Hirschman on the importance of the state and government policy among late developers, criticizes mainstream economic development theory of the last decades for its resistance to this basic reality.

International Economic Crises and National Politics

Over the past ten years, Peter Gourevitch has published a series of articles, and more recently a book, dealing with the impact of world economic crises of the last century on the politics of a number of European nations and the United States.[48] These studies represent a high point in rigor and theoretical sophistication in this international-national research tradition, and deserve to be treated in detail. Gourevitch traces the political and policy responses of five Western industrial nations (Germany, France, Great Britain, Sweden, and the United States) to the three world economic crises of 1870–90, 1930–40, and 1975–85. His major purpose is to explain why these five countries made different choices. In the course of doing this, he seeks to test the explanatory power of competing theories in the social sciences such as those emphasizing "state structure, social forces, ideology, international state rivalries, leadership, and the like."[49] He examines the impact of the three crises on different components of business, labor, and agriculture for each country, tracing the preferences and coalition responses of interest groups, their interaction with political parties, through to the choice of policies. Gourevitch's analytical scheme posits that their are five possible ways of coping with these crises: (1) a classical free trade market option, (2) a socialist-collectivist option, (3) a protectionist option, (4) a demand-stimulus "Keynesian" option, and (5) a "mercantilist" "industrial policy" option.

He tests a number of different theories seeking to explain the choice of policy option within individual countries. What he calls the "production profile explanation" attributes major explanatory power to the actual "situation" of the economic interests in the domestic and international economy. This theoretical approach starts with the impingement of the crisis on individual industrial sectors and groupings, then moves to pressure groups forming coalitions and interacting with political parties, through to policy choice and implementation. The particular structure of a national economy in relation to the international economy explains the outcome.

A second explanatory theory places emphasis on the characteristics of associational interest groups, their size, extent of membership, organizational characteristics, relationships to parties, and the like. As Gourevitch puts it, "Interest groups manage the evaluation of options, the articulation of opinions, the mobilization of collective action, and a variety of functional tasks, some in the economy, some conferred by the state. . . . The difficulty with this argument is the problem for any mediating variable—its effects require linkage to the terms of either side, to society and to the state."[50]

The third theory is the state structural explanation, the argument that policy outcomes are explained principally by the structure of the state, its centralization and concentration of authority, the characteristics of the bureaucracy, the powers of the judiciary, and the like. Here the main advocates of state-centered explanation are Krasner[51] and Skocpol.[52] For Gourevitch, attributing full explanatory power to state structure has the same problem as the argument from economic structure and intermediate associations. It is a only a part of the explanation.

The fourth explanation is that of economic ideology. Countries differ, and individual sociopolitical groupings differ, in the ways in which they analytically model the costs and benefits of economic policies. "Some have traditions of active government involvement to promote economic development; others emphasize laissez-faire. In some countries traditions of free trade are strong, unemployment is feared, and social services are accepted. Other countries are protectionist, fear inflation more than unemployment, and dislike social service systems. . . . The economic ideology interpretation of economic policy choices explains outcomes in terms of national traditions, and values concerning the economy."[53]

Finally, the international system explanation in its sweeping form would explain economic policy choices as completely constrained by international forces. And there are indeed situations—defeat in war, for example—where policy is fully constrained or limited. But Gourevitch argues that one needs all five variables to explain outcomes, and leadership, entrepreneurship, and chance as well.

Gourevitch does not claim that his studies have provided definitive answers as to the relative power of these explanatory variables. He describes his work as essentially a historical sociological analysis of national responses to fluctuations in the international economy. Not only does the power of the variables change over time, but their relationships are not constant. His work is a strong argument for an eclectic, dynamic, and indeterminist approach to the interaction of economy, society, polity, and international system in which human choice may be an important part of the explanation of the outcome.

International Impacts on Internal Political Stability

Social Revolutions

The international environment impinges on domestic politics not only through war and international economic crises, but in a number of other respects. Theda Skocpol, in *States and Social Revolutions*, stresses the importance of international strategic factors in explaining the classic revolutions of France, Russia, and China.[54] For Marx and his followers, political change was to be explained by internal changes in class and social structure. It was in Lenin's work that the international arena explicitly entered into revolutionary causality, but then only in a special way through conflicting capitalist imperialisms and the wars generated by them. Skocpol frees herself from this Marxist perspective by explaining the great social revolutions according to a three-way logic. She points out, "In France, Russia, and China, class conflicts—especially between peasants and landlords; were pivotal during the revolutionary interregnums. But both the occurrence of the revolutionary situations in the first place and the nature of the new regimes that emerged from the revolutionary conflicts depended fundamentally upon the structures of state organizations and their partially autonomous and dynamic relationships to domestic class and political forces, as well as their positions in relation to other states abroad."[55] Thus Skocpol departs from Marxism by stressing the causal significance of the "relative" or "potential" autonomy of the state vis-a-vis class forces. Class struggles are necessary conditions of social revolutions, but the efficient causes are the breakdown of the state attributable to the pressure of international crises and war. Skocpol points to the enormous costs of the military adventures of France under the *Ancien Regime*, the disintegration of the Russian army and the Russian economy under the impact of World War I, and the breakdown of Chinese political and economic cohesion under the impact of Japanese aggression and World War II as the efficient causes of these revolutions.

Skocpol makes progress over earlier Marxist analyses and the work of her teacher, Barrington Moore. But what is absent from her work is the appreciation of politics and political leadership in the explanation of revolutions. Her "structural perspective on social reality," which she views as essential to the analysis of social revolutions, leads her to downplay the explanatory significance of a Lenin, a Mao, or a Napoleon in the Russian, Chinese, and French revolutions. Leadership qualities and choices, political coalition making, and chance are eliminated from a causal scheme that explains social revolutions by a combination of class struggle and group conflict, military pressure and threat, and deteriorating governmental effectiveness.

Political Crises

The international environment has an important impact on national political development in less dramatic ways than through impingements on revolutions. Regime and major policy changes through other than revolutionary and military means may also in part be explained by international factors. Gourevitch's careful tracing of the impact of the economic crises of the late nineteenth and twentieth centuries on the politics of the major European nations and the United States has already made this point.[56] In a collaborative undertaking edited by Almond, Flanagan, and Mundt, eight historical episodes of the nineteenth and twentieth centuries were analyzed according to a common research design.[57] These were the British Reform Act of 1832, the British Cabinet crisis of 1931, the formation of the Third French Republic, the formation of the Weimar Republic, the Cardenas phase of the Mexican Revolution in the early 1930s, the Meiji Restoration of 1868, the fall of the parliamentary regime in Japan in 1932, and the Indian language and famine crises of the 1960s.

The central concern of these studies was a methodological-theoretical one. The prevailing theories explaining political development in the 1960s and 1970s were structural-functionalism, social mobilization theory, coalition theory, and leadership theory. The case studies demonstrated that these four approaches were essential parts of a more comprehensive logic of historical explanation. But for the purposes of this chapter the most important finding was the discovery that "the interchanges between the international security environment and political systems would seem to have been the most powerful exogenous variable in explaining system stability and change."[58] The theoretical framework used in analyzing the impact of international events on domestic politics distinguished between stabilizing and destabilizing effects, and differentiated among military, economic, and psychological impacts. The historical case studies in *Crisis, Choice, and Change* illustrate the variety of ways military factors can affect stability and change. "In Britain in 1832, a decline of military threat after the Napoleonic wars unsettled the British polity. In France in 1870–71, and Germany 1918–1919, it was catastrophic military defeat; in the Meiji Restoration in 1868 it was the threat of invasion and colonization by the Western powers that triggered revolutionary change. In Japan in 1930–36 it was the opportunity for expansion in China that united the Japanese behind militaristic goals, contributing to the fall of party government and stabilizing the polity under military control."[59]

The international economic environment entered into the historical case studies in the British crisis of the 1930s, when a generally deteriorating international trade situation peaked into a severe balance of payments crisis, and in the Indian case when the reduction of foreign aid intensified risk of famine, and indirectly in the Japanese crisis of the 1930s, when the collapse in foreign trade set off a depression.

In four of the cases there were significant international demonstration effects. During the crisis of the 1830s in Britain the French Revolution of 1830 had a mobilizing effect on British opinion. In Germany in 1918 the revolution in Russia contributed to political polarization. In mid-nineteenth-century Japan the European invasion and colonization of China dramatized the foreign threat. And again in the 1930s in Japan, opportunities for conquest in China, and the international trend toward military and totalitarian regimes, contributed to the collapse of the parliamentary party system.

This study makes the case that the penetration of domestic politics by the international environment is not only a matter of dramatic events, but a constant process at medium and lower levels of visibility, affecting political, economic, and social stability in both positive and negative ways.

Consociationalism and Democratic Corporatism

Two recent contributions to empirical democratic theory are consociationalism and neocorporatism. Both terms refer to types of democratic regimes common among the smaller European nations, the characteristics of which are in part explained by the international vulnerability of small nations to military invasion and fluctuations in the international economy. *Consociationalism*, first discussed in the late 1960s, refers to regimes in which internal accommodation is negotiated by party leaders. *Neocorporatism*, or democratic corporatism, first discussed in the early 1970s, refers to regimes in which internal economic accommodation is negotiated by interest groups, party leaders, and government officials.

Arend Lijphart is the principal consociational theorist,[60] while neocorporatism is the product of a number of scholars, including Philippe Schmitter and Gerhard Lehmbruch[61] and Peter Katzenstein.[62] Lijphart suggested a typology of democratic systems that went beyond the threefold classification then common in the discipline—two-party consensual, multiparty consensual, and multiparty fragmented and conflictual. Lijphart discovered a fourth variety, which he called "consociational democracy." This type of democracy had the properties of conflictual multipartism, but an elite accommodative pattern resulted in overcoming these divisions and maintaining stability. There were some five cases that fitted this pattern—the Netherlands, Belgium, Switzerland, Austria, and Lebanon, prior to its tragic breakdown of the last decade. In explaining the historical origins of these consociational systems, Lijphart points out:

> In the five principal consociational systems, the crucial steps toward this type of democracy were usually taken during times of international crisis or specific threats to the nation's existence. In Austria, Lebanon, and the Netherlands, the inception of consociational democracy can be traced plainly to a particular short span of time in their political histories, and it occurred without exception during, and also partly because of an international emergency. Austria's government by grand coalition was primarily a response to the civil strife of the First Republic, but it was inaugurated, significantly, while Austria was occupied by the Allied Powers after the Second World War. . . . And the comprehensive peaceful settlement of internal differences that paved the way for consociational democracy in the Netherlands was concluded in 1917 when the first World War was raging near its borders. In Belgium and Switzerland, consociational practices were adopted more gradually, but also under the influences of foreign threats. Belgian "unionism" (Catholic-Liberal grand coalitions) began during its struggle for independence, but became more infrequent when the nation's existence appeared to be secure. It was resumed again after the First World War, soon followed by the important step of admitting the Socialists to the consociational government. This final step of admitting the Socialists to the grand coalition was not taken until much later in Switzerland, but it also happened during a World War: in 1943.[63]

Consociational political arrangements follow the predicted Seeley-Hintze pattern. But here the response to external threat is the acceptance of policy accommodation, compromise and power sharing, and the adoption of institutions to that end, rather than bureaucratic and authoritarian centralization.

There are a number of definitions of corporatism. Peter Katzenstein's definition is the least restrictive and captures its different aspects. He describes it as "distinguished by three traits; an ideology of social partnership expressed at the national level; a relatively centralized and concentrated system of interest groups; and voluntary and informal coordination of conflicting objectives through continuous political bargaining between interest groups, state bureaucracies, and political parties."[64] He argues that "the interlocking crises of the 1930s and 1940s—depression, fascism, and World War II—fundamentally reorganized the politics of the small European states. The democratic corporatism that emerged has been reinforced since the 1950s by the pressures of a liberal international economy."[65] Since the economies of these small democracies are particularly dependent on international trade, the need for quick and efficient adaptation strengthens these patterns of bargaining and coordination. Here again, democratic corporatism can be interpreted in ways consistent with the Seeley-Hintze formulations. The response to external threat is an institutionalized accommodative pattern among interest groups and political parties and between these and the economic bureaucracy, and the emergence of supportive institutions.

Ilja Scholten, in a recent volume dealing with the relationship between corporatism and political stability, is the first writer to develop the consociationalism-corporatism connection systematically: "It may not be merely a coincidence or spurious correlation that the so-called 'consociational democracies' are together with the Scandinavian countries, most frequently cited for being examples of strong or well-entrenched neocorporatism, or that 'social pacts' are most frequently advocated as an efficacious means of overcoming crises during regime or political transitions. To juxtapose these cases will, it is hoped, facilitate further insight into the broader question of system stability in 'cleavaged' societies."[66] Scholten argues that the adoption of consociational accommodative patterns may have made the social pacting of democratic corporatism possible. He also makes the point that both consociational and corporatist practices may be responses to similar preconditions. But in the literature thus far produced by the consociational and neocorporatist writers, only Lijphart and Katzenstein explicitly place the emergence of these arrangements in the context of international military, economic, and political insecurity.

Conclusion

The literature reviewed in this chapter shows that the contemporary interest in international-national interaction has a substantial ancestry, and it was not influenced in any observable way by dependency and world systems theory. One looks in vain for references to Cardoso,[67] Wallerstein,[68] and their colleagues in the works of Lijphart, Schmitter, Lehmbruch, Tilly, Skocpol, Katzenstein, and others. The international environment has been treated in the dependency and world systems literature in as exaggerated a way as the domestic social structure was treated in the reductionist comparative politics of the late nineteenth century, against which Seeley and Hintze polemicized so vigorously. In Wallerstein there is perhaps a twofold reductionism. Both international and domestic factors are reduced to a global class struggle.

The arguments of the dependency theorists and of the researchers who sought to test their theories boil down to the very simple notion that the stagnation and "underdevelopedness" of Third World countries is explained simply and only by the exploitativeness of the dominant capitalist economies. By contrast, the research tradition reviewed here is based on an interactive analytical model – the international security, economic, political, and cultural environments shape and are shaped by the internal politics, economics, and culture of individual nation-states. The picture that emerges from the work of Hintze, Gerschenkron, Peacock and Wiseman, Hirschman, Lijphart, Almond and his collaborators, Tilly and his collaborators, Skocpol, Gourevitch, and Katzenstein is one of a complex dynamic process that offers no simple answers or solutions.

It is a mistake to underestimate the quality of the earlier part of this work. Hintze's rich and analytically sharp comparative analysis of the origins of the modern Western states has still to be fully translated from the German and appreciated. His work focuses more sharply on institutions than does that of Tilly, and is sounder in its explanatory logic than that of Perry Anderson. The "ratchet" theory of war, public expenditures, and the growth of the state was originated by Peacock and Wiseman in the early 1960s. Gerschenkron and Hirschman were writing about the consequences of lateness in economic development in the early 1960s. Rupert Emerson wrote about imperialism and decolonization in these same early years. Lijphart's insight into the role of international threat in the consociational democratic solution in the small democracies of Europe dates back almost two decades; and the case study research for *Crisis, Choice, and Change* was being done at around the same time. The search for the logical structure of political development explanation dates back to the nineteenth century and reaches a high point in the work of Hintze, who also employed a sophisticated and quite modern comparative methodology.

What one can say about the more recent literature is that it seems to have eliminated more thoroughly the "black boxes" that served as convenient boundary markers for some of the earlier literature. What one encounters in the work of Gourevitch, Skocpol, Lijphart, Katzenstein, and others is a model of political processes in which the boundaries between the national and international, the political and the economic have been removed, and important research programs demonstrating the improved explanatory power of this research strategy have gotten under way.

Peter Gourevitch, without so much as the flicker of an eyelid, crosses state boundaries, following the fluctuations of world prices of agricultural and industrial commodities as they affect the policy propensities of pressure groups and political parties in Britain, France, Germany, Sweden, and the United States, producing different political coalitions and different economic and security policies. Theda Skocpol, in her vivid efforts to reconstruct the onset and triumph of social revolution in France, Russia, and China, moves fluently from the wars of the eighteenth century to World Wars I and II and their impacts on the internal political economies of those countries. The entities that she deals with are armies and other military formations, bureaucracies, party and government organizations, economic groups, social classes, and the like. While she speaks of the decline and collapse of the Bourbon, Romanov, and Kuomintang states, it is the army, the party, the bureaucracy, the assembly (or parts of any and all of these) that are the political actors who carry her narrative. When Lijphart and Katzenstein describe how the international environment in the 1930s-1950s entered into the adoption of consociational and corporatist arrangements and practices in the smaller European democracies, they encounter no bulky "states" between the external and the internal processes that they are describing. And in his work on imperialism and decolonization, Miles Kahler describes how the French and British experience with decolonization spills back into French and British internal politics.[69] He similarly needs no research passport to cross over from the events in Indochina and Algeria, India, Burma, and Malaya into the politics of France and Britain.

This is what makes it perplexing that some of these same writers who have pioneered in this cross-disciplinary work should now be insisting on the reintroduction of the concept of the state, in the "black box" sense of the state, as an inclusive actor that may be either "strong" or "weak." This is a movement that sets aside the earlier effort to disaggregate the state concept, an effort that was by and large successful in reaching a higher level of analytic resolution in observing, measuring, and explaining things political. There is an egregious contradiction in arguing on the one hand for a cross-disciplinary perspective in order to observe the flows of actions and transactions across the international and national arenas while on the other hand mounting a campaign intended to "bring the state back in" as Skocpol,[70] Krasner,[71] and their collaborators have done.

In speculating about the prospects of this interdisciplinary movement it may be useful to return to Otto Hintze's explanation for the neglect of international factors by political and social theorists.[72] He points out that it is very difficult to grapple with these factors in terms of general propositions and regularities. At any given time during the past several centuries there has been but one central, international system, consisting of the interactions of the principal European states. Given variations in the political organization of these states in a singular international environment, it was the course of least resistance to assume the international environment to be a constant vis-a-vis all states, or simply to extract the state from its international environment and explain national political variation by internal economics, social structure, and culture. It was the virtue of Hintze to attribute spatial and temporal variability to the international environment, and to find in these variations some significant part of the explanation of internal variation. Those writers whose work is summarized above treat the international environment as varying over time and in its incidence on individual states. Hence they are able to generate propositions that systematically include aspects of the international environment as important variables.

This new generation of comparativists and international relationists has systematically and explicitly reintroduced this large comparative historical perspective. They select their problems and do their research with a historical consciousness that includes (1) the state-building processes of the fifteenth to eighteenth centuries; (2) the French Revolution and its national and international repercussions; (3) the economic growth, modernization, and economic fluctuations of the nineteenth and twentieth centuries; (4) the growth of empires and their later dismantlement; (5) the great wars, their origins, and their consequences; and (6) the Russian Revolution and its repercussions, still in such vivid evidence today. With this large historical perspective it is difficult for a scholar to evade the complex cross-penetration of national and world politics.

It is out of the crucible of international and internecine war that the Western state system emerged. The French and Russian revolutions are inescapable demonstrations of how individual national explosions can transform the world system and its component parts. The great wars confront us with the ways in which international interaction transforms the political characteristics of nation-states. Economic growth and crises transform the politics and policies of nation-states, which may in turn produce further changes in the condition of the international political economy. The First and Second worlds, through their internal and external policies, and through their interactions one with the other, transform the environments that constrain but do not determine the responses of Third World countries. This new generation of scholars draws its problems from these larger perspectives, and in addition brings to its work conceptual self-consciousness and methodological virtuosity. There is a record of substantial accomplishment, and greater promise.

Notes

1. Theda Skocpol, *States and Social Revolutions* (Cambridge: Cambridge University Press, 1979), p. 19.
2. Atul Kohli, "Introduction," in Atul Kohli [Ed.] *The State and Development in the Third World* (Princeton, NJ: Princeton University Press, 1986), p. 15.
3. Andrew Janos, *Politics and Paradigms* (Stanford, CA: Stanford University Press, 1986), p. 66.
4. Tony Smith, "Requiem or New Agenda for Third World Studies," in Ikuo Kabashima and Lynn T. White [Eds.] *Political System and Change* (Princeton, NJ: Princeton University Press, 1986), p. 376.
5. Peter Gourevitch, "The Second Image Reversed; The International Sources of Domestic Politics," *International Organization*, Vol. 32, No. 4, 1978, p. 882.
6. Robert A. Dahl, *Congress and Foreign Policy* (New York: Harcourt Brace, 1950).
7. Bernard C. Cohen, *The Public's Impact on Foreign Policy* (Boston: Little, Brown, 1972).
8. Raymond Bauer, Ithiel Pool, and Lewis Dexter, *American Business and Public Policy* (New York: Atherton, 1963).
9. Lester Markel [Ed.] *Public Opinion and Foreign Policy* (New York: Harper & Bros., 1949).
10. Gabriel A. Almond, *The American People and Foreign Policy* (New York: Harcourt Brace, 1950).
11. Richard Snyder, Henry Bruck, and Burton Sapin, *Decision-making as an Approach to the Study of International Politics* (Princeton, NJ: Princeton University, Organization Behavior Section, 1954); Richard Snyder, Henry Bruck, and Burton Sapin, *Foreign Policy Decision Making* (New York: Free Press of Glencoe, Macmillan, 1962).
12. Kenneth Waltz, *Foreign Policy and Democratic Politics: American and British Experience* (Boston: Little, Brown, 1967); Wolfram Hanrieder, *Comparative Foreign Policy* (New York: David McKay, 1971).
13. Peter Katzenstein, *Between Power and Plenty* (Madison: University of Wisconsin Press, 1978).
14. John Robert Seeley, *An Introduction to Political Science* (London: Macmillan, 1886), p. 133.
15. Otto Hintze, *Gesammelte Abhandlungen*, Band I, II, III (Gottingen: Vandenhoeck und Ruprecht, 1962–1967).
16. Woodrow Wilson, *The State: Elements of Historical and Practical Politics* (Boston: Heath, 1895).
17. Otto Hintze, *Soziologie und Geschichte* (Gottingen: Vandenhoeck und Ruprecht, 1964), pp. 19–20.

18. Otto Hintze, *The Historical Essays of Otto Hintze* (New York: Oxford University Press, 1975), p. 159.
19. Ibid., p. 162
20. Gabriel A. Almond, "National Politics and International Politics," in Albert Lepawsky, Edward Buehrig, and Harold Lasswell, *The Search for World Order* (New York: Appleton-Century-Crofts, 1971), pp. 284–85.
21. Gourevitch, "The Second Image Reversed," p. 882.
22. Peter Gourevitch, *Politics in Hard Times* (Ithaca, NY: Cornell University Press, 1986); Peter Gourevitch, "International Trade, Domestic Coalitions, and Liberty: Responses to the Crisis of 1873–1896," *Journal of Interdisciplinary History*, Vol. VIII, No. 2, 1977; Peter Gourevitch, "Breaking with Orthodoxy: The Politics of Economic Policy Responses to the Depression of the 1930s," *International Organization*, Vol. 38, No. 1, 1984.
23. Seeley, *Introduction to Political Science*, p. 131.
24. Ibid., p. 134.
25. Hintze, *The Historical Essays*, p. 164.
26. Ibid., p. 183.
27. Ibid., p. 266.
28. Hintze, *Staat und Verfassung*, p. 424.
29. Ibid., pp. 390ff.
30. Ibid., p. 428.
31. Ibid., p. 429.
32. Hintze, *Soziologie und Geschichte*, p. 202.
33. Gabriel A. Almond and G. Bingham Powell, *Comparative Politics: A Developmental Approach* (Boston: Little, Brown, 1966), pp. 314ff.
34. Perry Anderson, *Passages from Antiquity to Feudalism* (New York: Humanities Press, 1974); Perry Anderson, *Lineages of the Absolutist State* (New York: Humanities Press, 1974).
35. Anderson, *Lineages of the Absolutist State.*, pp. 15ff.
36. Ibid., pp. 197ff.
37. Charles Tilly [Ed.] *The Formation of National States in Western Europe* (Princeton, NJ: Princeton University Press, 1975).
38. Ibid., p. 73.
39. Adolph Wagner, *Finanzwissenschaft*, Vol. II. (Leipzig: Duncker und Humblot, 1890).
40. Alan Peacock and Jack Wiseman, *The Growth of Public Expenditure in the United Kingdom.* (Princeton, NJ: Princeton University Press, 1961).
41. Karen Rasler and William R. Thompson, "War-Making and State-Making; Governmental Expenditures, Tax Revenues, and Global Wars," *American Political Science Review*, Vol. 79, No., 3, 1985, p. 504.
42. Robert Wolfe, *Americans as Proconsuls: U.S. Military Government in Germany and Japan* (Carbondale: Southern Illinois University Press, 1984).
43. John Herz [Ed.] *From Dictatorship to Democracy: Coping with the Legacies of Authoritarianism and Totalitarianism* (Westport, CT: Greenwood, 1982).
44. Alexander Gerschenkron, *Economic Backwardness in Historical Perspective* (Cambridge, MA: Belknap Press of the Harvard University Press, 1962).
45. Albert Hirschman, *Journeys Toward Progress* (Garden City, NY: Anchor/Doubleday, 1965); Albert Hirschman, *Development Projects Observed* (Washington, DC: Brookings

Institution, 1967); Albert Hirschman, *A Bias for Hope* (New Haven, CT: Yale University Press, 1971).
46. Gerald Meier and Dudley Seers, *Pioneers in Development* (New York: Oxford University Press, 1984).
47. Gerald Meier, *Emerging from Poverty: The Economics That Really Matters* (New York: Oxford University Press, 1984).
48. Gourevitch, "International Trade, Domestic Coalitions, and Liberty"; Gourevitch, "The Second Image Reversed"; Gourevitch, "Breaking with Orthodoxy"; Gourevitch, *Politics in Hard Times*.
49. Gourevitch, *Politics in Hard Times*, p. 10.
50. Ibid., pp. 60–61.
51. Stephen Krasner, "Approaches to the State: Alternative Conceptions and Historical Dynamics," *Comparative Politics*, Vol. 16, No. 2.
52. Theda Skocpol, *Bringing the State Back in* (Cambridge: Cambridge University Press, 1985).
53. Gourevitch, *Politics in Hard Times*, p. 63.
54. Skocpol, *States and Social Revolutions*.
55. Ibid., p. 284.
56. Gourevitch, *Politics in Hard Times*.
57. Gabriel A. Almond, Scott Flanagan, and Robert Mundt, *Crisis, Choice, and Change* (Boston: Little, Brown, 1973).
58. Ibid., p. 628.
59. Ibid.
60. Arend Lijphart, "Typologies of Democratic Systems," *Comparative Political Studies*, Vol. 1, No. 1, 1968; Arend Lijphart, *Democracy in Plural Societies* (New Haven, CT: Yale University Press, 1977).
61. Philippe Schmitter and Gerhard Lehmbruch, *Trends Towards Corporatist Intermediation* (Beverly Hills, CA: Sage, 1979).
62. Peter Katzenstein, *Small States and World Markets* (Ithaca, NY: Cornell University Press, 1985).
63. Lijphart, "Typologies of Democratic Systems," pp. 28–29.
64. Katzenstein, *Small States and World Markets*, p. 33.
65. Ibid., p. 9.
66. Ilja Scholten, *Political Stability and Neo-Corporatism: Corporatist Integration and Societal Cleavage in Western Europe* (London: Sage, 1987).
67. Fernando Cardoso and Enzo Faletto, *Dependency and Development in Latin America* (Berkeley: University of California Press, 1979).
68. Immanuel Wallerstein, *The Capitalist World Economy* (Cambridge: Cambridge University Press, 1979); Immanuel Wallerstein, *The Modern World-System*, 2 vols. (New York: Academic Press, 1974, 1980).
69. Miles Kahler, *Decolonization in Britain and France* (Princeton, NJ: Princeton University Press, 1984).
70. Skocpol, *Bringing the State Back in*.
71. Krasner, "Approaches to the State."
72. Hintze, *Staat und Verfassung*, p. 424.

Appendix A

Harold D. Lasswell: A Biographical Memoir

Harold D. Lasswell ranks among the half dozen creative innovators in the social sciences in the twentieth century. Few would question that he was the most original and productive political scientist of his time. While still in his 20s and early 30s, he planned and carried out a research program demonstrating the importance of personality, social structure, and culture in the explanation of political phenomena. In the course of that work he employed an array of methodologies that included clinical and other kinds of interviewing, content analysis, para-experimental techniques, and statistical measurement. It is noteworthy that two decades were to elapse before this kind of research program and methodology became the common property of a discipline that until then had been dominated by historical, legal, and philosophical methods.

Lasswell was born in 1902 in Donnellson, Illinois (population ca. 300). His father was a Presbyterian clergyman, his mother, a teacher; an older brother died in childhood. His early family life was spent in small towns in Illinois and Indiana as his father moved from one pulpit to another, and it stressed intellectual and religious values. Although the regional milieu of his childhood and adolescence might suggest that Lasswell was raised in an intellectual backwater, in fact it was an unusually rich environment. He was especially influenced in adolescence by a physician uncle who was familiar with the works of Freud; by an English teacher in the Decatur, Illinois, high school he attended who introduced him to Karl Marx and Havelock Ellis;

---

and by a brilliant young teacher of high school civics, William Cornell Casey, who later became a professor of sociology at Barnard College in Columbia University. He excelled in high school, edited the school newspaper, gave the valedictory address at graduation, and was awarded a scholarship to the University of Chicago after winning a competitive examination in modern history and English.

When Lasswell entered the University of Chicago in 1918 – at age 16 – the university was in the third decade of its remarkable growth. At a time when sociology as a curriculum did not yet exist at most universities, Chicago had a major department that was staffed by such gifted theorists and researchers as W. I. Thomas, Albion W. Small, and Robert Park. Its philosophy department was dominated by realists and empiricists such as James Tufts and George Herbert Mead. Its economics department, in which Lasswell majored, included Jacob Viner, John M. Clark, Harry Alvin Millis, and Chester Wright. Its political science department was soon to begin its dramatic rise, but in Lasswell's undergraduate years the department was in transition, with Henry Pratt Judson soon to retire, and Charles Edward Merriam in the wings. Lasswell was a member of a graduate cohort that included Robert Redfield, Louis Wirth, and Herbert Blumer.

His graduate years in the Department of Political Science at Chicago coincided with the publication of Merriam's manifesto, *The Present State of the Study of Politics*, in 1921 and with Merriam and Gosnell's survey study of nonvoting in Chicago (1924). In *The Present State*, Merriam proposed that two steps be taken to make the study of politics more scientific: (1) the exploration of the psychological and sociological bases of political behavior, and (2) the introduction of quantification in the analysis of political phenomena. The nonvoting study was a demonstration of the uses of social psychological hypotheses and quantitative methods in the explanation of political phenomena. It was a survey of the "political motives" of some 6,000 nonvoters in the Chicago mayoral election of 1923; individuals to be surveyed were selected by a "quota control" sampling procedure that was intended to match the census demographic distributions. In the immediate aftermath of this study and during Lasswell's graduate student days, Harold Foote Gosnell (then a first-term assistant professor of political science) conducted the first experimental study in political science – and what may very well have been the first experimental study in the social sciences outside of psychology. This was a survey of the effects on voting of a nonpartisan mail canvass in Chicago that was intended to get out the vote in the national and local elections of 1924 and 1925. The experimental technique Gosnell devised was quite rigorous: there were carefully matched experimental and control groups, different stimuli were employed, and the results were analyzed with the most sophisticated statistical techniques then available. Reflecting the programmatic and comparative vision of these researches, follow-up studies of voting turnout were made by Gosnell in Britain, France, Germany, Belgium, and Switzerland.

While Harold Gosnell was chosen by Merriam to develop the statistical component of his early 1920s vision, it was Harold Lasswell who was encouraged to develop the clinical, psychological, and sociological components. As a young graduate student, Lasswell published an article in 1923 titled "Chicago's Old First Ward,"[1] and in collaboration with Merriam he published another in 1924 on public opinion and public utility regulation.[2]

Merriam threw out two challenges to the brilliant and ambitious young political scientist. The first came out of Merriam's wartime experience as chief American propagandist in Rome; the second arose from Merriam's interest in the characteristics of political leaders and the uses of the study of the abnormal and the psychopathological in explaining normal and typical behavior. Merriam's first interest—the importance of morale, propaganda, and civic training in the explanation of political behavior—led to Lasswell's 1927 doctoral dissertation, *Propaganda Technique in the World War*, and ultimately to his invention of systematic content analysis and its uses in World War II. Merriam's second interest—the psychological and personality aspects of leadership and the uses of the abnormal in the explanation of the normal—led to a series of articles by Lasswell on political psychology and personality in politics, culminating in his *Psychopathology and Politics*.

Lasswell's doctoral dissertation on propaganda in the 1914–1918 war was a systematic effort to place World War I propaganda experience in the context of a theory of politics. Although there was something of antiwar muckraking in its tone, it also had the marks of rigorous scholarship: careful operational definitions, specification of the techniques of propaganda, and the conditions that limit or facilitate their effectiveness. Lasswell had done field research in Europe for this study, interviewing scholars and governmental officials regarding aspects of the propaganda experience and the Great War. He also anticipated his later invention of content analysis in a simple quantitative study—"Prussian Schoolbooks and International Amity"—which was carried out in connection with his dissertation. (In the study Lasswell counted and evaluated the significance of the references to national superiority, military glory, foreign inferiority, military heroes, and the like in textbooks approved by the Prussian Ministry of Education after the establishment of the Weimar Republic.)[3]

Lasswell was appointed assistant professor of political science at Chicago in 1926 and soon embarked on researches in political psychology. Papers that he published from 1925 to 1929 showed him to be engaged in a search of the literature concerned with political psychology and political personality. One paper published in the *American Journal of Psychiatry* in 1929 recommended that psychiatrists keep adequate personality records and make them available to bona fide researchers; another published in the *American Political Science Review* the same year argued the case for the use of data on mentally ill persons with some involvement in politics as one approach to the analysis of the relationship between personality and politics. This literature search and his concern with the improvement of psychiatric record keeping were incidental to the preparation and publication of Lasswell's extraordinary book, *Psychopathology and Politics*, which appeared in 1930, when he was 28.

Lasswell's work in preparing the book was extensive. He had been granted a postdoctoral fellowship by the Social Science Research Council for 1927-1928 and spent most of that year in Berlin undergoing psychoanalysis at the hands of Theodor Reik, a student of Freud. There is a report that he made a presentation at a Freud seminar urging that psychiatric records be kept in order to facilitate research. He also discussed these ideas with leading psychiatrists in Vienna and Berlin. In late 1928 and 1929 he consulted with the psychiatric directors of the most important mental institutions on the eastern seaboard, tapping their memories of cases of politician patients. With their permission he examined psychiatric records at St. Elizabeth's in Washington, D.C.; Sheppard and Enoch Pratt Hospital near Baltimore; Pennsylvania State Hospital in Philadelphia; Bloomingdale Hospital of White Plains, New York; and Boston Psychopathic Hospital. He also gave depth psychiatric interviews to a number of "normal" volunteers.

Psychopathology and Politics was the first relatively systematic, empirical study of the psychological aspects of political behavior, and it coincided with the very beginnings of the culture and personality movement in anthropology and psychiatry. Lasswell was already in communication with anthropologist Edward Sapir, then a colleague at the University of Chicago, as well as with the New York psychiatrist Harry Stack Sullivan. The three of them began to plan an ambitious program of culture and personality research in the middle and late 1920s. Margaret Mead's *Coming of Age in Samoa* appeared two years before *Psychopathology and Politics*, and Ruth Benedict's *Patterns of Culture* appeared four years later. The first publication of the authoritarian personality research of the Frankfurt School—*Studien über Autoritt und Familie*—appeared in 1936, and the *Authoritarian Personality* of Adorno, Frenkel-Brunswick, Daniel Levinson, and Nevitt Sanford appeared only in 1950.

Chapters 6 through 9 of *Psychopathology and Politics* report Lasswell's case materials. These are not, and are not represented as being, findings or scientific explanations of political behavior. They are presented as clinically supported hypotheses regarding the personality-etiological bases of recruitment to different kinds of political roles and attitudes. Thus Lasswell draws on clinical material and his own depth interviews to suggest why some individuals become agitators and others become administrators. Similarly, he illuminates the relationship between personality variables and ideological propensities such as ultrapatriotism, internationalism, pacifism, socialism, and anarchism.

The rest of the book deals with methodological and theoretical issues. Among the methodological issues he treats are the uses of life histories in political science; the uses of the study of the deviant or the abnormal for the understanding of the normal; the dimensions used in typologies of politicians; the prolonged, "depth," or psychoanalytic interview as a mode of research in the psychological bases of social behavior; and the technique of free association as a method of getting data on politically relevant feelings and attitudes. He also presents a general theory of political behavior derived from a review of the various propositions of the psychoanalytic movement. This proposition, presented in the form of an equation, reduces political behavior – in the sense of choice of political roles and ideologies – to displacements of private, essentially "oedipal" and "libidinal" motives as rationalized in terms of political ideas and issues. It is a matter of some contention among Lasswell students as to whether this equation was literally intended or was a rhetorical exaggeration to draw attention to the importance of psychological motivation in the explanation of political phenomena. Supporting the reductionist position is the fact that the Freudian movement at this time took a similarly reductionist stand in the explanation of social, political, and aesthetic phenomena. Supporting the rhetorical interpretation is the fact that in this as in later work, Lasswell interprets unconscious oedipal and libidinal tendencies as powerful constraints on rational, object-oriented behavior, constraints that can be mitigated by psychotherapy. This was to be a theme of Lasswell's entire intellectual career; that professional political science had the obligation of discovering or inventing a "politics of prevention" of war and other evils; that there was a "commonwealth of human dignity" to which it ought to aspire; and that both of these required substantial psychotherapeutic inputs.

This dualism and ambivalence of reductionism and therapeutic optimism in some sense characterized the three principal influences on Lasswell's thought; the Presbyterianism of his family and childhood background, which deals with the question of how good may be wrested from an intractable evil; the Marxist-sociological background, which deals with the necessarily revolutionary confrontation of the traditional and reactionary with progressive forces; and the Freudian-psychoanalytic background, which deals with the confrontation of neurosis with psychotherapy. Lasswell's later contributions to political psychology took the constraint rather than the reductionist perspective. It is of interest that in an "Afterthoughts" he wrote for the 1960 edition of *Psychopathology and Politics*, he makes no reference to his equation; instead he tells us that at the time of writing the book he already shared in a revisionist ego-psychology trend, a movement in psychoanalysis that affirmed the importance of rational and cognitive processes.

In addition to the empirical and methodological parts, *Psychopathology and Politics* included a theoretical or metamethodological part. Chapters 12 and 13–"The Personality System and Its Substantive Reactions" and "The State as a Manifold of Events"–presented Lasswell's framework of politically relevant variables and a strategy of political explanation, which moves from intrapsychic processes and their etiology, to interpersonal and social processes, to domestic and international political processes, and back again. Personality, economy, society, and politics are considered and dealt with as interacting systems.

What Lasswell presented as a theoretical framework and set of hypotheses in *Psychopathology and Politics* became his research program during the decade of the 1930s. Consider the intellectual balls he was juggling during these years.

For the psychiatrists whom he had been urging to keep records of their interviews in the interest of scientific research, he set up a model laboratory in his own offices in the Social Science Research Building at the University of Chicago. Advised and encouraged by psychiatrists Harry Stack Sullivan of Sheppard and Enoch Pratt Hospital and William A. White of St. Elizabeth's, he devised a procedure under which skin conductivity, pulse rate, respiration, and body movements of experimental subjects were measured as the spoken word was recorded. Three articles describing this procedure and reporting preliminary results appeared in psychoanalytic journals in 1935, 1936, and 1937. Unfortunately, these research records were destroyed in 1938 in an accident that befell the vans moving Lasswell's effects to Washington on his departure from Chicago. This project, if not the first, was certainly one of the earliest efforts to link physiological, autonomic, and behavioral variables with communications and personality processes.

If this laboratory research was an effort to implement the methodological message of *Psychopathology and Politics,* then *World Politics and Personal Insecurity* (1934) was an elaboration of the theoretical perspectives spelled out in the final chapters of *Psychopathology and Politics.* Lasswell called his approach to political explanation *configurative analysis.* In configurative analysis the political process is defined as conflict over the definition and distribution of the dominant social values – income, deference, and safety – by and among elites. In his first paragraph he proposes the formula long associated with his name: "Politics is the study of who gets what, when, and how." Political science research hence requires the analysis of the social origins, skills, personal traits, attitudes, values, and assets of world elites, and their changes over time. Proper understanding of political processes calls for a combination of equilibrium and developmental analysis and the adoption of contemplative and manipulative attitudes toward political change. Equilibrium analysis emphasizes the systemic, the recurrent, the stable interaction of economic, social, political, and personality variables; developmental analysis stresses the dynamic, the dialectical and transformative aspects of social change. The contemplative attitude contributes to the discovery of "regularities," "laws," principles of social behavior. The manipulative attitude subjects these regularities to the test of imagination, tracing the consequences of changes in conditions and policies, extrapolating trends, and the like. What Lasswell had in mind by the manipulative attitude is not fully clear in these passages. From the beginning he had a commitment to a moral and consequential political science, but his earlier work focused on politics and power. In his early schematization of political values as income, deference, and safety, he describes them rather casually as illustrative and representative values – not a complete set of political goals. He did not begin to deal explicitly with the political value and public policy realm until his association with Myres McDougal and the Yale School of Law in the late 1930s.

The bulk of *World Politics and Personal Insecurity* illustrates his method and approach. In Chapters 2 through 6, conflicts among and within nations are related to human aggressive propensities, as well as the structural conditions of international relations and domestic societies. The consequences of economic and class structure, cultural diffusion, and the media of communication are the topics of Chapters 7, 8, and 9. In Chapter 10, politics, culture, and personality are related in an interesting discussion of trends in American society: he treats the possibilities of the emergence of right-wing extremism and fascism and the approach of political psychiatry in a politics of prevention. A final chapter deals – in sociological and psychoanalytic terms – with the prospects of peace and social justice.

A briefer book, *Politics: Who Gets What, When, and How,* was published in 1936; it presented much of what was argued in *World Politics* but in a more succinct and more schematic form. If Lasswell has written a textbook, then this is it. It defined politics as the struggle among elite groups over such representative values as income, deference, and safety. The actors in these conflictual processes are groups organized around skill, class, personality, and attitude characteristics; they employ in different ways and with different effects the political instrumentalities of symbol manipulation, material rewards and sanctions, violence, and institutional practices.

These three books, which were written over a six-year period, constitute Lasswell's most important contributions to political theory. In this same productive decade of the 1930s, Lasswell was involved in two other major enterprises. He consolidated his earlier interest in propaganda research by collaborating with R. D. Casey and B. L. Smith in the preparation of an annotated bibliography of some 4,500 items. It was published in 1935 as a book—*Propaganda and Promotional Activities: An Annotated Bibliography*—with an introduction on the theory of propaganda by Lasswell. Later editions continued to guide and codify the field of communications and public opinion research. In an effort to implement the research program laid out in *World Politics,* Lasswell and a number of his graduate students carried out a field study of propaganda and political agitators and organizers among the unemployed in the city of Chicago during the Depression and New Deal years. A book coauthored with Dorothy Blumenstock Jones reported these findings in 1939.

The first phase in Lasswell's career came to an end in 1938. He left the University of Chicago to join forces with psychiatrist Harry Stack Sullivan and Yale anthropologist Edward Sapir, under the auspices of the William Alanson White Psychiatric Foundation. There was both "push" and "pull" behind these plans to leave. Under the presidency of Robert Maynard Hutchins, the hospitality of the University of Chicago to the empirical social sciences had notably cooled. Merriam's department came under criticism on grounds of "number crunching" and "psychologizing," as well as internal recruitment. Hutchins's conception of political science was humanistic, deductive, even Aquinian. Although Lasswell had tenure—as did Gosnell—both men left the university: Lasswell in 1938 for Washington, D.C., and the William Alanson White Psychiatric Foundation; Gosnell a few years later, also to the capital but for government service. Merriam himself was approaching retirement and was unable to defend his younger men.

The "pull" of the eastern seaboard on Lasswell had an earlier origin. During the mid-1920s, when he was preparing for his study of psychopathology and politics, Lasswell encountered the maverick psychiatrist Harry Stack Sullivan during his visits at eastern psychiatric hospitals. He also made the acquaintance of Dr. William Alanson White, the director of St. Elizabeth's, who was strongly interested in research and in collaboration with the social sciences. (Lasswell, because of his association with Merriam, was in a position to facilitate access for Dr. White to the early organizational meetings of the Social Science Research Council, then being held in Hanover, New Hampshire.) During these same years, Sullivan had come to know the cultural anthropologist Edward Sapir, then a colleague of Lasswell's at the University of Chicago. The three men, although of different ages – Sapir was born in 1884, Sullivan in 1892, and Lasswell in 1902 – were attracted to one another out of the strongest interest in culture-personality themes. They dreamed of a research institute that would combine the study of culture, society, and personality and contribute to a better and happier world. The research institute never came to fruition, but these encounters surely influenced Lasswell's program at the University of Chicago, Sapir's Institute of Human Relations at Yale, and Sullivan's William Alanson White Psychiatric Foundation in Washington, D.C.

In 1938, however, it appeared that these plans for a social science-cum-psychiatry institute in either New York or Washington with Sapir, Sullivan, and Lasswell as the full-time core research faculty were about to mature. In April 1938 the trustees of the William Alanson White Foundation decided to seek funds to support a full-time permanent research staff in psychiatry and the social sciences. And the three men were ready to move: Lasswell was pessimistic about prospects at Chicago, Sapir was acutely uncomfortable at Yale, and Sullivan looked forward to creative research collaboration under the most favorable of auspices.

It was in this mood of high hopes that in the spring of 1938 Harold Lasswell packed and shipped his files and belongings in two moving vans – which were fated to collide and burn on a lonely Indiana highway. But this was only the beginning of misadventure and tragedy. The fund-raising plans were unsuccessful, and relations between Sullivan and Lasswell deteriorated. Sapir died in early 1939.

Lasswell thus began the second phase of his career at age 36, in Washington, D.C., with uncertain prospects. He improvised for a while, giving educational radio broadcasts on "Human Nature in Action" over NBC and consulting to foundations. Beginning in the academic year 1938–39 he taught seminars as a visiting lecturer in association with Myres McDougal at the Yale School of Law; he was appointed professor of law there in 1946. As the international crisis deepened, he became involved in research programs at the Library of Congress and the Department of Justice. The Library of Congress at Lasswell's recommendation established a war communications research project, drawing on his experience with World War I propaganda. And the Department of Justice set up a special war policies unit to help administer the Foreign Agents Registration Act and the Sedition Act. Both of these tasks involved content analysis of the media of communication: on the world scale, as the propaganda war heated up in 1939 and 1940, and on the domestic organizational scale, as Nazis and fascists infiltrated foreign-language groups and media in the United States. Lasswell gave expert testimony in a number of trials under this legislation; he was also instrumental in the effort to have quantitative content analysis admitted as evidence in the federal courts.

During the war years he played an active role as a consultant to the Office of Facts and Figures and its successor organization, the Office of War Information; the Office of Strategic Services; the Foreign Broadcast Monitoring Service of the Federal Communications Commission; and the Army's Psychological Warfare Branch. For the social sciences these various research divisions of the government departments constituted advanced training centers for young social scientists. Leading scholars such as Lasswell, Lazarsfeld, Samuel Stouffer, and Carl Hovland trained groups of specialists in survey research, experimental small group research, propaganda and content analysis, and the like.

The methodological and substantive payoffs of Lasswell's wartime research are reported in *The Language of Politics: Studies in Quantitative Semantics* (1949), which was jointly edited with one of Lasswell's most brilliant students, Nathan Leites. This volume places mass communications content in the context of domestic and international politics, offers solutions for the principal methodological problems of quantitative content analysis, and reports on a number of successful uses of content analysis, both as a judicial tool and as a technique of intelligence gathering.

It had been Lasswell's ambition during World War II to set up what he termed a "world attention survey": a continual quantitative analysis of the content of the principal print and broadcast media of the major nations—friend, neutral, and enemy. It was a project of immense proportions and was set aside in the war years in favor of a much more modest program of propaganda analysis located in the Office of War Information and the Federal Communications Commission. But in the aftermath of the war and working with wartime collaborators—particularly sociologist Daniel Lerner and political scientist Ithiel Pool—Lasswell pursued these research themes. Based now as a professor in the Yale School of Law, in collaboration with Lerner, Pool, and others at the Hoover Institute and Library at Stanford, he undertook a series of comparative studies of elites and political symbols. Several volumes reporting the findings of these researches appeared in the 1950s. But one of the most important products of these Stanford years was *The Policy Sciences*, a state-of-the-art analysis of social science methodology as of the early 1950s that Lasswell coedited with Daniel Lerner, with coauthors Ernest R. Hilgard and others.

The third phase of Lasswell's career began in 1946, when he joined the Yale Law School faculty as a professor of law. He had been teaching part-time at Yale in association with Myres McDougal since 1938, and was a visiting research associate in the Institute of International Studies during the war years. His permanent location in New Haven in 1946 made possible a fruitful collaboration between Lasswell and McDougal in teaching, research, and contributions to legal and political theory, a collaboration that continued for the next several decades. In a major monographic contribution to the *Yale Law Journal* of March 1943, Lasswell and McDougal recommended the fundamental reform of law school curricula. The monograph argued that lawyers were the principal policymakers in modern democratic societies and that traditional law school curricula failed to provide training for the variety of policy-making roles lawyers were called upon to perform. In this seminal article, Lasswell and McDougal sought to remedy these shortcomings. They formulated a curricular philosophy based on the assumption that law had to be understood as a process of authoritative decision by which the members of a community clarify and secure their common interests. They then elaborated a sequence of seminars and courses that would effectively implement this philosophy. Prominent in this and later collaborations with McDougal and other law school colleagues were two theoretical innovations—components of an "institutional and value map"—that are properly associated with Lasswell's Yale career. The first innovation was a functional scheme for the analysis of decision making. This became in its final form a seven-phase process beginning with intelligence, in the sense of knowledge, and proceeding to promotion, prescription, invocation, application, termination, and evaluation. The second innovation was a classification of goals or base values that included power, wealth, respect, well-being, affection, skill, rectitude, and enlightenment. These two theoretical schemes enabled the legal scholar to locate his research in the policy process and to specify its substantive value aspects. The theoretical categories served to place in context the various legal and other studies that Lasswell carried on in the next decades.

One of Lasswell's most influential contributions in legal studies was

Power and Personality (1948), in which he presented a series of case histories of judges to demonstrate the connection between personality characteristics and patterns of legal decision making. Other Lasswell contributions to legal research and analysis are contained in such volumes as *Studies in World Public Order* (with Myres McDougal, 1960); *In Defense of Public Order: The Emerging Field of Sanction Law* (with Richard Arens, 1961); *Law and Public Order in Space* (with Myres McDougal and Ivan A. Vlasic, 1963); and *Human Rights and World Public Order: The Basic Policies of an International Law of Human Dignity* (with McDougal and Lung-chu Chen, 1980). A final volume, *Jurisprudence for a Free Society: Studies in Law, Science, and Policy*, coauthored with McDougal, is still to appear.

Lasswell became Ford Professor of Law and Social Science Emeritus at Yale in 1970. The last seven years of his life were spent in New Haven, where he continued his research interests, and in New York City, where he was affiliated with the Policy Sciences Center that he had helped to found in the 1940s.

Quantitatively, Lasswell's productivity was enormous. He wrote, coauthored, edited, and coedited some sixty books. He also contributed more than 300 articles to a wide range of journals: political science, sociological, psychiatric and psychological, legal, journalism, and public opinion. His publications also include several hundred reviews and comments. Among the important works that have not yet been mentioned are *Power and Society* (with Abraham Kaplan, 1950); *Democratic Character* (1951); *The Decision Process: Seven Categories of Functional Analysis* (1956); *The Future of Political Science* (1963); *The Sharing of Power in a Psychiatric Hospital* (with Robert Rubenstein, 1966); *Peasants, Power, and Applied Social Change: Vicos as a Model* (with Henry F. Dobyns and Paul L. Doughty, 1971); and *The Signature of Power: Buildings, Communication and Policy* (with Merritt B. Fox, 1979).

These titles suggest the enormous range of Lasswell's interests, which he maintained throughout his life. *Power and Society*, which was written in collaboration with the philosopher Abraham Kaplan, was a propositional inventory and conceptual handbook for political science. Among its noteworthy contents was the elaborated version of Lasswell's classification of base values (see above). Lasswell's monograph *Democratic Character* was an important addendum to a 1951 reprint of his *Psychopathology and Politics* and *Politics: Who Gets What, When, and How*, neither of which dealt with the psychological aspects of democracy. This monograph sought first to define the value orientations that would be supportive of democratic institutions and then to spell out "democratic" personality characteristics and the social and family conditions that were likely to produce them. His monograph on the decision process (1956) spelled out more clearly his theoretical framework for the phases of policy-making and implementation discussed above.

In *The Future of Political Science* (1963), evocative of earlier visions of a world in which social science research has reached high influence, he draws on two social science research projects in which he was engaged in the 1960s. The first of these was an anthropological study of a hacienda in Peru. In this effort Lasswell collaborated with Allan Holmberg of Cornell and later produced a book (with Dobyns and Doughty) titled *Peasants, Power, and Applied Social Change: Vicos as a Model* (1971). The experiment involved giving increasing initiative in decision making to the peasants in the hacienda and attempting to measure the consequences of these and other experimental inputs of modernization and democratization. The second, done collaboratively with Robert Rubenstein, was a study of an experiment at the Yale Psychiatric Institute involving the participation of patients with staff and psychiatrists in decision making on the ward. The research was concerned with the effects of this participation on the effectiveness of the ward and on the therapeutic goals of the institute. (A book documenting the study appeared in 1966 under the title, *The Sharing of Power in a Psychiatric Hospital.*) *The Future of Political Science* proposes that the political science profession develop the capacity to administer comprehensive surveys of world political change in order to advise effectively in the avoidance of war and other social evils. Such a survey would be informed by Lasswell's decision process and goal-value conceptualizations. He also describes the kind of professional education that would be required to administer this kind of research program and cultivate the creativity essential for effective intervention.

Finally, in a book published after his death, *The Signature of Power: Buildings, Communication and Policy* (1979), Lasswell explores the relations among the architecture of public buildings, their public functions, and the surrounding political culture. Using photographs of public buildings and monuments from all over the world to illustrate his points, he demonstrates that the functions of buildings—civil or military, judicial, legislative, and bureaucratic—influence their structures. These structures in turn are influenced by national cultures, which produce their own structural variations.

Lasswell received many honors in the course of his career. He served as president of the American Political Science Association in 1956 and of the American Society of International Law from 1966 to 1968. He received honorary degrees from the University of Chicago, Columbia University, the University of Illinois, and the Jewish Theological Seminary. He was actively associated as officer, board member, or consultant to the Committee for Economic Development, the Commission on the Freedom of the Press, the Rand Corporation, the American Association for the Advancement of Science, and many other organizations. He was a fellow of the American Academy of Arts and Sciences and was inducted into the National Academy of Sciences in 1974.

Harold Lasswell suffered a massive stroke on December 24, 1977, from which he never recovered. He died of pneumonia in his apartment in New York City on December 18, 1978.

I wish to acknowledge the help I have received from a number of sources: from Dwaine Marvick's "Introduction" to his anthology, *Harold Lasswell on Political Sociology* (1977); from the various contributions to Harold Lasswell's festschrift, *Politics, Personality, and Social Science in the Twentieth Century* (ed. Arnold Rogow, 1969); the memorial volume, *Harold Dwight Lasswell 1902–1978,* which was published by the Yale Law School under the editorship of Myres McDougal; and Helen Swick Perry's *Psychiatrist of America: The Life of Harry Stack Sullivan* (1982), which contains information on the early collaboration of Lasswell with Sapir and Sullivan; and from personal communications and accounts provided by William T.R. Fox, Bruce L. Smith, Andrew R. Willard, Rodney Muth, and Myres McDougal.

Notes

1. *National Municipal Review*, 12: 127–31.
2. "Current Public Opinion and the Public Service Commissions," in *Public Utility Regulation*, ed. M. L. Cooke (New York: Ronald Press, 1924).
3. "Prussian Schoolbooks and International Amity," *Journal of Social Forces*, 3 (1925): 718–22.

Selected Bibliography

1925

Two forgotten studies in political psychology. *American Political Science Review*, 19: 707–17.

1927

Propaganda Technique in the World War (Ph.D. dissertation). New York: A. A. Knopf; London: Kegan Paul.

Types of political personalities. *Proceedings of the American Sociological Society*, 22: 159–69.

1929

Personality studies. In *Chicago: An Experiment in Social Science Research*, ed. T. V. Smith and L. D. White, pp. 177–93. Chicago: University of Chicago Press.

Problem of adequate personality records: A proposal. *American Journal of Psychiatry*, 7: 1057–66.

The study of the ill as a method of research into political personalities. *American Political Science Review*, 23: 996–1001.

1930

Psychopathology and Politics. Chicago: University of Chicago Press.

Personality system and its substitutive reactions. *Journal of Abnormal Psychology*, 24: 433–40.

Psychoanalytic interviews as a method of research on personalities. *Childs Emotions*, February: 136–57.

The scientific study of human biography. *Scientific Monographs*, 30: 79–80.

Self-analysis and judicial thinking. *International Journal of Ethics*, 40: 354–62.

1931

The measurement of public opinion. *American Political Science Review*, 25: 311–26.

1932

Triple-appeal principle: A contribution of psychoanalysis to political and social science. *American Journal of Sociology*, 37: 523–38.

1935

With R. D. Casey and B. L. Smith: *Propaganda and Promotional Activities: An Annotated Bibliography*. Minneapolis: University of Minnesota Press.

World Politics and Personal Insecurity. New York: McGraw-Hill.

Verbal references and physiological changes during the psychoanalytic interview: A preliminary communication. *Psychoanalytic Review*, 22: 10–24.

1936

Politics: Who Gets What, When, and How. New York: Whittlesey House, McGraw-Hill.

Certain prognostic changes during trial (psychoanalytic) interviews. *Psychoanalytic Review*, 23: 241–47.

1937

A method of interlapping observation in the study of personality in culture. *Journal of Abnormal Psychology*, 32: 240–43.

1938

What psychiatrists and political scientists can learn from one another. *Psychiatry*, 1: 33–39.

1939

With Dorothy Blumenstock Jones: *World Revolutionary Propaganda: A Chicago Study*. New York: A. A. Knopf.

1941

The garrison state. *American Journal of Sociology*, 46: 455–68.

1943

With Myres McDougal: Legal education and public policy: Professional training in the public interest. *Yale Law Journal*, 52: 533–61.

1945

World Politics Faces Economics. New York: McGraw-Hill.

Interrelations of world organization and society. *Yale Law Journal*, 55: 889–909.

1948

The Analysis of Political Behaviour: An Empirical Approach. London: Routledge & Kegan Paul.

Power and Personality. New York: W. W. Norton.

1949

With Nathan Leites, eds.: *The Language of Politics: Studies in Quantitative Semantics*. New York: George Stewart.

1950

With Abraham Kaplan: *Power and Society*. New Haven, CT: Yale University Press.

National Security and Individual Freedom. New York: McGraw-Hill.

1951

With Daniel Lerner, eds.: *The Policy Sciences: Recent Developments in Scope and Method*. Stanford, CA: Stanford University Press.

Democratic character. In *The Political Writings of Harold D. Lasswell*, pp. 465–525. Glencoe, IL: Free Press.

1952

With Daniel Lerner and C. Easton Rothwell: *The Comparative Study of Elites* (Hoover Institute Studies). Stanford, CA: Stanford University Press.

With Daniel Lerner and Ithiel de Sola Pool: *The Comparative Study of Symbols* (Hoover Institute Studies). Stanford, CA: Stanford University Press.

1956

The Decision Process: Seven Categories of Functional Analysis. College Park: University of Maryland Press.

The political science of science: An inquiry into the possible reconciliation of mastery and freedom. *American Political Science Review*, 50: 961–79.

1959

Political constitution and character. *Psychoanalytic Review*, 46: 3–18.

The qualitative and quantitative in political and legal analysis. *Daedalus: Journal of the American Academy of Arts and Sciences*, 88: 633–45.

With Myres McDougal: The identification and appraisal of diverse systems of public order. *American Journal of International Law*, 53: 1–29.

1960

With Myres McDougal: *Studies in World Public Order*. New Haven, CT: Yale University Press.

With L. Z. Freedman: The common frontiers of psychiatry and law. *American Journal of Psychiatry*, 117: 490–98.

1961

With Richard Arens: *In Defense of Public Order: The Emerging Field of Sanction Law*. New York: Columbia University Press.

With L. Z. Freedman: Cooperation for research in psychiatry and law. *American Journal of Psychiatry*, 117: 692–94.

1963

The Future of Political Science. New York: Atherton.

With Myres McDougal and Ivan A. Vlasic: *Law and Public Order in Space*. New Haven, CT: Yale University Press.

With Arnold A. Rogow: *Power, Corruption, and Rectitude*. Englewood Cliffs, NJ: Prentice-Hall.

1964

With Bruce M. Russett, Hayward R. Alker, Jr., and Karl W. Deutsch: *World Handbook of Political and Social Indicators*. New Haven, CT, and London: Yale University Press.

1965

With Daniel Lerner, eds.: *World Revolutionary Elites: Studies in Coercive Ideological Movements*. Cambridge: MIT Press.

1966

With Robert Rubenstein: *The Sharing of Power in a Psychiatric Hospital*. New Haven, CT: Yale University Press.

1967

With Myres McDougal and James C. Miller: *The Interpretation of Agreements and World Public Order: Principles of Content and Procedure*. New Haven, CT: Yale University Press.

1968

With Myres McDougal and W. Michael Reisman: Theories about international law: Prologue to a configurative jurisprudence. *Virginia Journal of International Law*, 8: 188–299.

1969

With Satish Arora: *Political Communication: The Public Language of Political Elites in India and the United States*. New York: Holt, Rinehart & Winston.

With Allan Holmberg: Toward a general theory of directed value accumulation and institutional development. In *Political and Administrative Development*, ed. Ralph Braibanti, pp. 354–99. Durham, NC: Duke University Press.

1971

With Henry F. Dobyns and Paul L. Doughty: *Peasants, Power, and Applied Social Change: Vicos as a Model*. Beverly Hills, CA: Sage.

1975

With Warren F. Ilchman, John D. Montgomery, and Myron Weiner: *Policy Sciences and Population*. Lexington, MA: D. C. Heath.

1979

With Merritt B. Fox: *The Signature of Power: Buildings, Communication and Policy*. New Brunswick, NJ: Transaction.

1980

With Myres McDougal and Lung-chu Chen: *Human Rights and World Public Order: The Basic Policies of an International Law of Human Dignity*. New Haven, CT: Yale University Press.

With Daniel Lerner and Hans Speier, eds.: *Propaganda and Communication in World History*, 3 vols. Honolulu: University Press of Hawaii.

Appendix B

Chicago Days

Mr. Brody: When did you attend the University of Chicago, and did you go in with the intention of being a political scientist?

Mr. Almond: I got to the university in 1928, and my aspiration was to be a journalist, a writer. In the middle of my undergraduate career, the depression hit – 1929 – I had been putting myself through college and it began to get more and more difficult to get any kind of job. The career of a journalist and writer was much more chancy than the career of a teacher, so I began to think in terms of teaching. And around that time I happened to take a couple of courses – this would be in my junior year, in other words, in 1930 – I took a couple of courses, one with Fred Schuman in international politics and one with Merriam. I got very good grades on my papers, and so that decided me for political science. I ended up my undergraduate career with two majors: one in English literature and composition and the other in political science.

Mr. Brody: Did you do work with Lasswell when you were an undergraduate?

Mr. Almond: Yes. It was in the end of my junior year or the first quarter of my senior year that I took Harold Lasswell's "Non-Rational Factors in Political Behavior." It was the first time he had given that course and it was organized around the case histories that were then being written up for *Psychopathology and Politics*. I was at the University of Chicago, then, from 1928 to 1938 when I got my degree – my Ph.D. – with one year out for field research.

Adapted from an oral history of Gabriel A. Almond conducted by Richard Brody for the American Political Science Association. Reprinted by permission.

But that would have been the flowering period of the Department of Political Science at Chicago. It would have been the time during which Lasswell's *Psychopathology and Politics* was published, Lasswell's *Politics: Who Gets What, When and How* was published, Schuman's *International Politics* was published. Actually, I did research on Schuman's *International Politics.*

Mr. Brody: Was Quincy Wright there?

Mr. Almond: Quincy Wright and L. D. White were also there. If you're thinking of the core group in the faculty of the university at that time, it really consisted of these five men. V. O. Key was still a graduate student. It would be Merriam, Wright, White, Lasswell, and Gosnell. And you have to remember that departments were small. I mean, that would represent half of the full-time equivalents of the department. Now, if you're thinking of how much of the time of these five scholars was going into the kind of innovative research that we associate with the Chicago school, you'd have to say that Harold Lasswell was full-time involved in this kind of creative work; Gosnell, similarly, was full-time involved in teaching and in research of this kind; Merriam mainly played the role of the mobilizer of resources and the picker of talent—he was really important in picking promising people and betting on them; Quincy Wright and Leonard White were, I would say, more marginal—that is, they had research interests of a conservative, solid, creative sort, but they were also men who were open to new ideas and possibilities and both of them—Quincy Wright in his *Study of War* and L. D. White in a number of things, his *Prestige Value of Public Employment*, which used survey methods to get at the problem of public attitudes toward public service, and then all the work he did on the Hoover, Recent Social Trends study, he did a lot of that kind of aggregate statistical data gathering on the development of American government and federalism, indicators of central, peripheral interaction. But, I'd have to say that those senior men, Wright and White, were more marginal; they accepted this kind of quantitative and sociological, psychological analysis, but they weren't as centrally involved or fully involved.

Mr. Brody: It's a long time ago, it's 50 years, but do you remember what the general shape of the graduate program was? Did you have to work with White and with Wright as well as with Schuman and Merriam?

Mr. Almond: There's one thing I don't want to forget—the whole question of the scale, not just of the department, but of the whole social science enterprise at Chicago, you can't really understand the political science part of it without the whole, but to come back to your question about how much of the department one had to be exposed to as a graduate student, you had to be exposed to it all. The department was not only a small department–it wasn't unusual in that respect, it was one of the major departments. I don't think Harvard and Yale and Princeton had more. But as far as fields were concerned, Ph.D.s. were examined in all the fields other than the one in which they did their dissertations, the assumption being that they would master that field anyway. So that to get your Ph.D. you had to go through the whole business of international relations, which meant politics, organization, law; public law; public administration; political parties and elections; and political behavior, when Lasswell was giving it.

Mr. Brody: Political philosophy, too?

Mr. Almond: Political theory. Merriam gave political theory, yes. I think there were five examining fields.

Mr. Brody: What about the history of political thought?

Mr. Almond: Merriam gave that. You had to pass an examination in the history of political thought, American political thought, and contemporary political thought.

Mr. Brody: Did you read Marx? I mean, was that part of the course of study?

Mr. Almond: Yes. I'm just trying to think where one would read Marx. You'd read it in two places. You'd read Marx in Merriam's history of political theory, modern political theory, that part of it, and you'd get him in Lasswell's work, Lasswell's courses. But, if I may just say a word or two about the larger context of the department.

Mr. Brody: Yes, please do.

Mr. Almond: In the late 20s and 30s, which is really my period there, this was the period in which the Social Science Research Building was built, the one over which there was great controversy about the Lord Kelvin motto which Ogburn had engraved on the front–what is it–the lintel?–of the entrance of the Social Science Research Building while Merriam was away. You know, our knowledge is meager if we can't measure it–I can't remember how it actually goes. When Merriam got back, he was quite upset about that. But this wasn't a very big building; it was five stories and it contained all the departments and with the exception of psychology, all the social sciences, including a substantial part of history. Some of history was in the neighboring Harper Library Building, they had their offices there.

Mr. Brody: Economics, too?

Mr. Almond: Economics, sociology, political science, anthropology were all in this five story building, and, you have to remember, assuming the department of political science was typical, there must have been roughly forty professors in that building with offices, kind of satellite offices, many of them if not most of them had research assistants. It would be typical of a graduate career, let's say of four to six years, that you would get to know at least by sight if not for purposes of actual acquaintance or friendship, the economics and the anthropology and sociology faculty as well as the political sciencc faculty, and there was a tea room, a lounge on the second floor, and every afternoon – it's interesting, coffee wasn't served, it was tea with cookies, little Lorna Doones if you can remember them, tea and cookies – and most faculty members and most of the graduate students made a practice of going to these teas at four in the afternoon. So, you might say, the physical setting was such that you thought of yourself as being both a political scientist and a social scientist. Graduate students who worked as research assistants, weren't necessarily housed only with colleagues who were in their field. My first office in the SSRC building I shared with Edward Shils and Leland Devinney, and Herbert Goldhamer, all three of them sociologists, so that I had as strong personal relationships with anthropologists and with sociologists as I did with political scientists.

Mr. Brody: How many graduate students did Chicago admit in a given year?

Mr. Almond: I think maybe the department at Chicago would have had roughly the same number of graduate students as we have here at Stanford; that is, roughly about eighty all told, at all levels, including those who are out teaching but hadn't finished their dissertations. The seminars were not only populated by graduate students, but they were populated by undergraduates. There was no sharp distinction drawn. As a junior and a senior as an undergraduate, I took courses with Frank Knight, with George Herbert Mead, of an advanced graduate sort. When I went east after I began teaching, the sharp distinction drawn between graduate and undergraduate courses struck me as anomalous.

You have to remember then, that this was a relatively intimate setting, and I think that that contributed something to the development of the social sciences at Chicago. Also, the fact that it was the first university which, in a sense, acknowledged the unity of the social sciences by building a building. I think it was the first social science building, as such, in an American university. But, on top of that, the faculty, and I think this was still the consequence of the talent search of the founder, Samuel Rainey Harper, with Rockefeller money, who went out and bought up the best professors there were – that he pulled together in a very dynamic setting: Chicago at the turn of the century, where there weren't many restraints, there wasn't much stratification. There were maybe half a dozen outstanding, intellectually creative men and the same number of excellent entrepreneurs, that is, men who were able to mobilize resources and make contacts in the community outside.

Mr. Brody: You put Merriam in the latter category?

Mr. Almond: Well, I would put Merriam – principally his impact was of an entrepreneurial sort and of a kind of prophetic, charismatic sort.

Mr. Brody: Rather than a creative, intellectual leader?

Mr. Almond: Rather than a creative, intellectual leader. His own work came out of the Dunning history of political theory. Dunning was his Columbia Ph.D. supervisor, and Merriam cherished all his life long the aspiration that had a kind of Germanic cast to it, of producing a kind of *Allgemeine Staatslehre* American style that would be – I think he had in mind the kind of thing that some of us refer to as empirical political theory, which would still be in continuity with the kinds of questions and issues that are raised in classical political theory. He had that aspiration, and toward the end of his career he produced a number of books that reflected the persistence of his ambition. But I think what had happened was he had just, in a way, exhausted his energies. It's hard to say what his ultimate talent would have been, but quite early on he came into a city at a time when there was a tremendous demand for leadership, when Chicago's money was just turning into the second generation with all the aspirations for civic improvement and that kind of thing. There was Julius Rosenwald and the Sears, Roebuck money and the Northside millionaires, I can't remember all their names, the stockyards people, the Armours, the Swifts, and so forth and so on. And Merriam came from Columbia at the turn of the century, a tall handsome man, to this new university and opportunities beckoned him from all sides. As a matter of fact, the domination of the Department of Political Science by Hewy Pratt Judson who was the first chairman of the Department of Political Science, was such that he couldn't really do very much in the department; he had his professorship there. So, he spent the first couple of decades of his – or first decade and a half – of his career teaching political theory, writing *American Political Ideas*, which was a breakthrough in looking at American political thought or the thought and expression of politicians as belonging somehow in the tradition of political theory. It was an innovative and not entirely acceptable thing to do. But in the reform movement in Chicago, Merriam was elected alderman in the Fifth Ward in Hyde Park in 1910. He was the lone voice speaking out for honesty and efficiency and so forth and so on, naturally coming to the attention of the Gold Coast millionaires; and at that time Hyde Park in the Woodlawn section had its own millionaires. His political career peaked in his candidacy for the Republican nomination for mayor, which, according to the story, was stolen in the counting. Merriam was widely looked upon as the Woodrow Wilson of the Midwest, but that came to a disappointing outcome in the 1915 mayoral election. It was shortly before our entrance into the war, and Merriam, of course, was drawn into that, into World War I, and was put in charge of American information in Italy, which made him interested in public opinion, in propaganda, in communication. I think it was this experience in the wartime public information program that ultimately led to Merriam's interest in the content of the media and impact of the media. Lasswell's dissertation was on propaganda in the First World War, directly following up on Merriam's experience at that time.

Mr. Brody: He was also – you were saying at lunch that he was one of the progenitors of the scientific public administration movement. Was there a lot of interaction between that kind of activity and the social science research center?

Mr. Almond: Yes. Associated with this involvement of Merriam in the reform movement was the development on the University of Chicago campus of a whole cluster of organizations, all of which were housed in a building across the midway – 1313 E. 58th St. – and staffed by young M.A.s and Ph.D.s. from the Department of Political Science. These organizations and associations were intended to professionalize public officials such as finance officers, assessors, county clerks, mayors, governors. There were eight or ten of them and then a top organization, intended to stimulate the development of other kinds of activities, including the formation of organizations of a professional sort among public servants, the Public Administration Clearinghouse, which was headed up by Merriam's close personal friend, Louis Brownlow. But, if one had been a student at the University of Chicago in the late 20s and early 30s, and you were asked to say, Now what is the most important activity going on around here? one wouldn't have said that it was the kind of work that Lasswell was doing and Gosnell was doing, or that Merriam encouraged in his *New Aspects of Politics*. It was that activity, that had its own building, that had much more money back of it, that was staffed by a whole generation of young political scientists in gray flannel suits who made better salaries and who were out on the road at a time when airplane travel was just in its beginnings. All these guys were flying all over the country and the guy with the greatest prestige was the guy who was at home least, like a later generation of professional political scientists or social scientists.

But, at any rate, to get the thing in balance from our perspective of the history of American political science, we would say that it was what Merriam encouraged and what these other people began to do, but Merriam really had all these different interests—I mean, there was this reform concern—he saw how it all fitted together. He was concerned with what he thought of as the professionalization of the public service, he thought of bringing to bear on the training of public officials and on their professional standards the knowledge that would be accumulated through the social sciences. This was very much the central theme of Merriam's life; he saw all these things as fitting together. It was science and it was civic activity; it was moral, not only in the local context, but in the national context, and in the international context. And he also saw these developments of an empirical and a practical sort somehow in continuous relationship with the history of political theory tradition, out of which he came. And it was his ambition that somehow he'd pull all this together when he retired in the early 1940s. But by that time, when he thought, now I'm going to sit down and do the *Allgemeine Staatslehre*, it just didn't come. In that sense, he felt somehow that his life wasn't fulfilled. I think it's an interesting thing about Merriam, he had an enormous need for affection, and his relationship with graduate students and with his younger colleagues, and with his older associates like Brownlow, were—they were as whole people. I know that Merriam was concerned about people like myself who had to work in order to get through college, who came from immigrant families. I think it gave him particular pleasure to see these young men and women coming out of these backgrounds, moving into mainstream careers. He was concerned about your parents if they were around. During Prohibition he always had a couple of bottles of Scotch in his filing cabinet and with close friends he would take a bottle out and have a drink toward the end of the day. Chicago's climate is one of the most impossible of all climates, and during my graduate student days, there was an air-conditioned bar in Hyde Park at the Shoreland Hotel, and he had a table, it was Merriam's table in this air-conditioned bar, and whenever one of his graduate students had, in a sense, made it, like passed his prelims or finished his dissertation, or got his first job, it was the mark of having made it for Merriam to invite you down to the Shoreland bar and give you a drink in this wonderful, dim, whiskey-smelling atmosphere.

Mr. Brody: I take it that his standing in the university was pretty strong since he did get all these things going?

Mr. Almond: Starting about 1900 he had just a marginal position; he was a young faculty member in a small department under a rather authoritarian chairman (Judson) who didn't really give him any leeway. And this authoritarian chairman later became president of the university, and he didn't give up the department chairmanship. So it was confining, and that was one of the reasons why Merriam—first, he was tempted to go, and if you look at his correspondence, you find that he had offers from here and there and was on the point of taking advantage of them because of the situation in Chicago, but he never did. And somehow, if he didn't have all that he wanted at the university, he had a tremendous amount of resonance outside of the university which kept him, so that explains his political reform career, and by the end of World War I, he was in the driver's seat in the department. Either Judson retired or died, I don't know what. He then proceeded to move, it was not long after that that he gave his famous . . .

Mr. Brody: What year was it that he was president of the Association? Twenty-five?

Mr. Almond: But it was in 21 when he gave the lecture that was the introductory lecture to the *New Aspects of Politics.* It was in 21; it appeared in one of the 21 numbers of the APSR. So he sounded that gun; he already was in a situation where he could call on Rosenwald or the Rockefeller family because of his record as a reformer; he could get support to fund the Local Community Research Committee in this little building, the Social Science Research Building. It wasn't only the building, it was the social structures that were invented, one of them being the idea of a kind of a local research fund that would be sufficiently close to the grass roots of the various departments to be able to fund the promising, risk-taking kinds of work. So he brought the Laura Spellman Rockefeller money into the support of creative research like L. D. White's *Prestige Value of Public Employment*, Gosnell's *Studies of Nonvoting*, or Harold Lasswell's *Psychopathology*. He could even pull in things that looked kooky at the time, like the applications of psychoanalysis to the study of political behavior, which somebody like Rosenwald or the Rockefeller family would have difficulty with. His general authority and prestige was such that he could get uncommitted money for these purposes.

Mr. Brody: Let's turn for a moment to your own thesis research during this period of time. Of course, the Depression had set in, as you said, shortly after you arrived at Chicago as an undergraduate, but by the time you were in graduate school it was pretty thoroughly in place. Now you did a study, I guess either as a beginning graduate student with Lasswell, on the client-welfare worker relationship. That was not your dissertation?

Mr. Almond: No, that wasn't. I had Lasswell as an undergraduate, and after graduating, I had to accumulate a little more money before I could go to graduate school. I got a job at the Unemployment Relief Service in the stockyards district. Lasswell had given me the idea of field research, and somehow I thought in what I was experiencing, I was up at the front desk of an Unemployment Relief office in 1932, which was at the peak of unemployment. This was a very exciting place; there were all the various ethnic groups, including blacks and Mexicans, and some groups were very angry, or sullen. Lasswell had told me that these things were important for politics, and we had case records on these people and they came up and they behaved in front of me and I know that the way they behaved affected the way I behaved. So I can remember when I got that job and had been doing it for a couple of weeks, I called Lasswell on the phone and said, "Gee, I think there's a chance that we can do some research." This was before I had really started graduate work. And he said he thought it was a good idea. And we got together and we kind of planned it out, that I would try to interest the other complaint aides to make records of the way in which they were approached by people seeking assistance and record this—we had to record all these contacts on slips; and the slips were kept; well, they were kept for a certain period of time and then thrown away, but I arranged to have them preserved. And I got the support of the people in charge of the office to do this study, and so I had three of us, over a period of six months, recording all these contacts. In the course of six months, you might have as many as half a dozen or a dozen contacts with a specific individual, and he would have been evaluated by one of the three of us, but usually by more than one of us. So that it would be possible at the end of a six-month period to classify these people by their approach to authority. Then it was possible to get demographic and other kinds of data on them from their case histories. It was as simple as that. Now, when I ended up after six months, I must have had data on a couple of thousand individuals and it was obviously going to be impossible to do them all. At that time, I didn't know anything about sampling, but Harold Lasswell did, and he said, well, look, you take every Nth case, and so I learned about Nth just as the king of Siam learned about et cetera; I learned about Nth, and for me that was a big jump. But we ended up, instead of having two thousand cases, maybe a hundred cases selected by the way in which they behaved, because we were interested in contrasting the independent variables. Let's say, they would explain aggression, or passive aggression, or submissive behavior. We then wrote that up and it was published in the *American Political Science Review.* Lasswell was very resourceful. The first version of it was to explain aggressive behavior on the part of clients on public relief, the idea being that aggressive behavior was kind of proto-political, it wasn't actually political, but it could be converted into political revolutionary behavior. This was the time when Lasswell was looking at the world revolution of our time and so, in a sense, this was grist for his mill; he was studying proto-revolutionary tendencies; who were the aggressives in a revolutionary situation like this. Well, the case histories gave us the correlates and the kind of things that went along with aggressiveness. I can't remember what they all were, but they were what you'd expect, but at that time it was novel. It got published in Ogg's *American Political Science Review.* This early success probably set me on a research course.

Lasswell was just beginning to write about the elites; this would have been the time of *Politics: Who Gets What, When and How,* early 30s. And Lasswell suggested that I do an elite study. I was interested in – I began to do papers on the elite in the city of Chicago, the political elite and the economic elite, and the social prestige elite and the philanthropic elite, and so forth and so on. And I was curious about how they overlapped; I was interested in, you might say, the structure of the elite in contemporary American society; this would be Depression America. It grew out of the basic Marxist challenge of whether or not American society or capitalist society in general was dominated by the capitalist class. Well, one could look at the various social positions, at least, as kind of a starter, and see how much overlap there was. If nothing else had happened, I would have done my dissertation on the elite in Chicago, but around this time Merriam was involved in getting the Social Science Research Council established – this is what he'd already been working on in the mid-20s and by the time I was doing graduate work, the SSRC was coming into full swing and they were offering in 1935, for the first time, a predoctoral field fellowship for the social sciences. I got recommended for one of those–$1,600–and I wrote my own ticket as to what I was going to do and what really struck me at the time and won my ultimate and undying loyalty to both the SSRC and the ideals of social science was the fact that I had this $1,600 fellowship and that the fellowship secretary, when I presented him my plans for my dissertation–what I proposed to do was utterly fantastic–I mean, I was proposing to make a comparative study of the elite in New York City, which is a big city as you know, and to compare that with Charleston, South Carolina, to get the opposite extreme, the premodern, insofar as anything premodern persisted in the United States. Everything went: What could they do to facilitate, how could they help? You know, that's–you win converts that way. Anyway, I went to New York and I tried, again, bringing my University of Chicago culture with me; I was going to study, not just as a political scientist but as an anthropologist and as a sociologist, not so much as an economist. But what that meant was that I had to look at New York City as an anthropologist would look at it–a field site. And I remember making contacts with the New York City elite and it presented some problems, because it meant that I had, in some sense, to give false credentials so that I'd get invited to a dinner or a social occasion, and I'd come there as a graduate student working for a Ph.D. and what I really was interested in was encountering these people and seeing at firsthand what their attitudes and their values were.

Well, my effort at being a participant observer as a way of researching the elite in New York City lasted until Christmas, as I remember. I just couldn't take it and at the same time do a full day's work at the New York Public Library. Actually, the New York Public Library had a whole room on New York people. That was another kind of incredible experience, you know. It was all full of the documentary material and all full of the old directories and everything else, the old *Who's Who*s. So, you might say after my experiment at participant observation, I went fully into this business of really putting together the data for an analysis of the transformation of the elite in New York City from the Revolutionary period to the modern period, but done by taking temporal cross sections and not really sampling the elite, but taking, for example, all of the politicians and all of the people at certain levels of social status and so forth and so on, and then comparing them. Well, it was an enormous body of material that I collected, and it was quantitative and it was pre-IBM cards and pre-calculators. I had them all on little slips of paper–you know, each biography–and I just calculated it myself by hand and then, of course, we had the simplest kind of calculator which computed percentages, and I think I ended up with a doctoral dissertation that had about 150 major tables in it. I don't know how many ideas there were in it, but when it was finally presented to people like Gosnell and Lasswell and Merriam, they just had to acknowledge the fact that I'd worked awfully hard and accumulated an enormous body of material.

Mr. Brody: You didn't do the South Carolina side of it?

Mr. Almond: No. That was hopeless. I bit off more than I could chew. No, I never did South Carolina.

Mr. Brody: You might have spiked Floyd Hunter in the bud before he ever got started.

Mr. Almond: That is possible. Well, there's a long story about what happened to that dissertation, but I don't know how far we've gotten today; have we . . .

Mr. Brody: Well, what is the story about what happened to the dissertation?

Mr. Almond: Well, it's—you might say the pain has long since gone out of the memory, but I finished the dissertation in 1938 and I took my first job at Brooklyn College and for the first couple of years there, 1939 and 1940, I didn't have time to do anything but go from one class to another. I taught five sections of Government 1, American Government, for the first three years of my teaching career, which came to a total of 30—I taught Government 1 30 times, and I must say that in the course of teaching it 30 times, just to keep from dying of boredom, I exhausted all the secondary literature on American government. It was possible to do it in those days—everything on parties, everything on legislatures, constitutional law, political theory as it bore on the constitutional system and all the rest. But I didn't have any time really to work on my dissertation. I had it there, you know, just kind of accumulating dust. We had to publish—although the stress on publication wasn't quite as sharp as it became later—but certainly for me to get a book out was the most important thing. I had been encouraged by Harold Lasswell and Merriam to see if I couldn't turn it into a book. Now the doctoral dissertation, as such, was concerned—it was mostly political sociology, historical political sociology, that is, tracing the social characteristics of the political, economic, and social elites of New York City from the Revolutionary period up until the then contemporary period, 1935-36. And I had this obsession—

somehow I wanted to come to grips with every aspect of the elite and I hadn't really drawn on my psychological, psychoanalytic side, which I had also gotten from Harold Lasswell.

So in whatever spare time I had in my first three teaching years, I began to accumulate biographical material on New York businessmen, prominent corporation executives, entrepreneurs, people like J. P. Morgan, John D. Rockefeller, corporation lawyers, men who were on the margin between economic power and political power. I collected maybe a couple dozen of those biographies and I was very much interested in seeing if I couldn't explain or get some kind of hold on the explanation of what kind of propensity they had—you know, ideologically speaking. What could explain a rich, economically powerful liberal, like Andrew Carnegie—at least he got to be a liberal, you know, from the point of view of standards of those days—as contrasted with a reactionary like William Randolph Hearst, who spent a considerable part of his career in New York. Was there anything in their psychological development that could illuminate this choice—the choice of a reactionary or a conservative or a liberal option on the part of people who, roughly speaking, came from the same economic stratum. So I had three or four major chapters which I decided to add to my doctoral dissertation which introduced this psychological dimension.

I went back to the University of Chicago in 1944 from Washington, where I was working in one of the war agencies—and I went back and presented the dissertation to the University of Chicago Press, and they were excited about it. You know, wealth and politics, the kind of book that both can be represented as a scholarly book and might sell. And they thought that it had some possibilities. Merriam, around this time, had become increasingly melancholy and depressed. Hutchins had taken over the university. Merriam had retired. The university was holding up on the appointment of a successor; that humiliated L. D. White, they never really permitted him to take the department chairmanship. The whole thing that Merriam had built looked as though it was on shaky foundations. Hutchins was ridiculing it. Mortimer Adler ridiculed this kind of fact-gathering, crude empiricism stuff. Merriam was an unhappy man and perhaps somewhat frightened at the time, too, and I know that he had my dissertation with the revisions in it and the press had it, and when I went to talk to him about it he said, "Well, take that psychological stuff out." What Merriam was concerned about was that I had done some psychologizing of John D. Rockefeller, who was the founder of the University of Chicago and the source of its funding; and I had gathered material on Carnegie and the Carnegie Corporation was becoming an important source of research funds.

After all, Merriam probably thought, here's this young whippersnapper; it isn't enough for him to do this dissertation on wealth and politics, which is a risky thing, but he wants to get all this stuff about their family life and how nasty their parents were to them and so forth and so on. So, he said take it out and he just kind of gestured with a sweep of his hand. It was quite unexpected. Really, the parts that he wanted to take out were the parts that I was proudest of; I mean, the stuff that I had just lovingly put together, you know. It didn't strike me as really being the heart of my contribution. But there it was, I remember it came at a point where the war was going badly and people in my age bracket—even though I had a pre-Pearl Harbor child—were being taken up in the draft, and I said the hell with it, I was just going to wait and get drafted, I wasn't going to seek any deferment.

In the meanwhile, Otto Klineberg came and asked me if I would go to work for USSBS, the Strategic Bombing Survey, so, choking back my disappointment and my wrath and anger at Merriam, I went over to England and later to Germany; and when I got back, instead of taking the chapters out, I rewrote them in the form of an article, and that was the only part of my doctoral dissertation that really got published; it's called "Political Attitudes of Wealth," and it was published in the *Journal of Politics*. So that's the story of my doctoral dissertation. In a sense it tells the story of what had happened to that wonderful department. I think political science took the worst beating—well, after philosophy was decimated, that is, the pragmatic school at Chicago was decimated when Hutchins came in—of the major social science departments, I think political science took the worst beating because Hutchins, I think, was resolved that he just wouldn't approve of appointments to full professorships for Harold Gosnell and Harold Lasswell. And both of them left around this time, and Merriam was on the margin, and so the department went into a period of mediocrity. It was just at that time that Merriam was sitting in judgment of my doctoral dissertation and I think it might have had a different outcome had it been completed at an earlier time. So that's the story of my doctoral dissertation.

Mr. Brody: Well, maybe we'll stop here for today, and pick it up with some description of some of the people who were your classmates and young faculty members at the University of Chicago.

Mr. Almond: I want to say a word or two about Harold Lasswell. Is [the tape recorder] on now?

Mr. Brody: Yeah.

Mr. Almond: Well, Lasswell was somewhat isolated. Let's say, we're talking now about the late 20s and early 30s, up to the time of his departure in 38.

He didn't have a lot of graduate students; most of the graduate students would take one of his courses, but what he was doing, even at Chicago, was a bit on the high-risk side and I think that the impression that somehow Lasswell and Gosnell and that kind of behavioral tendency in the department was the central or mainstream tendency of graduate training and research during those years is not really correct. There may have been half a dozen people who were doing their Ph.D.s under Harold's direction, but there were a considerably larger number whom he influenced and for whom the kind of work that he did legitimated that kind of research. When I first encountered Harold Lasswell his door was the only door in the Social Science Building that wasn't half glass. It was a solid wooden door, which, in a sense, was symbolic of what he was doing and the kind of mystery that was associated with his work. He, at the time, was a lay member of the Chicago Institute of Psychoanalysis. I don't know that he did any therapeutic analyses, but I think he was authorized to do that. He was doing psychoanalytic interviewing in connection with research that he was doing at the time. He was very much out in front—you've got to remember, this now is the early 30s and he is engaged in research attempting to relate the flow of communication between a therapist or an interviewer and a patient/respondent to the physiological changes in the patient/respondent. He was working with a psychology graduate student whose name slips my mind. The things that went on in his laboratory, where he had real machinery, and this door that didn't have a glass pane in it, and the kinds of issues and problems that he dealt with, and his—how would I put it?—his brashness, his lack of inhibition, let's say, in referring to processes that were kind of—in that Victorian era you just didn't talk about them—like toilet training, specific kinds of sexual activity, homosexuality and the like, things that are quite commonplace now, all had the effect of making him seem like a somewhat dangerous kind of person to be associated with, and he suffered somewhat from that. I know that the people who did work with him got a lot of his time and he was extremely generous, both in time and support, without which I couldn't really have continued in graduate work.

People like Bruce Smith, Dorothy Blumenstock, maybe three or four others, were much closer to him and often had dinner with him; there was a favorite place that he had on 63rd street below Cottage Grove avenue, a Greek restaurant, the Athens Cafe, where you could get Greek resin wine and good food—so that he had these very close relationships, often apprenticeships, with a small number of students and he had this more superficial impact on the larger group of graduate students. He was looked on then as a somewhat threatening figure.

On the other hand, Gosnell was a very shy and gentle soul and was quite undervalued at the time. It's a very interesting kind of indication of how things have changed. The fact that he was so preoccupied with quantitative analysis was viewed as a mark of his purely technical—his was viewed as a purely technical kind of accomplishment and it didn't really compare with the kinds of research that was done by other members of the department. He was a very unaggressive man.

Mr. Brody: What was the relationship between Gosnell and Lasswell like?

Mr. Almond: Well, Lasswell being a more powerful and effective operator, used to tease Gosnell, and so did Merriam tease Gosnell, and Gosnell was, as I say, such a gentle kind of person that he didn't really defend himself. It's a very interesting thing that later on it turns out that Gosnell—after he had left academic life—used to send Christmas cards that were extraordinarily revealing of a much livelier, much more imaginative kind of personality than we had associated him with. I remember on one particular Christmas card he sent around he had Harold Lasswell and Charlie Merriam as nudes in some kind of composition.

Mr. Brody: Oh, his cartoons?

Mr. Almond: You know about his cartoons?

Mr. Brody: Yeah.

Mr. Almond: Well, so much for Gosnell. As I say, he was doing—he was just solidly productive at the time, just one book after another on the Negro in politics, on parties and elections, surveys of attitudes toward voting, but he wasn't really taken seriously, he wasn't really viewed as a figure of creative and seminal importance. Lasswell was looked upon as somewhat dangerous, but everybody recognized his brilliance and his—almost his genius. V. O. Key was a stretch behind, of course. He was Merriam's favorite, at a time when Merriam was still under the influence of his foray into municipal politics.

Mr. Brody: He would have been a fellow student of yours?

Mr. Almond: V. O. would have been about two or three years ahead of me.

I think he got his Ph.D. probably in 35, 36, and I got mine in 38, so I was, you know, just coming in my first, second year, when he was finishing up. But, V. O., as I was saying, was close to Merriam and this dissertation came out of Merriam's reform side. He wrote his doctoral dissertation on the techniques of graft, never published—I'm not sure why. V. O.'s work habits—well, the work habits of all the people in the Social Science Building; it was a beehive, and I imagine that the work level in Chicago was substantially greater than would have been the case in comparable institutions. Research was taken very, very seriously, and it was organized research; it was research that was backed up by research funds, so to speak, and it was unlike the more gentlemanly relations between the professor and the students at a place like Yale or Harvard at that time. It was more the atmosphere of a science laboratory or business situation, you know. You really were under a good deal of pressure to be productive. I think one of the reasons was you were getting grants; I think Chicago probably innovated in the social sciences in having an organized body of resources for research—the Local Community Research Committee—and you got grants that enabled you to hire students who then became your research assistants and apprentices and you had to show some productivity if you wanted to get a renewal of that grant. I think it was just a very exciting place and people were stimulated to go off and to do things; people worked nights, they came on weekends, Sunday there were lights on.

Mr. Brody: Were they mostly unmarried?

Mr. Almond: Oh no, as a matter of fact, the unmarried ones—say people like Nathan Leites and Ed Shils who weren't married at the time . . .

Mr. Brody: And Harold wasn't?

Mr. Almond: Harold wasn't, but Gosnell was married, Merriam was married and had a family, V. O. Key wasn't married—he got married later to another graduate student. It wasn't that they didn't get married, but even if they were married, they all lived in the Hyde Park community, they were within walking distance of the building and they'd go over after Sunday dinner. There was a connection, you could walk without going outside from the Social Science Research Building right into the stacks of the Harper Memorial Library, so it was very convenient to work there. But always, as long as I can remember, there were big things going on in which graduate students were involved, like the Hoover Recent Social Trends Survey. When Hoover was secretary of commerce and then became president, I can't remember exactly when it was, he decided that we really needed to find out where we were in America in terms of the whole sweep of social, economic, and intellectual life, and he was a man who believed in research—he was an engineer. Merriam, L. D. White, and others were very much involved in this Recent Social Trends study and a lot of us graduate students got research jobs working on one or another of the major studies that were done for the Recent Social Trends study. And after that there was the Committee on Administrative Management and National Resources Planning Board research, which Merriam was involved in and which brought graduate students opportunities to do research and to do doctoral dissertations. This kind of thing is quite familiar today, but Chicago was a pioneer.

Mr. Brody: Was Herb Simon a fellow student of yours?

Mr. Almond: Oh, Herb Simon was a fellow student; he would be about the same distance behind me that I was behind V. O. Key.

Mr. Brody: Did you know him at the time?

Mr. Almond: I knew him very well. Herb Simon married the department secretary, Dorothea Pye, Dorothea Pye Simon. He worked in one of the public administration organizations across the midway.

Mr. Brody: So he was more closely associated with White?

Mr. Almond: He was a White Ph.D., but there's an interesting story about Herb Simon. Herb was in one of the organizations, the Institute for Municipal Research, and they were engaged in efforts of measurement, measurement of the performance of municipal functions. That's what got him into his later interests and work. But I can remember as a graduate student, a research assistant over in one of these 1313 outfits, he was working on the problem of quantitative measurement, of the performance of governmental functions—this reflects the early reaction at Chicago to what we now accept as important behavioral research—he had difficulty with L. D. White, even though L. D. White himself used quantitative methods, I can't remember all the details of this encounter but Herb Simon was put off by this early encounter, and it may have led to dropping his political science connection.

Mr. Brody: While he was still at Chicago or more recently?

Mr. Almond: More recently.

Mr. Brody: Oh yeah, he's in the Department of Psychology at Carnegie-Mellon.

Mr. Almond: Yes, I know, but I think that part of this alienation began at Chicago, and it was in part due to the fact that quantitative analysis and the kind of formal analysis that Herb Simon was getting into wasn't really appreciated by his professors.

Mr. Brody: Was it that, or are you thinking of the nonrational elements in administratiom . . .

Mr. Almond: Well, you see, when Herb was just coming in, Lasswell was on his way out. He would have had good sponsorship in the Department of Political Science a few years before. But at any rate, I think that it may be the story of why we lost Herb. I think Herb might have been more – he might have stayed a little bit closer to political science. I wouldn't say he'd be back in political science, but, for example, he's never, despite the important work that he's done, he was never a president of the Association. I think the reason being that he probably isn't a member – you know, you have to be a member.

Mr. Brody: Yes, I know that.

Mr. Almond: There was much more going on at Chicago. There was a group of graduate students involved in metropolitan regional studies. We viewed the community outside as a kind of laboratory, and at that time, interestingly enough, the urban problem was much at the center – the notion, really, of the artificiality of governmental jurisdictions – so there was a general research program on what was then called the metropolitan community. And there must have been a dozen dissertations done – one of them by Victor Jones on local government in the metropolitan community of Chicago showing that there were some 1,600 different units and all the problems of jurisdiction; Albert Lepawsky did one on the courts of the metropolitan community; John Vieg did one on education in the metropolitan community. At the same time that these studies were being done on the governmental and the political side, there were studies being done on the sociological side. There was the notion of ecology very much at the center of this research in the metropolitan community, particularly the work being done by Ogburn and others in the Department of Sociology, say the epidemiology of social and psychological phenomena, crime rates, insanity, delinquency, and so forth and so on—a whole series of studies.

Naturally, I've speculated about why the University of Chicago turned out to be such a creative place. I've often felt that while I suffered a bit at the beginning of my career because of the fact that a Ph.D. in political science from Chicago was a little unconventional, that I got an enormous advantage out of it in the period after World War II when I discovered that I was about a decade ahead in terms of my training as compared with colleagues in my age group. I've often wondered, you know, why was it that Chicago turned out to be such a creative place. There are some obvious, I'd say structural conditions, one of them being it was a new university, a university that started off with a lot of money. It didn't have a tradition to buck, it could be selective in deciding what particular lines to pursue. It was true that Chicago, itself, didn't have much tradition, it wasn't much of a city that set any kind of restrictive examples. But in addition to that, there were the accidents of just who were the people who were brought in, like Merriam, and Robert Park in sociology, Burgess and Ogburn and Wirth, all very ambitious, very imaginative men in a situation in which the institutional limits on what they could do were relatively loose. So it was a combination of a relatively open situation and aggressive, enterprising, imaginative scholars. But there were a couple of inventions, at least as far as the social sciences were concerned. One of them was the organized research umbrella—you know, this local community research committee. I think it was the first one of its kind that supported social science research and it wasn't a foundation far away, it was a source of funds right there where you could select risks with greater information. I think another social innovation was the relation between research-oriented faculty and graduate students; that is, the research assistantship as a typical part of a graduate student's training; a period of apprenticeship doing actual grown-up research with a creative scholar. I think that was an innovation. It wasn't true of the social sciences in other parts of the country.

Well, that really would cover the ground of special conditions that would help explain it.

Index

About the Author

Gabriel A. Almond was born in Rock Island, Illinois, on January 12, 1911. He received both his bachelor's and Ph.D. degrees from the University of Chicago, the first in 1932, the second in 1938. He has taught at Brooklyn College, Princeton and Yale universities, and Stanford University, where he is at present Professor Emeritus. He has also served as Visiting Fellow or Professor at the University of Tokyo in Japan, Cambridge University in England, the University of Minas Geraes in Brazil, and Kiev State University in the USSR. He is the author or coauthor of *The American People and Foreign Policy*, *The Appeals of Communism*, *The Politics of the Developing Areas*, *The Civic Culture*, *Political Development*, *Crisis, Choice, and Change*, *The Civic Culture Revisited*, and other books and articles in the fields of public opinion, comparative politics, political development, and political theory. He has served as Chairman of the Committee on Comparative Politics of the Social Science Research Council (1954–63) and as President of the American Political Science Association (1965–66). He is a member of the National Academy of Sciences, the American Philosophical Society, and the American Academy of Arts and Sciences. He received the James Madison Award of the American Political Science Association in 1981.

NOTES

NOTES